Series Editors Michael C. Meyer John D. Martz Miguel León-Portilla

University of Nebraska Press Lincoln and London

United States Policy

in Latin America

A Quarter Century of

Crisis and Challenge,

1961-1986

Edited by John D. Martz

Copyright © 1988 by
the University of Nebraska Press
All rights reserved
Manufactured in the United States
of America

First paperback printing: 1990
Most recent printing indicated by
the first digit below:
10   9   8   7   6   5   4   3   2   1
Library of Congress Cataloging
in Publication Data
United States Policy in Latin
America.
(Latin American Studies series)
Includes index.
1. Latin America – Foreign
relations – United States.
2. United States – Foreign
relations – Latin America.
3. United States – Foreign
relations – 1945-
I. Martz, John D. II. Series.
F1418.U715   1989   327.7308
87-25503
ISBN 0-8032-3097-4
(alkaline paper)
ISBN 0-8032-8193-5 (pbk.)

Contents

John D. Martz

Introduction

More than a quarter century ago the rise of Fidel Castro and the consummation of the Cuban Revolution served as a major stimulus to Latin American studies in the United States. Cynics of the day argued, in fact, that events in Cuba constituted the greatest boon to Latin Americanists since at least the advent of the cold war. Although this view was exaggerated, it contained more than a kernel of truth. The early 1960s saw the attention of the North American public captured by the Bay of Pigs, the Cuban Missile Crisis, and—to a less dramatic degree—the creation of the Peace Corps and the establishment of the Alliance for Progress. In academia, the National Defense Education Act supported area-studies centers and funded graduate education. Before the close of the decade a new generation of young scholars and experts had emerged.

In due course, however, both the political and institutional enthusiasm for Latin America waned. The national leadership minimized its attention to the Third World in general and Latin America in particular. Public interest inevitably declined, and those who studied and wrote about the area did so with scant encouragement from anyone but their peers. It was only with the advent of new problems and a different set of headlines that the pendulum began to swing back in the decade of the 1980s. The interminable civil war in El Salvador, the radicalization of the Nicaraguan Revolution, the South Atlantic War, the debt crisis—these and other events captured the attention of both the public and the political elites in the United States.

The renewal of concern after two decades has been reflected in an increased number of journalistic and academic works. Among the more popular—and more important for policy formation—have been collections dealing with the general topic of U.S. foreign policy in

Latin America. While these have incorporated chapters and essays drawing upon historical experience, their major emphasis has been upon immediate problem areas and policy disputes. Some of my own previous works have followed this course: with Lars Schoultz, *Latin America, the United States, and the Inter-American System* (1980), and with E. Michael Erisman, *Colossus Challenged: The Struggle for Caribbean Influence* (1982). If such works met a genuine need, they also tended to emphasize current events to such an extent that their value was soon reduced.

Rather than produce yet another such book, I have attempted to organize a volume with a more distinctive and less transitory value. What has emerged is an undertaking with several related but identifiable perspectives. Part 1 presents a chronological account of the years since 1960, with attention directed to the politics and policy making of a succession of administrations. The contributors carry us from the halcyon days of the New Frontier—that striking admixture of youthful idealism and grim anticommunism—to the eight Nixon-Ford years and the dominance of Henry Kissinger, ever the global strategist uninterested in the affairs of the Third World. We continue with an examination of the brief but eventful stewardship of Jimmy Carter, and thence to Ronald Reagan and the record still being written.

Part 1 is not, however, a mere listing of major events in order of their occurrence. Rather, it highlights the orientation and outlook of the various administrations, often incorporating treatments of the principal decision makers for each administration. This treatment in turn raises broader questions about the role of crisis management in the formulation and execution of U.S. policy toward Latin America, questions that are addressed in part 2. Ranging from examples of unilateral intervention at one extreme to effective multilateral negotiation at the other, the four cases presented in Part 2 offer insights into the policy-making process. The Dominican case in 1965 centers on military intervention, while the example of Chile illustrates a host of U.S. policies and actions, both overt and covert. In Panama we confront a lengthy diplomatic undertaking in which U.S. domestic politics were a crucial factor. Lastly, controversy over the Falkland/Malvinas Islands explodes into a war, one in which a state from outside the Western Hemisphere is involved.

Part 3 addresses current problem areas that can be expected to endure for years to come. The debt crisis, extant in the 1970s but suddenly discovered in the 1980s, may well prove to be the single most vexing and urgent subject of inter-American relations for the remainder of the century. At the same time, the brush fires and conflagrations of Central America can also be expected to rivet attention of the entire world for years to come, while difficulties between Cuba and the United States will endure long after the present leadership in both countries departs the scene. As with part 2, the selection of cases is not exhaustive, nor can it be. Rather, it provides an alert for those who care about the challenges and opportunities stretching ahead to the year 2000 and after. My essay concludes the volume by calling for renewed attention to and understanding of the meaning of democracy, its applicability to diverse societies, the strength of prevailing tradition, and the legacy of history.

The history of relations between the United States and Latin America has been tortuous and unsettled. For more than 150 years, politics in the America has been turbulent. Traditional cultural and societal tensions between Latin America and North America, along with the rapidity of change in the more volatile contemporary period, have contributed to the variegated tapestry woven over the years. But during the past quarter century, controversy and complexity have grown exponentially. Contentiousness in the North-South linkage has mounted, while issues of diplomacy and foreign policy lie increasingly matters of the public concern. The emergence of revolutionary Cuba has left an indelible mark, as has a long series of incidents and misunderstandings. The decade of the 1980s has seen relations further exacerbated at a time when divisions among foreign-policy elites in the United States have been drawn more sharply than at any other time during this era.

To examine and probe the substance of U.S. policy in Latin America is the fundamental purpose of this book and of its contributors. It is necessary to go beyond the headlines of the moment, although they, too, have their place in any quest for a meaningful understanding. In the analyses here, one encounters a kaleidoscopic array of problems and personalities. A long succession of U.S. decision makers has attempted to cope with often heterogeneous issues. Policies have changed; economic realities have shifted, growing ever more arcane and intricate; societal forces have unfolded in a strange or unpredicted fashion. Yet general *leitmotifs* recur, and a set of common attitudes or practices has affected policy toward the hemisphere. A few of the more important should be noted here because they help to provide a necessary perspective while also serving as a reminder that experience is scarcely irrelevant in considering the problems that may characterize U.S. policy concerns in the years ahead.

At least three broad thematic areas can be readily identified: (1) national policy objectives, (2) political perspectives, and (3) patterns of crisis management and decision making. The first incorporates those basic goals to which every administration in Washington has been committed. As will be seen, although emphases have varied over time, fundamental notions of the national interest have largely held constant. Moreover, there is little reason to anticipate significant change in the foreseeable future. Notwithstanding the inevitable tugging and hauling between allegedly idealistic and pragmatic approaches, in the final analysis the national policy objectives have held fast. As the dean of Latin Americanist political scientists notes in chapter 1, U.S. commitments have historically reflected a pair of interrelated concerns.

Federico G. Gil characterizes these preoccupations as historically unaltered. The first calls for the exclusion of extracontinental rivals or hostile powers from the Western Hemisphere. This policy can be traced all the way back to the 1823 enunciation of the Monroe Doctrine. It is writ large in the diplomatic history of U.S. policy toward Latin America, and today it is epitomized by the determination of the Reagan administration to prevent or eradicate the presence of Soviet supported and inspired regimes. Methods and techniques to sustain this objective can and will vary greatly. However, there is no questioning the fundamental conviction that external powers must be restrained. Whether with respect to the British in Central America in the mid-1800s, the French in Mexico in the 1860s, the Germans off the Venezuelan coast at the close of the century, or any of the more recent instances of extrahemispheric involvement, concern and opposition from Washington has been assured. Even the preoccupation with international communism, while seemingly an artifact of the post–World War II era, can be seen in earlier years. "Red scares" concerning a threat from Mexico in the 1920s are clear examples.

Second, as Gil also observes, the United States has engaged in an enduring effort to secure and maintain a dominant politico-economic presence in the region. It has not been enough merely to bar or constrain the presence of other states; rather, Washington has been determined to be actively dominant throughout the region. The ability of the United States to assert itself and to shape events, whether through action or inaction, has been a consistent objective, albeit pursued by a host of different political, economic, diplomatic, and military instrumentalities.

These basic priorities are first discussed with regard to the Kennedy-Johnson years. Although it was a period in some ways remarkable for U.S. policy toward Latin America, the two basic concerns were never forgotten. The experience of subsequent governments merely underscores Gil's argument. The presidency of Jimmy Carter, for example, adopted an ambitious agenda toward Latin America at the outset. Informed by a set of precise foreign-policy principles, the administration later found itself shifting toward basic crisis management in order to honor traditional security interests. Carter adviser Robert A. Pastor acknowledges as much in his chapter, noting the extent to which that administration found itself necessarily responding to events emanating from Latin America itself. This was also true of the first Reagan administration, as Hayes observes.

Similar perceptions of basic objectives form a part of Abraham F. Lowenthal's discussion. In his examination of the Caribbean Basin in the 1980s, Lowenthal describes U.S. interests as still revolving in large part about political and security concerns. Policymakers desire unhampered and total access to the region, with economic development and political stability standing as prerequisites for regional self-sufficiency. Underlying these fundamental objectives is an unending clash between what, for want of more felicitous labels, may be termed idealism and pragmatism. The dichotomy does not exist in pure form, but the impulses are clearly perceptible. Within the context of U.S. policy toward Latin America, this dichotomy is often addressed in terms of intervention and nonintervention. At least hypothetically, the latter is espoused by those who place particular emphasis on the democratization of Latin America. Proponents of this policy argue that the highest ideals of the revolution against the British—symbolized in the words of the Declaration of Independence and the writings of Jefferson, Paine, and others—must be projected across the Americas. This view was exemplified by the emphasis on democracy in President Kennedy's Alliance for Progress, in President Carter's human rights policy and opposition to military regimes, and in the rather belated championing of democratic regimes by the Reagan administration in the wake of Jean-Claude Duvalier's ouster from Haiti.

Yet the ambiguities and inconsistencies have always been pronounced, as the final chapter discusses at length. John F. Kennedy was quite willing to intervene with diplomatic and political pressure against some military seizures of power but not others. Lyndon B. Johnson resorted to direct military measures in the Dominican Republic in the name of protecting a democracy allegedly imperiled by international Marxism. The Nixon administration and Henry Kissinger had few qualms about adopting numerous interventionist measures to block the advent or penetration of the Allende government in Chile. Years later, Kissinger's erstwhile protégé Alexander M. Haig was an unsuccessful advocate of direct pressure and action against Cuba as a means of combating Soviet influence in the hemisphere.

Haig's efforts came at a time when the administration that he served was demonstrating more than customary complacency about authoritarian regimes that were friendly to the United States. A later change in the Reagan outlook came well after Haig's departure from Washington, thereby testifying further to the stresses experienced by any administration that attempts to balance security interests, an idealized vision of global democratization, and an exaggerated faith in its capacity to control events. If there are basic contradictions between an unrealistic vision of pristine nonintervention and equally extreme definitions of security interests, the fact remains that any administration will, in the final analysis, recognize its ultimate and ineradicable goal as one of preserving the U.S. presence, influence, and security interests in the region.

Accompanying such undeniable facts is the question of political perspective. For every foreign-policy maker and major actor in each presidential administration, there is a basic worldview that is important to the formation of specific policies. At the broadest level there is a distinction between those who would identify the East-West linkage and those who would identify the North-South linkage as fundamental to the international role of the United States. Inconsistency and ambiguity sometimes exist, but nonetheless, these perceptions of the shape of the world beyond national boundaries determine the thrust of policy decisions. The Kennedy-Johnson period, by way of illustration, was marked by more than a modicum of interest in the Third World, particularly Latin America. During the subsequent years of Republican government, the familiar intellectual and political inclinations of Henry Kissinger shifted the official perspective from one of a North-South emphasis to one of East-West priorities.

With the two most recent presidencies, worldviews are even more sharply different. When Jimmy Carter came to power, he did so in the wake of domestic repercussions from a decade of racial disturbances, assassinations, Watergate, Vietnam, and Kent State. The new president believed that the Third World was of great and increasing importance to the United States. Interestingly enough, as Pastor observes, Carter himself was more concerned with Latin America than either of his two major foreign-policy advisers, Cyrus Vance and Zbigniew Brzezinski. At least at the outset, traditional security interests as defined by East-West competition were subordinated to a restatement of the "special relationship" with Latin America. This focus on the North-South dialogue provided a framework for the application of human rights policies and related efforts designed to encourage a democratization of regimes in the Western Hemisphere. Only later in his term was Carter confronted with such knotty issues as Cuba and Mariel, Nicaragua, and El Salvador. The heady if difficult days spent in winning the fight for renegotiated treaties with Panama gave way to problems that gradually pressured the administration to move toward more orthodox expressions of an implicit East-West orientation.

With the inauguration of Ronald Reagan in 1981, the perspective shifted toward more traditional Cold War views and attitudes. Jeane J. Kirkpatrick was an eloquent spokeswoman for those in the administration who were most alarmed over Soviet and Cuban purposes. Security interests were couched exclusively in terms of East-West competition. It was believed that Jimmy Carter had conducted a long foreign-policy retreat that had to be reversed. There could be no real negotiations with Cuba, no patience with leftist revolutionaries, and as later became evident, no willingness to accept the Sandinista authoritarianism that emerged in Managua.

Margaret Daly Hayes explains the Reaganite conviction that the Central American quagmire required firm, decisive, and conceivably unilateral action on the part of the United States. If, as Hayes contends, the Reagan approach reflected an awareness that policy should and could be the art of the possible, thereby rebuffing the rhetorical righteousness of the true believers, it also mirrored the notion that, in the final analysis, Latin American problems were of urgent concern to national interests only because of the threat of international communism. There was the conviction, shared by many previous governments, that revolutionary regimes were by definition unpredictable, radical, susceptible to the wiles of external Marxism, and irrevocably dangerous to the presence and security of the United States. There was a sense that Washington was holding the line against international communism, an attitude that presumably influenced those who were most directly involved in the Iranian arms deal and contra fund-raising in 1985 and 1986 that shook the administration.

The prevailing worldview in Washington, in short, has very much affected the handling of specific disputes and the formation of policies. More often than not, Washington's willingness to deal with Latin America on the basis of North-South relations has been dependent upon its reading of potential Marxist involvement. Even in the heyday of Henry Kissinger, as discussed by Michael Francis, conflicts without seemingly global connotations were customarily treated with reasonable sensitivity, out of which emerged policies of a concessionary nature. Given the belief that Latin America was regarded as unimportant for the East-West competition, the Colossus of the North could afford to be generous, patient, and paternalistically understanding. Where a problem area incorporated Cold War features, however, the shaping of policy was likely to be far more harsh than concessionary toward Latin America.

National policy objectives and definitions of U.S. interests have consequently been articulated and refracted through the prism of Washington's prevailing worldview. These in turn have been converted into specific policy through the patterns of crisis management and foreign-policy decision making. Several themes have been readily evident in virtually all the administrations during this period. In the first place, at least in part as a consequence of a generalized national lack of interest in and an ignorance about Latin America, the region has usually received low priority. Only in times of apparent emergency has Latin America appeared in front-page headlines. Otherwise, media attention has largely been limited to reports of natural disasters, scientific curiosities, and an occasional political episode with sensational overtones. It is scarcely surprising that the public's lack of interest and understanding has been mirrored in high-ranking political leaders.

To consider the presidents since 1961, for example, is to concede that public posturing and well-intentioned expressions of concern have barely masked presidential ennui. John F. Kennedy, to be sure, was willing to receive the opinions of his advisers, but few of them possessed real expertise on Latin America. Although a fast learner, he cannot be said to have had more than a superficial comprehension of the region. Lyndon Johnson formed his opinions in the fashion of a Texan looking toward Mexico, with his ranking adviser, Thomas Mann, a Texas oil entrepreneur. For Richard Nixon it was never possible to demystify the mistrust that had been nourished by the traumatic receptions accorded his vice-presidential visits to Lima and Caracas in 1958. His announced presidential policy of the low profile, popularly referred to as benign neglect, dovetailed with his predilection for East-West policy making in foreign affairs. Following the brief interregnum of Gerald Ford, who characteristically made no pretensions of comprehending hemispheric affairs, Jimmy Carter finally personified a chief executive with a degree of insight, if relatively limited expertise. Carter's successor in the White House was a Californian whose only exposure to hemispheric concerns had been his opposition to "giving away" the Panama Canal during treaty renegotiations.

Granting the obvious maxim that no president can begin to master all the details of domestic and international affairs, it must lamentably be added that major foreign-policy advisers, those with authority and influence with a president, have themselves consistently demonstrated limited knowledge about Latin America. Secretaries of state, whatever their background and career, have possessed little expertise in the region. The emergence of preeminent national security advisers inside the White House has not rectified this situation. Such powerful personalities and thinkers as McGeorge Bundy, Walt W. Rostow, Henry Kissinger, Zbigniew Brzezinski, and Alexander Haig were multitalented advisers on international affairs whose ignorance of, and often lack of concern about, Latin America ranged from substantial to legendary. Positions of high authority in foreign affairs are not, as a general rule, filled by those with expertise in hemispheric relations.

This is not to denigrate the talents of the professional diplomats who serve in the region. However, those who are posted abroad in U.S. embassies do not customarily make the crucial decisions; much of their work is in a sense routine, notwithstanding its value. Moreover, even career professionals can run afoul of Washington elites.

In Chile in the early 1970s there were ambassadors who were systematically ignored, contradicted, misinformed, or not informed by the administration; Henry Kissinger chastised one of them for allegedly trying to "give him a political science lecture." Under Jimmy Carter, Frank Ortiz was dismissed from his post in Guatemala on the grounds of his unduly conservative sympathies; the Reagan administration relieved John Ferch after a brief stint in Honduras as a consequence of unenthusiastic implementation of policy directives.

Even the occasional political appointee who proves to be an effective ambassador, and who presumably has political mentors in the Washington establishment, is unlikely to play an important role in high-level decision making. Rare indeed is it for a person to enjoy direct access to, or even a longstanding friendship with, a president. John Gavin, Ronald Reagan's close Hollywood friend in Mexico City, was an exception. These and additional illustrations all demonstrate the fact that policy toward Latin America is essentially the work of powerful political leaders who, whatever their talents, are less than knowledgeable about the societies and governments toward which their decisions are directed.

Another trait marking decision making in hemispheric policy is its organizationally diffuse quality. To be sure, this is by no means unique to Latin American policy. However, outside observers, sometimes including Latin American leaders and analysts, often fail to recognize the fact that the number of relevant political actors is substantial. The institutional as well as informal political relationships are complex and changeable. Within the executive branch itself, responsibilities and preoccupations over Latin American policy extend beyond the State Department and the National Security Council. The Departments of Defense, Commerce, the Treasury, Agriculture, and Interior all have legitimate institutional and political interests in the region. This is also true of the attorney general's office, and the role of the Central Intelligence Agency is, of course, profoundly important.

Moving to the legislative branch brings us to a separate set of duties and interests. The constitutional responsibility may emerge in highly visible fashion, as with the battle over the Panama Canal treaties in the Senate. On some occasions, partisan lines are clear-cut, while on others the Republican-Democratic dichotomy is blurred. Certain senators or representatives may exert great influence for a time on a selected issue—until her 1986 electoral defeat, Paula Hawkins of Florida had a strong influence on drug matters, to cite a recent example. Those whose constituencies include growing numbers of Hispanics are predictably and properly devoting more attention to Latin American issues, and there are usually a few who take a particular interest in the region for idiosyncratic or circumstantial reasons. Thus North Carolina's Jesse Helms had demonstrated neither interest in nor knowledge of in Latin America during a lengthy career as a television commentator in Raleigh. When national attention focused on the Panama Canal renegotiations, however, he swiftly developed a commitment that brought him exceptional power during the Reagan years—sometimes to the dismay of leaders in both parties and in the White House itself.

The news media and the burgeoning number of think tanks and policy centers are also important to the foreign-policy process. In the case of communications, it remains true that, as James Reston once remarked, Americans will do anything about Latin America but read about it. Similarly, the press still concentrates on crises and natural disasters. Its attention span is limited, as is television's. Viewers do not require a long memory to recall the wave of media attention directed to El Salvador at the start of the 1980s. A veritable army from the networks and the press corps descended upon San Salvador, and viewers and readers were deluged with information, much of it superficial or at best repetitious. In due course, the "hot" story cooled and attention shifted. Although civil strife, violence, and economic depredation continue, the media have turned elsewhere, most notably to Nicaragua. Only a minority of reporters brought long experience and accumulated insight to reporting on Latin America.

The role of the think tanks has been an important one, with increasing visibility during the last decade. The Brookings Institution, RAND Corporation, and the American Enterprise Institute have been joined by a number of others, ranging in quality and consequence from outstanding to mediocre and in political outlook from one end of the spectrum to the other. The policy output has also been increasing from such academic affiliates as the Hoover Institution at Stanford and the Center for Strategic and International Studies at Georgetown University. Nor can one ignore such bastions of the traditional foreign policy establishment as the Council on Foreign Relations. The input of these groups varies in significance. The immediate point, however, is to substantiate further the basic observation about the multiplicity of potential actors and competing interests in the formulation of U.S. policy toward Latin America.

In light of the pluralistic character of the United States and its traditions of democratic government, particular emphasis must be placed on the role of public opinion. This draws upon the character relationships between the elite and the masses and the extent to which foreign-policy makers are responsible and responsive to the citizenry. There can be little question that the formulation of foreign policy is essentially an elitist process. Members of the public are usually unconcerned about international affairs unless they perceive the matter at hand to be central to war, peace, and national survival. This is certainly true with questions of hemispheric policy. Most of the time, problems arise and are addressed in light of only minimal awareness by the majority of the electorate.

Put another way, there are usually few if any natural constituencies to lobby for particular policies or to apply pressure on elected or appointed leaders. We have seen elsewhere that the Carter administration fought for the renegotiations with Panama without support from any significant public constituency. This made it difficult to counter the complaints of the small but vocal group that actively opposed the new treaty terms. This was an unusual case in that Carter chose to undertake a far-reaching and politically problematic reform that required senatorial approval and that did not enjoy significant support. Few administrations are willing to pursue such a course unless, as with Carter, the president is personally committed to it.

It should go without saying that the greatest likelihood of public attention accompanies apparent or alleged Marxist activity that is perceived as a threat to national security. Even then, however, it is far from certain that public opinion will be swayed, and if it is not, an incumbent government can be left with a contentious political problem. In the Dominican Republic in 1965, the Johnson administration initially did not raise the banner of anticommunism. Doing so soon became politically advisable, however, and thus the decision to intervene was heralded as an effort to combat the threat of "another Cuba" in the Caribbean. Whatever the wisdom or folly of the U.S. action, no president could afford the political risk of permitting another Marxist regime to be set up in its geopolitical backyard. It is also true, however, that the administration's best efforts were unable to generate a strong public sentiment in favor of the policy.

Even the more dramatic case of an elected socialist president in Chile did little to arouse public opinion. Indeed, Washington's preference in that instance to operate behind the scenes could be rationalized on the grounds that anti-Allende policies lacked any important public constituency. The attempt to design and direct a policy of destabilization over more than three years, informed by Washington's determination to save the voters of Chile from their own presumed stupidity, was not grounded on popular support. This is in contrast to the relationship between the United States and Nicaragua in the 1980s—a conflict still far from resolved as this is written. President Reagan, who initially denounced the Sandinista regime for providing arms to Salvadoran insurgents, had little success in persuading or arousing the public to this threat. A later stiffening of political rhetoric demanded a democratization of the regime. By 1986 Reagan conceded in a Mexican interview that, in the final analysis, the government in Managua might have to be removed. This was the presidential wish that helped to motivate those who undertook the disastrous Iranian arms arrangement and the diversion of funds on behalf of the Nicaraguan contras.

The Reagan determination that the Sandinistas be driven from power had long been implicit. It was within the context of the 1986 legislative battle over aid to the insurgents, however, that the administration launched a determined publicity campaign to sell the U.S. public on this policy. It proved to be one of the few instances in which the Great Communicator was rebuffed by popular opinion. A long succession of surveys amply documented that on this issue the vaunted communicatory magic of Ronald Reagan was weighed and found wanting. Setting aside the unsurprising fact that most citizens have difficulty in identifying individual Central American countries on the map, it was also evident that there was uncertainty about the identity and political goals of the contras and of the Sandinistas. More important was the unwillingness of the public to accept the premise that Central American upheaval constituted a major threat to the security of the Republic.

It is possible to project a scenario that might indeed arouse public opinion to a fever pitch: border fighting, the seemingly innocent involvement of U.S. citizens, the death of U.S. military personnel, and the like. The imagination can readily construct a course that would inflame the public, at which time an active interventionist policy incorporating military operations might enjoy broad support. Even so, however, the motivation would be less a widespread fear of Marxist penetration than a defense of national honor. In the absence of such exceptional circumstances, the reigning elites in Washington can scarcely proceed openly unless they are willing to pay a high price for ignoring or defying public opinion, and historically this has been a politically dangerous course within the context of the pluralistic U.S. system.

Even when looking for special-interest groups or targeted sectors of public opinion, the possibilities are limited. On most issues concerning policy toward Latin America, natural constituencies are either nonexistent or too small to have political significance. Short of questions perceived as bearing consequences for national security, attempting to create massive public support is unrealistic. Notwithstanding scattered church organizations and a peace movement that may deal with such questions as sanctuary for Salvadoran refugees, public influence is slight. Recent demographic shifts that have created areas with large Hispanic populations may well be more important. Certainly the influence and political potential has established itself in southern Florida, in southwestern border areas, and in the urban centers of the Northeast. For years Miami has been a center of vehemently anti-Castro Cuban expatriates, but the city is now swelling with Latin Americans from other countries. Statewide influence includes the recent election of Robert Martinez, a former Tampa mayor of Hispanic background, as the Republican governor of Florida. In other areas the number and influence of Hispanics are also on the rise, and in time they will constitute an important constituency whose voice will be heard and heeded in Washington.

In the pages that follow, thematic variations and refinements will become evident. This essay has attempted merely to call attention to selected topical areas of concern, ones that have proven germane to U.S. policy toward Latin America over a long span of years. It has been suggested that certain trends of the last twenty-five years have altered older patterns. At the same time, recognizable historical currents are still apparent. Even though the years since 1961 have been unsettled and marked with upheaval, consistencies of action and policy have appeared far more often than contradictions. The traits and circumstances stated in summary form above retain validity as policymakers face the approach of a new century. The discussion of enduring policy clusters in part 3 must inevitably take into account these factors. The debt crisis presents rather different problems than those traditionally associated with foreign policy. Yet, as Riordan Roett persuasively argues, the relationship between economics and politics is unbreakable. In the case of U.S. policy toward the Caribbean Basin, including specifically Castro's Cuba, classic questions of national priorities, political perspectives, and styles of decision making and crisis management again spring to the fore.

Set against the backdrop of these themes are the fascinating and challenging questions confronting policymakers for the present and near future. Lessons from experience, even if properly understood, must be viewed cautiously in order to provide flashes of insight for those who would solve contemporary issues. Consensus is difficult at best; its absence merely testifies to the complexities inherent in policy making. The following essays answer some questions but leave other unanswered. Can there be a single view about relations with Cuba? What about the past (or even present) role of the United States in Chile? What of responses to the debt crisis? What should be the mediate and long-range priorities for Central America? At what point should the limitations of U.S. control or influence be recognized? What are the alternatives to the historic tradition of domination by the *yanquis*?

If on few other points, there is doubtless unanimity among our contributors over the inevitability of dissent. Differences of opinion, some sharply articulated, emerge in the pages that follow. This is as it should be, for there is, after all, no easy road to understanding or to the resolution of controversy. Policy problems are not readily soluble, and some may never be satisfactorily untangled. But the effort to understand and to care, to seek possible answers and viable courses of action, constitutes a responsibility not to be shirked. It is a duty long since accepted by each of our distinguished writers, many of whom have served in a variety of public or private capacities or both. Their collective effort merits our attention in thinking about the policies and role of the United States in Latin America.

Part One

Politics and Policy Making

Federico G. Gil

The Kennedy-Johnson Years

Despite cyclical oscillations between serious concern and declining interest, U.S. policy in Latin America has constantly pursued two objectives. The first has been to exclude from the western hemisphere extracontinental rival or hostile powers. The second has been to secure the dominant politico-economic presence of the United States in the region. Implicit in these objectives is the maintenance in Latin America of stable regimes capable of safeguarding U.S. interests.

A Historical Overview

Many different political, economic, diplomatic, and even military instrumentalities have pursued of these goals. Thus the United States, engrossed at first in the process of developing its trade, restricted by the limitations imposed by belligerent European nations, and preoccupied mainly with its own security, accepted the newly born republics of Latin America into the international community in 1822, and the following year enunciated the Monroe Doctrine—the first political expression of the idea of spheres of influence—with the intention of restricting extracontinental meddling and establishing the foundation of U.S. continental hegemony. For Latin America there was never to be one Monroe Doctrine but several, each drawn up to serve a specific situation. For the United States, on the other hand, the Monroe Doctrine was to become not only the most influential expression of its policy during the nineteenth century but also a symbolic formula imbued with almost mystical overtones. During the next two decades the United States dedicated itself to its internal development and expansion, practically ignoring its neighbors to the south.

Later, as its power developed and its demographic, cultural, and economic superiority with respect to the Latin American nations became greater, the United States concentrated its efforts on converting Simón Bolívar's Pan-Americanism into an association of American nations. The primary goal was to obtain commercial advantages that would insure U.S. economic domination in the region.

The first phase of the imperialist era, that of Manifest Destiny (1845–1860), preceded this effort to secure hegemony and resulted in a renewed interest in the region. The United States used the concept of Manifest Destiny to extend itself along a broad front to the Pacific and to expand its territory by more than two-thirds. From 1861 to 1889 the Civil War, Reconstruction, the conquest of the West, and the process of industrialization absorbed all the energies of the United States, and there was a period of quiescence in U.S.–Latin American relations. Once these tasks were completed, there began, with the Spanish-American War, a second stage of the imperialist era, the strategic and economic expansion that converted the Caribbean into a U.S. *mare nostrum.*

With the rise of the United States as a world power at the turn of the century, it became necessary to reexamine its foreign policy. The result, as Robert Freeman Smith has noted, was a "pragmatic attempt to define the interrelated strategic economic interests of the United States in a world of competing empires and power blocs."[1] This approach was based on the premise that U.S. interests would be best protected in a stable world in which no one nation exercised absolute control over extensive regions. Thus the Latin American policy of the United States was formulated in the light of the conflict between the national interests of Latin America and the existing imperial systems. But orthodox implementation of this policy was made practically impossible by the rising economic and strategic interests of the United States in the Caribbean.

The new interpretation of the Monroe Doctrine was embodied in the Roosevelt Corollary and the construction of an inter-American system that would promote U.S. economic and political interests. To be sure, both were manifestations of the attempt to preserve the status quo, a paramount objective of U.S. policy, but they inevitably involved a contradiction for the United States for many years to come. The Roosevelt Corollary, justifying interventionism because of the "duty" of the United States to uphold European proprietary rights and the need to protect the increasing economic and strategic stakes of the United States in the Caribbean, could not be reconciled with the tenets of Pan-Americanism.[2] If the only effective means of assuring stability—the immutable goal of U.S. policy toward Latin America—was to be intervention, the possibilities of constructing Pan-Americanism were nil.

President William Howard Taft's "dollar diplomacy," which in his words "substituted dollars for bullets," was designed to insure stability through the use of economic devices. Dollar diplomacy was reshaped over the years in response to changing conditions in Latin America and the need for making an inter-American system dominated by the United States more palatable to the Latin American nations.[3]

The constant deterioration in U.S.–Latin American relations arising from the growing resentment against the Colossus of the North, along with the world economic crisis of 1929, which made it imperative for the United States to increase its trade with Latin America, were responsible for a significant change in course during the Hoover administration, a change that would culminate in the adoption of the Good Neighbor Policy by Franklin D. Roosevelt. During the Roosevelt administration the Monroe Doctrine underwent a transformation that made possible its acceptance by Latin America. In a historic speech in 1933, Roosevelt proclaimed the continentalization of the doctrine by rejecting the right of intervention. Under the impulse of the new policy, the inter-American system continued its rapid development from that time until the end of World War II.

The menace of European totalitarianism stimulated new U.S. efforts to strengthen and perfect the inter-American defense system. But, paradoxically, the creation of the legal structure designed to consolidate the regional system coincided with a notable deterioration in U.S.–Latin American relations and the reappearance of conflicts and frictions. The old fears and mistrust, which had partially dissipated during the era of the Good Neighbor Policy, returned with unexpected vigor as disinterest on the part of the United States in the great economic depression the Latin American nations suffered after the end of the war became evident. The United States' lack of concern over the economic aspirations of the region was accompanied by a total lack of comprehension of the emotional impact of development. This process of deterioration began with the shift in U.S. foreign policy from a North-South axis to an orientation toward Europe and Asia. At the systemic level in domestic American politics, debate developed on the theme of regionalism versus globalism. Though preserved at the 1945 San Francisco Conference, and later consolidated with the Reciprocal Assistance Treaty of Rio in 1947 and the adoption of the charter of the Organization of American States at Bogotá in 1948, the regional system was to settle into a languid existence.

Coincidentally with this there was a growing erosion of democratic processes in Latin America, to which U.S. policy responded with its historic inclination to favor strong-arm regimes for the sake of stability. During World War II, because of strategic considerations, the actions of the Roosevelt administration were directed at maintaining the status quo even if this meant supporting the most undemocratic governments. In the mid and late 1940s, however, as a consequence of the reorientation of its policy toward Europe and Asia, the United States started to reduce military and economic assistance to Latin America. There followed a series of revolutionary movements and changes in government throughout Latin America—in Guatemala and Cuba in 1944, in Peru, Venezuela, and Brazil in 1945, and in El Salvador in 1948.

The cold war brought a change in the Latin American policy of the United States, which again dedicated itself to the vigorous support of stable regimes regardless of their nature. With extensive U.S. military aid, dictatorial regimes such as those of Alfredo Stroessner in Paraguay, Fulgencio Batista in Cuba, Anastasio Somoza in Nicaragua, and Manuel Odría in Peru, were strengthened. This policy, defended by Secretary of State John Foster Dulles, was initiated with the 1954 intervention in Guatemala, an episode that inflicted a damaging blow to U.S. prestige. The Guatemalan episode was at least partly a consequence of the program of military defense that the Truman administration had started following the outbreak of the Korean War. Under the Mutual Security Act of 1951, the United States eventually negotiated numerous military agreements with Latin American nations. A basic assumption of this policy was that strengthening the Latin American military was the best insurance against Communist subversion in the region. The issue of military aid, combined with the aftereffects of the Guatemalan intervention, produced more suspicions and resentments in Latin America, and these eventually erupted in the late 1950s.[4]

The continuing deterioration of U.S.–Latin American relations was brought into sharp focus as a result of the violence attending Vice-President Nixon's Latin American tour in 1958. In 1953, in an effort to improve the U.S. image, President Dwight D. Eisenhower had commissioned his brother Milton to make a fact-finding journey to Latin America. This mission reported that Latin America urgently needed outside economic help. A reexamination and restatement of U.S. policy toward Latin America appeared imminent with the publication of the Eisenhower Report, but the only positive result was the eventual but reluctant acceptance by the United States of a long-cherished desire of the Latin Americans through the creation in 1960 of the Inter-American Development Bank.

Deep concern was growing in Washington. The Committee on Foreign Relations of the U.S. Senate began a long-range review of U.S. foreign policy. President Juscelino Kubitschek of Brazil and President Eisenhower exchanged notes concerning the critical conditions of U.S.–Latin American relations. Kubitschek suggested a twenty-year plan for large-scale joint hemispheric action to promote Latin America's economic development. To implement Kubitschek's Operation Pan-America, a special group—the Committee of 21—was appointed by the Organization of American States (OAS). This group submitted a series of recommendations embodied in a document known as the Act of Bogotá of 1960. This document contained a complete program of social and economic development while clearly recognizing the relationship between development and the strengthening of free and democratic institutions. Financing for the program was to be achieved by adding to the internal resources of each nation a special fund—to which the United States pledged $500 million—to be administered by the Inter-American Development Bank. The first indication of a shift in the U.S. attitude was its new readiness to discard its traditional policy, which maintained that private investment should carry the greater burden of Latin American development and that international governmental aid should be limited.

A chain of events in the 1950s led to the emergence in Latin America of what seemed to be a self-conscious democratic impulse, or at least a populist impulse. This trend was best articulated politically by the liberal progressive political parties that formed what was generally referred to as the Democratic Left. Beginning with *aprismo* in Peru, the Democratic Left was to gain currency and acceptability in several Latin American countries. By the advent of the Kennedy administration, the democratic ethic, as it was to be articulated in the new policies of that administration, seemed to be a reflection of what was taking place in Latin America at that time. As Arthur Schlesinger puts it: "Without the rise of the Democratic Left there would have been no Alliance."[5]

The New Frontiersmen

Subscribing to the Act of Bogotá was the last of the Eisenhower administration's minor adjustments in a foreign policy that had always aimed at balancing foreign and domestic claims on resources.[6] The work of the United Nations Economic Commission for Latin America, Brazil's advocacy of Operation Pan-America, the creation of the Inter-American Development Bank, and finally U.S. acceptance of the Act of Bogotá, laid the foundations for revitalized hemispheric relations and the emergence of new spirit of reform in the Latin American policy of the incoming administration of John F. Kennedy.

Most students of U.S. foreign policy will agree with Hannah Arendt's observation that a "fear of revolution has been the *leitmotif* of postwar American foreign policy in its desperate attempts at stabilization of the *status quo*, with the result that American power and prestige were used to support obsolete political regimes that long since had become objects of contempt among their citizens."[7] No other area of the world better illustrates the truthfulness of this assertion than Latin America, and in perhaps no other region of the world did the changes brought about by the Kennedy administration in the foundations of our foreign policy become clearer.

This basic and profound change came about as a response to a single event that had extraordinary repercussions on the international scene, namely, the Cuban Revolution. To be sure, revolutionary change in Latin America has been one of the most difficult and frequently recurring problems to confront the United States since the turn of the century. The first true social revolution of the twentieth century took place in Mexico in 1910 and presented U.S. policy makers with a new version of the old dilemma. The United States did not employ armed intervention, but it did insist that Mexico moderate its revolution. The next threat of social revolution occurred in Cuba in 1933. In keeping with the principles of the Good

Neighbor Policy, again there was no military intervention. Instead, the United States used economic measures as the key instruments of a policy designed to prevent undue changes and maintain the status quo. In 1952 the Bolivian social revolution provided a new test. The Bolivian revolutionary regime expropriated the tin mines and instituted a radical agrarian reform program. After some hesitation, the United States began to extend economic aid to the Bolivian regime, but not before Bolivia had reached a preliminary financial settlement with the mining companies.

From 1953 until the advent of the Cuban Revolution, the United States lost the opportunity for a policy of watchful waiting. Events beyond U.S. control were responsible for the revolution that shook the island republic. The United States could no longer wait on the sidelines for the revolutionary drive to slow down before extending aid and moral support to countries experiencing the traumas of revolutionary change. External forces were compelling the United States to develop a new kind of diplomacy, the diplomacy of social revolution. The traditional framework in which U.S. and Latin American foreign policies were shaped was broken. The Cuban Revolution's impact on international policies was far-reaching in that it gave rise to a model for development in Latin America and linked the cold war to the problem of underdevelopment.[8] Coincidentally, the foreign policy of the Soviet Union underwent an important shift in the mid-1950s, when Moscow proposed a policy of extending aid to revolutionary movements even when they were not of Communist origin and embarked upon a large program of economic aid to the underdeveloped world.

The Alliance for Progress

The Kennedy administration's response to this challenge in Latin America was embodied in the Alliance for Progress, which the president announced dramatically in his speech of 13 March 1961 and in a special message to Congress the next day. Kennedy's interest in Latin America was longstanding, but the rise of Fidel Castro in Cuba had done more than anything else to make Latin America a lively issue in the 1960 presidential campaign, since preventing other Latin American countries from "going Communist" proved to be a politically profitable campaign issue. Some of his intimates have felt that had there been no Cuban Revolution and no Cold War, Kennedy might not have made it an issue in the campaign. But he felt keenly about Latin America, having visited the region twenty years before becoming president. He had a new conception of American interests in the hemisphere and believed that it was necessary to distinguish between the interests of American private investors, so assiduously protected by preceding administrations, and the national interest of the United States. He strongly believed that the national interest would be more effectively protected by the extension of popular government and the promotion of democracy and reform.[9] With the exception of Franklin D. Roosevelt, Kennedy was the only president in this century with a genuine interest in U.S.–Latin American relations.

The general ambience in the United States and abroad was favorable for such a revolutionary approach. There were profound longings for a better life, and the belief was widespread that it was possible to utilize reason as an instrument of social change. Progressive democracy appeared to be moving forward irresistibly in Latin America and in the United States simultaneously. It was in the context of this domestic and international outlook that the Alliance for Progress was launched.[10]

The New Frontiersmen of 1961 shared Kennedy's convictions, but they were not necessarily experts on Latin America. With the exception of Adolf Berle, who had extensive experience acquired in the days of the Good Neighbor Policy, most of the members of the president's circle of advisers lacked any direct, intimate contact with the region. But they were willing to learn. C. Douglas Dillon, the secretary of the treasury, had gained some experience during the second Eisenhower administration as under secretary of state for economic affairs, but Richard Goodwin, Ralph Dungan, and Arthur Schlesinger, Jr., all intellectually indefatigable and capable, had to undergo a rigorous apprenticeship in the pursuit of the two basic goals of the new policy: the enlargement of democracy and the conquest of poverty in Latin America. Pursuit of these goals, according to Kennedy, was the answer to Castro and the Communist movement.

The Alliance for Progress was unprecedented in the history of hemispheric relations, for in essence the United States was offering to underwrite a social revolution for Latin America. "The great plan was expected," as Adlai Stevenson said, "'to take the bold, brave, difficult steps' to achieve peaceably and democratically reforms which in the past history of the world had been accomplished only through revolutions of blood and violence."[11] Its origins, as we have seen, were essentially ideas derived from Latin America's two closely related desires: (1) to modify drastically the obsolete social systems perpetuated by dictatorial civil-military regimes, and (2) to accelerate economic development and eradicate widespread poverty. Thus the Alliance was not a program imposed by the United States upon Latin America but a body of Latin American ideas and proposals that had finally been accepted by the United States.

Kennedy's Latin American policy was based on the idea of a partnership between those governments and political parties of Latin America that were willing to mobilize national resources and enlist the energies of their people, and a United States that would provide economic assistance and political support. Convinced that the United States, despite its economic and military might, could not realistically be expected to solve the problems of Latin America by itself, Kennedy considered that only a vast cooperative effort would have a chance of successfully carrying through a peaceful revolution, thus avoiding dislocations and turmoil in the social and economic fabric of the Latin American countries, with dire consequences for the interests of the United States.

The ultimate goal, as has traditionally been the case in U.S. policy, was of course the preservation of hemispheric stability and order. But Kennedy felt that U.S. interests in the region were being endangered by the American failure to understand the rapidly changing hopes and ambitions of the people to the south. As conceived by Kennedy and his New Frontiersmen, the Alliance for Progress was to pursue three mutually dependent goals: economic development, basic structural change, and political democratization. All of these goals could only be achieved through the most determined efforts of the Latin American nations themselves, with impetus from outside assistance.

Four months after President Kennedy's speech pledging the cooperation of the United States in this vast effort, the representatives of the American republics, convened by the Inter-American Economic and Social Council of the OAS, met at Punta del Este, Uruguay, to design a specific plan of action along the lines proposed by Kennedy. The Declaration of the Peoples of America, signed on 17 August 1961, set forth the following objectives: (1) the development and strengthening of democratic institutions, (2) the acceleration of economic and social development, (3) an anti-illiteracy program and higher educational standards, (4) the assurance of fair wages and working conditions, (5) the promotion of health programs and the eradication of contagious diseases, (6) the reform of tax laws and the encouragement of agrarian reform, (7) the curbing of inflation and the restoration of fiscal stability, and (8) the stimulation of private enterprise in order to provide jobs and thereby to reduce unemployment. The declaration also suggested that these changes could come about only through the self-help efforts of each country and the essential contributions of external assistance. The United States agreed to contribute a major part of the minimum of $20 billion, principally in public funds, that would be required during the next ten years from all external sources to supplement Latin America's own efforts. As an immediate contribution, the United States was to provide $1 billion by March 1962.

Another product of the conference was a lengthier document, which became known as the Charter of Punta del Este and which contained the operational plan for the Alliance. The plan carried the implicit assumption that in many Latin American countries the development of self-sustaining economics could be attained in a period of ten years. The charter also recognized the need for external capital to be applied to social goals such as education, health, housing, taxation, and agriculture, as well as to the growth of industry and other elements of economic development.[12]

Explicit in the charter was an emphasis on the principle of self-help and a requirement for the formulation of national development programs based on the nations' own effort and financed from domestic resources, with foreign aid supplying only the technological resources and capital that the countries were unable to provide. In order to achieve these goals, the Latin Americans were to raise their per capita income by a minimum of 2.5 percent annually. This meant that the region's gross national product would have to increase more than 5 percent in order to compensate for the expected 3 percent population increase per year.

A clause of the Charter of Punta del Este specified the commitment on the part of the Latin American nations to develop cooperative programs to prevent the often seriously damaging effects of fluctuations in the foreign exchange derived from export commodities, but it failed to suggest concrete actions. It simply gave a general endorsement of all international efforts to reduce market instability and instructed the OAS to convene a group of experts to study the problem and make recommendations. Reflecting the incipient strength of the movement for regional integration that was to gain considerable ground in the following decade, the charter expressed the need for agreements on economic integration aimed at creating a "Latin American Common Market."

But even this early, at the meeting at Punta del Este, which was held in the midst of almost euphoric expectations, some danger signals could be detected. The writing of the Declaration of the Peoples of America was no easy task. Some Latin American delegations became alarmed at the discussions on the redistribution of resources and attempted to water down the document in order to weaken the demands for structural reforms.[13]

Another task undertaken at Punta del Este was to determine the role to be played by existing international organizations in the extraordinarily complex machinery required to achieve the immediate goals of, for example, housing, health, and education, and the long-range objectives of socioeconomic reform and development encompassed by the Alliance. Coordination and cooperation were needed among inter-American organizations and between these and other international agencies. Consequently, in 1961 the OAS, the Inter-American Development Bank, and the UN's Economic Commission for Latin America (ECLA) signed a covenant under which each assumed its share of the responsibility for the direction and execution of the Alliance. Thus the OAS accepted the responsibility for providing basic studies, technical personnel, and task forces, and for evaluating the long-term national development programs the Alliance required of the Latin American governments. The Inter-American Development Bank was placed in charge of channeling the funds allocated to each national project, and ECLA provided many of the trained personnel required to direct new development projects.

In response to a joint proposal from the OAS secretary general, the president of the Inter-American Development Bank, and the secretary of ECLA, the Inter-American Economic and Social Council appointed a panel of nine high-level experts, who became known as the "nine wise men." This panel functioned as an independent body. In 1962 it recommended a revision in the Alliance's machinery, which led to the appointment of former presidents Alberto Lleras Camargo of Colombia and Juscelino Kubitschek of Brazil as a committee to recommend changes. The results led in turn to the creation in 1963 of the Inter-American Committee for the Alliance for Progress (CIAP) to provide liaison between the United States and the Latin American governments. With the creation of CIAP, the Latin

American role in determining priorities, channeling requests, and recommending expenditures was increased.

This brief description suggests the extraordinary complexity of the multilateral mechanisms required for continuing policy formation, programming, planning, testing, and review under the ambitious and massive program agreed upon in the Alliance for Progress.[14] To some extent, such complexity was unavoidable, since the program was injected into an existing multilateral administrative structure composed of three international agencies: the OAS, the Inter-American Development Bank, and ECLA. The involvement of these organizations was indispensable, because they made possible the acceptance in an international forum of key commitments to undertake reforms in areas traditionally reserved to the domestic jurisdiction of states.

To complicate matters further, the Alliance had two other basic aspects, one unilateral and the other bilateral. They first reflected the fact that social and institutional reforms could be achieved only by actions of the respective countries—even in financing. The bilateral aspect mainly concerned financing and technical aid and involved numerous agencies of the United States government, as well as banks and industrial enterprises in the private sector. Among the U.S. government agencies were the Agency for International Development (AID), the Export-Import Bank, the Food for Peace Program, and the Peace Corps. Many internecine conflicts among these agencies impeded the progress of the Alliance and contributed to its decline during the Johnson administration and its eventual demise under Nixon.

Once the Alliance was launched, Kennedy had to persuade the executive and legislative branches of the government to support his new approach to Latin American policy. There was little consciousness in the bureaucratic apparatus of the gravity of the situation south of the border. In the State Department the "old Latin America hands" were highly suspicious of the Alliance's revolutionary rhetoric, and throughout the government there was an instinctive resistance to new directions.

Why the Alliance Failed

Organizationally, the United States simply lacked adequate experience, instruments, and the requisite skills for promoting and managing a socioeconomic revolution of the magnitude to which it had committed itself. At another level, by redefining the issues and objectives, the Alliance did succeed in the beginning in altering the political consciousness and the social agenda of Latin America. Ultimately, however, neither the United States nor the Latin American countries presented the program to the people as a multilateral cooperative partnership rather than a conventional foreign-aid program. Among the masses of Latin America there was little popular awareness of the revolutionary import of the Alliance, notwithstanding Kennedy's amazing popularity throughout the region. Not since the Roosevelt era had a U.S. president enjoyed such enthusiastic approval.

In the United States, big-business—which had received sympathetic and ample support during the Eisenhower administration, often exerting a dominant influence on foreign policy—were less than happy with the new directions. Big business did not participate in any meaningful way in the formation of the Alliance, though some prominent business leaders expressed sympathy for its goals. In fact, during the Kennedy years there was an unusual but temporary decline of corporate influence in the foreign-policy process, accompanied by a reduction of U.S. private investment in Latin America.[15] An example of conflicting views between the administration and big business was the passage in 1962 of the Hickenlooper Amendment, which required that economic sanctions be imposed when Latin American governments nationalized or imposed discriminatory taxation on U.S. owned enterprises.[16]

In Latin America the forces opposed to reform began an implacable campaign of resistance to and sabotage of the new policy. The Latin American oligarchs, with few exceptions, reacted to Kennedy's foreign policy with almost pathological fear. Remembering with nostalgia the U.S. diplomacy of the past, they concluded that Kennedy had aligned himself with the radicals in their countries, and they felt betrayed by the revolutionary thrust of the Alliance, particularly by its emphasis upon tax and land reforms. The oligarchs were, of course, opposed to any reforms that threatened their wealth and political power, and they refused to accept Kennedy's thesis that the choice was between peaceful and violent revolution. More often than not, the emerging middle classes, content with adopting the values and aping the manners and customs of the upper class, were unable to develop any class consciousness or unite in defense of reforms. The lowest stratum of the society, living in poverty and misery, was

too apathetic and indifferent to mobilize against the traditional social order. Finally, the Latin American radical left opposed the Alliance with a vigor equal to that of the oligarchy. Latin American leftists feared the Alliance as much as the oligarchs on the right did,
because they felt that if the democratic revolution were to succeed,
theirs would have no future.

The political parties of the Democratic Left were the chosen instruments to implement the Alliance. They were the logical vehicle
for political action. Based in the rising middle sectors in the 1930s,
the Democratic Left had provided the vital functions of leadership,
production, and investment in efforts toward social and economic
reforms. But by 1960 their capacity and willingness to provide these
functions were in doubt. By then the movement had lost the drive
and zealous spirit that it had possessed because of its origins in the
student and trade union movements of earlier decades. It is ironic
that at the time of its greatest strength, U.S. foreign-policy makers
had viewed the Democratic Left as too radical and therefore as a
threat, not a potential ally. By the advent of the Kennedy administration, the parties of the Democratic Left were in political decline,
having lost touch with the younger generation. For them the Alliance had come ten years too late.[17] Many of their younger followers
were beginning to think that the progressive democratic way was too
slow and was incapable of restructuring society.

A source of difficulty for the Alliance was the failure of governments and political leaders to develop an ideological content, as Rosenstein-Rodan (one of the "nine wise men") remarked, a mystique
that "could overcome the normal inertia and resistance to change. . . .
To create a heroic spirit of mission, an enthusiasm for a peaceful revolution is the main task confronting Latin American leadership."[18]
The spirit of mission that characterized Roosevelt's New Deal was
absent from the New Frontier's Alliance for Progress. This is not to
say that a psychological element was entirely absent in Latin America. Such a spirit did exist then as it does today, but it was linked
with strong nationalistic feelings born of Latin America's earnest desire for self-determination and economic independence. The Alliance's inability to identify itself with this potent force was perhaps
inevitable, since nationalism in Latin America feeds on anti-Americanism.[19] The problem arose from the newness of the image of the
United States as a champion of reform. In the minds of the Latin
American masses, the stigma of broken promises and domination in

the past was much stronger than the image of a United States devoted to freedom and social justice for all.[20] Inevitably, Latin American nationalism defines itself as opposed to the United States.

In the United States, the administration of the Alliance was entrusted to a segment of AID, which was designed to carry out the objectives of the Point IV Program and therefore was definitely inappropriate, structurally speaking, to undertake such a dramatic task as that of bringing about peaceful revolution. The new program, using as vehicles for action gigantic and slumbering organisms such as the Department of State and AID, was perhaps inherently incapable of making the important changes and adjustments required by the revolutionary crusade.

The Dream Begins to Fade

Two years after the Alliance was launched, disillusionment, frustration, and at times even resentment were voiced in Latin America and the United States alike. Kennedy himself recognized the difficulties and limitations. "We face extremely serious problems in implementing the principles of the Alliance for Progress," he said in 1963. "It's probably the most difficult assignment the United States has ever taken on. . . . There are greater limitations upon our ability to bring about a favorable result than I had imagined."[21] To be sure, the Alliance achieved considerably less than Kennedy had hoped. Although it registered substantial progress toward its social and political objectives and was not entirely ineffective in promoting economic growth, such gains in social and economic development were offset by Latin America's basic problem, the population explosion.

The Punta del Este declaration had set forth the goal of a yearly increase of 2.5 percent per capita in the combined gross national product of Latin American countries. In the first seven years of the Alliance, Latin America showed an average annual increase of 4.5 percent per year, but because of the staggeringly high population growth, the per capita increase was actually only 1.5 percent. In 1968 the overall rate of growth was 5.5 percent, and the per capita increase had risen to 2.5 percent.[22] Though it is not possible to claim that this improvement was entirely the result of the Alliance, undoubtedly some portion of it must have been due to the Alliance's efforts. Though Kennedy was aware of the problem and had mentioned it on several occasions, population control was a delicate political subject, given the overwhelming strength of Catholicism in Latin America, so much so that it was not even mentioned in the Charter of Punta del Este.[23]

A 1968 AID report said that in spite of the difficulties, some progress had been made in some areas. Tax collections had increased, and governments had made outstanding improvements in public health and in the building of schools, low-cost housing, sewage disposal facilities, water supply systems, and so on. But progress in agrarian reform had been slow, the region's share in world trade had not improved, neither unemployment nor inequalities of income distribution had decreased, and illiteracy rates continued to be high.[24] The flow of new foreign capital was more than offset by large repayments of past loans and profit remittances sent abroad.

What had gone wrong? Some have suggested that the United States overrated the demand for change and ignored the strength of structural barriers and the depth of inertia that pervaded the entire region. This is, of course, true. Others have rightly emphasized that there existed an intrinsic contradiction in the Alliance. Che Guevara had predicted that the United States, by setting loose the forces of change, could end by losing control of a revolution that could be its enemy.[25] Schlesinger maintains that "no one could doubt an intrinsic contradiction between the Alliance and the rest of the United States government," which was concerned, to the exclusion of any other considerations, with national security and the Communist threat. In his view the "unrelenting pressure of the national security bureaucracy led to a perversion of Alliance programs."[26] He shared the opinion of others that it would not be fair to conclude that the Alliance had failed since it had not really been tried except for the very short period of the one thousand days of the Kennedy administration.

Above all, there is the fact that the goals of the Alliance were unrealistic. The idea of accomplishing in ten years a task that could easily take several generations reflected how much Kennedy and his men underestimated the structural obstacles in the path of reform and overestimated the ability of the United States to foster and lead revolutionary change in other societies. In their innocence, perhaps they also forgot that in spite of protestations to the contrary, the United States' most consistent goal in foreign policy was to preserve stability, to oppose communism, and to foster favorable conditions for financial investment. These goals are not always compatible with reform.

The Counterinsurgency Policy

Guerrilla movements seeking to overthrow established governments appeared in a number of countries in the 1960s. Some of these governments were dictatorial; others had a reformist democratic inclination. Nor were the revolutionary movements of the 1960s all alike. But generally the guerrillas of the 1960s tended to be opposed to the United States and, inspired by the Cuban Revolution, to stand for radical programs of change. They shared the view that reformism was doomed to fail and that the United States was not sincere in its advocacy of social change.

The security preoccupation combined with an authentic concern for the well-being of the Latin American peoples prompted the framework of the Kennedy administration's two-pronged response to social revolution in Latin America. Through the Alliance, the United States could provide support and encouragement for social reform within the existing political systems, and through counterinsurgency programs, the U.S. government could sponsor the elimination of rebel movements that threatened political stability and that were hostile to the United States. This component of Kennedy's Latin American policy was perhaps its weakest. The policy was partly the result of Kennedy's tenuous assumptions about the "Soviet connection" with national liberation movements and partly the result of his personal confrontations with Khrushchev. The Soviet leader repeatedly assured national liberation movements of the support of the USSR. Kennedy, personally confronting Khrushchev at the Vienna summit meeting, felt compelled to respond forcefully to the Soviet challenge with counterinsurgency programs. Thus the goal of military aid to Latin America evolved from the prevention of outside aggression to the suppression of internal subversion externally supported.[27]

Through AID a public safety program was launched under which Latin American internal security and police forces were provided with a variety of arms and special equipment. Military advisers provided special training in counterinsurgency operations for the Latin

American armed forces. The total number of Latin Americans trained under U.S.-sponsored military assistance programs during the twenty-year period 1950–1970 came to nearly fifty-five thousand.[28] The State Department established an International Police Academy to offer training in modern methods.[29]

By 1967 most of the guerrilla movements had been eliminated. The most dramatic episode in the antiguerrilla campaign was the death of Che Guevara and his small band in Bolivia in 1967. Guerrilla activities, however, persisted sporadically in other countries and reappeared with more vigor in the 1970s and 1980s in Central America and some South American republics.[30]

The counterinsurgency policy led to some difficulties related to the recognition of new governments. The question was this: What should the United States do when a military coup overthrows a duly elected regime? The traditional U.S. policy was to extend automatic recognition to any government able to maintain order and to meet its international obligations, regardless of its origin. In the Western Hemisphere, U.S. recognition often could make or break governments and had often been used as a form of intervention. The question faced by the Kennedy administration was not new, but it was a difficult one if the United States was to be faithful to the democratic principles of the Alliance.

Answers to the dilemma were not always the same. When the Argentine generals turned out the constitutional president Arturo Frondizi in 1962, Kennedy accepted the State Department's recommendation to recognize the new military regime on the basis that the chief justice of the Argentine supreme court had been constitutionally named his successor. On the other hand, when *aprista* leader Haya de la Torre won a presidential election in Peru the same year but the military took over to prevent him from assuming the office, Kennedy suspended diplomatic relations and all forms of assistance. Later, when the Peruvian military restored civil rights and promised new elections, the United States restored relations.

In 1963 a series of military coups overthrew the governments of Guatemala, Ecuador, the Dominican Republic, and Honduras. Kennedy decided to continue aid to the military juntas in Guatemala and Ecuador but pursued the same course of action he had followed in Peru in suspending relations and all aid programs to the counterrevolutionary regimes of Honduras and the Dominican Republic. This time, however, the policy proved unsuccessful. Convinced that non-recognition was not palatable to the Latin American nations when most of them hastened to recognize military governments, he decided to resume relations with those two countries.[31]

The Cuban Problem

The most spectacular failure of Kennedy's Latin American policy was, of course, the Bay of Pigs episode. This affair was clearly a reflection of the contradiction, already discussed, between the bureaucratic approach and preoccupation with national security, and the Alliance's grand design for development and democratic reform.

The Bay of Pigs disaster had been an initiative of the Eisenhower administration that Kennedy, with considerable misgiving, agreed to continue after taking office. The whole operation was incredibly mismanaged, and the invasion on 17 April 1961 ended in total disaster. The popular uprising anticipated by the CIA never occurred, and U.S. support was not sufficient under the restrictions Kennedy had placed on it. In a matter of hours the expeditionary force of anti-Castro Cuban exiles, which had been trained in collusion with Guatemala and Nicaragua, had been crushed, and the episode turned into an impressive victory for Fidel Castro.[32] Clearly, the United States had flagrantly violated the principle of nonintervention included in the charter of the OAS and in numerous other hemispheric agreements. President Kennedy promptly assumed total responsibility for the tragic fiasco, which cast doubt not only on the integrity of the United States but also on its leadership and military ability. It also gave new weight to the propaganda efforts of anti-American forces throughout Latin America at a time when U.S. prestige on the continent had reached a new low. It was chiefly as a result of this debacle that the Kennedy administration decided to embark upon the counterinsurgency program.

Now that Cuba was clearly committed to the Soviet camp and to a policy of spreading its revolution to the rest of Latin America, the administration turned to a multilateral approach to the Cuban problem. At the instigation of the United States, a meeting of foreign ministers of the American republics was held in January 1962 at Punta del Este. At the meeting the United States urged a collective break of diplomatic relations with Cuba and a total embargo. These proposals encountered the opposition of the most important nations. Finally, with six nations (Argentina, Bolivia, Brazil, Chile, Ecuador, and Mexico) abstaining, the meeting suspended Cuba from participation in the inter-American system and also suspended trade with Cuba in arms and implements of war, a measure that proved to be highly ineffectual.[33]

Meanwhile, Cuba was faced with the question of whether to encourage Latin American revolutions or to build up and strengthen its own regime. Its answer was that it should do both but that Cuba must come first. Castro's emphasis during the Kennedy years, however, was more on Cuba as the citadel of Latin American revolution, a citadel that must not be endangered. As Cuban zeal to convert the Andes into another Sierra Maestra was reaching new heights, Soviet military support, not only in armaments but also in personnel, became a cause of concern for the Kennedy administration. In October 1962 photographic evidence and air reconnaissance revealed that a number of offensive missile sites were being constructed on the island. President Kennedy ordered a quarantine on all offensive military equipment destined for Cuba and a blockade of ships carrying such equipment.[34] Twenty-four hours after Kennedy's speech announcing these measures, the council of the OAS endorsed his position, and some Latin American countries immediately contributed naval forces to the blockade. Others mobilized their armies and offered the use of bases to the United States.

The missile crisis ended after an exchange of messages between Kennedy and Khrushchev, but Cuban efforts to extend revolutionary activities over Latin America resumed. There was little that Kennedy could do except to tighten the economic boycott, though it failed to damage Cuba, because it was receiving substantial assistance from the Communist bloc. Latin Americans were reluctant to join in any punitive action against their sister republic, and some countries (Brazil, Mexico, Bolivia, Uruguay, and Chile) still maintained relations with the Castro regime. It was not until after Kennedy's death that Cuban subversive activities in Venezuela provoked action by the OAS in 1964, and this eventually led to the nearly complete economic and political isolation of Cuba in the Western Hemisphere.[35]

Johnson and Latin America

Soon after Lyndon Johnson took the oath of office onboard Air Force One in Dallas, it became evident that Latin America had lost the preeminent place on the priority list of the foreign-policy makers that it had enjoyed during the Kennedy years. President Johnson's knowledge of and interest in Latin America were very limited. The image of Latin America he was familiar with was one that can only be seen on the borderlands of the United States. As Schlesinger said, Johnson "thought that Latin America ended with Mexico."[36] His administration was not only unable but also unwilling to provide the Alliance for Progress with the intellectual and political leadership, the spiritual élan, which had disappeared with John F. Kennedy's death. The Alliance was not officially abandoned, but it was left in a moribund state until it finally died during the Nixon years.

Absorbed in domestic issues, particularly in developing his plans for the Great Society, and obsessed with the Vietnam conflict, Johnson demonstrated little interest in Latin American policy. Disillusioned with the slow pace of Latin America's development, Congress began to make large cuts in funds for the Alliance in 1967. At the same time, political instability, an ever-growing rate of inflation, and a general uncertainty inhibited the flow of U.S. private capital into the region. Latin America's private capital, for the most part in the hands of the oligarchic strata of the society, preferred the security of deposits abroad to the risks of domestic investments.

As we have seen, the last days of the Kennedy administration witnessed a resurgence of military coups throughout much of the continent. At the end of 1963 the Johnson administration, much more concerned with security matters and anticommunism than with the undemocratic nature of Latin American military regimes, decided not to continue to use recognition as a way of encouraging democratization, and it extended recognition to the military regimes of the Dominican Republic and Honduras. In striking contrast, Johnson halted aid to the democratic government of Fernando Belaúnde Terry in Peru, a defender of the Alliance, in order to coerce that government into reaching a settlement favorable to the International Petroleum Company in its dispute over nationalization.

In April 1964 the constitutionally elected government of João Goulart in Brazil was overthrown by a military uprising. The Johnson administration, which suspected Goulart of softness toward communism, quickly extended recognition to the new authoritarian regime. Recognition of the Dominican military junta on 14 December 1963 came about in response to both strong pressure on President Johnson from his advisers and his own conviction, arising from his political anxieties, that there was an urgent need to prevent the emergence of a revolutionary movement modeled on Cuba. Subsequent events and the Johnson administration's increased fear that the Dominican situation might result in a Communist takeover and in the establishment of a Castro-like regime led to the 1965 U.S. military intervention and the enunciation of the Johnson Doctrine, both of which are discussed elsewhere in this volume.

By once more playing the role of international policeman in the Caribbean, the United States aroused a storm of reaction in Latin America and caused a group of nations to refuse to support the United States' anticommunist policy at the expense of the fundamental principle of nonintervention. It is significant that of the five countries that supported the American intervention, only one, Costa Rica, had a democratic government. The others—Brazil, Guatemala, Honduras, and Paraguay—had unrepresentative and military-controlled regimes.[37]

The Dominican affair was not only a serious setback to the regional system. It also dealt a damaging blow to the Alliance for Progress. Johnson focused his Latin American policy on the political and military aspects of anticommunism in the hemisphere at the cost of further serious deterioration in U.S. relations with its partners in the Alliance by thus making a radical break with Kennedy's policies. As William D. Rogers, assistant secretary of state for inter-American affairs during the Ford administration, has said, "a more dramatic shift in tone and style of U.S. Alliance leadership would have been difficult to imagine."[38]

Johnson's new assistant secretary of state in charge of Latin American affairs, Thomas Mann, was an advocate of using the Alliance principally as a political instrument of U.S. foreign policy to solve short-range problems and as an economic arm at the service of U.S. business. He replaced not only the able career diplomat Edwin Martin, who had served Kennedy in that capacity, but also Teodoro Moscoso, the great champion and spiritual leader of the Alliance, who had so devotedly headed the program since its inception. With Mann, business corporations, which had played only a minor role in foreign-policy making during the Kennedy years, began to reassert their influence. Under Mann's stewardship the Latin American policy of the United States was reoriented toward supporting any government, regardless of its nature and origins, that opposed communism and that was well-disposed toward U.S. business interests. Under the Johnson administration, the Alliance was deprived of its social content and became more and more a conventional aid program, featuring loans conditioned on purchases in the United States.[39]

Conclusion

To use the words of Chile's President Eduardo Frei, the Alliance "lost its way."[40] All in all, it yielded more discord than harmony and more frustration than satisfaction. Progress was slow and painful. The economic growth that was achieved, since it was rarely accompanied by an authentic restructuring of the existing pattern of income distribution and by social and political reforms, tended to benefit primarily those who already held wealth and power and strengthened a corrupt status quo.[41] Without the Alliance, Latin America might have suffered even more, but the fact remains that the Alliance, a generous and noble gesture, was unable to implement solutions to the fundamental conflicts it sought to resolve.

Notes

1. Robert Freeman Smith, "The Role Played by the United States in Latin American Social and Economic Revolutions of the Last Half Century" (Paper presented at the Eighth Southeastern Conference on Latin American Studies, Miami Beach, 29 April 1961).

2. Federico G. Gil, "Latin American Social Revolution and United States Foreign Policy," in Marian D. Irish, ed., *World Pressures on American Foreign Policy* (Englewood Cliffs, N.J.: Prentice-Hall, 1964), p. 133.

3. Ibid.

4. Gil, *Latin American–United States Relations* (New York: Harcourt Brace Jovanovich, 1971), pp. 214–15.

5. Arthur M. Schlesinger, Jr., "The Alliance for Progress: A Retrospective," in Ronald G. Hellman and H. Jon Rosenbaum, eds., *Latin America: The Search for a New International Role* (New York: John Wiley and Sons, Sage Publications, 1975), p. 61.

6. R. Harrison Wagner, *U.S. Policy toward Latin America* (Stanford: Stanford University Press, 1970), p. 150.

7. Hannah Arendt, *On Revolution* (New York: Viking Press, 1963), p. 47.

8. Gustavo Lagos, *International Stratification and Underdeveloped Countries* (Chapel Hill: University of North Carolina Press, 1963), p. 120.

9. Schlesinger, "Alliance for Progress," pp. 58–59.

10. Ibid., p. 57.

11. Gil, *Latin American–United States Relations,* p. 240.

12. The texts of the Declaration of the Peoples of America and of the Charter of Punta del Este are reprinted in *Special Report on Latin America,* Sen. Doc. no. 80, 87th Congress, 2d sess., 1962 (Washington, D.C.: U.S. Government Printing Office, 1962), pp. 33–43.

13. Schlesinger, "Alliance for Progress," p. 65.

14. Figure 3 in J. Warren Nystrom and Nathan A. Haverstock, *The Alliance for Progress: Key to Latin America's Development* (Princeton, N.J.: D. Van Nostrand, 1966), has a useful organizational diagram of the Alliance.

15. It is worth mentioning, however, that some revisionist historians, in the perspective of today, suggest that the Alliance was a shrewdly devised product of U.S. economic interests and was designed to expand their markets and protect their investments in Latin America.

16. A. F. Lowenthal, "United States Policy toward Latin America: 'Liberal,' 'Radical,' and 'Bureaucratic' Perspectives," *Latin American Research Review* 8 (Fall 1973): 3–25.

17. Schlesinger, "Alliance for Progress," pp. 70–71.

18. Paul Rosenstein-Rodan, "Latin America," *Challenge* 3 (May–June 1967): 10–11.

19. Arthur M. Schlesinger, Jr., *A Thousand Days: John F. Kennedy in the White House* (Boston: Houghton Mifflin, 1965), pp. 791–92.

20. Gil, "Latin American Social Revolution," p. 152.

21. *Public Papers of the Presidents of the United States: John F. Kennedy . . . 1962* (Washington: U.S. Government Printing Office, 1963), pp. 880, 889.

22. *A Review of Alliance for Progress Goals (A Report by the Bureau for Latin America, Agency for International Development),* 91st Congress, 1st session, House of Representatives (Washington, D.C.: U.S. Government Printing Office, 1969), p. 1.

23. Schlesinger, "Alliance for Progress," p. 69.

24. *Review of Alliance Goals,* p. 16.

25. Richard Goodwin, "Our Stake in a Big Awakening," *Life,* 14 April 1967, p. 83.

26. Schlesinger, "Alliance for Progress," pp. 73–74.

27. Cole Blasier, *The Hovering Giant: U.S. Response to Revolutionary Change in Latin America* (Pittsburgh: University of Pittsburgh Press, 1976), pp. 241–42.

28. Ibid., p. 243.

29. Schlesinger, "Alliance for Progress," p. 74.

30. Blasier, *Hovering Giant,* p. 246.

31. Gil, *Latin American–United States Relations,* p. 250.

32. Ibid., p. 233. For a detailed account of this affair, see Tad Szulc and Karl E. Meyer, *The Cuban Invasion: The Chronicle of a Disaster* (New York: Bal-

lantine Books, 1962); also Gil, *Latin American–United States Relations*, p. 233.

33. Jerome Slater, *The OAS and United States Foreign Policy* (Columbus: Ohio State University Press, 1967), pp. 152–61.

34. "The Soviet Threat to the Americas," Address by President John F. Kennedy delivered on 22 October 1962, *Department of State Bulletin* 47, no. 1220 (12 November 1962): 715–19.

35. Gil, *Latin American–United States Relations*, p. 235.

36. Schlesinger, "Alliance for Progress," pp. 82–83.

37. Gordon Connell-Smith, *The Inter-American System* (New York: Oxford University Press, 1986), p. 342.

38. William D. Rogers, *The Twilight Struggle: The Alliance for Progress and the Politics of Development in Latin America* (New York: Random House, 1967), p. 226.

39. Schlesinger, "Alliance for Progress," pp. 78–80.

40. Jerome Levinson and Juan de Onís, *The Alliance That Lost Its Way: A Critical Report on the Alliance for Progress* (Chicago: Quadrangle Books, 1970).

41. Ibid., pp. 307–8.

Michael J. Francis

United States Policy toward Latin America during the Kissinger Years

Finding some order in the mountain of small and large decisions that comprised Washington's policy toward Latin America during the presidencies of Richard Nixon and Gerald Ford is a confusing task. Only one broad, official statement of policy toward Latin America was made during the period. In his highly publicized presidential speech on 31 October 1969 to the Inter-American Press Association, Nixon claimed to "offer no grandiose promises and no panaceas" but rather to offer "action" in constructing a new hemispheric policy of "a more mature partnership in which all voices are heard and none is predominant."[1] However, as one looks at the record of the years that followed, it is difficult to argue seriously that this speech really laid out a blueprint of the policy. It was more a talk that set a rather condescending tone: Latin American countries had finally matured enough to be treated as equals.[2]

After that speech, most of the statements of policy toward Latin America are hidden away in various foreign-aid messages and press conference comments. Late in 1973 there was a brief flurry of excitement over a possible new policy as a result of Secretary of State Henry Kissinger's calling for a "new dialogue," and in April 1974 he claimed that "the policy of the good partner" would be the new approach. In 1974, people in Washington were saying that Kissinger was going to make it the "Year of Latin America,"[3] but by January of the following year the Latin American policy was described as being in shreds.[4] In February of that year, the *Christian Science Monitor* reported that there was "a growing tendency [among Latin American leaders] to doubt that Dr. Kissinger really is sincere in his efforts to set up a 'new dialogue.' "[5] Then suddenly, with the Ford political campaign facing problems, in October 1976 Kissinger asserted that

Latin American concerns were Washington's first priority, although he admitted that the problem was being recognized somewhat late.[6]

So how can we speak of a Latin American policy on Washington's part during the Nixon and Ford administrations? It is the thesis of this discussion that there were two levels of treatment, two kinds of policies. If a matter was perceived as having no East-West aspects or serious domestic political implications, it was handled within the foreign policy bureaucracy (largely the Department of State) by individuals who had the furtherance of good relations between countries as their highest priority and who were quite willing to make substantial concessions in order to assure cordial relations. If somehow the issue had Cold War or domestic political significance, it received the attention of Kissinger and Nixon, and they were willing to play very rough (as in the case of Chile) or make substantial concessions (as in Panama), depending on what action they thought would be most effective. But in the cases in this second category, the goal of good relations with Latin American countries was not highly valued—the stakes were the competition with the Soviet Union and the political future of the Republican administration, and in these situations the sensibilities and sovereignty of the Latin American states were of little concern to the White House.

To grossly oversimplify what is doubtless already an oversimplification, the following heuristic schema is offered:

Perception of Dispute	Level of Decision Making	Type of U.S. Policy
economic or political dispute within the hemisphere	professional foreign service officers and other members of the foreign policy bureaucracy	concessionary to Latin American countries
dispute with possible Cold War implications or political aspects	President and Kissinger	decision determined by perceptions of implications for East-West relations, not by interests of Latin American countries; action could be concessionary or harsh

The degree to which we are speaking of "perception" in this schema is important to keep in mind. The question of how these perceptions come to be is a preoccupation of political scientists,[7] and it clearly involves such things as access to leadership, the role of interest groups, domestic political situations, and psychological factors. Thus, even if this schema is completely accurate, an important facet of the process—the origin of the perceptions—is not within our framework.

Kissinger: The Geopolitical Vision

The platitudes of the broad policy statements are not the place to start in order to explain this dichotomy. Rather, the distinction is rooted in the geopolitical perceptions that dominated Henry Kissinger's view of the world. And to illuminate how that applied to Latin America, the place to begin is with a comment that Kissinger, who was then President Nixon's national security adviser, made in June 1969 to Chilean foreign minister Gabriel Valdés.[8]

The context of the statement was a meeting held in the Oval Office between visiting Latin American foreign ministers and President Nixon, who had then been in office about six months. The visitors were presenting the recommendations of a meeting of Latin American representatives that had taken place in Viña del Mar, Chile, and the recommendations were generally critical of U.S. trade policy and foreign assistance programs. At the session the aristocratic Valdés took it upon himself to speak rather harshly to the president and his national security adviser about Washington's historic abuse of its power in hemispheric relations. Apparently the Valdés comments marred what the White House had intended to be a pleasant exchange of platitudes and a photo opportunity.[9] Kissinger, doubtlessly encouraged by the president, asked Valdés to lunch the following afternoon. At that meeting he spoke harshly to his guest, and in so doing he revealed a good deal about his perception of the world. The best-known Kissinger comment from that meeting is the following:

Mr. Minister, you made a strange speech. You come here speaking of Latin America, but this is not important. Nothing important can come from the South. History has never been produced in the South. The axis of history starts in Moscow, goes to Bonn, crosses over to Washington, and then goes to Tokyo. What happens in the South is of no importance. You're wasting your time.[10]

Later, when accused by Valdés of knowing nothing about the South, Kissinger replied "No, and I don't care."[11]

It is easy to express dismay at such a heavy-handed statement, but getting beyond the obvious pique that prompted the comment, Kissinger's view is consistent with his worldview, and it is that vision that brings coherence and order to our understanding of U.S. policy toward Latin America during the Kissinger-Ford-Nixon years.

Kissinger was broadly influenced by such thinkers of the power politics/realism school as Hans Morgenthau, whose textbook on international politics and other writings dominated the intellectual debate after World War II, and George Kennan, the scholar-diplomat whose statement of the containment policy neatly fit the prevailing diplomatic outlook of his day. In essence, the Kissinger view is that power underlies all international relations.[12] Nations protect their national interests via the pursuit of power. Although economic might is important, the bottom line is military might. Force is the final arbiter in international affairs. The system, Kissinger would presumably argue, worked reasonably well (when in the hands of good leadership) in keeping the peace or controlling violence through the European balance of power, but with the nuclear age more stability is required because the results of a breakdown are more disastrous.

From Kissinger's perspective, the most obvious contemporary threat to the needed stability was created by the emergence of the Soviet Union as a world power. This was made difficult by two factors: (1) the problem of integrating any new great power into the system because the existing powers would have to come to terms with a new, and often less favorable, distribution of power, and (2) the ruthless, totalitarian nature of the Soviet government. This latter factor was due both to historical factors within the Soviet Union and to the banner of Marxism-Leninism, which placed a particular "twist" on the Soviet actions and led Moscow to have destabilizing perceptions of certain international situations.

As the most powerful nation on earth at the end of World War II, the United States, in Kissinger's eyes, had a responsibility, both in its own interest and in the interest of others, to combat Soviet expansionism while at the same time allowing the Soviet Union to gain a place in the hierarchy of international affairs that reflected its great-power status. Because of the savage nature of nuclear war, the kind of wars or skirmishes that had characterized the traditional balance of power was no longer acceptable—stability had to be the highest concern. The proper role for Latin America would be to cooperate with the initiatives of the hemispheric hegemonic power.

Within this rather broad intellectual abstraction, factors such as bureaucratic bargaining and personality factors helped to shape the actual policy decisions. In Kissinger's case, his expertise was in western European affairs, and his ignorance of the Third World (and of international economics) heavily influenced his sense of priorities. But what distinguishes Kissinger from most other recent American foreign-policy decision makers is the degree to which he stuck to his priorities rather than trying simultaneously to please everyone or solve all the world's problems at once. No evidence is more convincing as to the White House's disinterest in Latin American problems than a reading of Nixon's, Ford's, or Kissinger's memoirs.[13] Latin American matters are almost totally ignored.

Some critics of Kissinger point to this lack of interest as a major failing. This is a defensible criticism, but it can also be argued that foreign-policy decision makers have limited amounts of time and attention, and that the more serious immediate threats to the national interest were in the Middle East, Vietnam, and the Soviet Union, and hence that Latin America should *not* have been a region that consumed much of the president's or Kissinger's time.

For its part, the foreign-policy bureaucracy in Washington had no master plan for Latin America. Rather, it had a tendency to attempt to solve discrete problems as they arose with individual Latin American governments. This is not to say that there were no generally shared perceptions within the foreign-policy bureaucracy.[14] Of particular importance for the Third World was the widely held U.S. belief that free trade and foreign investment were important for economic development. This investment, via such institutions as multinational corporations, was under attack from Third World leaders. Increasingly, Latin Americans were expressing the fear that their economic development was being thwarted by the structure of the international economy. Within that broad complaint, many schools of thought existed, ranging from reformist to Marxist.

Many in the Department of State had no problem believing that American foreign investment had at times behaved badly in Latin America or had been exploitative, and foreign service officers saw the protectionist elements in Congress as seriously undermining a liberal international trade system. But representatives of the foreign-policy bureaucracy were generally solid in their belief that, whatever its disadvantages, foreign investment was a prime engine of growth in Latin America and that heavy government intervention in the economy inevitably became political and disrupted rational economic decision making by individual entrepreneurs. Of course, in such agencies as the Department of Commerce, the liberal prescription was taken particularly seriously. Nixon shared this belief. In his 1969 speech to the Inter-American Press Association, he argued:

We will not encourage U.S. private investment where it is not wanted or where local conditions face it with unwarranted risks. But I must state my own strong belief and it is this: I think that properly motivated private enterprise has a vitally important role to play in social as well as economic development in all of the nations.[15]

So Kissinger and Nixon did not question the conventional wisdom that a liberal economic order worked to the benefit of all parties concerned. Given the importance of the multinational corporations in the U.S. economy, there were few voices of criticism of the multinationals in high levels of government. But to think that Kissinger placed a high priority on the protection of the specific interests of multinationals is to misunderstand his viewpoint. He was quite willing to sacrifice their interests, or the interests of allies, if he felt it served the higher goal of stability. However, since his views of international politics included a belief in the advantages of a liberal trade and investment regime, there were few situations in which his actions would be to the detriment of the multinational corporations. And certainly he had been a protégé of that pillar of corporate America, Nelson Rockefeller.

So it is difficult to strike a balance when discussing this question of the influence of multinationals on American foreign policy in Latin America. Publicly and privately, officials gave much lip service to the glories of multinational-fueled development. What this essay suggests is that Kissinger's worldview carried with it many advantages for the multinationals. The big corporations had largely supported the Republican president even though it was a vision of a stable world (rather than a world dominated by them) that shaped Kissinger's actions. The implication that there is a deep difference between the two approaches can be misleading. Stability was of prime importance to *both* the multinationals and the geopoliticians.

If Kissinger did not particularly care about the interests of multinational investors in Latin America, what vision did he have of the area? What Kissinger wanted was a kind of liberal hegemony in which the area was stable and the United States stood willing to step in from time to time and straighten out situations that threatened stability. Because this was the U.S. sphere of influence, he felt justified in behaving aggressively in appropriate situations in order to stop Moscow from stirring up trouble in Latin America. Although he could not say so publicly, the rules of the game as Kissinger saw them were that the United States could fund dissidents in Eastern Europe and generally stir up trouble, but we would not intervene militarily if the Russians enforced their hegemonic authority through the use of force. Similarly, we could expect the Russians to exacerbate problems in the hemisphere, but the United States could play an active role (as in Guatemala in 1954 and the Dominican Republic in 1965) without fear of Russian military retaliation. In fact, stability in the system required an activist role for the United States, and the logic of this line of thought suggests that the Russians could be expected to do the same in Eastern Europe. Whether the countries had democratic governments or not was of no concern to Kissinger—in fact, in his Inter-American Press Association speech, Nixon went far out of his way to make it clear that the United States, while preferring democracy, would deal with the Latin American governments "as they are" rather than testing them for democratic development.[16]

To support this thesis, this paper will discuss four cases. They are (1) U.S. relations with Cuba, (2) the Panama Canal negotiations, (3) the Allende election and downfall in Chile, and (4) the International Petroleum Company's dispute with Peru. I have chosen these cases because they deal with particularly important problems of the period and because they illustrate the thesis.

Cuba: The Mouse That Roared

The flaw in Kissinger's world of geopolitical spheres of influence was Cuba, a country ninety miles off the coast of Florida that had managed to fall into the Soviet orbit. The United States had made major efforts to reverse this "historical accident" at the Bay of Pigs and later through continual harassment of the island via cooperation between CIA operatives and Cuban exiles.

On the other hand, Castro's initial efforts to export his revolution to the rest of Latin America had slackened during the mid-1960s— presumably in part as a result of the disastrous attempt by Ernesto "Che" Guevara to overthrow the Bolivian government in 1966 and 1967. So by the time Nixon and Kissinger came into office, Castro's optimism about toppling governments in the hemisphere had been cut back to some minor opportunistic support. This diminished effort may have been an attempt to win the favor of the Soviet Union, which had long been critical of Castro's aggressive and naive belief in his revolution's ability to influence events in the hemisphere. Certainly during the late 1960s the Cuban-Russian relationship had become increasing cordial and trade had increased.

Although Kissinger had few preconceptions about the Cuban situation, it is clear that a number of experiences had shaped Nixon's thinking about Cuba. After his 1959 conversation with Castro during the Cuban leader's tour of the United States, for example, Nixon had begun warning that Cuba was going Communist unless something was done. He had not handled the topic well in the 1960 presidential debates, and there was his friendship with "Bebe" Rebozo, a strongly anti-Castro exile who frequently shared his thoughts on the Cuban situation with Nixon. All this resulted in, to use Kissinger's words, Nixon's having "a neuralgic problem" on the topic of Cuba.[17] The Cubans, or at least Castro, may well have had a similar phobia regarding Nixon, since he was continually held up in the Cuban press as a particularly malevolent force, and the "x" in his name was replaced by a swastika. Despite these factors, the first two years of Cuban-U.S. relations during the Nixon presidency were comparatively calm.

But the serenity ended in August 1970 with the discovery by photoreconnaissance of a new installation in Cienfuegos harbor that some intelligence analysts saw as a base for nuclear submarines. Kissinger was immediately convinced of the worst—in part because a soccer field had been constructed near the base, and Kissinger "knew" the Cubans didn't play soccer.[18] The installation of a major submarine facility in Cuba had a potential for influencing the strategic balance and hence was immediately seen as an East-West issue. One of the weaknesses of the Soviet strategic nuclear missile deterrent has been that it keeps a far lower proportion of its submarines at sea at any one time than does the United States. Its submarines patrolling the North American coasts have to return to Russia in order to undergo maintenance. A facility in Cuba could help the Russians to keep more submarines with nuclear missiles off the Atlantic coast.

Kissinger concluded that building such a base constituted a repudiation of the understanding upon which the settlement of the

Cuban Missile Crisis had been based, that is, that in return for a U.S. promise not to invade, offensive weapons were not to be reintroduced to the island. Kissinger also saw the building of the base as a test of American resolve and hence, believing that the United States was obligated to react with vigor, urged Nixon to push the Soviets on the matter.

Ironically, Nixon showed a great deal of reluctance. The fate of the Moscow summit was in the balance, and at the time the facility was discovered, there were important confrontations taking place in the Middle East. Furthermore, Nixon argued that a Cuban crisis in the midst of a congressional campaign would trigger public cynicism about the political process.[19]

Nixon's hope of holding off a controversy over the Cuban facility until he returned from his European trip proved futile, because leaks to the press raised the issue in a sensational way. Seymour Hersch's extremely critical biography of Kissinger claims that the national security adviser himself manipulated the press in order to force Nixon to confront the issue,[20] and even Kissinger in his memoirs refers to the press leaks as providential, although he makes a great deal out of precisely how the story came to be public, an explanation that leaves him blameless.[21]

Whatever the catalyst, the United States and Russia were again in confrontation over Cuba, and as was true during the Cuba Missile Crisis, the opinion of Havana was to matter little. In an attempt at firm but quiet diplomacy, the United States warned Moscow that it would not allow the presence of strategic nuclear missiles on submarines being serviced by the facility. The Soviet response was vague, but it indicated a recognition that Washington's position was consistent with the surprisingly imprecise terms of the 1962 missile crisis settlement.

According to both Nixon's and Kissinger's accounts, the Soviet Union at this point backed down and removed the offending facilities at the naval base. Other observers have concluded that the facility had not been set up for the purpose Kissinger feared and that the Soviet Union essentially assured Washington of this and went about its previously planned course of action.[22] This is a controversy that was totally controlled by the interests of Soviet-U.S. relations. Washington perceived U.S. hegemony as being under challenge.

Four years later, in September 1974, Cuba again became an issue because Colombia, Costa Rica, and Venezuela jointly asked the Organization of American States to drop its sanctions against Cuba, which barred diplomatic relations and trade by member countries with the Cubans and participation by Havana in the OAS. Although the administration had been vocal in support of ostracizing Castro, it went to the meeting in Quito at which the issue was to be considered "without a defined position" and finally abstained in the vote.[23] However, the removal of sanctions fell two votes short, and the United States was criticized by several Latin American countries for a failure to exercise leadership at the meeting.[24] Then in July 1975 the administration shifted its position to support readmission.[25]

This came in the midst of a flurry of stories indicating that relations might improve between Castro and Washington. The *Washington Post* described a series of minor U.S. concessions as "part of a slow, guarded turn toward normalizing U.S. relations with the Communist government of Premier Fidel Castro."[26] James Reston, after an interview with Castro, observed that he was obviously getting ready for such discussions.[27] The idea of normalizing relations between Havana and Moscow made sense from Kissinger's point of view because it would have represented a wooing of a loyal Soviet satellite. On the other hand, during this period Kissinger was primarily involved in the continuing Middle East crisis, although between November 1974 and November 1975 there were four secret meetings in New York and Washington between U.S. and Cuban officials.[28]

With a general settlement with Castro very much in the air by late 1975, the hard realities of dealing with Castro began to dawn on those who hoped for better relations. There are several major difficulties. First, there are a host of discrete problems connected with any settlement, such as the amounts due various U.S. investors who lost holdings due to Castro's nationalizations.[29] Second, there are the personality and belief system of Castro himself. His self-righteous anti-Americanism, his support for Puerto Rican independence,[30] and his vision of being a Third World leader made rapprochement with Washington difficult on both sides. And there was the electorally important and extremely vocal Cuban community in the United States, which largely opposed concessions to the man who they felt had ruined their native island.

But the factor that finally killed any prospect for a settlement was Cuba's sending of troops to Angola. That decision brought Castro into direct conflict with a CIA-sponsored effort and allowed Castro to be seen in Africa as fighting the racist South Africans—and fighting them effectively. The long training and experience of the Cuban soldiers made them more effective than African soldiers. Here was an arena in which Castro could become an important actor on the international stage. Thanks to Russian support, rather than being simply another mouse in the world of global politics, Cuba had become a lion (at least in the context of the struggle in Africa). The intervention had the further benefit, from the Cuban perspective, of giving Havana more leverage with Moscow for economic, military, and political support.[31]

This enraged Kissinger's sense of power politics because it seemed impossible to believe that the small island could extend its influence into Angola, then Ethiopia, and then elsewhere. It was a violation of the rules of geopolitics and hence made no sense. Seeing the very foundations of power politics being violated in Africa, he spoke ominously of the Cuban troops there in a February 1976 press conference: "There are matters to which we cannot be indifferent, because it can lead to enormous instabilities all over the world, especially when it is done by a small Caribbean country backed by revolutionary zeal and Soviet logistics."[32] At another news conference the same month, he again spoke of a broad significance for Cuba's actions: "This is a pattern which, as one looks at other parts of the world, would have the gravest consequences for peace and stability, and it is one which the United States treats with indifference only at the risk of buying graver crises at higher cost later on."[33]

After advising the Cubans to be wary in their African moves, at a news conference in Dallas in March 1976 (Texas was a key primary state in the Ford campaign), Kissinger said the United States would not tolerate further Cuban intervention abroad, but within three days he was softening his stance and claiming that there was "no crisis."[34]

Ford and Kissinger were frustrated by the situation, but the costs of teaching Castro a lesson in power politics outweighed the psychic benefits of such an initiative. Also, the secretary of state was busy trying to get congressional support for his collapsing Vietnam peace settlement. So in this case Cuba was able to do as it pleased. To Kissinger, in matters regarding a possible direct confrontation with the Soviet Union, discretion was needed in the name of stability.

Panama: Negotiations and Politics

The Panama Canal treaty negotiations are an interesting case, in part because, contrary to much public rhetoric at the time, Nixon and Kissinger did not even see the waterway as central to U.S. national interests. They were initially quite willing to let the Department of State handle the issue. However, due to its complexity and the fact that there were potential domestic political implications for each decision, they were inevitably drawn into the talks.

Under pressure triggered by the January 1964 riots in Panama, the Johnson administration had managed to negotiate a new treaty to replace the 1903 arrangement and its later modifications. With Ellsworth Bunker as Washington's negotiatior, the new documents were completed late in Johnson's term. But the political costs of Vietnam and the confusion resulting from the impending U.S. presidential and congressional elections caused those agreements to be shunted aside. Additionally, a presidential campaign was in full swing in Panama, and in May 1968—half a year prior to the U.S. election—Arnulfo Arias was elected. Arias, an unpredictable and opportunistic politician, had strongly opposed the new agreement on the general grounds that the Panamanian delegation had conceded too much.

We know a good deal about the detailed inner workings of the decision-making process relating to Washington and the Canal as a result of a remarkable book by former Kissinger National Security Council aide and former ambassador to Panama William J. Jorden.[35] In it he details the White House's initial lack of interest in the Canal question. The "panorama of great power politics left little room for developments south of the border," as Jorden put it.[36] Thus the matter fell into the hands of the lower echelons of the foreign-policy bureaucracy. Assistant Secretary of State Charles Meyer, fearful of the harm the Panamanian deadlock was doing to U.S. prestige in Latin America (and fearful of another embarrassing explosion such as occured in 1964), pushed Secretary of State William Rogers on the matter. Then, through a chain of circumstances, the civilian president of Panama (and confidant of strongman Omar Torrijos) managed to raise the matter in a direct conversation with President Nixon.[37] Nixon expressed a reluctant and limited interest, but his vague promise to pursue talks was enough to restart the negotiations. On the U.S. side, Charles Anderson, a former secretary of the treasury under Eisenhower but not a friend of Nixon's, represented the United

States. Progress was difficult because Nixon never talked with Anderson on the matter.[38] As Jorden observes:

For the president, the Panama negotiations were a political complication. He knew any fair settlement would have only a small constituency in the American body politic. Any change would encounter opposition in the Pentagon. He had been on Capitol Hill long enough to know the resistance the treaty would meet there. He had given his word to try to solve the problem, but he was not enthusiastic. Kissinger took his lead from his boss, and Anderson's repeated requests for meetings or for decisions were unanswered.[39]

In fact, however, the Panamanian delegates were having a similar problem in that Torrijos wanted to remain aloof from the talks, which left technical experts in charge who had no political or decision-making responsibility.

Torrijos, frustrated by the lack of progress, formulated another strategy—or second track—for influencing the United States. Put in the vocabulary of this essay, he purposefully set about converting the Panama question from a bureaucratic concern to a geopolitical question. He did this in a calculating manner and caused great discomfort in the White House and the bureaucracy. Besides making highly publicized visits to such anti-American Third World leaders as Fidel Castro and Muammar al-Qaddafi, the military leader sought an international occasion to dramatize the situation. Finally he managed to get the UN Security Council to meet in Panama and discuss the Canal in March 1973. Left alone in its opposition to the resulting resolution, the United States was forced to cast its third Security Council veto in thirty-seven years to defeat a resolution that criticized U.S. reluctance to settle the issue with Panama.[40] As Jorden observes:

I believe that what really made Kissinger understand he was sitting on a potential powder keg was the U.N. Security Council meeting. . . . It was, after all, a gathering not of the Western Hemisphere but of the world. Votes against the United States came not only from Panama and Peru but also from the Soviet Union and China and even France. That was enough to awaken any geopolitician. Bangladesh and Cambodia were on the other side of town; Panama was in the backyard. Kissinger saw the danger and acted. A bemused president, focused on survival, was brought along more by acquiescence than by strong conviction at that point.[41]

There was the fear of a possible bloodbath due to rioting in Panama, but there was also the fact that the Nixon landslide of 1972 had emboldened the administration to move onto tackling a list of unsolved foreign policy problems.[42] Coupled with what Jorden saw as the beginnings of Kissinger's realization that "great power politics, which shaped the 1950s and 1960s, was no longer adequate in coping with rising, assertive, ambitious, demanding peoples and nations from Thailand to Tierra del Fuego,"[43] the upper leadership of the foreign-policy establishment took an interest in the matter.

Another factor was a Kissinger promise at an October 1972 luncheon in New York of the Latin American representatives to the UN for the opening of a new session. At that time Kissinger unexpectedly pledged to begin "a new dialogue" on hemispheric affairs. Although seen publicly as the beginning of a new policy, Jorden (then a Kissinger aide) provides a more whimsical account. He claims that "warmed by the evident good fellowship in the room, Kissinger had waxed eloquent" and ended up promising the new dialogue.[44] The Latin American diplomats were astute enough not to let the remarks go unnoticed, and they quickly began to plan for the new dialogue in a manner more serious than Kissinger had anticipated.[45] The fact that Washington was under a good deal of criticism from Third World countries at the time and that OPEC was making itself felt probably also pushed Kissinger to take Latin America a bit more seriously.

So with that impetus, Ellsworth Bunker was returned to the negotiating table and Kissinger staff member Jorden was made ambassador to Panama. When Nixon resigned, Kissinger quickly wired Panamanian foreign minister Juan Antonio Tack to tell him that the change in leadership would not stall the talks. These discussions were incredibly complicated and hinged on how titular sovereignty was to be handed over, the amount of land in the Canal Zone the United States would control, the management of the Panama Canal Company, yearly payments, defense, the termination of various privileges, and a host of other concerns. Kissinger largely stayed out of the negotiations and gave Bunker great latitude, and with this assurance of support from the White House, Bunker made genuine progress toward an agreement. Substantial concessions were made on both sides.

But then the political calendar began to complicate the issue. Extremely strong opposition to any settlement with Panama stirred in the ranks of American conservatives (ironically, matched by opposition to any concession by Panama on the part of the Panamanian left). During the Republican primary, candidates Ronald Reagan and

John Connally began to blast the Ford administration for the pending "giveaway" of the Canal. Connally's candidacy soon drowned in an ocean of voter apathy, but the Reagan forces became an increasing threat to Ford's hopes for the nomination.

The heat of the issue, and its complexity, led both Kissinger and Ford seemingly to repudiate concessions that had privately been made to the Panamanians, and Ford's backpedaling on the issue caused the administration to put the entire issue aside. Even after the president narrowly defeated Reagan for the nomination, during the presidential campaign Ford and Carter's efforts to seem resolute in the face of Panama's demands made the situation worse. Part of the problem was that neither candidate understood the technicalities involved well enough to be consistent in his statements on the issue.

As one tries to understand Kissinger's foreign policy by analyzing the Canal issue, we find further support for the contention that Kissinger was essentially uninterested in the area. Only geopolitical arguments (a possible bloodbath in the area or threats to U.S. assured hegemony via anti-American propaganda and international resolutions) attracted his attention—coupled with such idiosyncratic elements as his overly gracious promise of a new dialogue and the political factors that provided a "window of flexibility" when Nixon obtained his 1972 landslide. But he was never interested in the details of the talks, and soon the presidential campaign placed such controversial issues on the back burner, and it remained for Carter eventually to negotiate the treaties and to see the Senate ratify them by the narrowest of margins.

Chile: Playing International Hardball

All international situations have historical backgrounds, but in the case of the United States' relationship with Chile during the Kissinger days, that prelude is important to understand. Chile, a geographically misshapen country with a relatively small population of 10 million, had become the focus of Washington's attention during the 1960s, and that interest and commitment continued on through the 1970s.

The Kennedy administration had seen the political and economic development of Chile, which was virtually an island of democracy in a continent of upheavals during the 1950s and 1960s, as an important anticommunist showcase. When the far left demonstrated consistent electoral power and the possibility of winning the presidential election in 1964, the Central Intelligence Agency and the Agency for International Development were given approval for large expenditures to assure the victory of Eduardo Frei, the reformist head of the Christian Democratic party.[46] In what was virtually a two-man contest, Frei garnered 56 percent of the vote to defeat the socialist-Marxist candidate, Dr. Salvador Allende.

The success in electing Frei was not matched by success in accomplishing quick reforms. The Chilean economy and social structure had too many bottlenecks to permit rapid growth. Political bickering, mismanagement, and a number of other problems plagued the Christian Democrats when they had power, although the CIA continued various operations (primarily campaign and media support) in the country to help keep the Marxist elements out of power. The Frei administration of 1964 to 1970 certainly was not a failure, but it seems fair to call its record mixed. During this period, the United States was quickly becoming deeply involved in the domestic political processes in the country.

Unlike 1964, when a Marxist victory seemed a real possibility, the intelligence agencies were more optimistic as to the 1970 presidential contest. The centrist Christian Democrats eventually nominated Radomiro Tomic from the left wing of that large party, the leftist coalition again nominated Salvador Allende, and the conservative forces believed they had a particularly strong candidate in Jorge Alessandri, president of the republic from 1958 to 1964. In part because polls showed the aging former president well in the lead, the CIA and elements in the Department of State were reluctant to urge a major electoral effort of the type undertaken in 1964.[47]

The problem of support was made more difficult by the nature of the three-man race. Throwing CIA money behind Alessandri would have meant supporting the most conservative elements in a society with a strong reformist center. What was finally approved was a propaganda effort that was simply anti-Marxist in nature (and of highly dubious impact) and a contingency fund to support efforts to prevent the Marxist candidate from being approved by the Chilean Congress if he were to finish strongly (if no candidate had a plurality, the constitution allowed the Congress to choose one of the top two finishers, although there was a strong Chilean tradition that the Congress would approve the top vote getter). But the U.S. ambassador in Santiago, Edward Korry, had a distaste for the Chilean political right and believed that financially supporting that group—which, he argued, could afford to support its own campaign—was inconsistent with a commitment to change in Latin America. Korry's argument carried the day and helped dilute the U.S. government's pro-Alessandri effort,[48] although U.S. corporations with operations in Chile did funnel support to the conservative candidate.

The clamor of the campaign, however, obscured a hard fact of Chilean political life at the time: all recent elections had shown that the left was almost surely capable of attracting 33 to 39 percent of the vote. The significance was that if the non-Marxist vote split more or less evenly, even 34 percent could win the popular vote total. At the end of Election Day on 4 September, the world press was electrified by the news that Allende, a self-described Marxist, had won a plurality in the election with 36 percent of the vote. The right-wing candidate got 35 percent, and the Christian Democratic candidate obtained 28 percent. The cliché that Marxists cannot win in free elections was shattered. Washington was surprised and Nixon incensed at this turn of events.

At the time, there were many ways of viewing the events in Chile. Academics specializing in Latin American politics seemed to see the Chilean left as relatively indigenous and to view the election as more or less politics as usual, although it was clear that Chile would be an interesting political laboratory over the following years. But from the first, Nixon did not see it that way, and neither did Kissinger. To quote Kissinger, "Nixon was beside himself."[49] And Kissinger, typically using the vocabulary of geopolitics, later put his concerns then as follows:

Allende's election was a challenge of our national interests. We did not find it easy to reconcile ourselves to a second Communist state in the Western Hemisphere. We were persuaded that it would soon be inciting anti-American policies, attacking hemispheric solidarity, making common cause with Cuba, and sooner or later establishing close relations with the Soviet Union.[50]

Although he omits the quotation from his memoirs (while quoting other portions of his briefing to a group of midwestern newspaper editors), he also claimed at the time that "I have yet to meet somebody who firmly believes that if Allende wins there is likely to be another free election in Chile."[51]

So what we have is a leadership in Washington convinced that the

United States had an important stake in Chile that would be lost unless it intervened. As it turned out, in fact, there were free and hotly contested municipal elections the following year and bitter, unfettered congressional elections in 1973. Allende's record of preserving democratic procedures—which he consistently promised he would—was relatively good by normal standards. This is not to say that Allende, like Chilean political leaders before him, would not have liked to soften criticism of his regime. Kissinger makes a good deal of such efforts—conveniently forgetting his own administration's continual efforts to soften criticism.[52] But until the day of the coup there was a vigorous free press in Chile, to some extent due to CIA financing, and most democratic procedures were respected.

In Nixon's memoirs he devotes only one page to his policy toward Chile. In that account he makes an issue of the fact that money had come in from the outside to finance Allende's campaign.[53] It is true that there was a good deal of outside money coming to all the political parties, but certainly the Allende campaign was not nearly as lavishly financed as the Tomic or Alessandri effort, so if the Cubans or Russians underwrote Allende's campaign, they were parsimonious in their support.[54]

There are three major alternative explanations as to why Nixon and Kissinger viewed the Chilean election as a matter that demanded action. First, there is the corporate-interest argument, which states that U.S. foreign policy is dominated by the interests of the multinationals. Seymour Hersch's biography of Kissinger is careful to document the access businessmen had to Nixon.[55] There is no question that ITT was goading the government into action (even during the campaign), and Pepsi-Cola leader Donald Kendall used his considerable influence with the Nixon administration to obtain a personal presidential hearing for Agustin Edwards, the conservative publisher of *El Mercurio* (Santiago's most prestigious newspaper), who immediately fled Chile upon learning the results of the election.[56] Hersch concludes: "There is compelling evidence that Nixon's tough stance against Allende in 1970 was principally shaped by his concern for the future of the American corporations whose assets, he believed, would be seized by an Allende government."[57]

A second explanation would be the political realism/power politics argument that was explained above and which doubtless fueled Kissinger's thinking. However, the problem with that argument is that it does not inexorably lead to vigorous action in the case of Chile.

Why not simply let things develop and see what happens? The CIA apparently was not interpreting the elections as threatening, and Ambassador Korry, although employing the vocabulary of catastrophe, in fact favored a noninterventionist policy.[58] One of the problems with using political realism as a guide to foreign policy is that it finally rests on the good or bad judgment of decision makers. How pessimistic an interpretation is one to put on events in other countries? Too pessimistic and one is surrounded by a sea of potential Hitlers and Castros and hence constantly engaged in intervening in the affairs of other countries. Too optimistic a viewpoint and one's foreign policy ceases to defend the abstract national interest.

But whichever of these first two explanations one wishes to apply to the Chilean case, the same policy direction is suggested (assuming one places a dark interpretation on projections of U.S.-Chilean relations). Kissinger had an alarmist view, and it may well be that the ability of the multinationals to present their interpretation of the future reality of Chile helped to shape his perception. Kissinger is a classic example of how the logic of realism is similar to the corporate-interest explanation because he depreciated the importance of multinationals and their leaders even though he had risen to the heights of power by having ideas that were consistent with the protection of their interests.

A third possible explanation for U.S. actions in Chile during the Allende period is to account for the policy in terms of American domestic political considerations. Truman had been criticized for "allowing" Mao Tse-tung to come to power, Eisenhower for Castro, and so forth. One of the most convincing explanations for the prolonged U.S. involvement in Vietnam was that no president wanted to be the one who lost the war, even though winning the struggle did not seem worth the blood and treasure needed to accomplish that difficult end.

If Allende became a thorn in the side of the United States, Nixon might well be held politically accountable. Hence there was considerable pressure within the White House to rid itself in advance of the potential Allende problem. One suspects that this motivation and the business community's access to the president were the primary factors in Nixon's response. In the case of Kissinger, his belief that U.S. hegemony in Latin America was essential doubtless justified his support of the measures the U.S. government utilized, although this is one issue where Kissinger's memoirs seem to suggest a sliver of difference between the president and him, perhaps resulting from

Nixon's deeper commitment to the interests of the multinational corporations.

The first effort Washington decided upon was to try to pressure the Chilean Congress to go against tradition and deny Allende inauguration. A scheme was suggested that would involve the Congress's selecting Alessandri, followed by his resignation, followed by another presidential election, in which Frei presumably could run and win.[59] Money was allocated to help pressure or bribe the Congress to adopt this course of action. Appropriately enough, the plan was referred to as the Rube Goldberg ploy[60] after the cartoonist whose drawings presented elaborate machines based on oddly rigged everyday mechanisms. The plan, however, was quickly shown to be unworkable—the Chilean tradition was too strong, and the Christian Democratic candidate, Tomic, had previously made a secret agreement with the Allende forces regarding congressional support.

But if that approach (often referred to as Track I) seems interventionist, in fact there was an even darker set of schemes underway—Track II. CIA Director Richard Helms was summoned to a meeting with the president, Kissinger, and Attorney General John Mitchell on 15 September 1970 in which Helms was given a blank check to move against Allende in secret. Not even Ambassador Korry was to be informed of the operation. Helms's notes from the meeting include such jottings as "no concern risks involved," "full-time job—best men we have," "make the economy scream."[61] Whether he was also given a green light for a possible assassination, either implicitly or explicitly, is unclear. Helms later told the Senate Intelligence Committee that he left the meeting with the "impression . . . that the President came down very hard, . . . that he wanted something done, and he didn't much care how."[62] Questioned by a senator as to whether or not that included assassination, Helms said, "not in my mind"—an answer that leaves open or actually suggests that other minds could have been thinking differently. Hersch later quotes a Helms confidant as saying Helms told him that there was no doubt Nixon included assassination as an option.[63]

This mandate resulted in several agents skilled in undercover operations being sent into Chile to make contact with military leaders who were plotting coups of one variety or another to head off the inauguration of Allende. One of those plots in which the United States was involved, although U.S. material support was withdrawn late in the operation, resulted in the killing of General René Schneider, the Chilean equivalent of the chairman of the Joint Chiefs of Staff.[64] The assassination infuriated Chilean public opinion, and when it was quickly traced to right-wing military officers, it became inevitable that on 3 November 1970 Allende would be sworn in as president.

In a rather defensive tone, Kissinger writes in his memoirs:

> There was always less to Track II than met the eye. As I have shown many times in this book, Nixon was given to grandiloquent statements on which he did not insist once their implications became clear to him. The fear that unwary visitors would take the President literally was, indeed, one of the reasons why Haldeman controlled access to him so solicitously. In the case of Track II, for example, . . . no specific sum was ever set aside. The expenditures, if any, could not have amounted to more than a few thousand dollars. It was never more than a probe and an exploration of the possibilities, even in Helms's perception.[65]

The form Track II took after Allende came to office is difficult to discuss with much certainty. The Senate Intelligence Committee's report on covert action in Chile honored the CIA's request that it not publish details of the post-1970 operations. Hersch claims that new agents were sent, information essential to a military dictatorship was collected, and disinformation and propaganda efforts were made to undermine the government.[66] Kissinger indicates that Track II ended when Allende came to power, although there is ample evidence now to suggest that the lower levels of the CIA did not know this.[67] As former U.S. ambassador to Chile Nathaniel Davis observes, "Apparently, Kissinger—no doubt reflecting President Nixon's preference—would have liked to have indefinitely perpetuated the Track II arrangement, where neither the ambassador nor the secretaries of state and defense were informed."[68] But Davis is also convinced that Track II (which we can define as actual attempts to overthrow the government, as opposed Track I, which was clandestine but which aimed more at helping the opposition to remain active) was not important during the last two years of Allende's government and was, in fact, rather conveniently lost in the CIA bureaucracy. The policy was not to "destabilize" the Allende government but to keep democracy alive until the 1976 presidential election. The realities of the situation forced that policy on the White House, and Ambassador Davis expended a great deal of bureaucratic effort to keep government officials from seeming to favor a coup.

The efforts that were aimed at supporting the opposition, based on the rationale that this was preserving democracy (Track I), involved the allocation of more than $3.5 million for CIA activities in Chile in 1971. In September 1973 (the time of the coup) the CIA officially reported that it had spent more than $6 million in Chile on its anti-Allende plotting. The defenders of this action imply that the bulk of the money went to support the opposition press, which was encountering difficult economic problems due to pressure from the Allende government. But money also went to help opposition business and labor organizations, and a small amount of money may have very indirectly "leaked" over to help finance two nationwide strikes (those in October–November 1972 and July–September 1973), which were instrumental in Allende's fall.

The U.S. embassy monitored coup plots (which were abundant), and it was widely known in Chile that Washington would welcome a coup. Whether North American intelligence and military personnel were active partners in the plots is hard to prove.[69] They were at least cheering them on. Guilt in such situations, as Davis points out, is a difficult concept.[70]

Washington was also trying to deny Chile international loans, as shown in the contents of National Security Decision Memo 93, "Policy toward Chile," although the disarray in the Chilean economy bolstered the argument that the economy was simply not creditworthy.[71] The United States did press for the repayment of the loans Washington had made to Chile through the years, and ironically some of the loans Allende was being asked to repay had been made in order to prop up the economy so that he would not be elected in the first place.

Kissinger, in his memoirs, discusses the failure of Chile to repay its debts and to obtain further financial assistance as if it were this lack of creditworthiness that was the problem with the Chilean requests.[72] With the perspective of the experience following the refinancing of debts in the 1980s, one realizes that political considerations can play a major role in deciding whether to press for repayment and that had Allende been a more friendly government, the United States would probably have made an effort to stabilize the economy.

So we can say of the U.S. policy toward Allende that despite the public posture of neutrality, it was one of trying to weaken the economy and the government. Many scholars who have studied the situation argue that the economic errors of the Allende administration were more fundamental causes of the eventual coup than were the actions of Washington.[73] This does not change the fact, however, that it was the specter of a Marxist government in Chile that precipitated the forceful, and largely covert, anti-Allende policies on the part of the administration.

In September 1973, a military coup toppled Allende. Doubtless there was some sense of relief over this operation in the White House, but as is often true, the solution created another problem. Most observers had assumed that Chile's democratic tradition would soon force the holding of free elections. However, the behavior of the military after the coup became outrageously brutal. The foreign assistance that had been cut off during the Allende administration was soon resumed, but so many details of the terror being employed by the military appeared in the Western world's press that throughout the rest of Kissinger's term, maintaining a placid relationship with noncommunist Chile proved difficult.

Spurred on by reports of the Chilean government's brutality, U.S. church, labor, and human-rights groups pressured Congress to stop assisting the government of General Augusto Pinochet. There is little evidence to suggest that Kissinger took these international criticisms seriously. When Ambassador David Popper raised the issue with the Chilean government, he was reportedly told by Kissinger "to cut out the political science lectures."[74] But by the end of President Ford's term, even Kissinger was voicing some support for human rights, although it was not a position he took easily, because his fundamental concept was that such issues had no place in the world of power politics. Domestic aspects of a government, such as its treatment of its citizens, were not considered proper subjects of conversation among those guided by the principles of political realism. It was only candidate Jimmy Carter's skillful use of the issue that brought about some statements of concern from the White House.

The final action between the Pinochet regime and the White House was the assassination of Orlando Letelier, Allende's ambassador to the United States, in Washington in September 1976. At the time, Kissinger, who called it an "absolutely outrageous act," observed that there was no evidence as to who was behind it.[75] Within a year it had become clear that right-wing Cuban assassins working for the Chilean intelligence service had done it.[76] The violent nature of Chile's military dictatorship had spilled over into the streets of Washington, D.C.

Peru: The Expropriation Issue

In the closing months of the Johnson administration, a military junta headed by General Juan Velasco took power in Peru. Although this happened against a backdrop of serious economic difficulties, the immediate catalyst was the decision of the democratic government of Fernando Belaúnde Terry to make certain concessions in order to settle one of the long-standing points of conflict between Lima and Washington: the International Petroleum Company (IPC) controversy.

The dispute traced its roots far back into Peruvian history and had become a major political issue. When, under urging from the United States, the Belaúnde administration (which had strong U.S. support) finally reached an agreement on the matter, politicians from the right and left orchestrated a national outcry over the settlement. In the name of Peruvian independence and nationalism (specifically mentioning the IPC case), the military moved into power, renounced the agreement, and promptly nationalized the IPC holdings in October 1968. The new government offered to provide compensation for the takeover only after IPC had paid an enormous amount in back taxes the government claimed was owed to Peru—an amount far in excess of the value of the holdings.

The merits of the case do not affect our analysis, although it seems fair to say that the role of the IPC in Peru had its unethical moments and that the claim for back taxes was clearly a bargaining ploy on the part of the military government. It was an issue, to use the words of Jessica Einhorn, of legal complexity and political intensity.[77]

The State Department immediately began to seek solutions to the question and, rather typically, showed an unwillingness to press Peru too much, both because the department had a general responsibility to maintain relations and because the IPC takeover was popular in other Latin American countries. However, there was another factor that gave the matter a sense of urgency, and that was the Hickenlooper Amendment. This was a requirement in the 1962 Foreign Assistance Act that mandated a complete cutoff in funds to nations that nationalized U.S. property without just compensation. The purpose of the amendment, which had been consistently opposed by the Department of State for being excessively rigid, was to deter countries from such confiscatory nationalizations.

There was a six-month deadline, which meant that if the problem were not settled by April 1960, the ban on assistance was to go into effect. The date for the enforcement of the law fell early in the Nixon administration, and it seemed inevitable, given the intransigence of the military government. But several forces were quietly pushing for a "softening" of the amendment: other American business interests in Peru opposed the implementation of the amendment out of fear for their own interests, the CIA felt that sanctions would help trigger further Latin American radicalism,[78] and Henry Kissinger was interested in preserving Nixon's flexibility on the issue of expropriation until the administration had decided on a policy.[79] Furthermore, according to Einhorn, although "Kissinger was perceived to be a hard liner in matters of foreign policy; . . . [he was] more lenient in economic issues where he had less interest."[80]

Ultimately, the Hickenlooper Amendment was simply ignored[81]— an action of dubious legality, but since there were few bureaucrats or members of Congress who strongly favored its application, the decision was politically acceptable. After all, the amendment was intended as a deterrent, and when it failed to work, it seemed counterproductive to enforce it.

On the other hand, after publicly announcing the nonapplication of the amendment, at Nixon's order the United States did begin quietly to oppose further Export-Import Bank credits for Peru, to make no further AID authorizations, and to try to prevent loans from international agencies from going to Peru. This quiet sanction was favored by many, particularly those who opposed the military junta's violation of democratic processes in Peru.

As time went on, the initial successes and the reformist nature of the Peruvian junta began to win some friends in Washington, but the January 1971 Bolivian expropriation of IPC again spotlighted the need for a policy on expropriation. In June 1971 the National Security Council decided that a study of the expropriation issue and a statement of policy were needed. Apparently Nixon and Kissinger hoped that there was a consensus in the government on how to handle the issue.

This passive, almost uninterested, response of calling for a study unleashed bureaucratic infighting,[82] with the State Department no longer being the only agency actively interested. The Treasury Department, whose responsibilities were concerned with maintaining the domestic economy rather than with trying to keep good relations with other countries, became more involved. The reason for the department's new influence lay with the January 1971 appointment of John Connally as secretary of the treasury.

Connally combined two qualities: strongly held views and access to Nixon. His views were fiercely probusiness and xenophobic. He is said to have observed at one point that the United States should get tough with Latin American countries that expropriated U.S. holdings because "we don't have any friends down there anyway."[83] Nixon greatly admired the self-assured, macho Connally and wanted to name him vice-president after Spiro Agnew decided to resign. Connally had far more access to the White House than his predecessor, David Kennedy. Connally's get-tough aura also had its supporters in Congress. Henry Gonzalez, the chairman of the House subcommittee dealing with foreign aid, agreed that on a tactical basis a strong public stance was needed in order to convince the members of Congress that foreign assistance was not going to help enemies of the United States. Conservatives had mounted increasing attacks on the program, and liberals were becoming disillusioned with the results.

Given these factors, it is remarkable that the final statement that came out of the National Security Council was as moderate as it was. Its bland nature was testimony to the ability of the Latin Americanists in the Department of State "to consistently package conciliatory or compromising proposals in terms of their long run contributions to achieving tough objectives."[84] In the atmosphere of Kissinger's own support for an aggressive U.S. foreign policy, State managed to protect its traditional stance by changing its vocabulary.

The statement the White House issued in January 1972—which doubtless was formulated to a large extent for its domestic political appeal—concluded with the following:

When a country expropriates a significant U.S. interest without making reasonable provision for . . . compensation to U.S. citizens, we will presume that the U.S. will not extend new bilateral economic benefits to the expropriating country unless and until it is determined that the country is taking reasonable steps to provide adequate compensation or that there are major factors affecting U.S. interests which require continuance of all or part of these benefits.

It also said that the U.S. government would withhold its support in multinational development agencies for loans to such countries.[85]

The influential *Latin America Report*, published in London, termed the statement the "little stick."[86] Einhorn comments that "the U.S. government never viewed the Peruvian situation through the harsh eye that had been focused on Cuba in the early 1960s or with the opposition directed against Chile a few years later."[87] The explanation for the differing treatment of Chile and Peru is geopolitical; that is, the East-West conflict was not perceived as being part of the issue. Kissinger saw no reason for decisive action here because it was obvious that the Peruvian junta, however undemocratic and radical, was not Communist. The issue of communism surrounded the Chilean case but not the Peruvian case, and hence the decision was left to the outcome of the bureaucratic power struggle between the compromise-minded Department of State bureaucrats, with their interest in good relations with all countries, and the Department of Commerce officials, who saw trade as the answer to everyone's problems.

Conclusion

Other aspects and other cases could be discussed, of course, as part of an examination of the years in question. For example, Brazil played a key role in the U.S. interest in South American stability. Four days before the 1968 election, candidate Nixon sent a warm message to the Brazilian government.[88] When the military president of Brazil visited Washington in December 1971, Nixon called Brazil one of America's "closest friends" and referred to "vitally important" consultations with the president prior to Nixon's trips to China and Russia.[89] During the last year of the Ford administration, Kissinger called for regular Brazilian-U.S. consultations,[90] an action that miffed Argentina and Chile.[91]

The cordial Brazilian connection was made in spite of a very poor human rights record on the part of the military government. But until late in the Ford term (and then presumably in response to a challenge from Jimmy Carter), public pressure on the Brazilian government in regard to human rights was conspicuously absent. Given Brazil's size and potential power, the special treatment made geopolitical sense and needs little in the way of explanation. The high degree of support given the military government of Brazil is primarily interesting in that it shows the degree to which Kissinger was willing to disregard the nasty internal elements of repression (and the international and domestic outcry it stimulated) in order to curry favor with a potentially important ally in South America.

One could also discuss the ups and downs of foreign assistance to Latin America during the Nixon years. In some ways the administration was relatively generous, but there was always the underlying tone that free enterprise—not foreign aid—was the key to development and that the president's public foreign aid proposals were part of the bargaining process with Congress rather than a reflection of a deep concern for the area.[92]

It may be argued that in essence the thesis of this chapter is no more than a statement that minor matters were handled routinely by State Department bureaucrats and important matters were brought to the attention of the president and the secretary of state. This is, of course, an accurate view of how the foreign policy bureaucracy generally functions. But the Kissinger years represent a different era in terms of what was thought to be important enough to justify the White House's time. One must remember that the Kennedy administration—and the Johnson administration too, in the sense that Johnson inherited Kennedy's foreign-policy advisers—believed the Third World (and Latin America in particular) to be the important future battleground in the East-West struggle. Kissinger and Nixon had no such perception. Their view was that Latin America counted for little in the world of power politics and should remain the passive supplicant of Washington's favors and wishes.

Though it is fair to argue that Kissinger's disdain for Latin American issues lessened during his years in power as he learned more about the region, the content of Latin America's demands was particularly unsuited to Kissinger's taste. The Latin Americans were furious over the 10 percent surcharge, concerned about the U.S. tariff structure, and critical of the levels of foreign assistance. Quite correctly, Kissinger realized that these policies were deeply rooted in the domestic political process and that he could do little about them. Furthermore, Kissinger, by his own admission, found these economic issues to be outside his area of expertise or interest.

So for eight years, terms such as "mature partnership" and "new dialogue" masked a fundamental lack of interest in Latin America on the part of the Nixon and Ford administrations. It may well be that the greatest flaw in Kissinger's policy toward Latin America was that the difficult question of defining the U.S. national interest vis-à-vis the hemisphere was not seriously discussed or openly debated.[93]

Perhaps the long-term interests of world peace and Latin American economic development are best furthered by a Latin America obedient to the hemispheric leadership of the United States. But though the Kissinger years saw much public posturing about hemispheric solidarity, the realities of power politics were considered too brutal for the sensibilities of North American or Latin American public. Hence the policy was hidden behind platitudes, and it was only in an occasional slip in off-the-record comments, such as Kissinger's scorching observations to Chilean foreign minister Valdés in 1969, where one glimpses the real mind-set.

Notes

1. "Action for Progress for the Americas," *Department of State Bulletin* 61, no. 1586 (17 November 1969).

2. Undoubtedly, one reason for the lack of a warm reception for the speech is that the words had all been heard before in Latin America. For example, the basic statement of Washington's policy toward Latin America in 1950 had said that U.S. public opinion now "formally accepted the other American republics as adults and our equals in dignity." See Y, "On a Certain Impatience with Latin America," *Foreign Affairs* 28 (July 1950): 571.

3. "Latin America: Planetary Metternich," *Latin America Report*, 25 January 1974.

4. "Latin America: Some More Equal than Others," *Latin America Report*, 31 January 1975.

5. James Nelson Goodsell, "New Low for U.S. Ties with Latin America," *Christian Science Monitor*, 14 February 1975.

6. James Nelson Goodsell, "Diplomats Kept Guessing," *Christian Science Monitor*, 12 October 1976.

7. E.g., Robert Jervis, *Perception and Misperception in International Politics* (Princeton, N.J.: Princeton University Press, 1976).

8. We have only the Valdés version of the luncheon, but there is a ring of truth to what he says, and it is consistent with the picture of Kissinger painted by the various biographies of him.

9. The first meeting is described in Armando Uribe, *The Black Book of American Intervention in Chile* (Boston: Beacon Press, 1975), pp. 30–33.

10. Seymour M. Hersch, *The Price of Power* (New York: Summit Books, 1983), p. 263.

11. Ibid.

12. What follows is based on a reading of Kissinger's memoirs, particularly chapter 3 of *The White House Years* (Boston: Little, Brown, 1979), and such biographies of Kissinger as Roger Morris, *Uncertain Greatness* (New York: Harper and Row, 1977); Marvin Kalb and Bernard Kalb, *Kissinger* (Boston:

Little, Brown, 1974); Stephen R. Graubard, *Kissinger: Portrait of a Mind* (New York: Norton, 1974); David Landau, *Kissinger: The Uses of Power* (Boston: Houghton Mifflin, 1972); and R. J. Vincent, "Kissinger's System of Foreign Policy" in *The Yearbook of World Affairs, 1977* (London: Stevens and Sons, 1977) pp. 8–26.

13. Richard Nixon, *RN: The Memoirs of Richard Nixon* (New York: Grosset and Dunlap, 1978); Gerald Ford, *A Time to Heal* (New York: Harper and Row, 1979); Henry Kissinger, *The White House Years;* and *Years of Upheaval* (Boston: Little, Brown, 1982).

14. See Morton Halperin, *Bureaucratic Politics and Foreign Policy* (Washington, D.C.: Brookings Institution, 1974), pp. 10–11, although the matter of a liberal trade and investment regime is not precisely one of Halperin's "shared images."

15. "Action for Progress in the Americas," p. 412.

16. Ibid., p. 413.

17. Kissinger, *White House Years,* p. 633.

18. Ibid., p. 638. It is not true that Cubans didn't play soccer. Although baseball had gained great popularity on the island, Castro had worked at strengthening interest in soccer as one of a multitude of actions he took to move his country out of its relationship of dependency on the United States.

19. Ibid., pp. 641–43.

20. Hersch, *Price of Power,* p. 254.

21. Kissinger, White House Years, pp. 643–45.

22. Hersch, *Price of Power,* chap. 20.

23. "O.A.S. Meets in Ecuador Today on Issue of Cuban Sanctions," *New York Times,* 8 November 1974.

24. Joseph Novitski, "U.S. Approach to OAS Shifts after 14 Years," *Washington Post,* 16 November 1974.

25. David Binder, "Cuba Sanctions, In Force 11 Years, Lifted by O.A.S.," *New York Times,* 30 July 1975.

26. Murrey Marder, "U.S. Curbs on Cuba Relaxed," *Washington Post,* 22 August 1975.

27. James Reston, "Reporter's Notebook: Castro Readies Himself for Negotiations with U.S.," *New York Times,* 25 August 1975.

28. David Binder, "U.S. and Cubans Discussed Links in Talks in 1975," *New York Times,* 29 March 1977.

29. James Nelson Goodsell, "U.S.-Cuba Talks Likely to Snag over Expropriated Property," *Christian Science Monitor,* 24 July 1975.

30. James Nelson Goodsell, "Cuba Backs Off From U.S. Ties," *Christian Science Monitor,* 17 November 1975.

31. Edward Gonzalez, "Cuba: The Impasse," in Robert Wesson, ed., *U.S. Influence in Latin America in the 1980s* (Boulder, Colo.: Westview Press, 1982), p. 211.

32. "Questions and Answers following the Secretary's Address at San Francisco," *Department of State Bulletin* 74, no. 1913, (23 February 1976).

33. "Secretary Kissinger's News Conference of 12 February," *Department of State Bulletin* 74, no. 1915 (8 March 1976).

34. David Binder, "Kissinger Advises Cuba to be Wary of African Moves," *New York Times,* 5 March 1976; Bernard Gwertzman, "Kissinger Says U.S. Will Not Tolerate Any Further Cuban Intervention Abroad," *New York Times,* 22 March 1976; Murrey Marder, "Kissinger on Cuba: No Crisis," *Washington Post,* 27 March 1976.

35. William J. Jorden, *Panama Odyssey* (Austin: University of Texas Press, 1984).

36. Ibid., p. 147.

37. Ibid., pp. 150–52.

38. Ibid., p. 159.

39. Ibid.

40. "U.S. Vetoes U.N. Security Council Resolution on Panama Canal Negotiations," *Department of State Bulletin* 68, no. 1765 (23 April 1973).

41. Jorden, *Panama Odyssey,* pp. 206–7.

42. Ibid., p. 182.

43. Ibid., p. 206.

44. Ibid., p. 218.

45. Alan Riding, "Latins Seeking Common Front," *New York Times,* 19 February 1974.

46. We know a good deal about the history of the CIA in Chile through official government publications of various sorts. For example, see U.S. Congress, Senate Committee on Foreign Relations, Subcommittee on Multinational Corporations, *Multinational Corporations and United States Foreign Policy: Hearings on the International Telephone and Telegraph Company and Chile, 1970–71,* 2 vols. (Washington, D.C.: U.S. Government Printing Office, 1973); U.S. Congress, Senate, Select Committee on Intelligence Activities, *Alleged Assassination Plots Involving Foreign Leaders,* Interim Report (Washington, D.C.: U.S. Government Printing Office, 1976); and U.S. Congress, Senate, Select Committee on Intelligence Activities, *Covert Action in Chile, 1963–1973* (Washington, D.C.: U.S. Government Printing Office, 1975).

47. Kissinger, *White House Years,* pp. 664–66.

48. Hersch, *Price of Power,* pp. 266–68.

49. Kissinger, *White House Years,* p. 671.

50. Ibid., p. 654.

51. Richard Fagen, "The United States and Chile: Roots and Branches," *Foreign Affairs* 53 (January 1975), 297.

52. See Kissinger, *Years of Upheaval,* chap. 9.

53. Nixon, *RN,* pp. 489–90.

54. Michael J. Francis, *The Allende Victory* (Tucson: University of Arizona Press, 1973).

55. Hersch, *Price of Power,* chaps. 21, 22.

56. During the period of the Allende government, *El Mercurio* continued to publish. A major recipient of CIA funding, it was a strong voice of opposition to the Allende government. Edwards himself had been the outgoing head of the Inter-American Press Association at the time Nixon first presented his "mature partner" speech, and he knew the president reasonably well.

57. Hersch, *Price of Power,* p. 270.

58. Ibid., pp. 269–73.

59. Under the Chilean constitution, a president cannot succeed himself.

60. Kissinger, *White House Years,* pp. 670–74.

61. Thomas Powers, *The Man Who Kept the Secrets: Richard Helms and the CIA* (New York: Alfred A. Knopf, 1979), pp. 234–37.

62. Hersch, *Price of Power,* p. 274.

63. Ibid.

64. Hersch details this in *Price of Power,* pp. 277–90.

65. Kissinger, *Years of Upheaval,* p. 574.

66. Hersch, *Price of Power,* p. 295.

67. This matter is well discussed in Nathaniel Davis, *The Last Two Years of Salvador Allende* (Ithaca, N.Y.: Cornell University Press, 1985), chap. 12.

68. Ibid., p. 313.

69. Thomas Hauser, *The Death of Charles Horman* (New York: Harcourt Brace Jovanovich, 1978). This is the book upon which the popular movie *Missing* is based. Davis discusses the weaknesses of the Hauser book in *The Last Two Years of Allende,* pp. 352–53.

70. Davis has an interesting discussion of this matter in *The Last Two Years of Allende,* chap. 15.

71. Hersch, *Price of Power,* p. 294.

72. Kissinger, *Years of Upheaval,* chap. 9.

73. E.g., Cole Blasier, *The Hovering Giant* (Pittsburgh: University of Pittsburgh Press, 1976), p. 266; and Paul Sigmund, "Chile: Successful Intervention?," in Wesson, ed., *U.S. Influence in Latin America,* p. 27.

74. Sigmund, "Chile," p. 30.

75. *Department of State Bulletin* 75 no. 1950 (8 November 1976): 578.

76. For an excellent account of the case, see Taylor Branch and Eugene M. Popper, *Labyrinth* (New York: Viking, 1982).

77. Jessica Pernitz Einhorn, *Expropriation Politics* (Lexington, Mass.: Lexington Books, 1974), p. 16. Most of the following account of the IPC case is based on Einhorn's excellent book. Also see Adelberto J. Pinelo, *The Multinational Corporation as a Force in Latin American Politics* (New York: Praeger, 1973), and Richard Goodwin, "Letter from Peru," *New Yorker,* 7 May 1969, pp. 41–109.

78. Einhorn, *Expropriation Politics,* p. 53.

79. Ibid., p. 62.

80. Ibid., p. 61.

81. "Peru: How William Rogers Created a Popular Front," *Latin America Report*, 11 April 1969.

82. This is well documented in Einhorn, *Expropriation Politics*, chaps. 4 and 5.

83. "Loans: 'We Don't Have Any Friends Anyway,'" *New York Times*, 15 August 1971.

84. Einhorn, *Expropriation Politics*, pp. 61–62.

85. "President Nixon Issues Policy Statement on Economic Assistance and Investment Security in Developing Nations," *Department of State Bulletin* 66, no. 1702 (7 February 1972).

86. "USA: Little Stick," *Latin America Report*, 28 January 1972.

87. Einhorn, *Expropriation Politics*, p. 49.

88. "Nixon: Latin American Doubts," *Latin America Report*, 15 November 1968.

89. Benjamin Welles, "Brazilian President Welcomed by Nixon," *New York Times*, 8 December 1971.

90. Jonathan Kendall, "Brazil and U.S. to Consult Regularly, Kissinger Announces on Brasilia Visit," *New York Times*, 20 February 1976.

91. James Nelson Goodsell, "Kissinger Makes Brazil Keystone of U.S. Policy," *Christian Science Monitor*, 23 February 1976.

92. Yale Ferguson, "The Ideological Dimension in United States Foreign Policies toward Latin America, 1945–76," in Morris J. Blachman and Ronald G. Hellman, eds., *Terms of Conflict: Ideology in Latin American Politics* (Philadelphia: Institute for the Study of Human Issues, 1977), pp. 215–20.

93. The matter of what the U.S. national interest is in regard to Latin America is intelligently and provocatively discussed in Margaret Daly Hayes, *Latin America and the U.S. National Interest* (Boulder, Colo.: Westview Press, 1984), and U.S. Congress, House of Representatives, Committee on Foreign Affairs, Subcommittee on Inter-American Affairs, *United States National Interest in Latin America, Hearings* (Washington, D.C.: U.S. Government Printing Office, 1981).

Robert A. Pastor

The Carter Administration and
Latin America: A Test of Principle

There are no natural points to divide a nation's foreign policy. Sometimes the crucial turning points in U.S. foreign policy have coincided with a specific domestic or foreign event, like the Depression or the Cuban revolution. Sometimes the policy of a particular president differs so much from his predecessor's or his successor's as to justify a separate designation in the history books. More often, a president leaves a distinctive imprint—often a slogan—on his policy that will permit historians to distinguish it from others.

Few American presidents have focused on Latin America and the Caribbean. Those who have formulated policies have felt compelled to do so by events, most often by a security crisis, whether it be instability in Nicaragua, Haiti, or the Dominican Republic; the approaching storm of world war; or the Cuban Revolution. Jimmy Carter was the first U.S. president to forge a policy of his own choosing in the absence of a security crisis, or as it turned out, before rather than after a crisis.

The Carter administration's policy toward Latin America can be divided into two parts. During its first two years, the administration addressed an extensive agenda and formulated a new approach to the region based on a set of principles. By the end of 1978 the administration had implemented most of the initiatives begun the previous year. In its last two years, the administration was compelled to address a more traditional security agenda and to focus its attention on the Caribbean Basin. The administration was largely preoccupied with crisis management, though it also tried to develop some longer-term approaches.

Obviously, history is not as neat as a system of abstract classifications. Attention shifted to security issues in late 1977 as the Cubans expanded their military presence in Africa, and in 1979 and 1980 the administration was still trying to implement the key elements of its first agenda—for example, legislation implementing the Canal treaties and democratization in the Andean countries. Nevertheless, there was a discernible division between most of the issues and the policies chosen by the administration in the first two years and those that preoccupied it in its last two years.

The following section describes the background to the administration's policy toward Latin America and the Caribbean. Then the two periods of the administration's policy are discussed. Finally, the chapter concludes with an assessment of the continuity and change involved in the Carter administration's policy and an evaluation of its successes and failures.

Background

Like its predecessors, the Carter administration did not have a policy toward Latin America when it took office, but it did have a predisposition toward a new approach. The ingredients included (1) the views of the president and his senior advisers, (2) their reaction to the policies of the departing president, (3) the agenda and positions recommended by the Democratic party's specialists on Latin America, and (4) the current problems and issues on the national agenda.

Jimmy Carter had a deeper interest in Latin America and the Caribbean than either of his two principal foreign-affairs advisers, Cyrus Vance and Zbigniew Brzezinski. This was partly because Carter had less experience in other areas, but also because as a farmer from the South, Carter had a special sensitivity to the borders and to Latin America. He had also studied Spanish at the Naval Academy and had visited Brazil, Colombia, Argentina, Costa Rica, and Mexico.

Carter's emphasis on human rights was a central element of his policy toward Latin America because of a deep personal commitment, the massive human rights violations in the region, and the apparent lack of interest by the previous administrations. Carter viewed the need to restore faith in government at home and its policies abroad as the point of departure for his administration:

In the aftermath of Vietnam and Watergate and the C.I.A. revelations, our Nation's reputation was soiled. Many Americans turned away from our own Government, and said: "It embarrasses me." The vision, the ideals, the commitment that were there 200 years ago when our Nation was formed, have somehow been lost. One of the great responsibilities that I share with you is to restore that vision and that degree of cleanness and decency and honesty and truth and principle to our country.[1]

Even before his election, Carter had already shaped this concern for human rights into a framework for policy, and he outlined it in a speech on 8 September 1976:

I do not say to you that we can remake the world in our own image. I recognize the limits on our power, but the present administration—our government—has been so obsessed with balance of power politics that it has often ignored basic American values and a common and proper concern for human rights.

Ours is a great and a powerful nation, committed to certain enduring ideals, and those ideals must be reflected not only in our domestic policy but also in our foreign policy. There are practical, effective ways in which our power can be used to alleviate human suffering around the world. We should begin by having it understood that if any nation . . . deprives its own people of basic human rights; that fact will help shape our own people's attitude toward that nation's repressive government. . . . Now, we must be realistic . . . we do not and should not insist on identical standards. . . . We can live with diversity in governmental systems, but we cannot look away when a government tortures people or jails them for their belief.[2]

Although Washington expected an immediate clash between Carter's senior advisers, both Vance and Brzezinski entered the administration with almost the same substantive agenda and no important differences on the key issues of U.S. policy toward Latin America.[3] When differences did emerge in early 1978, they were largely confined to the question of how to respond to Cuba's expanding military presence in Africa. As the differences between the two men on the Soviet Union, China, and Iran became more serious, they often tried to minimize their differences in other areas—such as Latin America—in order to preserve their personal relationship.[4] Moreover, Vance tended to delegate most of Latin American policy to his deputy, Warren Christopher.

This is not to suggest that there were no differences between the State Department and the National Security Council (NSC)—the two key institutional actors with respect to Latin American policy during the Carter administration. But the differences between the heads of both institutions were trivial at the beginning, when the administration was shaping its new approach. Much of the debate on U.S. policy between the staff of State and the NSC subsequently stemmed from the natural bureaucratic tension between the State Department, which emphasizes diplomacy and good relations with other governments, and the NSC, which has a more political and strategic outlook and which is more assertive of the specific interests that the president considers to be of the highest priority.

In converting its predisposition into a policy, the new administration had the benefit of the research done by two private commissions. Carter, Vance, and Brzezinski were all members of the Trilateral Commission, which offered the administration a conceptual framework for the full gamut of international issues. However, with regard to setting an agenda and an approach to Latin America, the most important source of influence on the Carter administration was the Commission on U.S.–Latin American Relations, chaired by Sol Linowitz. A bipartisan group of about twenty-five distinguished leaders, the commission issued two reports recommending both general and specific changes in U.S. policy.[5]

The commission analyzed the changes that had occurred in Latin America in the previous decade and concluded that U.S. policy should be adapted to take into account "an increasingly interdependent world in which Latin American nations seek to be active and independent participants." The group urged the new administration to remain "sensitive to the unique qualities of inter-American relations" but to approach the region with "a consistent pattern of global economic policies."[6] Soon after he was appointed secretary of state, Cyrus Vance met with Sol Linowitz to discuss the report and to ask him to be one of the two negotiators for new Panama Canal treaties along with Ellsworth Bunker. Michael Blumenthal, another member of the commission, became secretary of the treasury. Other staff were appointed to key positions in the Treasury Department and the National Security Council. The reports helped the administration define a new relationship with Latin America, and twenty-seven of the twenty-eight specific recommendations in the second report became U.S. policy.

Ideals, principles, human rights—these were the themes that moved Carter from Georgia to the White House, and these themes were the bedrock upon which he constructed a new approach to Latin America.

Carter's Agenda

Because of Watergate, the transition from Nixon to Ford, and then the presidential campaign of 1976, the U.S. government had postponed addressing a multitude of issues. Among the most difficult issues were Panama and energy. The new administration was faced with the question of whether to confront all of these issues, some of them, or none of them. A person who delighted in accomplishing much more than anyone thought possible, Carter insisted on tackling almost all of these difficult issues at once.

In a five-hour conversation with Cyrus Vance on 30 November 1976, as Carter was deciding whether to appoint him as secretary of state, Vance insisted that negotiating a new Panama Canal treaty was an urgent issue, and Carter agreed.[7] Carter asked Vice-President Walter Mondale to chair a small meeting of the new administration's senior appointees on 5 January to prepare a foreign-policy agenda. The group decided to place Panama first. Three days later, Brzezinski appointed the staff director of the Linowitz commission to take charge of Latin American affairs on the NSC, and his first responsibility was to draft two Presidential Review Memorandums (PRMs)— PRM-1 was on Panama, and PRM-17 was to include all other Latin American issues. (PRMs defined the terms of reference for interagency options papers that would be used by the NSC to decide on new policies.)

Panama: The Most Urgent Issue

In its final report, the Linowitz Commission had described the Canal negotiations as "the most urgent issue" in inter-American relations. This assessment was shared by the presidents of Venezuela, Colombia, Mexico, Costa Rica, Honduras, El Salvador, and Nicaragua, all of whom endorsed a cable sent to President-elect Carter, urging him to expedite negotiations for new Canal treaties. The cable described the treaties as "the crucial test of the degree of sincerity of a good inter-American policy of the U.S. . . . The Panamanian cause is no longer the cause of that nation alone. Its intrinsic merits have made it the cause of all Latin America." The presidents underscored the point that a failure to negotiate new treaties would create a barrier to good relations. Characteristically, Omar Torrijos, Panama's leader, described the situation more graphically, saying that "Panama's patience machine" was running out of fuel.

The president formally signed PRM-1, on the Canal issue, on 21 January 1977, but by that time the interagency group had almost completed the paper for the administration's first meeting of the Policy Review Committee (the PRC was one of the two NSC committees), which was scheduled for 27 January 1977. The PRC recommended to the president that Vance meet with the Panamanian foreign minister soon to declare the administration's intent to negotiate a new treaty in good faith and rapidly.[8] The PRC decided that if Panama was forthcoming on the combined issues of the defense and the neutrality of the Canal, then the U.S. would accept a termination date for the new treaties of the year 2000.

When the negotiators reported to the president on 2 March, they talked about the need for some ambiguous language on the key defense issues, like UN Resolution 242, but Vice-President Mondale argued persuasively that ratification of the treaties by the Senate would require very clear language on these issues. In May the two sides agreed to language that would permit the United States to defend the Canal beyond the duration of the principal Canal treaty. The remaining questions related to when the United States would transfer lands and waters in the Canal Zone to the Panamanians and how much and what kinds of benefits would accrue to Panama. Negotiating both sets of issues was difficult, but on 10 August 1977 the two sides announced agreement.

After consulting with Senate Majority Leader Robert Byrd, Carter decided to sign the treaties in a formal ceremony in Washington on 7 September, shortly after Congress returned from recess. Brzezinski recommended that instead of inviting all the Latin American presidents, Carter should only invite the *democratic* Latin American presidents, who had advised Torrijos, and the foreign ministers of the other countries. Carter decided to invite all the Latin American presidents, however, to demonstrate to the American people that the treaties enjoyed complete hemispheric support.

The two treaties signed by Omar Torrijos and Jimmy Carter at the OAS on 7 September 1977—the Panama Canal Treaty and the Neutrality Treaty—established a partnership between the United States and Panama to operate the Panama Canal together until the year 2000, at which time Panama would be solely responsible for operation and maintenance. The Neutrality Treaty declared the Canal permanently neutral and indicated that Panama and the United States had responsibility to ensure that it remained open.

Describing the treaties as unpopular would be an understatement. David McCullough explained that many people felt that relinquishing the Canal was saying "that we have reached a turning point in our growth as a nation." Ronald Reagan effectively portrayed the treaties as a retreat of U.S. power.[9] Carter tried to respond to this argument by describing the treaties as a sign of "confidence in ourselves now and in the future. . . . We do not have to show our strength as a nation by running over a small nation."[10] But the basic public relations problem was that it was intuitively difficult to argue that the Canal could be best protected by giving up control.

The Neutrality Treaty was voted first on 16 March 1978. The administration's political strategists—primarily Vice-President Mondale, Hamilton Jordan, and Robert Beckel—judged that the treaty would not pass unless the administration accepted an amendment (technically a "condition") introduced by a freshman senator from Arizona, Dennis DeConcini. With the amendment, the treaty passed 68 to 32, but the amendment, which asserted the U.S. right to intervene in Panama's internal affairs, was more than the Panamanians were willing to accept.

The administration was reluctant to lose DeConcini's vote by trying to dilute his amendment in the second treaty, but Panama left the administration with no choice, and Senator Robert Byrd submitted a revised amendment. The National Security Council and the Pentagon were instructed to develop contingency plans. If the treaties were rejected, many believed that the Canal might be closed by sabotage or riots and that U.S. embassies in a number of Latin American countries would be vulnerable to attack. Fortunately, the second treaty passed, by the same vote.

PRM-17, on Latin America

On 26 January 1977, Brzezinski sent PRM-17, on U.S. policy toward Latin America and the Caribbean, to the Departments of State, Defense, and the Treasury and every agency with a program that touched the region. The terms of reference were as broad as inter-American relations: analyses and policy recommendations were requested on economic issues, human rights, nonproliferation, arms sales, territorial disputes, illegal migration, and other issues. The memorandum also requested papers on special country or subregional concerns, including Cuba, Mexico, and the Caribbean.

The bureaucracy does not respond either constructively or creatively to such a request, but it can provide sufficient raw material for staff people to piece together a concise options paper for the Policy Review Committee. The State Department, which was charged with coordinating the exercise, was therefore instructed to weave the various papers together into a conclusion that included basic options for an overall U.S. policy toward the region. The PRC was scheduled to meet on 24 March 1977 to discuss the issues.

The key overall issue was whether the United States should assert a "special relationship" with Latin America or adopt a single global policy for the developing world that could be adapted to the unique characteristics of the region's past relationship with the United States. Since President James Monroe's message to Congress in 1823 announcing that the Western Hemisphere was closed to European colonization, U.S. policy had been premised on the existence of a special relationship, or what Arthur Whitaker called, "the Western Hemisphere idea."[11] A certain mythology naturally grew up around this idea, but in essence the special relationship was premised on special U.S. security interests due to proximity. In the postwar period, to obtain Latin American acquiescence or support for those interests, the United States needed to be responsive in some way to the region. The Alliance for Progress during the Kennedy administration was the most visible illustration of this relationship, which was inherently and unavoidably paternalistic: for its generosity, the United States expected special behavior.

The major institutional bastion of the special relationship in the U.S. government was the Bureau of Inter-American Affairs (ARA) in the Department of State, and its opposition to the global policy ensured that the debate would be joined. To a certain extent, the debate was theological and unrealistic, because one could argue that in the postwar period the United States always applied global policies to the region with a special sentimental or national security twist. After the decade of "benign neglect" (1966–1976), the United States seemed to cling only to the rhetoric of the special relationship. Still, some argued that the rhetoric remained important to Latin America—in some cases, more important than the reality of the policy itself. If we abandoned the rhetoric, according to this argument, Latin America would abandon us in a security crisis.

Those in favor of a global approach argued that Latin America had already gone its own way; the rhetoric no longer bound anyone but

OAS historians. The key issues of concern to Latin America were economic, and beginning in the mid-1960s the leaders in the region had indicated by their actions that they considered the Western Hemisphere too limited for their interests. Raúl Prebisch, an Argentine, used the United Nations Conference on Trade and Development (UNCTAD) to press all the industrialized countries—not just the United States—to open their markets on a preferential basis to the products of all the developing world—not just Latin America's. Venezuela took the lead in pressing for a worldwide North-South dialogue, not just one between the United States and Latin America. The United States, according to the "globalists," ought to aim for more balanced relationships with Latin America, and this could not be achieved within the context of an inherently paternalistic special relationship.

These were essentially the arguments made at the PRC meeting on 24 March 1977, with the foreign service officers of ARA and some of the career people in the Defense Department arguing for the special relationship, and the new Carter administration appointees—led by Brzezinski and Christopher but including General George Brown, chairman of the Joint Chiefs, and officials of the Treasury Department—arguing for a new approach.

The PRC discussed the other "theological" issue of inter-American relations—nonintervention. Franklin D. Roosevelt's acceptance in 1934 of the principle of nonintervention, which a number of Latin American governments had been advocating, enshrined Roosevelt in Latin America as one of the most respected U.S. presidents. Since then, every U.S. president has pledged his support for the principle, but few, if any, have taken it seriously when they perceived U.S. security interests to be threatened. Carter was not exceptional in this regard, having said several times that he opposed intervention in the internal affairs of other countries *unless* U.S. security interests were directly threatened.[12] The dividing line among the presidents relates to differences in the perceived threats, not basic support for the principle of nonintervention. Nevertheless, the PRC discussed this issue and concluded that since Latin American governments had a good sense of their own independence, the prospect for intervention was not great, and U.S. policy should be contingent on the way other Latin American governments, particularly the democracies, responded.

The PRC discussed all the key issues, and Carter largely accepted the recommendations and articulated them in his second foreign-policy speech, an address to the Organization of American States on Pan American Day, 14 April 1977. As Carter told the OAS, "As nations of the 'New World,' we once believed that we could prosper in isolation from the 'Old World.' But since the Second World War, in particular, all of us have taken such vital roles in the world community that isolation would now be harmful to our own best interests and to other countries." After describing the dramatic changes in inter-American relations, Carter concluded that "a single United States policy toward Latin America and the Caribbean makes little sense. What we need is a wider and a more flexible approach, worked out in close consultation with you."

In those sentences, Carter opened the hemispheric envelope, and whereas the previous administration had been equivocal or hostile toward a North-South dialogue, Carter said: "We count on you to contribute your constructive leadership and help guide us in this North-South dialogue." On "the great issues which affect the relations between the developed and developing nations," Carter announced "a positive and open attitude" on commodity agreements and a commitment to fulfill U.S. pledges to the international development banks. He promised an effort "to provide special and more favorable treatment" to developing nations in the multilateral trade negotiations, and he expressed interest in exploring new modes of cooperation in the areas of science and technology to substitute for less bilateral aid to the middle-income Latin American countries. On private investment, he encouraged U.S. corporations to be flexible and adaptable in responding to the needs of Latin America, and he promised to try "to avoid differences and misunderstandings." Finally, he pledged early and full consultation on all economic issues.

Carter reaffirmed his commitment to human rights: "Our own concern for these values [on human rights] will naturally influence our relations with the countries of this hemisphere and throughout the world. You will find the United States eager to stand beside those nations which respect human rights and which promote democratic ideals." He announced that he would sign the American Convention on Human Rights and urged other governments to join the United States in increasing the support for the Inter-American Commission on Human Rights and for assisting political refugees.

Carter also expressed his support for conventional arms-control initiatives and said the United States would show restraint in its own arms sales. He announced that he would sign Protocol I of the Treaty of Tlatelolco, which banned the placement of nuclear weapons in Latin America. Ironically, the two most specific decisions announced by Carter at the OAS—to sign the American Convention on Human Rights and Protocol I of the Treaty of Tlatelolco—had not been discussed at the PRC meeting; they had been proposed by the NSC staff two days before the speech.

Finally, Carter signalled a determination to resolve the old problem of the Panama Canal treaties and a willingness to improve relations with Cuba "on a measured and reciprocal basis."[13]

Consultations

After a decade of disinterest by the United States, Latin Americans generally were encouraged by the energy and ideas of the new administration, but they were still skeptical about whether the United States would really consult them on key economic issues. To try to dispel this skepticism, Carter dispatched a number of personal emissaries to explain his overall approach and to seek comments and advice on how common goals—in human rights, economic development, and peace—could best be implemented.

He undertook the first consultation himself. On 3 May, two days before his departure for the Summit of Industrialized Countries, Carter met with the ambassadors of Brazil, the Dominican Republic, Peru, Costa Rica, and Trinidad-Tobago to discuss a series of decisions that he had to make on whether to help the ailing U.S. sugar industry and if so, how. Although briefed beforehand, the ambassadors were still so surprised by the meeting that they were not as helpful as they might have been. Nevertheless, in preparing for the meeting Carter was sensitized to the impact of U.S. sugar policy on these and other Latin American countries, and his decisions reflected that. The next day, the White House announced that the United States would vigorously pursue an international sugar agreement as the best means for helping the U.S. sugar industry. Carter also rejected the recommendation of the International Trade Commission for import quotas on sugar, and he rejected the petition of the American Farm Bureau Federation for dropping sugar from the generalized system of tariff preferences.[14]

At that meeting, Carter announced that he was sending his wife to seven nations in Latin America to conduct "substantive talks with the leaders and to report" to him. The idea of sending Rosalynn Carter as the president's personal emissary was inspired, although no one would have described it as such then. Carter's election and subsequent statements and decisions had raised expectations in Latin America to unrealistic levels. The decision to send Rosalynn Carter lowered those expectations, and her performance then exceeded them.

In her travels from 30 May to 12 June, Rosalynn Carter used her public statements and private conversations to repeat and expand the main themes in Carter's Pan American Day speech.[15] She also pressed each leader to use his influence on the governments that had not signed or ratified the Treaty of Tlatelolco and the American Convention on Human Rights. In Jamaica she assured Michael Manley, who thought the Republican administrations had tried to destabilize him, that the Carter administration was prepared to support a social democratic experiment that was in fact democratic. In Peru and Ecuador she used every opportunity to reinforce the democratization process promised by the military governments, and in Brazil she sought the same objective, although more delicately.

On her return, she briefed the president and Secretary of State Cyrus Vance, who then left for the OAS General Assembly meeting in Grenada. That meeting was dominated by the human rights issue, marking, as a *Washington Post* reporter put it, "a new phase in U.S.-Latin American relations." Instead of a lack of interest or a resistance to Latin American resolutions, the United States assumed joint leadership with its democratic friends. One OAS diplomat said it was "the first time a U.S. representative was both positive and publicly and privately consistent." The United States joined with Venezuela, Costa Rica, and the Caribbean to pass narrowly a resolution that strengthened the Inter-American Commission on Human Rights and affirmed that "there are no circumstances that justify torture, summary execution, or prolonged detention without trial contrary to law." When Southern Cone governments tried to change the resolution to justify violations against terrorism, their amendment was rejected.[16]

Probably the most energetic and determined president of a democratic Latin American government was Carlos Andrés Pérez of Venezuela, and Carter decided to cultivate him, believing that Pérez's support for human rights, the North-South dialogue, arms control, and nonproliferation could be critical to achieving these objectives. Pérez also played a central role in helping both the United States and Panama to reach agreement on new Canal treaties. Carter therefore wrote to him regularly and met with him in June and September 1977 in Washington and in March 1978 in Caracas. In February 1978, when the Uruguayan military government tried to obtain the thirteen votes in the OAS necessary to host the next General Assembly, Venezuela joined with the United States and Panama to block that effort.[17]

Human Rights and Democratization

While the decision to abandon the rhetoric of the special relationship in favor of a more openly internationalist approach probably represented the sharpest break from past policy, and the Canal treaties were the most difficult aspect for Carter's policy for the American people to accept, the policies that came to dominate the public's perception of Carter's approach toward Latin America were on human rights and democratization. Arthur Schlesinger, Jr., commented that "nothing the Carter administration has done has excited more hope, puzzlement, and confusion than the effort to make human rights a primary theme in the international relations of the U.S." By and large, the confusion was in the United States, where critics either found the policy too punitive, too soft, or simply inconsistent. The policy was understood in the developing world even before Carter's inauguration. For example, Haitian president-for-life Jean Claude Duvalier released political prisoners and improved the atrocious conditions in his jails shortly after Carter's election.[18]

A National Security Council directive established an Inter-Agency Committee, to be chaired by Deputy Secretary Warren Christopher, to ensure that human rights criteria were fully integrated into U.S. foreign-policy and foreign-aid decisions. One of the first decisions by the administration was to modify the Ford budget for the 1977 fiscal year to reduce aid to three countries for human rights reasons; two of the three—Argentina and Uruguay—were in Latin America. Richard Fagen wrote of the decision: "The amounts involved were not large, but symbolically the initiative was important, for it marked the end of an executive branch undercutting of legislative intent, as well as a partial declaration of independence by the Carter administration from past policies."[19]

Despite criticism from within the United States and abroad, senior administration officials scheduled and announced meetings with democratic opposition leaders. Vice-President Walter Mondale, for example, met with former Chilean president Eduardo Frei on 25 May

1977 to affirm U.S. support for democracy in Chile. The administration also complied with the law and sent human rights reports on each country to Congress. Both of these decisions generated divisions within the administration, as the regional bureau in the State Department often opposed steps that would be viewed negatively by Latin American governments. Also, several military governments—those of Brazil, Argentina, El Salvador, and Guatemala—chose to end their military assistance agreements with the United States as a way to protest the policy. Such actions stirred their conservative defenders in the United States, like Ronald Reagan, who wrote: "Little wonder that friendly nations such as Argentina, Brazil, Chile, Nicaragua, Guatemala, and El Salvador have been dismayed by Carter's policies."[20] Each of these governments was then a military dictatorship.

What was the impact of the Carter human rights policy? First, the consciousness of the world was raised with regard to violations of human rights, and leaders came to recognize that there was an international cost to be paid for repression and a corresponding benefit to be gained by those governments that respected human rights. Second, international norms and institutions were strengthened. In part because of the Carter administration's lobbying, the American Convention on Human Rights was transformed from a moribund treaty that only two nations had ratified by 1977 to one that came into force with fourteen ratifications by 1980. The budget and staff of the Inter-American Commission on Human Rights quadrupled, and its activities expanded commensurately.

Third, violations of the integrity of the person substantially declined throughout the hemisphere. Disappearances declined markedly in Argentina, from five hundred in 1978 to less than fifty in 1979; and there were no confirmed disappearances in Chile or Uruguay after 1978. Political prisoners were released in substantial numbers in many countries—including 3,900 from Cuba and all those previously held in Paraguay. The use of torture declined markedly. By the end of the Carter administration, no one questioned its commitment to human rights, although many criticized the policy's inconsistency, and some continued to doubt its impact.[21] William F. Buckley, Jr., who was skeptical of the policy at the time, reexamined his position in the light of the evidence that emerged during the trials of the Argentine military leaders. In 1985 he admitted he had been wrong, that "the advertisement by American agencies official and nonofficial, of the plight of missing persons as often as not had concrete results. Pressure was felt by the criminal abductors. The man scheduled for execution was, often, merely kept in jail."[22]

Carter also sought opportunities to strengthen and reinforce the trend toward democracy in the hemisphere. In May 1978 he issued a strong private statement and a clear public statement directed at Dominican president Joaquín Balaguer that U.S. relations with his government depended on his noninterference in the election results. This involvement may have been decisive in compelling Balaguer to permit the election to go forward.[23] Similarly, through letters and special emissaries, Carter sought numerous opportunities to reinforce the democratization process in Ecuador, Peru, and other countries in the region.

North-South Relations and Multilateral Cooperation

During the first six months of 1978, Carter personally devoted more time to ensuring the ratification of the Canal treaties than to any other issue, and he also made two trips to Latin America. In March 1978, as a demonstration of his commitment to the developing world, Carter undertook a tour to Latin America (Venezuela and Brazil) and Africa (Nigeria). He spoke on North-South relations before the Venezuelan Congress, stressing the need for the developing world to participate more fully in decisions that shape the international economy. He declared that "Just as all people should participate in the government decisions that affect their own lives, so should all nations participate in the international decisions that affect their own well-being. The United States is eager to work with you, as we have in the past, to shape a more just international economic and political order."[24] He also used the opportunity of his visit to Caracas to announce a new fellowship program, named after the late Senator Hubert H. Humphrey, for young professionals from the developing world to come to the United States for a year of postgraduate study.

In early 1977, undiplomatic efforts by the Carter administration to alter the German-Brazilian nuclear agreement incensed the Brazilian government. Partly to assuage bruised feelings, Carter visited Brazil and offered new forms of cooperation in the areas of science and technology, particularly as they related to energy. A U.S.-Brazilian committee was established to pursue this issue, and as AID began to develop new programs in science and technology, the administration chose to focus on Latin America and the Caribbean as the first region to implement these. In 1979 Frank Press, the president's science adviser, led a large delegation of U.S. scientists and government officials to several Latin American countries to forge specific arrangements.

The culmination of Carter's effort to seek a multilateral strategy appropriately occurred in Panama on 16 and 17 June 1978, on the occasion of the exchange of the Canal treaties. Omar Torrijos and Carter invited the presidents of Venezuela, Colombia, and Costa Rica, and the prime minister of Jamaica—all democratic nations that had helped in the Canal negotiations—to Panama to discuss a wide range of issues. There was a remarkable degree of consensus among the leaders on the central objectives in inter-American relations, and therefore the group focused on what it could do individually and collectively to achieve these objectives. When Carlos Andrés Pérez recommended at the end of the first day's conversation that the presidents issue a joint declaration, they readily agreed in principle, and the next morning they accepted the U.S. draft with minor changes.

The Joint Declaration of Panama praised the treaties as "an historic step forward in inter-American relations." The declaration then listed three goals and set out specific steps that the leaders pledged to take and urged others to take. To promote world peace, the leaders recommended ratification of Tlatelolco, strengthened peacekeeping machinery in the OAS, limiting arms sales and expenditures, and resolving territorial disputes. To promote human rights, the leaders pledged to bring the American Convention into force, strengthen the Inter-American Commission on Human Rights, reinforce democratic trends, and "speak out for human rights and fundamental freedoms everywhere." To develop a more just and equitable international economic system, the leaders promised to bring multilateral negotiations on the Common Fund (on commodity price stabilization), debt, and trade to a favorable conclusion and to support the multilateral development banks and the World Bank–led Caribbean Group. This was as clear a statement of support for U.S. policy toward Latin America as one is likely to find in inter-American relations in the postwar period, and it was endorsed by four independent democratic leaders.

Carter returned to Washington, and on 17 June 1978 he addressed the opening session of the OAS General Assembly. He summarized the results of the Panama declaration and urged other governments to contribute to realizing its common goals. He encouraged those countries involved in territorial disputes to follow the example of the Canal treaties in seeking a peaceful resolution: "Just as the nations of this hemisphere offered support to Panama and the United States during the Canal negotiations, I pledge today my government's willingness to join in the effort to find peaceful and just solutions to other problems."[25]

A new, unanticipated agenda in the last two years of his administration deprived Carter of the time he would have liked to spend on boundary disputes and arms control. Instead, he encouraged the pope to play the leading role on the Beagle Channel dispute, and the Peruvian president to play the same role in a territorial dispute between El Salvador and Honduras. On arms control, the administration gave strong support and staffing to two regional initiatives (by Mexico and by Venezuela), and it made a preliminary effort to discuss the issue with the Soviets. None of these initiatives succeeded.

Special-Country or Subregional Issues

Besides Panama, the other countries or subregions that engaged the Carter administration at the beginning were Mexico, the Caribbean, and Cuba. José López Portillo assumed office at a moment when Mexico's financial and political situation was desperate. Carter recognized the importance of Mexico's political stability and development for the United States, and one of his main objectives in inviting the new Mexican president as his first state visitor, on 14 February 1977, was to help restore the financial community's confidence in Mexico. The conversations went exceedingly well, and both presidents decided to establish a U.S.-Mexican consultative commission to track the numerous issues in the relationship and ensure that these issues would receive presidential attention on both sides.

The discovery of tremendous oil reserves in Mexico did more than Carter's encouraging words to restore Mexico's self-confidence and the confidence of the international community in the nation's future. But the personal relationship between the presidents deteriorated markedly as a result of an unfortunate misunderstanding. The Mexican government began negotiations with a number of U.S. gas companies to sell natural gas to the United States. The Carter administration informed Mexico that it should negotiate an agreement with the U.S. government rather than the gas companies, for three reasons. First, the interests of the gas companies were different from those of the U.S. government; the companies did not mind paying a high price for gas since they could roll it into their domestically regulated price. Second, such a deal would have to be approved by the regulatory agencies, and the chance for this would be reduced if the U.S. government had not participated in the negotiations to ensure that the national interest was protected. Third, the administration was in the process of negotiating the long-term deregulation of the price of natural gas with Congress, and it feared that the entire energy bill would be endangered if Mexico received a higher price than it was trying to obtain for domestic gas producers.

López Portillo chose to ignore the warnings of the Carter administration; perhaps the gas companies convinced him that the administration would have no choice but to approve the deal. They were wrong, but having staked his position on the deal, López Portillo never forgave Carter for not accepting it. This incident might have been ameliorated or prevented had López Portillo been able to attend the Canal treaties signing ceremony and speak with Carter, but despite Carter's phone call (only one of two he made to try to secure the attendance of a head of state), López Portillo said he could not come. (The signing coincided with the week of the "Informe," Mexico's State of the Nation address.)

In January 1978, Vice-President Walter Mondale visited Mexico, but by then López Portillo had concluded that he had been "left hanging by the paintbrush" on the gas negotiations, and Mondale was unable to put the relationship on a better track. In August 1978, Carter initiated a major review of U.S.-Mexican relations (PRM 41), which would culminate with three cabinet-level discussions prior to Carter's visit to Mexico in February 1979. As a result of that trip, both presidents decided to resume new gas negotiations—this time between the governments—and an agreement was signed in 1980. Other issues were resolved, but the relationship remained strained through the rest of the Carter administration.

The Canal signing ceremony on 7 September 1977 not only permitted Carter to get to know seventeen presidents and prime ministers of the Americas and to master a wide range of complex issues, it was also an opportunity for him to make some decisions—for example, on a new Caribbean policy. One of the recommendations from Mrs. Carter's trip to Latin America was to send the U.S. ambassador to the United Nations, Andrew Young, to the Caribbean to consult on the best way for the United Staes to assist in the region's development. Young visited ten countries in August 1977, and based on his report, the National Security Council staff sent Carter a memorandum recommending the establishment of a new organization that came to be called the Caribbean Group for Cooperation in Economic Development. This organization would be directed by the World Bank and would include thirty-one nations and fifteen international institutions. In order to reduce the dependency of the small, vulnerable nations of the Caribbean, the group would be multilateral at both the donor and the recipient ends, and it would encourage regional projects and cooperation.

After his meetings in September, the president asked his wife to unveil the plan in a speech she was giving at a UPI editors conference in Puerto Rico on 11 October 1977. The ideas obtained a favorable reception, and in December the World Bank hosted a conference, which voted to establish the group. By 1980 the group had rationalized and quadrupled foreign aid to the region to about $1 billion and encouraged greater regional cooperation. It also produced over a hundred separate development reports for the countries and for the region.[26]

The Carter administration sent an early and clear signal to Cuba that it was prepared to negotiate the terms of a more normal relationship. In his confirmation hearings as secretary of state on 11 January 1977, Cyrus Vance said that "if Cuba is willing to live within the international system, then we ought to seek ways to find whether we can eliminate the impediments which exist between us and try to move toward normalization."[27]

The administration initially considered Cuba to be within the terms of PRM-17 but then dealt with it separately at a PRC on March 9. The PRC recommended an approach along the lines Carter had sketched four days before in an answer to a question during a telephone call-in program:

I would like to do what I can to ease tensions with Cuba. . . . Before any full normalization of relationships can take place, though, Cuba would have to make some fairly substantial changes in their attitude. I would like to insist, for instance, that they not interfere in the internal affairs of countries in this hemisphere, and that they reinforce a commitment to human rights by releasing political prisoners that have been in jail now in Cuba for 17 or 18 years, things of that kind.

But I think before we can reach that point, we'll have to have discussions with them. And I do intend to see discussions initiated with Cuba quite early on reestablishing the anti-hijacking agreement, arriving at a fishing agreement between us and Cuba, since our 200-mile limits do overlap between us and Cuba, and I would not be averse in the future to seeing our visitation rights permitted as well.[28]

After the successful conclusion of negotiations on fisheries and maritime boundaries, Cuba and the United States decided to establish interests sections—rather than open embassies, which would have signified diplomatic relations—in each other's capitals on 1 September 1977. Both sides took several other steps, but on the central issue of security, Cuban president Fidel Castro made clear that he was not prepared to meet the U.S. conditions:

They [the U.S. officials] say we must stop giving our solidarity to the revolutionary movements in Africa. We feel these issues are not matters for negotiation. . . . We haven't organized subversion against or sent mercenary invaders to the U.S. They are the ones . . . they must lift the blockade. . . . We will not make any concessions on matters of principle in order to improve relations with the U.S.[29]

Though the United States cautioned Cuba in May 1977 that an expansion of its new military advisory group in Ethiopia would jeopardize the improvement of relations with the United States, by the fall of 1977, there were reports of more Cuban troops and military advisors in several countries in Africa. The United States again communicated its concern, but as it had little effect, Carter decided to publicly criticize the Cubans on 11 November 1977:

The Cubans have, in effect, taken on the colonial aspect that the Portuguese gave up in months gone by. . . . [They] are now spreading into other countries in Africa, like Mozambique. Recently, they are building up their so-called advisers in Ethiopia. We consider this to be a threat to the permanent peace in Africa.[30]

Castro gave higher priority to his foreign activities in Africa than to normalizing relations with the United States. In November 1977 there were four hundred Cuban military advisers in Ethiopia; by April 1978 there were seventeen thousand Cuban troops there, serving under a Soviet general. In an interview on 12 May 1978, Carter harshly criticized the Soviet-Cuban intervention:

There is no possibility that we would see any substantial improvement in our relationship with Cuba as long as he's committed to this military intrusion policy in the internal affairs of African people. There is no doubt in my mind that Cuba is used by the Soviet Union as surrogates in several places in Africa.[31]

The Cuban and U.S. governments had begun to talk to each other but not to listen. The United States refused to accept Castro's statement that his international activities were matters of principle, and Castro refused to accept Carter's statement that such activities precluded normalization.

Castro thought he could reverse Carter's position by responding to his concerns about Cuban political prisoners. In the summer of 1978, Castro informed U.S. officials that he was prepared to release as many as 3,900 political prisoners to the United States. During the next year he also released all U.S. prisoners—both political and criminal—and people with dual citizenship. This represented a reversal from a position he had taken in an interview with Barbara Walters one year before.[32] Castro also tried to do the impossible: to transform the Cuban-American community from his enemy to his lobbyist. He invited a group to Havana in November 1978 and left them believing they had persuaded him to release the prisoners. Cuba's military cooperation with the Soviet Union in Africa, however, not only precluded any further improvement in relations with the United States, it also began to affect American strategic perceptions of the Soviet Union.

The Old World Revisited

In 1977 the Carter administration decided to alter its approach to Latin America because it concluded that U.S. policy toward the region could no longer be made as if in a vacuum. By 1979, as the international political climate darkened, the new premise returned to haunt the administration. The expansion of Soviet-Cuban activities abroad, together with the emergence of an anti-American fundamentalist regime in Iran, left many Americans with a feeling of disquiet, which in turn reinforced the arguments made by an increasingly powerful conservative movement in the United States. One symptom of this change in mood in 1979 was that the Senate, for the first time in a decade, voted a 10 percent increase over the administration's defense budget.

Compared to the rest of the world, Latin America had little impact on these trends; still, the trends did affect the U.S. view of the world, including Latin America and the Caribbean. While the Carter administration continued to pursue the basic approach toward Latin America that it had established two years before, most of its energy in its last two years was consumed in managing a series of crises—Nicaragua, Grenada, Cuba (the Soviet brigade in Cuba and then the Mariel boatlift), and El Salvador.

The Carter administration anticipated the first major security crisis it would face in the region and tried to prevent it, but it was unsuccessful.[33] Since the mid-1930's, Nicaragua had been run by the Somoza family almost like a fiefdom. By the mid-1970s, the Somozas' greed and repression had alienated every group in the country not under their control, and the children of the middle class began joining the Sandinista National Liberation Front (FSLN), a guerrilla group inspired by the Cuban revolution and established in 1961.

The Carter administration's human rights policy impelled Anastasio Somoza to lift the state of siege in September 1977. The middle class, encouraged by U.S. policy, took full advantage of the political opening. Pedro Joaquín Chamorro, the leader of the opposition and the editor of *La Prensa,* published scathing editorials on corruption of the Somoza dictatorship. On 10 January 1978, Chamorro was assassinated, and Managua was closed down by a general strike led by businessmen, who demanded Somoza's resignation. The Sandinistas were caught off guard, but in a daring move they seized the presidential palace in August 1978 and recaptured the initiative. The spontaneous cheering they received on the way to the airport surprised and awakened the Carter administration to the realization that opposition to Somoza could easily be transformed into support for the Sandinistas.

There was a consensus in the administration that if the United States did nothing, Somoza would remain in power, the country would polarize even further, and the Sandinistas would eventually win a military victory. Although the Carter administration recognized the broadening of the Sandinistas' base of support, it viewed the key leaders as Marxist-Leninists who looked to Cuba and the Soviet Union as allies and who saw the United States as the enemy. Therefore the administration decided to encourage a political transition in Nicaragua, subject to two conditions. First, Carter believed that he should not ask a sitting president to step down, nor should he try to overthrow him. Second, Carter insisted that U.S. policy should not be unilateral. A solution would have to emerge from a multilateral effort.

With the Dominican Republic and Guatemala, the United States established a negotiating group under the auspices of the OAS to try to bring the opposition and the Somoza government to an agreement on a transitional process. The group recommended a plebiscite on Somoza's tenure, but the negotiations collapsed in late January 1979 when Somoza rejected the conditions that would have permitted a free election. The United States had warned Somoza that it would take tough actions to dissociate itself from his regime if he blocked the plebiscite. On 8 February 1979, the United States therefore reduced its embassy by half, ended the aid program, and terminated its AID and military missions. Somoza had almost doubled the size of the National Guard and evidently believed he was secure.

By May 1979, with Castro's help, the three Sandinista factions united and established a secure, continuous, and ample arms flow from Cuba through Panama and Costa Rica. In early June the FSLN launched first its military offensive and then a political offensive with Mexico and the Andean Pact nations aimed to strip Somoza of formal legitimacy and transfer it to them. As the war intensified, the question of whether Somoza would leave was gradually replaced with the question of what would follow.

After consultations in the region, the United States called for a meeting of the OAS and proposed a cease-fire between the FSLN and the National Guard that would coincide with Somoza's departure and then lead toward a negotiated coalition government. An inter-American Force would oversee the cease-fire and assist in the integration of the armed forces. Nicaraguan moderates failed to see this proposal as a way to strengthen their position and rejected it. The Sandinistas correctly saw it as an attempt to deny them exclusive power, and with the help of Panama, Costa Rica, Mexico, and Venezuela, they succeeded in blocking the U.S. proposal. Carter had no intention of undertaking unilateral action when democratic friends in the region were so clearly aligned against the U.S. position. On 17 July 1979, Somoza fled Nicaragua for Miami, and the Sandinistas arrived to a joyous welcome two days later.

Having failed to create a democratic center or to prevent a military victory by the Sandinistas, the United States shifted its strategy once they came to power. The United States was determined to avoid in Nicaragua the mutual hostility that had characterized early U.S.-Cuban relations and had led to a break in the relationship. At considerable political cost, Carter requested $75 million for the new revolutionary government, despite its hostile rhetoric. With the increasing power of conservatives in Congress, the issue of aid to Nicaragua was debated at great length and with considerable heat.

The administration succeeded in obtaining the funding, but only after the Congress imposed a series of explicit conditions on the use of the aid. The principal condition was that the president could only disburse aid after he submitted a certification to Congress that the Nicaraguan government was not aiding any foreign insurgency. Both Congress and the executive were concerned about the impact of the Nicaraguan revolution on the rest of Central America and the Caribbean. As a result of the revolution, Central America's guerrillas became emboldened; the military and the right, more intransigent; and the middle, more precarious.

In the spring of 1979, before the climax of the Nicaraguan revolution, the Carter administration had turned its attention to the rest of the region. The administration's approach was based on its view that the status quo in Central America was neither defensible nor sustainable; the only way to avoid violent revolution, which the United States judged to be in neither its own nor in Central America's best interest, was to encourage the opening up of the political process. Honduras, Nicaragua's northern neighbor, seemed most intent on pursuing a democratization process, and therefore the administration decided to put its aid and support there as an example to the other countries. El Salvador and Guatemala had repressive military governments. The United States decided to intensify its efforts to communicate to these regimes that while it shared their concern about revolution, U.S. support was possible only if they ended repression and eased their controls on the political process.

The Carter administration had no discernible impact on the Guatemalan regime, but after numerous efforts, on 15 October 1979 an opening appeared in El Salvador. A group of young army officers seized power and invited a number of moderate and leftist civilians to help them implement a full range of social, economic, and political reforms. The United States viewed this as a breakthrough, but Carter decided to make U.S. support conditional on the new government's making progress in implementing the reforms—particularly an agrarian reform—and stopping the repression.

In 1979 revolution also came to the Caribbean. On 13 March a group of fifty members of the New Jewel Movement (NJM) seized power in a nearly bloodless coup on the small island of Grenada. It was the first unconstitutional change of government in the English-speaking Caribbean, and it unsettled the region. The New Jewel Movement reassured everyone of its moderate and constitutional intentions, but after securing recognition the new regime invited Cuba to help build a people's revolutionary army and postponed elections indefinitely.

After the U.S. ambassador delivered a message of concern to the new regime about its growing military relations with Cuba, Prime Minister Maurice Bishop publicly denounced the United States for trying to dictate Grenada's destiny.[34] Relations deteriorated, and the revolutionary regime no longer concealed its predisposition toward Cuba and the Soviet bloc, although they never revealed that they considered themselves Marxist-Leninists.

The administration adopted a very different strategy toward Grenada than it did toward Nicaragua, although largely for the same reasons. In both cases, the administration consulted widely and placed great weight on the views it received from friendly democratic neighbors. What it heard in Central America was that the United States had to support a nationalist revolution to keep it from being seized by Marxists. What it heard in the Caribbean was that it ought to help the other islands more than Grenada, or it might unwittingly send a signal to local radicals on each of the islands to seize power and confront the United States. Therefore, the main thrust of U.S. policy was to help the democratic governments in the area in matters concerning economic development and regional security rather than to confront Grenada.

When Fidel Castro hosted the Summit of the Non-Aligned Movement in September 1979, he was flanked by the leaders of the two new revolutionary governments in the region—Nicaragua and Grenada. Together they tried to steer the Non-Aligned Movement (NAM) toward a "natural alliance" with the Soviet Union. The Carter administration took the NAM seriously and devoted about six months before the Summit to consultations with NAM governments. Rather than encourage moderate leaders to remain outside the debate on the future of the NAM, the United States encouraged them to participate and to try to prevent Cuba from seizing control of the movement. Whether U.S. consultations helped or not, the moderate leaders were decisive in preventing Cuba from shifting the NAM's direction. However, from the perspective of American public opinion, the overall image of the summit was that of a large group of leaders who had journeyed to Havana to condemn the United States.

Moreover, a few friendly leaders like Michael Manley of Jamaica gave speeches that left many questioning their friendship and democratic intentions. In his speech, Manley condemned every U.S. intervention and overlooked every Soviet or Cuban intervention, and the underlying theme was decidedly favorable to the Soviet Union and Cuba. "All anti-imperialists know," he said, "that the balance of forces in the world shifted irrevocably in 1917 when there was a movement and a man in the October Revolution, and Lenin was the man." He praised Castro as "always humane" and credited him with the fact that "the forces committed to the struggle against imperialism [in the Western Hemisphere] were stronger today than ever before."[35]

The NAM summit coincided with the "discovery" in Washington of the Soviet brigade in Cuba. Castro thought that the United States had concocted the entire incident to embarrass him at the Summit, but he overlooked the fact that the incident was even more embarrassing and politically costly to the Carter administration. As with each of the strategic confrontations in Cuba, the Soviet brigade issue had almost nothing to do with Cuba and almost everything to do with the perceived balance of power between the Soviet Union and the United States.

In June 1979, Presidents Carter and Brezhnev signed the second Strategic Arms Limitation Treaty (SALT II). Conservatives in the United States argued that the only effect of an arms agreement was to soften the will of the United States. This view was gaining strength, and many senators facing reelection in 1980 were uneasy about the political consequences of voting for the treaty. One such senator, Richard Stone of Florida, pressed the administration in the spring of 1979 about reports that the Soviets had sent soldiers to Cuba. Secretary of State Vance responded in a letter that there was no evidence of this. At that time, most officials in the administration discounted the report because it was implausible that the Soviets would send soldiers to Cuba on the eve of the NAM summit. Nonetheless, the administration promised to conduct more extensive surveillance, and as a result, in August it detected a Soviet combat unit. As most of the administration's senior officials were on vacation at the time, the government did not have an opportunity either to ascertain the nature and origin of the brigade or to try to quietly negotiate the issue with the Soviets before the information was leaked to *Aviation Week and Space Technology*. Frank Church, chairman of the Senate Foreign Relations Committee, was in a tough fight for reelection at the time. Upon learning of the report he announced that SALT II would not pass the Senate unless the brigade was withdrawn.

The incident occurred at a time when the differences between Vance and Brzezinski had become significant. A genuine crisis would have united the administration, but the brigade issue was only a political dilemma. As such, it exacerbated the contradictions within the administration. Vance believed that the brigade issue required some face-saving gesture from the Soviet Union but that it was "definitely not a reason to interfere with the ratification of the SALT Treaty." Brzezinski saw SALT as only one element in a wider strategic relationship; he thought the brigade issue should be used to "stress Cuban adventurism worldwide on behalf of the Soviet Union." To Brzezinski, this was "the main problem."[36] Neither wanted the issue to interfere with the ratification of SALT, but Vance thought prospects for ratification would be improved if the United States played down the brigade, while Brzezinski thought the administration's position would be strengthened if it puffed up the issue and showed that it understood the increasing threat of Soviet-Cuban expansionism.

Senate Majority Leader Robert Byrd told Carter that the only way to pass the treaty was to realize that the brigade was of relatively little consequence, and Carter took his advice. On 1 October 1979, Carter addressed the nation on the Soviet brigade, noting Brezhev's assurances that the brigade was a training unit and that the Soviets would not change its structure. Carter's major objective was to persuade the nation of the need to ratify SALT II, but he did so by sharply criticizing the Soviet Union and Cuba. He also called for expanding the U.S. security presence in the Caribbean.

There was a special poignance to the fact that Carter delivered the speech on the same day that the Canal treaties came into force. Vice-President Mondale was in Panama at that moment with several democratic presidents from the region to celebrate the passing of an old era in inter-American relations, and yet the speech served as a powerful reminder that the old era was not entirely history. And indeed, one of the Latin presidents commented to Mondale about the unfortunate symbolism.

If the domestic or global political environment had been sunny, these regional events—the Nicaraguan and Grenadian revolutions, the Havana summit, and the Soviet brigade—would have been less troubling and less trouble. However, the opposite was the case. In July 1979, at the moment that the Sandinistas were coming to power in Managua, the United States felt the full impact of the second oil shock. The price of gas soared, the supply declined, and the nation saw the longest lines of cars waiting for gas since World War II.

When Carter's popularity fell below that of Nixon in the last two months before he resigned, he decided to go to Camp David for near-ly two weeks of consultations to assess the state of his presidency and to decide how best to proceed. His energy speech on 15 July helped him to recoup some of his popularity, but he lost it again with the subsequent dismissal of four members of his cabinet. Inflation, which began to climb into double digits, contributed to the percep-tion that Carter was not in control, and other international events reinforced that perception. In November the staff of the U.S. embas-sy in Teheran was taken hostage, and the next month more than ten thousand Soviet troops marched into Afghanistan. Carter realized that the SALT treaty would be defeated if the Senate voted on it, and he therefore requested that the Senate postpone debate or a decision. He also imposed a range of sanctions against the Soviet Union.

With the domestic political, the regional, and the international trends all so ominous, the Carter administration focused its atten-tion on the Caribbean Basin, and increasingly on security issues. The administration did not alter its basic approach, but it did intensify its efforts. Among other things, the United States significantly ex-panded its aid program to the region and began exploring ways either to expand the Caribbean Group to include Central America and Mexico or to encourage the formation of a parallel group for Central America. Drawing from his own personal experience, Carter also proposed a dramatic expansion of people-to-people programs in the Caribbean Basin. He encouraged the establishment of Caribbean/ Central American Action in April 1980 with the intent that it would represent the full gamut of nongovernmental groups in the United States and the region—businessmen, church groups, labor, and oth-ers. Carter believed that, in the long run, such contacts were the best way to reduce misunderstanding and promote balanced relation-ships.

In El Salvador the war worsened. With all the leverage the United States and Venezuela could provide, the government did manage to decree and implement an agrarian reform and the nationalization of the banking and export trading sectors. But each positive reformist step was followed by murders by right-wing death squads. After the murder of four U.S. religious workers in November 1980, Carter suspended all economic and military aid as a way to provide additional leverage for the ultimatum given to the military by José Napoleón Duarte, the Christian Democratic leader of the junta. A major leftist attack was expected in January 1981, but Carter did not release any of the aid until the military agreed to take specific steps to pursue the investigation of the murders, dismiss several officers from the security forces, and strengthen Duarte's position.[37]

After the election of Ronald Reagan, but before his inauguration, the Salvadoran guerrillas persuaded the Nicaraguan government to support their final offensive in January. This proved a fatal error for both. The final offensive was a complete fiasco, and the evidence of Nicaraguan support for it was so conclusive that it in effect destroyed the relationship that the Carter administration had been trying to nurture.

While Central America was unsettled by the Nicaraguan revolution, democracy in the eastern Caribbean was, if anything, strengthened after the Grenadian revolution. Not only did elections go ahead as scheduled in six countries, but moderates defeated radicals by large margins. The only country in the Caribbean to experience instability in 1980 was Cuba. As a result of the Carter administration's dismantling of the embargo on travel between the United States and Cuba, more than 110,000 Cuban-Americans visited the island in 1979. They brought money, presents, and success stories, and left in their wake the first visible signs of discontent Cuba had seen in a generation. In a speech in December 1979, Castro acknowledged the discontent and its link to the more open relationship developed during the previous two years:

Nowadays, the counter-revolution . . . has begun to appear. . . . [Why?] Is it because we let down our guard? . . . Is it because the absence of the enemy has caused us to lose our faculties? Is it because we have felt . . . too much at ease? Perhaps, in a certain way, we have been needing an enemy; because when we have a clearly defined enemy, engaged in hard-fought combat, we are more united, energetic, stimulated.[38]

In late 1979, Cubans began breaking into Latin American embassies in Havana seeking asylum. After an incident involving the death of two Cubans at the Peruvian embassy in early April 1980, Castro decided to teach Peru a lesson by removing the guard from the embassy and informing the people of Havana that they were free to go there if they wished. Within twenty-four hours more than ten thousand Cubans crowded into the small compound of a poorer nation than Cuba. Castro was surprised and embarrassed.

Charter flights began taking the Cubans to Peru via Costa Rica. When television recorded their joy at leaving Cuba, Castro stopped the flights. He then invited Cuban-Americans to Mariel Harbor outside Havana to pick up their relatives. Within a few days, thousands of boats of all sizes were sailing to Mariel. The Carter administration wanted to stop the boats but deferred to the Coast Guard's judgment that it would risk too many lives. The administration tried to discourage Cubans from sailing, but to no avail. The boats returned with a few relatives and many others, including mental patients and criminals, whom Castro decided to deposit in the United States. By the time the boatlift finally halted in September, 125,000 Cubans had arrived.

An Assessment

One could say that, in a symbolic way, the Carter administration arrived *pursuing* the Panama Canal and left *fleeing* from Mariel. It arrived with a preferred agenda that reflected its view of what inter-American relations should become. The agenda contained those issues that the Carter administration judged most important—the Canal treaties, human rights, democratization, a North-South dialogue, nonproliferation, arms control, and conflict resolution. In addition, Carter chose to pursue these ends differently from his predecessors: instead of unilateral or covert actions, Carter insisted on openness and multilateral cooperation.

Yet in its last two years the administration was impelled to address a traditional security agenda—war, revolution, and instability in the Caribbean Basin, and the prospects of Soviet-Cuban expansion. This was an uncomfortable agenda for the Carter presidency, and it split the administration. The split was exacerbated—if not caused—by other, even more disturbing international events and the popular reaction to them in the United States. By 1980, according to two public opinion analysts, the United States "felt bullied by OPEC, humiliated by the Ayatollah Khomenei, tricked by Castro, out-traded by Japan, and out-gunned by the Russians. By the time of the 1980 Presidential election, fearing that America was losing control over its foreign affairs, voters were more ready to exorcise the ghost of Vietnam and replace it with a new posture of American assertiveness."[39]

No administration leaves office the same as it arrived. It must adapt, as the Carter administration did, to changes in the region and in the global economic, political, and strategic landscape. U.S. foreign policy is the product of what an administration sets out to achieve and what Congress (articulating U.S. public opinion) and the world will permit. Congress forces each administration to give greater weight to certain national interests that it perceives the administration is ignoring; as such, it functions as a kind of compensator, a balancer of the national interest.[40]

Let us review the successes and the failures of the Carter administration and assess Congress's role. Carter pursued a new Panama Canal treaty and achieved it, but Congress left its imprint. In anticipation of Congress, the executive insisted on permanent rights to protect the Canal and resisted Panama's efforts to receive compensation for prior use of the Canal. During the ratification, the Senate clarified two obligations—on whether the United States had the unilateral right to protect the Canal, and on whether U.S. warships had the right to go to the front of the line in times of emergency.

Probably the second most important achievement of the Carter administration was in the area of human rights. Congress had tried to give higher priority to human rights, but an effective policy had to await an administration that had the same commitment as Congress. With Carter's personal leadership, the United States became identified with a hemispherewide movement for freedom and democracy. This movement gained strength, and within ten years military governments would be swept from power in all but two nations in South America.

The Carter administration's decision to deliberately set U.S. policies in a global context was significant theoretically but was unknown to the general public. The administration prided itself on not having a slogan, but in retrospect this was probably a handicap, depriving analysts of a handle to describe the policy. Without a slogan, the administration's approach became known not by its principles but by its salient features—human rights and democracy by those who were sympathetic to the administration, and the revolutions in Nicaragua and Grenada and the problem of Cuban refugees by those who were not.

The Carter administration did not go nearly as far on a North-South agenda as many had hoped, but it went further than Congress did. The United States negotiated an agreement on a Common Fund, replenishment of the international development banks, and new cooperative programs in science and technology. Congress, however, passed only a single foreign-aid bill, that in 1977, during the four years of the administration. Interest also seemed to have declined in the Third World, and by the end of the term the North-South dialogue was virtually mute.

During the Carter years, Congress's role was generally that of conservative watchdog, forcing the president to give greater weight to security interests. Jeane Kirkpatrick has argued that despite Congress, the Carter administration's policy in the first two years created the security problems of the last two, but this argument distracts from the main issue.[41] Undoubtedly, people in repressive societies— whether Nicaragua, Argentina, or Cuba—were encouraged by Carter's human rights policy and made new demands on their governments. The issue, which Kirkpatrick sidesteps, is whether the United States should encourage the pressures or defend the dictators. The Carter administration believed that the dictators were the problem and that human rights was the solution, whereas Kirkpatrick's argument implies that the opposite is the case.

Others have argued that the Carter administration retreated under pressure to the traditional Cold War agenda in its last two years.[42] But this implies that either the United States should be unconcerned about Soviet-Cuban expansion or that the administration abandoned its principles as it responded to the region's crises. No administration could be unconcerned about Communist advances, which inevitably involve a national interest.

It is true that as the administration tried to adjust to a changing agenda, Carter's commitment to three principles—human rights, nonintervention, and multilateral cooperation—was tested. In the case of Nicaragua, when the administration realized that its democratic friends in Nicaragua and in the region preferred the Sandinistas to the U.S. strategy of seeking an alternative to either Somoza or the Sandinistas, Carter decided against unilateral intervention. In the case of El Salvador, as the left grew stronger, Carter resisted pressure to offer unconditional support to the government. The United States, he said, would provide economic and military aid only if the government implemented land reform and took steps to ease repression.

Even his final decision in January 1981 to approve $5 million in military aid to El Salvador was taken partly because the military had responded to U.S. concerns on human rights. If the judgment on Carter's policy depends on whether he adhered to his principles during these crises, he clearly passes the test.

Despite continuous consultations, the administration's effort to forge a coalition of like-minded democracies to pursue a common policy in the Caribbean Basin did not bear fruit. Perhaps the approach was so different from past U.S. policies, which were unilateral or which wore a mask of multilateralism, that Latin American governments were skeptical. Perhaps conceptions of national security diverge so sharply within the region that individual Latin American governments were simply not prepared to cooperate with the United States. It may take a long time for such conceptions to change enough to permit such cooperation. Carter believed it was worth the time and the investment.

If one accepts Carter's goal to work closely with America's democratic friends in the region, then perhaps the final judgment on his policy should come from them. Henry Forde, the foreign minister of Barbados, offered such a judgment at the OAS General Assembly in Washington on 19 November 1980, after Carter's loss to Reagan. First, Forde listed the many criticisms leveled at Carter's human rights policy, but then he said: "It is our view that it has been the single most creative act of policy in the hemisphere in many a long year. It has raised the consciousness and stirred the consciences of many a leader in this region; it has given hope to many an oppressed citizen; it has helped, perhaps more than any other element of policy, to correct the image of the United States as an unfeeling giant, casting its shadow over its neighbors."[43]

Notes

1. "Address to a Democratic Party Campaign Luncheon, 20 September 1978," in *Public Papers of the Presidents of the United States: Jimmy Carter, 1978*, vol. 2, p. 1554 (hereafter cited as *Public Papers, Carter*).

2. The speech is reprinted in Jimmy Carter, *A Government as Good as Its People* (New York: Simon and Schuster, 1977), pp. 166–71.

3. Robert Kaiser, "Brzezinski, Vance Are Watched for Hint of a Policy Struggle," *Washington Post*, 28 March 1977, p. A2. Both Vance and Brzezinsky had read and substantially agreed with the Linowitz Commission's reports, which will be discussed shortly. Vance's memorandum to Carter in Oc-

tober 1976, reprinted in his memoirs, reflects many of the views in the reports; see Cyrus Vance, *Hard Choices: Critical Years in America's Foreign Policy* (New York: Simon and Schuster, 1983), pp. 444, 451–53. Several years before, Zbigniew Brzezinski had developed some of the same ideas. He had proposed that the United States abandon the Monroe Doctrine and the "special relationship" with Latin America, place U.S. relations with the region "on the same level as its relations with the rest of the world," and approach revolutionary change in "the developing countries with a great deal of patience." *Between Two Ages: America's Role in the Technetronic Era* (New York: Viking Press, 1970), p. 288.

4. This was sometimes done unconsciously; interview with Zbigniew Brzezinski, Washington, D.C., 18 July 1985. Excluding the issue of Cuba, during the entire administration Vance and his deputy, Warren Christopher, seemed to differ less with Brzezinski on Latin American policy than they did with the Bureau of Inter-American Affairs in the Department of State.

5. Commission on U.S.–Latin American Relations, *The Americas in a Changing World*, October 1974; and *The United States and Latin America: Next Steps*, 20 December 1976. Both were published by the Center for Inter-American Relations in New York.

6. Commission on U.S.–Latin American Relations, *The United States and Latin America: Next Steps*, p. 1.

7. Vance, *Hard Choices*, p. 33.

8. For two superb narratives and analyses of the Canal treaty negotiations within the administration, with Panama, and with the Senate, see William J. Jorden, *Panama Odyssey* (Austin: University of Texas Press, 1984), and George D. Moffett III, *The Limits of Victory: The Ratification of the Panama Canal Treaties* (Ithaca, N.Y.: Cornell University Press, 1985).

9. For McCullough's explanation, see "Ceding the Canal, Slowly," *Time*, 22 August 1977, p. 13. For an excellent description of the conservatives' strategy to try to prevent ratification of the treaties, see William J. Lanouette, "The Panama Canal Treaties—Playing in Peoria and in the Senate," *National Journal*, 8 October 1977, pp. 1556–62.

10. *Public Papers, Carter, 1977*, vol. 2, pp. 1889–90.

11. Arthur P. Whitaker, *The Western Hemisphere Idea: Its Rise and Decline* (Ithaca, N.Y.: Cornell University Press, 1954).

12. In an interview with Bill Moyers on 13 November 1978, Carter said, "We don't have any inclination to be involved in the internal affairs of another country unless our security should be directly threatened." *Public Papers, Carter, 1978*, vol. 2, p. 2019. But in his Pan American Day speech on 14 April 1977, Carter had redefined the principle of nonintervention in a way that connected Latin America with the United States: "We will not act abroad in ways that we would not tolerate at home."

13. For the entire Pan American Day speech, see *Public Papers, Carter, 1977*, vol. 1, pp. 611–16.

14. He also instructed the secretary of agriculture to institute an income support program for sugar farmers. *Public Papers, Carter, 1977*, vol. 1, pp. 797–801.

15. She describes the trip in some detail in her memoirs, *First Lady from Plains* (Boston: Houghton Mifflin, 1984), chap. 7.

16. Fourteen governments voted for the U.S. resolution, eight abstained, and three were absent. Thirteen votes are necessary for passage of a resolution. Karen DeYoung, "Human Rights Motion Passes, Underlines Divisions in O.A.S.," *Washington Post*, 23 June 1977, p. A20.

17. This decision stands in contrast to the acquiescence by the United States and Latin America to the initiative in 1976 by Chile to host the General Assembly. Lewis Diuguid, "O.A.S. Refuses to Meet in Uruguay," *Washington Post*, 3 February 1978, p. A23.

18. Arthur M. Schlesinger, Jr., "Human Rights and the American Tradition," *Foreign Affairs: America and the World, 1978*, vol. 57, no. 3, p. 503. For a compelling description of the personal impact of Carter's human rights policy on Haiti, see Patrick Lemoine and Erich Goode, "Living Hell in Haiti," *Inquiry*, 3 March 1980, pp. 12–19. In late 1976 the treatment of political prisoners improved dramatically, according to Lemoine, who was arrested in 1971 and released in February 1977. By September 1977, after a visit to the island by the U.S. ambassador to the UN, Andrew Young, all 104 political prisoners were released and granted amnesty. Interestingly, U.S. Ambassador Ernest Preeg later wrote that the political opening begun in November 1976 closed on 28 November 1980 because Duvalier and most Haitians expected Reagan to give "a lower priority to human rights." *Haiti and the CBI: A Time of Change and Opportunity* (Miami: University of Miami Graduate School of International Studies, 1985), pp. 17–21.

19. Richard R. Fagen, "The Carter Administration and Latin America: Business as Usual?" *Foreign Affairs: America and the World, 1978*, vol. 57, no. 3, p. 658.

20. Ronald Reagan, "The Canal as Opportunity: A New Relationship with Latin America," *Orbis* 21 (Fall 1977): 560.

21. See Abraham M. Serkin, "Can a Human Rights Policy Be Consistent?" in Peter G. Brown and Douglas MacLean, eds., *Human Rights and U.S. Foreign Policy* (Lexington, Mass.: Lexington Books, 1980).

22. William F. Buckley, Jr., "Lessons from Argentina," *Washington Post*, 9 June 1985, p. D7.

23. See Michael J. Kryzanek, "The 1978 Election in the Dominican Republic: Opposition Politics, Intervention, and the Carter Administration," *Caribbean Studies* 19 (April–July 1979): 51–73.

24. Jimmy Carter, "A Just International Order," Department of State News Release, 29 March 1978.

25. For the Panama Declaration and Carter's address at the OAS, see *Public Papers, Carter, 1978*, vol. 1, pp. 1123–25, 1141–46.

26. For a more complete description of the Carter administration's policy toward the Caribbean, one that places it in its historical context and contrasts it with that of the Reagan administration, see Robert Pastor, "U.S. Policy toward the Caribbean: Continuity and Change," in Peter M. Dunn and Bruce W. Watson, eds., *American Intervention in Grenada: The Implications of Operation "Urgent Fury"* (Boulder, Colo.: Westview Press, 1985), pp. 15–28.

27. U.S. Senate, Committee on Foreign Relations, *Nomination of Hon. Cyrus R. Vance to Be Secretary of State,* January 11, 1977, p. 17.

28. *Public Papers, Carter, 1977,* vol. 1, pp. 293–94.

29. Castro's statement was at a press conference in Tanzania on 21 March 1977. It was cited in an article by Edward Gonzalez in Cole Blasier and Carmelo Mesa-Lago, eds., *Cuba in the World* (Pittsburgh: University of Pittsburgh Press, 1979), p. 29.

30. *Public Papers, Carter, 1977,* vol. 2, p. 2011.

31. *Public Papers, Carter, 1978,* vol. 1, pp. 903–9.

32. Castro had said that he would not take any of these human rights steps until the United States freed all of its prisoners, since they were all victims of capitalism. He had also said that he would not release U.S. political prisoners because "some of them are important C.I.A. agents." Excerpts from Barbara Walters's interview with Castro in May 1977, in *Foreign Policy* 28, (Fall 1977): 929.

33. This subject of Nicaragua is developed more fully in my book *Condemned to Repetition: The United States and Nicaragua* (Princeton, N.J.: Princeton University Press, 1987).

34. For a detailed description and analysis of U.S.-Grenadian relations from 1979 to 1983, see Robert Pastor, "Does the United States Push Revolutions to Cuba? The Case of Grenada," *Journal of Inter-American Studies and World Affairs* 28 (Spring 1986): 1–35.

35. Foreign Broadcasting Information Service, "Speeches at the Sixth Nonaligned Summit Meetings, Part I, Supplement, 18 September 1979, Speech by Michael Manley on 5 September 1979," pp. 43–46

36. This section reflects my own perceptions as a participant in the decision-making process at the time, but it also borrows from the memoirs of Vance, Brzezinski, and Carter. See Vance, *Hard Choices,* pp. 358–64; Zbigniew Brzezinski, *Power and Principle: Memoirs of the National Security Adviser, 1977–1981* (New York: Farrar, Straus and Giroux, 1983), pp. 346–52; and Jimmy Carter, *Keeping Faith: Memoirs of a President* (New York: Bantam, 1982), pp. 262–64.

37. For a description of the steps taken at that time, see Robert Pastor, "Continuity and Change in U.S. Foreign Policy: Carter and Reagan on El Salvador," *Journal of Policy Analysis and Management* 3, (Winter 1984): 179–80.

38. Fidel Castro, "Address to the National People's Government Assem-

bly," 27 December 1979, mimeographed, pp. 49–55. (This secret speech became available in the United States and was the subject of a number of articles in the Miami Herald.)

39. Daniel Yankelovich and Larry Kaagan, "Assertive America," *Foreign Affairs: America and the World, 1980*, vol. 60, p. 696.

40. Congress's influence varies with the degree to which the president must obtain its support for administration policies. Congress therefore has less influence on the president when foreign policy relies on diplomacy (as in Nicaragua from 1978 to July 1979) than when the administration needs aid (as for Nicaragua in 1980) or the ratification of a treaty (as in Panama). For a more complete development of this thesis, see Robert Pastor, *Congress and the Politics of U.S. Foreign Economic Policy* (Berkeley: University of California Press, 1980).

41. Jeane Kirkpatrick, "United States Security and Latin America," *Commentary* 71 (January 1981).

42. See, for example, William LeoGrande, "The Revolution in Nicaragua: Another Cuba?" *Foreign Affairs* 58 (Fall 1979): 28–50; and Abraham Lowenthal, "Jimmy Carter and Latin America: A New Era or Small Change?" in Kenneth Oye, Donald Rothchild, and Robert Lieber, eds., *Eagle Entangled: U.S. Foreign Policy in a Complex World* (New York: Little, Brown, 1979).

43. Address to the OAS General Assembly by the Hon. Henry deB. Forde of Barbados, November 19, 1980, Washington, D.C.

Margaret Daly Hayes

Not What I Say, but What I Do: Latin American Policy in the Reagan Administration

When Ronald Reagan assumed the presidency in 1981, he came with the goal of changing things—reversing trends that he and fellow conservatives believed had served U.S. interests badly for a long time. He particularly targeted areas in which he believed that the Carter administration's policies had failed. In accepting the Republican nomination in July 1980, candidate Reagan said:

Never before in our history have Americans been called upon to face three grave threats to our very existence, any one of which could destroy us. We face a disintegrating economy, a weakened defense and an energy policy based on the sharing of scarcity. The major issue in this campaign is the direct political, personal and moral responsibility of Democratic Party leadership— in the White House and in the Congress—for this unprecedented calamity which has befallen us.[1]

The Reagan team, and conservatives in general, saw the Carter administration policies as the culmination of a long process of retreat in foreign policy that had been accelerated by the Vietnam War and Watergate but that had origins in the combined wisdom of an established (read liberal) foreign-policy elite. Conservatives believed that this group had dominated the foreign-policy decision process, to the United States' detriment, since the 1950s. However unfairly and inaccurately, the suspect tradition was personified by the Trilateral Commission, the Council on Foreign Relations, and— in the Latin American area—the two Linowitz commissions. Conservatives found these groups to be "soft" on communism, weak on defense issues, and wishy-washy in defending U.S. interests and values.

The change of course that Reagan advocated was not out of tune with broad public opinion. The political climate in the country and in Congress was changed in 1981. New members elected to the House and the Senate were younger and more conservative than in previous Congresses. The foreign policy crises of the Carter administration had taken their toll of confidence in the public and Congress. The Iranian hostage crisis had left an image of a foundering and impotent United States that political leaders were anxious to overcome. The fall of Somoza in Nicaragua raised the specter of a succession of revolutions with undesirable outcomes in the United States' own backyard. The American public was angry about the United States' being pushed around and was eager to change that course.

Critics of Reagan administration conservatism predicted early crisis and certain failure for the administration's efforts to cope with the conflict in El Salvador, to stop Nicaraguan and other Communist aggression against Nicaragua's neighbors, to renew relations with the military governments of Argentina, Guatemala, and other authoritarian regimes and dictatorships. Failure was not the outcome, however. With the encouragement of the U.S. government, democratic governments have emerged in every Latin American country except Chile, Paraguay, Nicaragua, and, of course, Cuba. In spite of the worst auguries, democratic forces dominate in both Guatemala and El Salvador, where five years ago it appeared that the guerrilla forces were facing certain victory. The same guerrillas are now are on the defensive in both countries.

In contrast, however, the situation in Nicaragua today appears more difficult than ever. Hopes that the Sandinistas might lead Nicaragua to peace, prosperity, and pluralism have been exhausted. The Reagan administration's efforts to pressure or topple the Sandinistas with counterinsurgency have not succeeded. To date, no viable alternative to the Sandinistas has emerged. The U.S. nemesis in Cuba has less influence in the region today than in 1979 and 1980, and the Sandinistas are increasingly isolated even from their Latin American neighbors, who have opted for democratic pluralism instead of Marxism. On another dimension, the economies of Latin America and the Caribbean are seriously threatened by low world commodity prices and a continuing inability to resolve a crisis of high debt, chronically inadequate growth, and the rise of protectionism in their principal markets. This chapter describes the evolution of U.S. policies toward Central American insurgencies, the advance of communism in the region, and the emerging Latin American economic crisis in order to demonstrate how successes emerged from failures.

The Reagan Administration's View of Latin America

The Reagan team's view of Latin America and of U.S. interests in the region differed sharply from those of the previous administration on the intellectual level but ultimately proved not to vary much from Carter's policies in practice. The early Reagan administration viewed U.S. security interests in the region as threatened not only by the advance of insurgencies in Central America and the increasing number of leftist and Marxist governments in the Caribbean region but also by the deterioration in U.S. relations with many governments in Central and South America. As a Californian, Reagan was sensitive to the poor relationship that had developed between the United States and Mexico largely because of a difference in personalities. The Reagan team thought it better to build bridges to friendly governments that had poor human rights records so as to promote both U.S. interests and human rights improvements than to make human rights the sole test of a bilateral relationship. They advocated "quiet diplomacy" (and some arm-twisting) to accomplish improvements in human rights. They were eager to get back into the commercial arms market and advocated a more open attitude toward Latin American countries seeking to upgrade their military arsenals with state-of-the-art weaponry.

The Reagan team saw no ground on which the United States and Cuba could find common cause. They did not believe the Cubans could be trusted, and they were convinced that Cuba and the Soviets were on the march in the hemisphere. They also were convinced that the multilateral development banks were undermining the United States by lending to left-leaning and statist countries. The administration's policy goals did not vary significantly over the years after 1981. However, as administration policymakers grew more sophisticated about the actors with whom they had to deal in Latin America, and about the complexities of the political processes unfolding in the region, policy itself became more nuanced, less naive, and more middle of the road—to the dismay of administration hard-liners. Ultimately, with a combination of steady insistence and a good measure of luck, the administration achieved some remarkable policy successes. It secured for the United States and the Latin American countries goals that democrats in the region, and Democrats and Republicans in the United States, could all support.

Three major themes occupied the attention of Reagan administration policymakers during the first term and into the second: (1) El

Salvador, (2) Cuba and Nicaragua and the problem of containing communism in the hemisphere, and (3) belatedly, the debt crisis. The following pages trace the evolution of the Reagan administration's policy in each of these three areas, assess the administration's record in coping with these problem areas, and review the play of forces that influenced policy-making and policy outcomes in each.

Coping with the Central American Quagmire

El Salvador and the broader Central American question dominated the administration's Latin American policy well into the second term. Three key events influenced U.S. policy toward Central America as Ronald Reagan took office in January 1981. They were (1) the 1979 revolution in Nicaragua, (2) the slaying of four U.S. churchwomen and two American workers in the Salvadoran land reform program in December 1980 and January 1981, and (3) the "final offensive" of the Salvadoran armed opposition against the Salvadoran government, also in January 1981. The first and last events made credible the conservatives' contention that indeed there was a new and concerted Communist drive to take over the hemisphere. The slayings confirmed the administration's liberal critics' certainty of the essential cruelty and unredeemable viciousness of the "old elite," especially the military. The nuns' murders mobilized U.S. church opposition to both the Salvadoran government and the U.S. government that supported it in a unique, highly personalized, and emotional way. The murders were the single aspect of U.S. policy that kept El Salvador constantly before the public for four long years.

Assistant Secretary of State for Inter-American Affairs Thomas O. Enders announced administration policy toward El Salvador in July 1981. The solution was to be political and was to be arrived at by Salvadorans. Carefully paralleling legislation then being discussed in Congress, the assistant secretary insisted that the solution included fulfilling the land reform announced in 1980, controlling violence from left and right, and holding elections (a timetable had been announced in 1980) that would include "all parties that renounce violence." Finally, Enders maintained that "the search for a political solution will not succeed unless the United States sustains its assistance to El Salvador" because, he argued, "should members of the guerrilla command believe that they can make gains by military means, no participation in elections, no meaningful negotiations, no political solutions are likely to be forthcoming. The point is not that sustained U.S. assistance might lead to a government military victory. It is that a political solution can only be achieved if the guerrillas realize they cannot win by force of arms."[2] In spite of the political rhetoric, the public fulminating, the highly emotional debate, and the battles within the administration itself for direction of the policy, this essentially modest policy toward the Salvadoran situation and similar Central American imbroglios prevailed throughout the first Reagan term.

Enders's Central American policy evolved through three phases. The first lasted from 1981 through 1982 and was a period of learning for both the administration and its critics. With the brief distraction of the Falklands War between Argentina and the United Kingdom, El Salvador was almost the exclusive focus of U.S. attention in Latin America. The second phase, 1983, began at the nadir of U.S. fortunes in El Salvador and was a time of desperation and transition. In El Salvador, the policy seemed to be failing; sanctions against Nicaragua were increased; Enders was replaced by Langhorne Motley; and aid requests were increased dramatically in an effort to gain the upper hand militarily. Demonstrations of U.S. resolve—as in Grenada—were used to strike fear in the region generally and to raise morale at home. By the end of 1983 the tide had turned in El Salvador and phase three ensued, a period of increasing confidence in the success of administration policies.

Working the Political Solution in El Salvador

When Reagan took office in 1981, all but three countries in South America—Colombia, Peru, and Venezuela—were military dictatorships of long standing. The Central American countries were embroiled in the process of political change, with powerful forces simultaneously struggling to reject old-line military governments, to promote democracy, and in some cases to experiment with Marxist formst of government.[3] In spite of their long parliamentary tradition, the Caribbean countries seemed almost as threatened by violence as did Central America. Under such circumstances, democracy rather than human rights became the Reagan administration's noble theme for Latin America, and democratic elections were defended as a key goal for every country. The electoral process, not the force of arms, was to be the appropriate way to bring about change.

As Enders announced in July 1981, El Salvador already had set a timetable for elections, and the administration's goal was to see that they occurred in as propitious a climate as possible. Throughout 1981 and more intensely between December 1981 and March 1982, the guerrilla movement engaged in sabotage of the economic infrastructure of the country in an effort to persuade the peasants that neither they nor their livelihood could be defended by the incumbent regime. Simultaneously, the guerrillas sought to make the elections impossible, burning town halls where the rolls of voters were kept, threatening and killing party organizers, and finally threatening death to those who voted. At the same time, elements of the Democratic Revolutionary Front (FDR), the political arm of the Farabundo Martí National Liberation (FMLN) guerrilla movement, sought to persuade opinion in the United States that fair elections were impossible because of the endemic violence. If representatives of the FDR / FMLN were not able to participate, they argued, the preferred choice of a large segment of the Salvadoran people would not be represented.

The 1982 Salvadoran elections should have marked the turning point in public opinion about El Salvador. The prevailing view was that voter turnout would be light and irregularities common. On the eve of the elections, Archbishop Rivera y Damas told Father Theodore Hesburgh of the U.S. observer team, led by Senator Nancy Kassebaum of Kansas, that the Salvadoran people would prove the skeptics wrong. Instead of boycotting the elections, as the guerrillas were urging them to do, they would "vote with their feet."[4] Indeed, more than a million people turned out to vote, some in the most difficult of circumstances, and over three hundred official observers failed to find any grave faults in the voting process itself.[5]

Five parties were represented in the Constituent Assembly. The Christian Democrats were the strongest, with twenty-four seats, but next in order, with nineteen seats, was ARENA, the new right-wing party of Roberto D'Aubuisson. This flamboyant, sometimes charismatic, former army officer with suspected ties to death squads had campaigned on the promise of a quick and decisive end to the guerrilla war. If anyone questioned whether the United States controlled the political situation in El Salvador in 1982, the results of the Constituent Assembly elections should have disabused them of the thought. It would be more accurate to say that the U.S. authorities were disappointed. The assembly was an unwieldy body that reflected the political divisions of the country. Though the Christian

Democrats had a plurality of votes, ARENA was a too-close second. As a consequence, several small parties of the center right, including a small urban middle-class party (Acción Democrática) and the party of the old political oligarchy, the Party of National Conciliation (PCN), held the balance.

The U.S. ambassador engaged in obvious politicking to wrest from the confusion a government that could govern and that would pursue reformist policies that would continue to enjoy U.S. congressional support. Leaders in the assembly disliked a good number of the policies advocated by the U.S. administration. An ongoing fight over continuation of the wide-ranging land reform promulgated in 1980 was only one example of the political tug of war, one that practically cost El Salvador its 1983 foreign-assistance budget.[6] Ultimately the political forces themselves split into warring factions. The cautious and consensus-building leadership of Interim President Alvaro Magaña led the country over the shoals of transition. By 1984, the Salvadorans were ready for a government with the authority to make decisions and an assembly that could be held politically responsible. José Napoleón Duarte was elected president in a two-stage runoff election that presented voters with a clear choice between the left-of-center Duarte and the conservative right of D'Aubuisson. In 1985 voters replaced the Constituent Assembly with a permanent assembly and gave Duarte a wide margin of support to carry out his political program.

Throughout the building of the democratic government in El Salvador, the FDR/FMLN argued for a negotiated solution. From the guerrilla's point of view, negotiations ultimately meant bringing them into the government at the expense of the Salvadoran military. For many in the United States who supported negotiations, such a solution meant ending the annoyance of El Salvador by bringing some moderate leftists into the government while ousting some hard-liners. The FDR/FMLN demands remained fairly constant across a series of documents announced to the public or sent to key members of Congress, whose support they hoped to enlist. Throughout, they insisted on the ouster of a number of military officers and the formation of a government prior to elections. They refused to run in elections, claiming their security could not be ensured; they also sought to sabotage elections so that they would not seem to be legitimate tests of the public will.

After the 1982 elections, the guerrillas' claim to represent a necessary choice within the Salvadoran political spectrum waned. They recognized as much, and their negotiating positions and rhetoric hardened. Nevertheless, at the nadir of the military campaign in 1983, some members of Congress still viewed a negotiated solution as a way to eliminate the continuing headache of El Salvador. Few were willing to risk the failure of the moderately successful Salvadoran political program for another coalition like that which had failed in Nicaragua, however. The administration, moreover, remained steadfast in insisting that a political solution in El Salvador could not be forced at gunpoint but had to be won in a democratic competition for votes. After the 1984 elections it appeared to most that a political solution in El Salvador had been found without the insurgents' participation. Increasingly, elements of the political arm of the FDR/ FMLN began to return to El Salvador to take up their lives again, and the guerrilla leadership renewed its commitment to a prolonged war.

Implementing the Land Reform

The Salvadoran junta decreed a far-reaching land reform in March 1980. The program would affect holdings in three categories: those over 500 hectares (Phase I), which would be expropriated and turned into cooperatives run by peasant dwellers; those between 50 and 500 hectares (Phase II), disposition of which was not determined; and those under 50 hectares (Phase III), title to which would be transferred to those who had rented and worked the land.

There were a number of problems associated with the program. The expropriation of both Phase I farms and Phase III properties was accompanied by extreme violence. The bonds offered to former landowners in Phase I were nearly worthless, and those owners who did not resist took their capital out of the country. Phase II farms were among the most productive in El Salvador. The government's indecision over their disposition also encouraged owners to disinvest. Other owners simply failed to plant or harvest, causing a severe impact on El Salvador's foreign-exchange earnings. Phase III was the program with the most potential for political impact, because it provided title to a plot of land to some 100,000 landless peasant families.[7] Establishing title was difficult, however, for El Salvador had no cadastral survey to establish either the legal title to or the extent of property holdings. Moreover, many of the tillers had worked a large number of plots over the years.

The government had little technical assistance to offer the new owners in either Phase I or Phase III of the system. Neither did it have the resources for crucial financing, and in many cases even those co-operatives that produced successful crops were not paid for their harvest, because the government marketing boards had no cash in the bank. Many of the new peasant owners did not know how to deal with the banking system itself. Moreover, during the interim government of President Magaña (from June 1982 to June 1984), the administration of the land reform institute was put under representatives of the ARENA party, which had opposed the reform.

In 1982, shortly after the newly elected Constituent Assembly was installed, it undertook to modify the land reform program in ways that appeared to terminate Phase III. The U.S. Congress reacted swiftly and strongly, threatening that if the land reform was terminated, "not one cent" of aid would be provided to the government. The reaction sent a strong signal to the Salvadoran assembly and to the government. A military officer was placed in charge of land distribution in Phase III. The chief of staff of the army, General José Guillermo García, himself participated in the first distribution of titles. Military personnel were instructed to "protect" peasants who had entered claims to the land. The Agency for International Development brought in a computer to sort out conflicting title claims. In 1982 some 22 final Phase I titles and some 34,674 provisional Phase III titles were distributed. By September 1985, 96 final Phase I titles, 65,676 provisional Phase III titles, and 15,228 final Phase II titles had been handed down.[8] Nearly three-fourths of the potential claimants to Phase III titles had been provided for, and agricultural production was up in most of the country. By 1985 the impossible land reform was a fact.

Improving Human Rights Performance

When the administration took office in 1981, violent deaths were oc-curring in El Salvador at the rate of between two hundred and five hundred per month and rising. Much of the violence was out of con-trol of the authorities, conducted by officers who made decisions on their own. Senior officials did not discourage "revenge" against left-ists. Rumors (and evidence) of death squads were rampant, but there was not enough evidence to establish responsibility and bring the culprits to justice. Key figures in the government protected suspect friends and relatives. The court system was inadequate to handle the difficult issue of human rights violations.

The Reagan administration's message on human rights was clouded by its own rhetoric and actions. The first candidate for assistant secretary for humanitarian affairs was Ernest Lefever, whose words on the subject won him the early distrust of Democrats and moderate Republicans alike. Lefever was forced to withdraw his name from nomination, and his replacement, Elliott Abrams, enjoyed much greater respect on Capitol Hill. Nevertheless, the experience left profound suspicions about the White House's commitment on the subject. Congress reacted by imposing certification language in the foreign aid authorizing legislation of 1981 which forced both the administration and the Salvadoran authorities to confront the statistics of violence directly.

As they grappled daily with the issue, administration dealings with the Salvadorans became increasingly tough. With violence levels declining by nearly every account, the administration could have relaxed its pressures. But its own prestige and credibility became entangled in the improving human rights situation. Moreover, human rights improvements became incorporated into the administration's own interpretation of the reforms that were required if El Salvador was ever to return to political stability. The approach reflected the U.S. authorities' growing understanding of their Salvadoran friends— without firm pressure they simply would not take difficult steps. In October 1982, Ambassador Deane Hinton spoke heatedly about the "rotten" Salvadoran legal system and challenged Salvadoran political leaders to get violence under control. He referred directly to the death squad issue, saying that a "rightist mafia" that kidnapped and murdered political opponents posed as great a threat to the country as the leftist guerrillas. Hinton's speech reflected the State Department's growing conviction that government human rights abuses were an obstacle to a political solution to the crisis, but conservatives within the administration rejected his efforts to twist the arms of the Salvadoran right. In seven months Hinton was gone, replaced by career diplomat Thomas R. Pickering.[9] In December 1983, Vice-President George Bush took his personal list of human rights "goons" to San Salvador authorities and demanded their removal. The individuals were replaced and violence declined dramatically.

It became increasingly apparent that the Salvadoran institutional system itself inhibited, even prohibited, any remedy for human rights abuses. Authorities testifying in the first certification hearings remarked that El Salvador had a legal system that had not evolved beyond the sixteenth century. Expressing frustration over the inability to obtain any action on the murder of the land-reform workers, another witness observed that the legal system had been devised to catch pig thieves, not to prosecute murderers.[10] Judges, on whom the burden of gathering evidence falls in systems based on the Napoleonic Code, had no staff to assist them and were subject to both threats and bribery. Moreover, justices tended to be political appointees with no necessary qualifications. They enjoyed a sinecure, and were not necessarily devoted to the administration of justice. El Salvador's bar association functioned as a social club, not as a standard-setting organization for the legal profession. To make matters worse, the Salvadoran budget permitted approximately $1.00 per month to the courts for supplies like pencils and typewriter ribbons.

The real test of U.S. public tolerance of the situation in El Salvador was the disposition of the churchwomen's murder case. Americans were incensed that four churchwomen could be so brutally murdered and that so little effort would be made to find and prosecute the murderers. Salvadorans, accustomed to hundreds of deaths a month, including churchpeople, were perplexed and angered by the North Americans' emphasis on "their" dead. They had trouble understanding why the churchwomen's murder case was so important.

The administration threatened, argued, and cajoled to get action from the Salvadorans, who always promised something "within weeks." With each failure to show any progress, political frustration in the United States increased. Both the U.S. and Salvadoran authorities were suspected of dallying.[11] The problem was more complex, however. Salvadoran law required that no detail of evidence be omitted in the prosecution's case to the judge, or it would be thrown out of court. With U.S. help, the Salvadoran attorney general's office slowly sought to build an airtight case against the five soldiers responsible for the slaying of the four women. On 24 May 1984 a jury found the five enlisted men accused of the murders guilty as charged. They were given maximum sentences of life in prison. Rumors persisted that senior officers of the army were responsible for ordering the slayings, but there was insufficient evidence to justify prosecution.

Public attention was never drawn so insistently to the case of the murder of the two American employees of the American Institute for Free Labor Deveopment (AIFLD) and the director of the Salvadoran land reform institute. Church groups in the United States tended to ignore the case, which was infinitely more complex than the church-women's case and was closely entwined with the privileges and immunities accorded members of the Salvadoran elite. Though evidence pointed strongly to the explicit involvement of two Salvadoran army officers and the complicity of others, the Salvadoran supreme court, presided over by the uncle of one of the accused, threw out the case for lack of evidence.[12] This underscored more than ever the weaknesses of the Salvadoran judicial system.

Providing the Military Shield

Enders's 1981 policy statement said that U.S. assistance would be required to prove to the guerrillas that they could not win by force, but the success of the policy depended on the skills of the Salvadoran army. In 1981 the United States sent a delegation of experienced army personnel to El Salvador to work with General García's staff to devise a training program and determine military hardware requirements. What the team found was discouraging: incompetent soldiers who did not understand battlefield, counterinsurgency, or civic-action tactics; an absence of staff functions to coordinate the military effort; low morale; corruption; and a hatred of politicians that pointed clearly to continuing problems of governance for any civilians who might inherit the political leadership of the country.

Initially, the U.S. government's principal concern was to assure that the Salvadoran military did not lose to the guerrillas. An army had to be built up, trained, and tested. Advisors initially envisaged a program that would last from three to five years. The more the U.S. trainers worked with their Salvadoran counterparts, the more assistance they found to be necessary. For three years the Salvadorans performed poorly and unsuccessfully. They engaged in useless chases over the countryside after the guerrillas, rarely finding any. They failed to gather intelligence and did not take prisoners. Moreover, with a few notable exceptions, they behaved imperiously toward the population. The press quickly dubbed the Salvadorans the "9-to-5 army," and deservedly so.

The United States trained Salvadorans in El Salvador, at Fort Benning, Georgia, at the School of the Americas in Panama, and briefly in Honduras. This training paid off, but more slowly than the advisers would have liked. The Salvadoran army gradually learned to deal with the guerrillas and with most elements of the local population.

As the army gained new skills, however, the guerrillas changed tactics. By early 1983, as the Salvadorans became a credible threat in the field, the guerrillas took to assaulting distant garrisons where the defending units, always short of ammunition, shot up their supplies and were then offered safe passage out of the area in exchange for their weapons. The guerrilla strategy was immensely successful until some guerrilla units began to kill their hostages.

As with other issues, 1983 was the critical year for U.S. policy on El Salvador. As it began, though violence was down to a degree, the Salvadoran army seemed to be falling behind in its effort to keep control of the countryside. The Pentagon argued for more trainers and more money to turn the war around. Congress, which had for two years constrained the military assistance budget for El Salvador, was confronted with the nasty choice of nickel-and-diming the army to defeat or giving it more than many felt it needed or could use. Skeptics in the House and Senate had forced a stalemate for two years, but the threat of possible defeat gave impetus to a more liberal gamble. Members remained torn between a concern that more military assistance would lead inevitably to intervention by U.S. troops and a fear that insufficient U.S. assistance would assure the need for direct military intervention.

In April 1983 the president was obliged to step in personally to turn the tide of negative sentiment. In his speech to a joint session of Congress, President Reagan recalled President Harry S. Truman's 1947 request to Congress for bipartisan support for the Marshall Plan, and quoted from Truman's speech to another joint session: "I believe that it must be the policy of the United States to support free peoples who are resisting attempted subjugation by armed minorities or by outside pressures." Reagan dismissed concerns about a repeat of Vietnam, saying, "There is no thought of sending American combat troops to Central America: they are not needed." He reiterated Enders's goals of support for democracy, reform, and human rights; economic development; the security of threatened nations; and "dialogue and negotiation—both among the countries of the region and within each country." The president then asked for prompt approval of his full request for aid for 1983 and 1984 and closed by throwing down the gauntlet before Congress: "This is not a partisan issue. . . . It is a duty that falls on all of us—the President, the Congress, and the people. We must perform it together. Who among us would wish to bear responsibility for failing to meet our shared obligation?"[13] The speech broke the stalemate over aid to El Salvador and marked the beginning of a dramatic shift in support for administration policies.

Changes also began to take place on the ground in El Salvador. In the spring, following a dispute with his more aggressive commanders, General García was forced to resign as commander in chief. His replacement, General Eugenio Vides Casanova, was more open to suggestions from his commanders and the U.S. military advisory team. He agreed to move some of the worst human rights offenders in the Salvadoran army out of sensitive positions. Moreover, he put his most capable commanders in the most conflictive areas, where they could take on the guerrilla force directly.

Over the summer and fall of 1983, the tide began to shift, at first imperceptibly, against the guerrilla force. The Salvadorans began to acquire and use intelligence; an amnesty program won them a number of informants; new tactics permitted them to keep the guerrillas on the run. The guerrillas made mistakes. Following a spectacular raid on the army's El Paraíso garrison in December, the guerrillas did not win another major battle. When Duarte came to the United States in December 1983 for his last visit before embarking on his election campaign, he had the sympathy and hope of most politicians and the public. Elections in March and May 1984 proved less dramatic than those in 1982, but they showed that the system worked. The members of Congress who observed the elections increasingly became persuaded that El Salvador did indeed have the beginnings of a democratic political process.

Duarte followed his May election victory with an official visit to the United States as president-elect to urge Congress to vote full funding of economic and military aid for El Salvador. Given his own heroic commitment to democratic processes, his demonstrated support from the people, his record of fighting against human rights abuses, and the positive military and economic situation in El Salvador that spring, it was impossible for Congress to deny him support, and all but $20 million in military assistance was approved for El Salvador for 1985. El Salvador rapidly ceased being front-page news, and few reacted with surprise when Duarte's Christian Democratic party swept the legislative assembly elections in March 1985. The U.S. administration had won its political victory.

Containing Communism

One of the most profound and visceral criticisms that the Reagan team had of the Carter administration concerned the latter's view of the Soviet-Cuban purpose in the world.[14] Carter's first major foreign-policy speech in May 1977 had stressed a new U.S. vision of its relations with the developing world in which it was no longer obsessed with the fear of communism. Jeane J. Kirkpatrick wrote in 1981 that

American policies have not only proved incapable of dealing with the problems of Soviet/Cuban expansion in [Latin America], they have positively contributed to them and to the alienation of major nations, the growth of neutralism, the destabilization of friendly governments, the spread of Cuban influence, and the decline of U.S. power in the region.[15]

Of course, the Carter administration was not responsible for all of the changes that were taking place in Third World countries. The Soviets had adopted a conscious policy of courting Third World clients during the 1970s. The process of detente and the U.S. foreign policy retreat following Vietnam also contributed to the Soviet disposition toward adventure. With the ideological battle in Europe stalemated, the Soviets knew better than the United States at the time that the contest between the superpowers was for the leadership of the Third World.[16]

The Reagan team, heavily staffed and counseled by ardent anti-communists, was committed to a new approach in its dealings with the Soviets on the strategic and political fronts. The Reagan team saw the Caribbean Basin as a major theater of U.S.-Soviet competition for the Third World. Cuba had been quiescent in its overseas commitments, particularly within the Western Hemisphere; by mid-decade, however, it was politically active again, especially among the countries of the Caribbean Basin. Carter had sought to pursue a rapprochement with Cuba but ceased when Castro sent troops to Angola and later to Ethiopia. At approximately the same time, 1975 and 1976, Cuban relations with the Manley government in Jamaica changed. Michael Manley became steadily warmer in his relations with Castro, and by 1979 Cuban activities on the island were a serious concern to Jamaicans and to the United States.

Also in 1979, a pro-Cuban faction of Maurice Bishop's New Jewel Movement seized power in a palace coup on Grenada. Marxist candidates vied for office in a number of the small Caribbean states in a process that was marked by increasing violence. Elsewhere, Castro had been decisive in his Johnny-come-lately support for the Sandinistas, and he entertained members of the governing junta almost immediately after the 17 July takeover in Managua. Castro demanded the union of rival Salvadoran guerrilla factions in 1979 and 1980, and the result was the FMLN. Throughout, the prevailing U.S. rhetoric lambasting authoritarian regimes with human rights problems and later promoting controlled evolution toward democracy suggested to those wanting to hear it a greater tolerance for radical change than in fact was present in either the Carter administration or the American body politic.

Historical events require that the United States tolerate a Communist Cuba on its Caribbean doorstep. It is a simple political fact, however, that the United States will never be complacent with a Marxist-Leninist regime in Nicaragua, nor with a Nicaragua closely allied with Cuba or the Soviets or committed to revolutionary movements elsewhere in the hemisphere. U.S. policy toward Nicaragua has evolved over a series of phases, but the essential elements emerged early on as first the Carter administration and then the Reagan administration got to know the Sandinista government. Carter, under pressure from congressional conservatives, had stopped assistance to the Sandinistas in 1980 because of their support for the Salvadoran guerrillas. On 1 April 1981 Reagan announced the termination of $15 million in assistance authorized after a long congressional battle the previous year.[17] Project funds already in the pipeline were not touched. The cutoff of aid was accompanied by a statement that the Sandinistas indeed had halted the majority of overland supply to the Salvadorans, the reason Carter had stopped aid months before. The decision sent confusing signals. On the one hand, it put the Sandinistas on notice; on the other, it suggested an intransigence and lack of trust on the administration's part that made negotiations with the Nicaraguans very difficult. The decision reflected the hard-line influence and unbridled enthusiasm of the tough-on-communism line of advisers in the administration.

Thomas Enders laid out the bottom-line U.S. position on Nicaragua in his secret August 1981 meeting with the Sandinista government. That included, as the *sine qua non*, the Sandinistas' cessation of all aid to the Salvadoran guerrillas.[18] In addition, Enders demanded a number of other concessions from the Nicaraguans and in exchange offered renewed assistance and some assurances against U.S. actions against the regime.[19] When confronted with Sandinista intransigence, Enders's approach was to apply increasing political, economic, and diplomatic pressure. More hard-line voices in the administration and in Congress proposed stronger measures, up to and including military action, but these were not seriously considered. From the administration's perspective, the situation in Central America could be handled with other policy tools.

The Reagan administration and the Sandinistas did not like one another. The inherent mistrust between the two governments contributed to lost opportunities for rapprochement, if there were any, and certainly to the impression that neither side was really interested in an agreement. Sandinista hubris also made negotiations difficult. The Nicaraguans repeatedly slammed shut doors that had been left partially open by the U. S. diplomats; the U. S. diplomats refused to accept anything but full capitulation from the Sandinistas.

The U.S. policy of pressure on Nicaragua was a long-term one with which hard-liners in the administration had little patience. Sandinista intransigence made it increasingly difficult to hold policy to a mere backdown for the Nicaraguans. A consensus began to emerge slowly about the Sandinistas' real political stripes. By 1982 they had lost the support of most liberal members of Congress who had welcomed the Sandinista victory over Somoza. Moreover, as the situation in El Salvador worsened throughout 1982 and 1983, it became more important that the Nicaraguans' ability to help the FMLN in the field be constrained.

The United States' minimal demands for containment increasingly became entwined with demands for a change in the regime.[20] This policy shift relied on the Sandinistas' own statement to the Organization of American States in which they indicated their intention "to convoke the Nicaraguans to the first free elections they will have in this century, so that they can elect their municipal officials and a constituent assembly, and, later, the supreme authorities of the country."[21] More important, it reflected the administration's conclusion that the regime in Nicaragua would not compromise and was not healthy for the region.

Whether it was or is realistic to think that the Sandinistas would modify their political stripes, the U.S. government's rationale for its insistence on pluralism was clear to its proponents. The historical record of Marxist tolerance of pluralism, support for private enterprise, noninterference in the affairs of neighbors, and independence from the Soviet bloc was not at all promising. The Sandinistas would be unique if they did not follow the model, and there were no signs that they were even trying. Sandinista rhetoric was stridently anti-American and replete with the rhetoric and logic learned only by careful study of Marx and Lenin. In 1980 they joined only five other countries in the world in supporting the Soviet invasion of Afghanistan. After spurning offers of assistance from Panama, Venezuela, and the United States, increasingly the technical advisers brought in to help with reconstruction came from the Eastern bloc—including East Germany and Bulgaria, among others.

The situation in Central America was not going well in 1983. The Latin American countries became so concerned that the United States might launch an invasion of Nicaragua through Honduras that four of them—Venezuela, Colombia, Mexico, and Panama—launched their own effort—the Contadora process—to resolve the Central American crisis. Important elements in the administration were initially skeptical of the Latin Americans' ability to work a solution in the region but were persuaded to give the effort a chance. After a tortuous eight months of intermittent negotiations, the group finally succeeded in announcing its "Document of Objectives," a statement of political, economic, and security goals for the region. In language, the objectives were fully consistent with U.S. goals for the region, but there was no mechanism for implementing them. An initial draft treaty circulated in the region in July 1984. However, it was not until the fall of 1984 that the group was able to achieve agreement on a draft treaty. Still, even that treaty did not have the teeth to implement the provisions of the security section, and it skirted the key issue for the other Central American nations: the problem of Nicaragua's Marxist ideology and the absence of pluralism in that country.

Contadora's fatal flaw was the failure to appreciate the real tensions that had developed between Nicaragua and its neighbors.[22] The Contadora four were further hamstrung by the Latin American's hesitancy to "interfere in the internal affairs" of others. For the Reagan administration, the problem in Central America was precisely the internal makeup of the Nicaraguan government.[23] The president announced in his April 1983 speech to Congress that the United States would support any "verifiable, reciprocal" agreements for withdrawing of foreign military advisers, for ending support for cross-border insurgencies, and for ending the Central American arms race. He slipped casually over a fourth point: "We want to help opposition groups join in the political process in all countries and compete by ballots instead of bullets." By 1984 the question of political reconciliation and reenfranchisement for the Nicaraguan opposition became the key issue around which solutions in Central America would turn.[24] U.S. government support for Contadora was frequently called into question. Indeed, not everyone in the administration did support the process, but it was agreed that Contadora should be given a chance. Gradually, however, as negotiations continued but without a solution, Contadora became less and less relevant to the overall search for peace in the region.

In 1983 the public and Congress were growing impatient. Hardliners in Congress and in the administration argued for stronger measures. Critics threatened to impose their own political formulas. The administration responded with a bizarre series of demonstrations of power in the region that seemed to suggest that it was about to invoke its military option. Military exercises on a grand scale were planned with Honduras for the spring and summer of 1983.[25] Several seemed to threaten the Honduras-Nicaragua border. In the course of preparations, U.S. Seabees and the Army Corps of Engineers arrived to set up "temporary" housing and build airfields at strategically located points. When the exercises were over, they left most of the hardware behind, including radar facilities that vastly improved the U.S. ability to monitor the airspace between Nicaragua, Honduras, and El Salvador. The radar facility was intended to provide intelligence to the Salvadoran armed forces. In July the president ordered the aircraft carrier *Ranger* to patrol the Pacific coast of Nicaragua. A destroyer was also diverted from the eastern Caribbean to the Honduran coast for a time, raising concerns that a blockade was being contemplated. The covert war, begun in 1981, escalated through 1982 and into 1983. In October the contras, with substantial support from the CIA, blew up a major Nicaraguan refinery.

In October 1983 U.S. forces were sent into military action in Grenada. There is little reason to believe that the invasion of Grenada was not the result of a felicitous coincidence of events. It is true that the administration wanted to end the Marxist government of Grenada and justified its military assistance requests for the Caribbean by noting the "Cuban-built" airfield being constructed on the island. It took the collapse of the Grenadian government in internecine fighting and a direct request for assistance from the leaders of the eastern Caribbean for the United States to act, however. The results of the military action surprised even the administration. The Cubans were armed and, with the Soviets, resisted much longer than the Grenadians. The Grenadian people cheered the invaders.

The propaganda impact of the Grenada operation was tremendous. On the one hand, the administration won tremendous public support for the successful operation. On the other, anyone who questioned whether the administration was a paper tiger had an answer. Finally, the truckloads of documents captured from the Bishop government proved beyond doubt that both the Cubans and the Soviets had interests in the region and that there had been the clear intention of establishing a Marxist-Leninist government on the island.[26] Leftist revolutionaries mouthing Marxist slogans would be looked at differently after Grenada. Grenada measurably closed the maneuvering room for the Sandinistas.

Both Cubans and Nicaraguans modified their postures in discussions with the United States following the Grenada episode. The pressure seemed to have worked.[27] In October, almost simultaneously with the Grenada operation, Nicaragua presented the United States with draft bilateral treaties outside the framework of Contadora. In the heady aftermath of Grenada, they were ignored by both the administration and Congress. Later, Nicaragua submitted a series of proposals to the Contadora negotiators and subsequently joined with the other Central American countries in endorsing the January 1984 Contadora "Principles for Implementation of Objectives." In principle, the endorsement committed Nicaragua to discuss elections and political reconciliation with its internal opposition as well as a military de-escalation, though the Sandinistas probably did not interpret the document in this way.

Administration thinking in the spring of 1984 seemed to be that if pressure was working, more pressure might bring success. In El Salvador the administration used strong-arm tactics to insure the continued transition to democracy in that country. In Nicaragua the administration used stronger tactics to force the Sandinistas to make changes. Whether these changes meant modifications in their policies and politics or a change in government remained an unresolved question. At the heart of the matter was the profound suspicion on the part of both the advocates of overthrow and those of accommodation that the Sandinistas were incapable of change.

Hard-line tactics ranged from the mining of the Nicaraguan harbors in January 1984 to increasing requests for funding for the contras. The harbor mining almost guaranteed congressional opposition to the funding request, for increasingly Congress was concerned that the covert operation was out of hand. Artful negotiations on Capitol

Hill postponed votes on contra aid through most of 1984, but finally congressional patience with duplicitous explanations wore out and aid was cut off. The hard line resulted in elections on schedule in 1984 but failed to assure sufficient concessions so that an opposition could run. The Sandinistas won 60 percent of the vote and became a "legitimate" government but lost most of their moderate friends in the process.

Administration policy had to achieve two goals in Nicaragua. The first was to contain Nicaragua's influence and limit or cut off its support for insurgencies elsewhere in the region. For the most part this was successful. While the administration claimed that supplies continued to be shipped to the Salvadorans throughout 1984 and 1985, they were clearly below levels provided before. The Nicaraguans had to concentrate their energies on an internal insurgency of their own. Moreover, as the Salvadoran conflict turned against the guerrillas, the latter became less attractive allies for the Sandinistas. Containment worked in part but at the cost of continued pressure on the Nicaraguans.

The administration's second goal—a wish as much as a goal—was to achieve the downfall of the Sandinistas without actually overthrowing the government. The same tactics—economic, political, and military pressures—were used to attain this goal, but with the consequence of increased Sandinista resistance to sharing power with any other elements in the country. Military pressures gave the Sandinistas an excuse to impose a state of seige, censor the independent press, and impose a highly unpopular draft. The internal situation became increasingly difficult for dissidents, and the more difficult the internal situation became, the more moderates left the country, depriving Nicaragua of a political alternative to Sandinista leadership. The 1984 elections, which were expected to show the Sandinistas as unpopular with their own people, gave them legitimacy, just as the 1982 elections had made the Salvadoran government legitimate. The Reagan administration's policy was essentially as flawed in its failure in the early years to consider a successor to the Sandinistas as the Carter policy had been from the outset in failing to understand the Sandinistas' drive to control the government.

The contras could not provide a solution, for their leaders were unable to command the respect and loyalty of the moderate politicians, professionals, and bureaucrats, people who had been small in number in Nicaragua even before the fall of Somoza. These people would be essential to the effective governance of the country, and they were the core of the democratic alternative that the administration so fervently wanted. Just as in El Salvador, the right-wing supporters of the previous regime could not maintain power in a democratic situation. The somocistas (the title is probably unfair) could not form a winning coalition in the Nicaraguan opposition. As a consequence, while the contras could bring military pressure to bear on the Sandinistas, they did not represent a viable political alternative. Without that more attractive alternative, aid to the contras could not succeed in bringing democracy to Nicaragua.

Setting Economic Policy

When the Reagan administration came to office, the Latin American economies were on the brink of an economic precipice. Most countries in the region had grown at record rates for a decade; commercial bank lending remained high and, despite the warnings of some doomsayers, seemed to indicate a continued degree of confidence. But those good times were at an end. The Reagan administration's economic policy was oriented domestically. Inflation in the United States was the administration's number one target; renewing economic growth at home was its second. Few if any advisers focused on the developing world's economic situation. The administration's principal economic message to the developing world was "reliance on the market place," a phrase that mirrored its policies for the domestic U.S. economy.

The Caribbean Basin Initiative

Circumstances required that the administration rapidly turn its attention to the deteriorating political and economic situation in Latin America. In 1981 the president offered a model economic development program—the Caribbean Basin Initiative—that reflected the administration's market preferences. By the end of 1982, with the onset of the debt crisis among the major Latin American debtors, the administration intervened bilaterally to help a number of troubled Latin American debtors. It did an about-face in its support for multilateral institutions by lobbying hard for an International Monetary Fund (IMF) capital increase in 1983. Throughout the first term, the executive branch used a number of policy tools to benefit Latin

American economies both directly and indirectly. Among them were increased use of Economic Support Funds (the AID-administered balance-of-payments support account), a series of Treasury Exchange Stabilization Fund lendings, increased bilateral assistance, and a series of actions on the trade front that directly benefited Latin American exports, sometimes at the expense of U.S. producers. By 1985 and the second term, administration policy encompassed both support for enhanced roles for the IMF and the World Bank, more aggressive U.S. government efforts to promote private bank lending to Latin America, and strong administration support for a liberal international trade regime.

On the economic as on the political front, the worrisome region in Latin America in 1981 was the Caribbean Basin, where economic deterioration had been rife for most of the 1970s. The Caribbean islands had been in particular trouble, and recent political turmoil exacerbated their problems. Central America had also experienced economic stagnation during the latter half of the 1970s as commodity prices sagged and oil import costs rose dramatically. The civil war in Nicaragua and mounting guerrilla activities in both El Salvador and Guatemala contributed further to the economic decline in Central America. Growing uncertainty about the Sandinista government's policies discouraged more investors.

When Edward Seaga, the prime minister of Jamaica, who had been advocating a "mini–Marshall Plan" for the Caribbean countries, came to Washington in April 1981, the administration had no plan to offer. Secretary of State Alexander Haig observed in his memoirs that Seaga "expressed disappointment and frustration" at the lack of new ideas coming from the White House. In response, Haig said "I went back to my desk and, with the help of the staff, put together overnight a package that provided for trade opportunities, tax incentives to U.S. firms to locate in Jamaica, and aid."[28] The Caribbean Basin Initiative (CBI), which the President announced before the Organization of American States on 21 February 1982, was of necessity too little to bring the Caribbean economies out of their deep doldrums. Each of the countries claimed a need for between $300 and $500 million to cover its balance-of-payments deficits. The sums were clearly beyond the U.S. government's ability to provide. Moreover, administration architects of the CBI recognized that money alone would not cure what ailed the Caribbean countries. Most of them depended heavily on commodities that enjoyed minimal demand elasticity and were subject to erratic price fluctuations. Unemployment was high, but few countries seemed attractive to investors. In keeping with the administration's preference for market solutions, planners preferred a program that would bring about some profound economic changes in the region through incentives to get out of the primary-export-commodity mold. The U.S. market was clearly the most available prospect. With the United States itself increasingly besieged by cheap imports from the Far East, the Caribbean seemed an appropriate place to promote the Taiwan/Singapore model. Trade, based on simple assembly operations and agricultural production for the U.S. market, seemed to offer the greatest promise of foreign exchange earnings, employment, and diversification.

The speech in which President Reagan announced the Caribbean Basin Initiative brilliantly reflected the forces struggling for control of the direction of U.S. policy toward Latin America. The first half of the speech underscored the threat of Cuban-inspired Marxism, which was on the move in the region; the second emphasized the challenge of economic development necessary to provide a sound basis for democracies to flourish. The Latin American ambassadors assembled at the OAS were torn. They wanted to cheer the development emphasis but not the tirade against Cuba. Their response was cool. And that response was repeated as the program was debated in public forums and in Congress. Ultimately the easy argument—the anti-Cuban argument—was given much more emphasis than was that for a relaxation of complex barriers to trade and investment as an initial step in stimulating appropriate economic development in the region.

The CBI was complex and ill-understood. Once launched, it lacked a clear advocate within the administration. The president and his legislative advisers became involved in tax and budget reform. Without an advocate, there was no one to push the bill through Congress. The confusion over purpose poisoned the public debate by focusing attention on the administration's supposed problems with Cuba. The potential impact that investment and trade might have on the region were rarely discussed. When they were, the emphasis was on the minimal amount of money involved in the program, the number of persons leaving the region and plants closing down, and the threat that unbridled production in the Caribbean might have on employment in the United States. Few commentators noted that unemployment in the Caribbean was about 40 percent and that any kind of job creation would help the economies.

It was rumored that even after legislation was written, elements in the Treasury Department were lobbying privately against the 5 percent investment tax credit with which they had always quarreled in the interagency meetings. The trade subcommittees of the House and the Senate were loathe to take up the question of one-way free trade because of the special interests that might be involved. Senate Finance Committee chairman Robert Dole declared that the Senate would not take up the bill until the House had passed its version, and by doing so, he put the Democrats in control of the process. It was December 1983 before the trade package for the CBI passed Congress.

The Kissinger Commission: More Aid for Central America

The Caribbean Basin Initiative had been developed in an atmosphere inimical to large increases in foreign aid. Its architects presumed early passage in Congress, because the package included only $350 million in economic aid (in project and balance-of-payments assistance) in the first year and $300 million in the second. Investment, not aid, was to be the engine of growth.

By early 1983 it was clear that in addition to the CBI's trade package, which remained to be approved by Congress, massive new aid would also be required. The president indicated the new consensus within the administration in his April 1983 speech to a joint session of Congress when he recalled the Marshall Plan. Massive amounts of new aid, however, would require strong bipartisan support in Congress. It was that support that the Bi-Partisan National Coalition on Central America (the Kissinger Commission) was organized to mobilize. The commission was launched in June 1983, a time of despair over the outcome of U.S. Central American policy, and was instructed to provide a report in six months. By the time the commission report was published in January 1984, circumstances had changed dramatically in El Salvador, and prospects for the commission's recommendations brightened perceptibly.

The Kissinger Commission operated under a number of handicaps, including scrutiny by political forces from the White House that sometimes was too close, conservative opposition to Henry Kissinger's chairmanship, and liberal concerns about the political balance of the commission's membership. In spite of its handicaps, the commission arrived at conclusions that made sense to a broad majority of legislators and public opinion leaders. Its message in brief was that Central America was in trouble and the United States must play an active role in ameliorating that trouble in defense of its own national interests. The commission report, with its long discussion of the problems of containment, presented in sharp contrast the choices on Central America confronting the policy community. While the commission's recommendations for action looked suspiciously like an AID planning document, they made sense to the growing numbers of legislators who had visited Central America and had seen firsthand the abject poverty there.

Critics sought to discredit the Kissinger Commission report by focusing on its tough and uncompromising position on Nicaragua and its regrettable acceptance of Defense Department military assistance planning figures. Others sought to carve up the assistance package in different ways, some penalizing El Salvador, others channeling all assistance through private organizations. A major clash between the administration and the commission and between conservatives and others occurred over the proposed Central American Development Organization (CADO). In the end, opponents were able to prevent passage of the policy framework the commission had sought to give to the U.S. assistance program, but funds were nevertheless authorized in their entirety.[29] José Napoleón Duarte's electoral victory in El Salvador in the spring explained the administration's success more than any other effort or action the executive took on its own behalf.

The Debt Crisis

In August 1982, while the CBI was still very much in jeopardy and before the Kissinger Commission's plan was believed to be necessary, the administration was forced to confront a new problem of an entirely different magnitude. At midmonth, Jesús Silva Herzog, the finance minister of Mexico, placed a surprise call to the U.S. Treasury Department to say that his country was no longer able to meet the repayment of principal on the external debt of its public and private sectors. Mexico's international debt at the time amounted to $80 billion dollars, much of it due in the next several years. The Mexican phone call came as a profound and unpleasant surprise to the U.S. government and to the commercial banking community. Mexico had played its economic cards very close to its chest, unlike Brazil, the developing world's largest debtor, which in 1980 had unilaterally

undertaken a series of severe austerity measures to bring its burgeoning domestic inflation under control.

A long weekend of negotiations between the Mexicans, the Treasury, Federal Reserve Board chairman Paul Volcker, and the commercial banks resulted in their piecing together an emergency package for Mexico.[30] However, that country's crisis had far-reaching
consequences for other debtors in Latin America; following the refinancing of the Mexican debt, commercial bank lending to Latin
America simply stopped. A sharp cutback in trade financing occurred as well, as banks sought to protect their short- and long-term
exposure in the region. With the vast majority (about 70 percent) of
commercial bank exposure concentrated in two countries, both of
which were in difficulty, banks had second thoughts about their
lending to *any* Latin American country. Throughout the region,
countries were required to make sharp adjustments in public spending and currency valuation, in effect imposing a recession on their
economies.

Even with adjustment measures in place, the Latin Americans required continued new flows of money to make payments on their
outstanding debts. With good demand for their products in the industrial world, they still needed trade financing to import critical
parts of the products they produced for export. The economic reality
of 1982, however, was one of deep recession in most of the developed world (by 1983 the U.S. economy was in recovery, but Western
Europe and Japan remained depressed). Demand for products from
the developing world was sharply down, and U.S. interest rates remained high, attracting flight capital. The makings of the debt crisis
were in place, and by November, Brazil, with $100 million in out-
standing obligations, was forced to declare itself unable to repay its
debt. Unlike Mexico, Brazil's dilemmas were well known, and the
administration willingly put into place a package of assistance—$1.4
billion and a $400 million bridge loan to be available until Brazil
could work out an arrangement with the IMF. The president announced the package, which had quietly been put in place in October, during his November state visit to Brazil.

Somewhere between Mexico's crisis and Brazil's, the administration began to rethink its approaches to the developing world debt.
Treasury Secretary Donald Regan returned from Brazil convinced that
a better way to manage the debt problem should be devised. In part,
his change of viewpoint may have resulted from the intense lobby-

ing efforts during the trip by Secretary of State George Shultz, an economist with a keen sense of the implications of the developing world's crisis for the prospects for political stability. In any case, Reagan announced U.S. plans to support an IMF capital increase—an initiative long advocated by European creditors—and supported a larger-than-anticipated assessment for the soft-loan window of the World Bank, the International Development Administration.

In spite of a new look at the multilateral institutions, the administration's policy toward the debt crisis remained short term. The IMF approach—to bridge an immediate problem with highly conditioned money and to insist on deep economic reforms to assure against a repeat of the crisis—suited the administration's philosophy that "correct" domestic policies, with minimal government intervention and maximum freedom for market forces, would solve all the problems. The adminstration saw austerity and reform as tough but necessary medicine to get out of the dilemma brought on, many thought, by a too-rich diet of spending during the 1970s and 1980s. With Brazil and Mexico taken care of, the U.S. financial community seemed secure for the time being. If those two countries could be kept afloat, no other country could sink the ship. Banks began putting up reserves against loans to the weaker economies. When the IMF capital increase was achieved in November 1983, after a tough battle in the House of Representatives, funding for future crises seemed to be in place. The policy of muddling through seemed to be sufficient.

More than a policy of choice, however, muddling through was also a policy of convenience and necessity. The administration had few other policy instruments with which to attack the Third World debt. Philosophically and politically, it was difficult for the conservative-led Republican party to promote more activist funding programs for the World Bank and other development institutions. The president's conservative supporters did not approve of those institutions. Moreover, the Inter-American Development Bank had just achieved a capital increase in 1901. The IMF fight had been tough, and in the 1984 congressional elections it cost some of the leading congressional proponents of that institution their jobs.[31] The energy for tackling the problems of the international economy was nearly exhausted. In 1983 the U.S. economy was recovering from its deep recession, but employment levels remained high and the memory of the recession was still fresh. The administration continued to pursue sharp reductions in domestic spending. Any proposals for spending money to bail out the banks or to cover the debts of profligate developing countries, many of which were taking jobs away from workers in the United States, was doomed to failure.

The administration did make use of those tools over which it exercised exclusive authority to ease the burden of the debtor countries, and principal among these was trade. The U.S. trade balance had been negative for some time as a result of the overvalued dollar. By 1983 it was almost $70 billion. While historically the trade balance with Latin America historically had been positive, owing to Latin America's tremendous demand for U.S. goods and services, in 1983 and again in 1984 it became sharply negative. Part of the shift was caused by a reduced demand from Latin America as governments cut spending to meet IMF targets, but there were also increased Latin American sales in the U.S. market.[32] Faced with rising competition from abroad, U.S. producers brought complaints against Latin American copper exporters (principally Chile and Peru) and shoe manufacturers (Brazil) to the U.S. International Trade Commission (ITC), the agency established to evaluate whether imports are unfair and are causing injury to U.S. producers. The ITC found in favor of the U.S. producers, and in both cases the administration rejected the finding, thus protecting Latin American access to the U.S. market.

The trend did not go unnoticed in Congress, where increasingly negative protectionist sentiments prevailed. Throughout 1984 Congress debated new and much tougher trade bills to replace the Trade Act of 1976. The administration sought to promote as liberal a trade perspective as possible, but it was an uphill fight. In the end, it succeeded in eliminating the most egregious sections of the bills, but the Trade Act of 1984 was, by any reckoning, a much stricter law. It gave the executive a mandate to go after countries that discriminated against the United States.

The State Department also sought to provide as much foreign exchange assistance to the Latin American governments as was within the realm of feasibility.[33] The department's foreign-assistance requests in 1983, 1984, and 1985 contained unusually large requests for Economic Support Funds (ESF). Only countries eligible for U.S. assistance could receive ESF, and the bulk of funds were targeted for the Caribbean Basin countries. Nevertheless, Congress added Peru, Bolivia, and Ecuador, and the move received the tacit support of State Department officials.

For a time, muddling through seemed to work. No one would call the situation in Latin America tolerable, and those responsible for studying the unfolding debt problem in Latin America were not blind to the deepening recession in the region. Lack of policy tools and of a consensus on how best to deal with the problem impeded dramatic efforts. The administration's approach to the debt was adequate to avoid a crisis, if not sufficient to solve the problem. With U.S. economic activity at a recent high in 1984 and Latin American exports vigorous, the Latin Americans posted a $47 billion trade surplus overall, the bulk of it with the United States. By the end of 1984, many were saying that a crisis had been averted. The next problem to tackle was a return to growth, and that was to be a task for the second term.

Conclusion

The Reagan administration's policy was expressed in high rhetoric that caught its audience's attention. The administration flexed its muscles to satisfy hard-line supporters but used those muscles infrequently. The press delighted in baiting the administration and making much of its most extreme statements. However, while the rhetoric kept the targets of administration policy worried about imminent U.S. invasions of Cuba or Nicaragua, administration policy was played out for the most part on another level. Behind the scenes, policy evolved slowly into a process of steadily, increasing pressure in areas where the administration sought a response—Argentina and El Salvador, and later Guatemala and Nicaragua. Even the debt crisis was managed with a delaying process that imitated the same sets of pressures for reform. Success varied according to the importance of the issue or country to the United States, to various constituencies in the United States, or to factions within the Reagan administration itself. After five years of Reagan government, Nicaragua appeared to be the only crisis with which the Reagan team had not been able to cope adequately.

Reagan policy successes resulted from compromise between the ideological beliefs of some of the strongest spokesmen in the administration and the art of the possible. Reagan rhetoric raised concern in the public and in Congress that the administration might go off half-cocked, resulting in legislated restraints on administration policy initiatives. Out of a concern that other issues, like human rights or political negotiations, would be ignored, Congress refused to grant requests for military assistance to El Salvador. The administration compromised, accepted the constraints, and then used the congressional club to bring recalcitrant right-wing Salvadorans into line. When the administration wanted to lift restrictions on military assistance to Argentina in 1981, Congress reluctantly agreed, but it imposed requirements that the Argentine military government could not fulfill without dramatic changes in its policies at home. In short, the test of the policy was its success, and on balance the administration enjoyed considerable success.

Notes

EDITOR'S NOTE: It should be emphasized that Dr. Hayes's chapter covers only the first term of the Reagan administration and thus does not deal with events from 1985 forward.

1. *New York Times,* 18 July 1980, p. A-6.

2. Thomas O. Enders, "El Salvador: The Search for Peace," Remarks before the World Affairs Council, 16 July 1981, Department of State, Current Policy No. 296. U.S. Department of State.

3. I have developed the thesis of the political "choices" made by Central American countries in "Understanding United States Policy toward Latin America and the Central American Crisis," in Jack Child, ed., *Conflict in Central America: Approaches to Peace and Security* (London: C. Hurts & Co. (Publishers) for the International Peace Academy, 1986).

4. Senator Nancy L. Kassebaum, *Report of the U.S. Official Observer Mission to the El Salvador Constituent Assembly Elections of March 28, 1982: A Report to the Committee on Foreign Relations, United States Senate* (Washington, D.C.: U.S. Government Printing Office, 1982).

5. Over eight hundred representatives of the international news media covered the Salvadoran elections, and these professional skeptics were profoundly surprised by what they saw. The story was not one of imminent failure of the government and massive support for the guerrillas but of a difficult struggle to reestablish order and to achieve basic rights that had never belonged to most Salvadorans. The guerrilla political front, operating from Mexico City, tried to discredit the elections by offering objections to the procedures designed to inhibit fraud. Elements of the right challenged the elections because D'Aubuisson had not won. Some picked up these stories, but too many reporters had been in El Salvador for them to gain any credence.

6. The morning of 20 May 1982 the day on which the Senate Foreign Relations Committee was to mark up foreign assistance for El Salvador, news arrived that the Constituent Assembly was about to eliminate Phase III of the land reform. As discussed below, Chairman Charles H. Percy announced at the start of the session that "not one cent of aid" would go to El Salvador if the assembly undid land reform. It was that fall before committee members

were convinced that the reform was intact. Stenographic Transcript of United States Senate, Committee on Foreign Relations, Markup of S. 2227, The International Security and Development Cooperation Act.

7. The rationale for the Phase III program is discussed by R. Prosterman, in R. Prosterman, J. Riedinger, and M. N. Temple, "Land Reform and the El Salvador Crisis," *International Security* 6 (Summer 1981): 53–74.

8. U.S. Dept. of State, "Report on the Situation in El Salvador," Seventh Report on the Situation in El Salvador pursuant to Public Law 98-332, September 30, 1985.

9. Pickering was the State Department candidate to replace Hinton. His nomination signaled that the right, which had sought Hinton's ouster, had been blocked in its effort to take over Salvadoran policy.

10. Testimony presented at Hearings before the Committee on Foreign Relations, United States Senate, see W.C. Doherty, "Presidential Certification on Progress in El Salvador," Senate Hearing 98-99, 98th Congress, 1st Session, 2 February 1983 (Washington, D.C.: U.S. Government Printing Office, 1982).

11. Charges that the U.S. government or embassy had been less than enthusiastic in pursuing the nuns' murderers were laid to rest following a detailed report of the investigation by Judge Harold G. Tyler. The State Department requested the report at the urging of members of Congress who were concerned that no stone be left unturned in the effort to prosecute the parties guilty of the murders. The report was circulated in classified form to members of Congress before being made public. See Judge H. R. Tyler, Jr., "The Churchwomen Murders: A Report to the Secretary of State," New York, 2 December 1983, typescript.

12. The heaviest penalty levied against the two accused was a dishonorable discharge from the army without rank or pension for Captain Avila. In 1986 efforts were still being made to bring charges against Lieutenant López Sibrian.

13. Ronald Reagan, "Central America: Defending Our Vital Interests," Address by the President before a joint session of Congress, 27 April 1983, Department of State, *Current Policy No. 432*.

14. This section emphasizes the administration's struggle to define a policy toward for the Sandinista regime. I have wittingly and somewhat uncomfortably chosen not to detail the variable policies toward Cuba. Space limitations prohibit adequate treatment of the administration's sometimes schizophrenic efforts to threaten and pressure Cuba into desisting from support for Central American insurgencies, to challenge Cuba domestically with Radio Martí, and to improve relations by finding a solution to the Mariel "excludables" problem.

15. Jeane J. Kirkpatrick, "U.S. Security and Latin America," *Commentary* 71 (January 1981): 29–40.

16. American misunderstanding of the Soviet challenge to the Third World

is dealt with in R. Legvold, "The Super Rivals: Conflict in the Third World," *Foreign Affairs* 57 (Spring 1979): 755–778; also Donald S. Zagoria, "Into the Breach: New Soviet Alliances in the Third World," *Foreign Affairs* 57 (Spring 1979): 733–754.

17. Curiously the administration had included $35 million in aid for Nicaragua in the 1982 fiscal year aid request submitted to Congress in March 1981. The funds were only to be used if Nicaragua fulfilled its promise to cease support for the Salvadoran guerrillas. In other words, they were the "carrot" to lure Nicaragua from its errant ways.

18. In the spring of 1981 the Sandinistas could claim that overland supply to the Salvadorans had ceased, or at least fallen off, but they still continued to host the FMLN command center and to allow guerrilla leaders easy transit back and forth across the border.

19. Enders's dealings with the Sandinistas are reviewed in his testimony before the Senate Foreign Relations Committee in April 1983. U.S. Senate, *The Situation in Nicaragua and Central America,* Hearings before the Committee on Foreign Relations, S. Rpt. 98:1, April 12, 1983.

20. The argument is made persuasively by R. Gutman, "Nicaragua: America's Diplomatic Charade," *Foreign Policy* 56 (Fall 1984): 3–23.

21. Shirley Christian, *Nicaragua: Revolution in the Family* (New York: Random House, 1984), p. 27.

22. For a description and analysis of the evolution of the Contadora process, see Susan Kauffman Purcell, "Demystifying Contadora," *Foreign Affairs* 64 (Fall 1985): 74–95.

23. This issue emerged on the Central American agenda, too, in May 1986, when the Contadora participants met in Esquipulas, Guatemala. The democratically elected Central American presidents openly voiced their disillusionment with the Contadora process and complained that the Nicaraguans "defined democracy in different terms" than they did."

24. For an analysis of U.S. attitudes toward Contadora, see Hayes in Child, ed., *Conflict in Central America,* pp. 21–41; also Margaret Daly Hayes, "U.S. Security Interests in Central America: Implications for Contadora," paper prepared for the conference "Contadora, the United States and Central America," sponsored by the Johns Hopkins University School of Advanced International Studies, 3–4 February, 1986.

25. The exercises had begun the year before but were upgraded in scale and purpose in 1983.

26. For a summary of the documents, see Jiri and Virginia Valenta, "Leninism in Grenada," *Problems of Communism,* July–August 1984, pp. 1–23.

27. Gutman in "Nicaragua: America's Diplomatic Charade" noted that "Even Nicaragua officials concede that these signals came in response to American pressures."

28. Alexander M. Haig, Jr., *Caveat: Realism, Reagan, and Foreign Policy* (New York: Macmillan, 1984), p. 91.

29. With authorizing policy legislation blocked, funds were appropriated in the 1984 Continuing Resolution for Fiscal Year 1985. In 1985 essential elements of the policy framework were included in the 1985 Foreign Aid Authorization Bill (for fiscal 1986).

30. The package consisted of the U.S. commercial banks foregoing repayment of the principal on $10 billion in loans due within the next ninety days and agreeing to an additional $500 million to $1 billion in new loans; a $1 billion advance payment on purchases of Mexican petroleum for the U.S. Strategic Petroleum Reserve; $1 billion in Commodity Credit Corporation loans; a $1.5 billion short-term credit with the Bank for International Settlements; and a $4 billion IMF standby loan plus a possible $800 million from the IMF's oil facility, a fund intended for oil-importing nations.

31. For example, Congressman Jerry Patterson of California, chairman of a House banking subcommittee, was defeated for reelection in California when his opponents used his record of support for multilateral institutions as a specific source of criticism.

32. There was also a dramatic flow of capital from Latin America into the United States, estimated at well over $100 billion.

33. The realm of feasibility was substantially constrained by the Office of Management and Budget's efforts to cut federal spending. The OMB rejected a number of State Department requests in preliminary budget-writing exercises before they could be presented to Congress.

Part Two

**Crisis Management:
Interventionism and
Negotiation**

Michael J. Kryzanek

The Dominican Intervention Revisited: An Attitudinal and Operational Analysis

It is now over twenty years since President Lyndon B. Johnson sent 23,000 American troops into the Dominican Republic in the spring of 1965.[1] For nearly six months the U.S. troops served as an occupation force charged with "pacifying" the opposing groups in and around the capital city of Santo Domingo. When the American forces left this Caribbean nation, they and their commander in chief were convinced that the American presence had not only protected lives and property but had stabilized a country that had fallen into a bloody civil war. Since those days twenty-three years ago, much has been written about this relatively brief intervention of the United States in Dominican affairs, ranging from accounts of our foreign policy establishment and the intricacies of the diplomatic efforts to reach a peace accord to detailed analyses of the political climate that precipitated the war and created a divided nation.[2] In fact, despite the brevity of our involvement, the Dominican crisis of 1965 has been our most studied intervention, with a veritable library of primary and secondary source material documenting this Caribbean police action.

But amidst this deluge of research and analysis there is a strange contradiction. The Dominican civil war and the U.S. intervention have consistently been viewed as relatively minor incidents of little importance outside of Dominican affairs. The fact that American forces stayed for a short period of time, suffered few casualties, and successfully completed their mission of pacifying and reconciling the warring parties has contributed to a downplaying of the intervention. Furthermore, the Dominican crisis is often examined in light of our emerging involvement in Vietnam. Strangely enough, because we "won" in the Dominican Republic, and won very quickly, our intervention is seen in a rather limited manner, as a foreign-policy event that offers little insight into our approach to social change, revolution, and Marxism. It is Vietnam where we "lost" and got mired down for a decade that is often viewed as holding the answers to the deficiencies of our foreign policy in the Third World.[3]

Even though the Dominican crisis has already been extensively investigated and analyzed, revisiting it can still be helpful as an explanatory tool, especially to those interested in exploring the manner in which the United States formulated and executed its policy during this period and the impact of the American intervention on future responses to revolution and political unrest. In many ways, the Dominican intervention of 1965 was a test case of how this country hoped to deal with instability and opposing ideologies in its sphere of influence. The evaluation of the civil war made by the Johnson administration, the manner in which the president chose to act, and the objectives that he sought to achieve through the intervention were not merely momentary reactions to a problem in our backyard. Rather, the U.S. involvement in the Dominican revolution served to highlight an emerging set of beliefs and perceptions about the character of political developments in this hemisphere and the strategies that would have to be employed to insure our continued control over these developments.

It is important to remember that the Dominican intervention was the first use of force by the United States in the hemisphere in over thirty years. Because this intervention occurred in a Latin America much removed from our first occupation of the Dominican Republic in 1916, the internal decision-making dynamics that carried this country into a renewal of its caretaker role were undoubtedly different.[4] The Dominican intervention of 1965 was a truly contemporary foreign-policy challenge spurred on by the changing nature of modern Latin America and, more important, undertaken by a country only beginning to understand the pressures building in the region.

In retrospect, the Dominican intervention is best understood as a starting point in this country's attempt to regain control of a sphere of influence that was rapidly changing and that was no longer prepared to comply with U.S. dictates. After six years of Fidel Castro and numerous signs of unrest all over the hemisphere, the United States decided to take the initiative and do something about revolution and the drift toward what it viewed as communism. The importance of the Dominican intervention, however, is not only as a critical point in the evolution of U.S. foreign policy in Latin America but also as an example of how the United States intended to solve revolutionary crises in a manner that protected our interests and asserted our domination over events in this part of the world. The Dominican intervention thus offers an excellent opportunity to examine the mind-set of the decision makers and the formation of a new counterrevolutionary policy involving military, diplomatic, economic, and public-relations initiatives.

The following discussion of the Dominican intervention therefore seeks to describe the key events, personalities, and decisions of that period from a somewhat different perspective. Rather than restating the history of U.S. policy in the Dominican Republic in 1965, the emphasis is on presenting some of the key perceptions, motivations, prejudices, and tactical considerations that served as the foundation for the Johnson administration's policy response to the crisis. By examining the attitudinal and operational influences on U.S. policy during the Dominican crisis, it is possible to evaluate the American intervention not only in terms of its merit and effectiveness but also as an action reflective of a nation's struggle to maintain control in the new Latin America.

Fear of the Unknown

The events of the spring and summer of 1965 in the Dominican Republic have been characterized in a number of ways. Some have called the unrest a revolution, others a civil war, and still others a localized political dispute. From the Dominican perspective, defining precisely what was at stake in the fighting is important as a means of understanding the contemporary history of their country. But for policymakers in Washington, there was little interest in delving beneath the surface of the fighting to determine the nature of the conflict or its connection to the governing values of the United States. To be sure, the Johnson administration knew that forces loyal to deposed president Juan Bosch had taken over the National Palace and that numerous groups in old Santo Domingo were demanding a return to constitutional democracy as practiced before a civilian puppet regime was placed in power in 1962. The administration also knew that arrayed against these "constitutionalists" were most of the frontline military units, which remained loyal to the government and which represented the interests of the conservative elites. But such details were less important than the reality of a country, long our closest ally, on the brink of transferring power from a group of pro-American generals and their conservative associates to a diverse group of self-proclaimed democrats led by a charismatic poet-politician who had lasted but seven months at the helm of national power. The fact that the constitutionalists espoused democratic principles, advocated a return to the constitution of 1962, and were supported by many middle-class professionals with favorable views of the United States had little bearing on the Johnson administration's approach to the unrest.

Faced with the predicament of a constitutional victory and the unknowns that it could bring, the administration opted for the established order. President Johnson was simply not interested in getting to know the rebels or, for that matter, in permitting the fighting to follow its own course and possibly permit a new democratic regime to take hold.[5] The uncertainty of government under the constitutionalists was enough to trigger the intervention and stabilize a war zone that was increasingly coming under the control of the rebels.

Maintaining the status quo and a stable political order have long been hallmarks of U.S. policy in Latin America. But with the Dominican intervention, fear of the unknown was added to the list of concerns that could stimulate aggressive action. Policymakers were reluctant to take some risks with the constitutionalists despite their public pronouncements of liberal democracy. Instead they decided to support what was familiar despite the obvious deficiencies of the conservative generals and their lack of popular backing. In light of the fact that in 1965 the United States was still smarting from its dealings with another unknown named Fidel Castro, the refusal to take a risk on an unknown band of urban rebels is perhaps understandable. Yet the Johnson administration had little interest in moving beyond a cursory examination of a very complex process of social and political change. In the end, what really mattered was that the United States simply could not and would not accept the possibility of a new government that it neither knew nor cared to find out about.

A Revolutionary Must Be a Marxist

Linked closely to this country's concern about working with the unknown in the Dominican crisis was our tendency to rely on political labels as a shortcut to defining the participants in a foreign-policy event. During the early days of the fighting, this reliance on labels played a significant role in charting official policy. Once the fighting reached a critical point and the rebels seemed to be gaining the upper hand, the battle between the constitutionalists and the conservative military became a contest of Communist sympathizers bent on gaining control of the government and supporters of the United States who were anxious to restore order and stave off the threat from the left.

From the American embassy in Santo Domingo, the reports to Washington grossly inflated the numbers and the influence of Communist sympathizers in the ranks of the constitutionalists and misrepresented the democratic commitment of many key rebel leaders. Piero Gleijeses's outstanding study has made clear that the Communists and Fidelistas were marginal participants in the rebel movement and hopelessly disorganized. Despite a few visible leftists in the command hierarchy of the constitutionalists, there was no real basis for the embassy officials' contention that the rebels were capable of turning the revolution toward Marxism.[6]

Labels, however, make life easier to understand and help to justify actions to key constituencies. In the case of the Dominican crisis, labeling the constitutionalist camp as heavily infiltrated by Marxists and Communist sympathizers bolstered the administration's claim that intervention was a necessity. Public declarations that sending U.S. troops to the Dominican Republic was required to protect American personnel and property quickly gave way to statements that the troops were saving the country from slipping into the hands of the Communists.

The erroneous and prejudicial reporting that emanated from the U.S. embassy is often attributed to the limited contacts of foreign-service personnel; the inability to assess adequately the war situation, especially in terms of leadership, and the commitment that the United States had made to the military-civilian government that was under siege. But the real problem with the U.S. evaluation of the character of the rebel camp was the refusal of the embassy and Washington to find out more about these constitutionalists, their backgrounds, their politics, and their vision of the future. The policymakers in Santo Domingo and Washington were content to rely on their preconceived notions that revolutionaries must be Marxists and that any evidence to the contrary was irrelevant. It was this attitude that left many liberal democrats among the constitutionalists bitter after the war, including Juan Bosch, who gradually embraced Marxist principles and frequently castigated the United States for failing to recognize the democratic nature of the constitutionalist movement.[7]

Neutralizing the Revolution

Over the years, much has been made of the so-called "No Second Cuba" doctrine that many observers see as the primary rationale for the U.S. intervention in the Dominican crisis. In the prevailing view, American military forces were dispatched to the Dominican Republic in 1965 to insure that Cuba would be the last Communist stronghold in the Western Hemisphere and that this country would no longer be perceived as unwilling and unable to stand up to Communist expansionism.[8] As Lyndon Johnson boasted to Republican congressional leaders Everett Dirksen and Gerald Ford on the eve of the intervention, "I have just taken an action that will prove that Democratic presidents can deal with Communists as strongly as Republicans."[9]

But although there is little doubt that the No Second Cuba doctrine was a critical factor in the Dominican intervention, what is often not stressed sufficiently is the choice of strategy the Johnson administration employed to insure the failure of another Marxist enclave in the region. In the case of the Dominican Republic, the important point to remember is not only that the United States decided to take a stand against communism but also that it opted for a strategy of intervention that emphasized wearing down the revolutionaries rather than crushing the rebels in a heavy-handed display of American power. In a key tactical move, the Johnson administration positioned its occupation forces in such a way as to establish a "neutral" zone through the capital city of Santo Domingo, thereby driving a wedge between the constitutionalists in the northern sections of the city and those in the central or old section. The establishment of the "neutral" zone in effect isolated the rebels in smaller pockets of resistance and denied them the opportunity to mount a major offensive.

An even more significant decision in terms of weakening the rebels was the active cooperation between the American troops and the loyalists under the command of General Antonio Imbert Barrera. Despite the United States' outward claims of neutrality, there is ample evidence that from the initial stages of the intervention the American troops had little intention of being impartial referees. The men of the Eighty-second Airborne who were sent into the Dominican Republic received orders while still in the United States to provide support to the loyalists against the constitutionalists, who were described as Communists or supporters of Fidel Castro.[10] Once in Santo Domingo, American troops on a number of occasions permitted loyalist units to enter into rebel-held territory and stage attacks.

The decision to create the "neutral" zone and deploy our armed forces in such a way as to split the constitutionalists into two groups, along with the quiet favoritism accorded the loyalists, reveals a more sophisticated approach to unrest than had previously been seen in this region. The Johnson administration was conscious of its image as an interventionist and was therefore willing to follow the more subtle approach of controlling the revolution rather than immediately reaching for the Big Stick. By appearing to be a peacekeeping force interested in protecting lives and property, the Johnson administration gained an important domestic edge and directed attention away from the more central objective of stopping what was viewed as another Cuba in the making.

With the Dominican intervention it is possible, perhaps for the first time, to see a presidential administration actively concerned with appearances and unwilling to be perceived as a heavy-handed interloper in the internal affairs of a neighboring country. Yet at the same time, policymakers were fearful that the revolution could get out of hand and further threaten our reputation as a controlling force in the Western Hemisphere. Faced with these two concerns, the Johnson administration decided to present its intervention in a new light and to employ tactics that would deflect criticism. The rebels, despite their alleged leftist leanings, were not crushed but isolated, and the loyalists were encouraged to expand their hold on Santo Domingo by a not-so-impartial peacekeeper.

Managing the Negotiations

Although the Johnson administration redesigned its military strategy to accomodate the occupation of the Dominican Republic, it relied on more traditional approaches in the diplomatic negotiations that were undertaken to end the fighting. The record of the U.S. diplomatic efforts during the Dominican crisis is one marked by manipulation and intimidation of both the major combatants in the struggle and the international organizations that sought to lend their services to a peaceful resolution of the conflict. It was clear very early on that the United States wanted to settle this problem its way and was prepared to use a diverse arsenal of diplomatic maneuvers to accomplish its objectives.

From the onset of the occupation, the United States was hampered by deep-seated mistrust on the part of both the constitutionalists and the loyalist forces. Constitutionalist leaders Francisco Caamaño Deño and Rafael Molina Ureña were outraged with U.S. ambassador W. Tapley Bennett's refusal to endorse a cease-fire and move quickly to begin negotiations during the height of the fighting in Santo Domingo. Instead, Bennett brushed aside the constitutionalists' request, branded the rebels as Communists, and made it clear that the wise move now was for them to surrender. The constitutionalists left the U.S. embassy with a new resolve to fight on and an unwillingness to deal with the Americans.[11] On the loyalist side, the problem was not anger over a failure to cooperate for peace, but an intense wariness that the United States would make its own deal with the rebels and shut out key military leaders who saw the revolution as a means of enhancing their own power and reputation. Conservative military leaders such as Elías Wessin y Wessin and Antonio Imbert Barrera were thankful for the American presence, especially when the fighting turned against the loyalists, but were suspicious of a negotiation process that permitted the participation of the constitutionalists and supported the idea that certain concessions might have to be made to the rebels.

Faced with this mistrust and skepticism, the United States resorted to an old negotiating tactic used in past crises in this region—it began to push its weight around. First the United States, through the efforts of presidential assistant McGeorge Bundy, tried to construct a provisional government under former agriculture minister Antonio Guzmán. Although Guzmán was a respected politician, this bold attempt to bypass the two sides and create a new leadership group was rejected by the combatants and abandoned by the American negotiators. Next the United States used its considerable influence in the Organization of American States (OAS) to pressure that body to endorse a multilateral peacekeeping force called the Inter-American Peace Force (IAPF). The OAS was extremely reluctant to become involved in the peacekeeping venture and on a number of occasions criticized the United States for its partiality toward the loyalists and its footdragging on establishing cease-fire agreements. But intense pressure from the Johnson administration eventually persuaded the OAS leadership to support the IAPF and to continue its efforts at arranging a suitable and fair peace. Despite the establishment of the IAPF, the attempt to create a multilateral peacekeeping force was tarnished by the behind-the-scenes pressure of the Johnson administration and the composition of the forces, which were made up of units from many of Latin America's most repressive dictatorships.

But as spring turned to summer in the Dominican Republic, it became clear that the success of the negotiations depended on the ability of the American troops to isolate the constitutionalists, drive them further into the old city of Santo Domingo, and make them realize that their only real option was to accept a settlement.[12] In August the efforts of an OAS-sponsored ad hoc committee led by U.S. ambassador Ellsworth Bunker proved successful as an Act of Reconciliation and an Institutional Act was signed by both warring parties. Although concessions and guarantees were granted to the constitutionalists, the settlement reflected the realization on the part of the rebels that they could no longer hold out against the American troops and their allies in the Dominican military. Their only hope was a settlement and the prospect of participation in national elections to be held in June 1966.

What the United States proved with its negotiation of the Act of Reconciliation and Institutional Act was that perseverance mixed with a favorable military position and a willingness to use raw power politics can create a winning combination. Although the Dominican civil war was ultimately settled through diplomacy, it is important to remember that the negotiations were conducted among unequals. All the other parties to the crisis were overshadowed by the United States, which was unwilling to allow either internal negotiators or external organizations to dictate the outcome. The final settlement was in large part our settlement with the constitutionalists; the loyalist forces played a secondary role in the formation of a new Dominican Republic.

Knowing How to Quit

Once U.S. troops left the Dominican Republic in September 1965, the physical intervention ended, but there was still the critical matter of the future direction of the country and the level of influence that the United States would enjoy. The OAS-sponsored elections quickly became a contest not only between Juan Bosch the proconstitutionalist candidate of the Partido Revolucionario Dominicano (PRD) and conservative Joaquín Balaguer of the Partido Reformista (PR) but also between two starkly different perceptions of the future direction of the Dominican Republic. Bosch, who returned from exile in Puerto Rico, represented a continuation of the revolution through the democratic process. If elected, it was certain that Bosch would attempt to institute reforms abhorrent to conservative elites and place rebel leaders in positions of administrative responsibility. Balaguer, on the other hand, would follow a distinctly different path. Himself exiled in New York after holding the presidency of the country during the waning years of the Trujillo regime, Balaguer was viewed by many in Washington as someone who would return the Dominican Republic to normalcy and reformulate the ties to the United States that had been so severely damaged during the civil war. Based on background and past performance in office, it was clear that in terms of American interests, Bosch was just too risky as a presidential aspirant, but Balaguer, with his mild scholarly demeanor and conciliatory politics, seemed to mesh with our desire to quiet the voices of revolution and move to a new level of national politics.[13]

It is important to stress, however, that despite the obvious preference of the Johnson administration for Balaguer and the fears that it harbored with respect to Bosch, policymakers in the White House and at the State Department were extremely cautious about publicly playing favorites or in giving even a hint of interfering in the electoral process. The word went out to embassy officials in Santo Domingo that the United States was maintaining a neutral stance in the elections despite its reservations about the Bosch candidacy.[14] Staying aloof from the election proved to be a wise strategy that aided the process of restoring confidence in the United States.

Luckily for the United States, Joaquín Balaguer was victorious in the June 1966 elections. Combining his strong support among the more conservative rural population with his promise of peace and reconstruction, Balaguer easily defeated Bosch by a margin of 57 percent to 39 percent. Bosch, who barely left his house out of fear of reprisal from the police and the military, was perceived by many Dominicans as a divisive leader who would only reopen the blood bath and perhaps even force the United States to intervene again.

The involvement of the United States in Dominican affairs during the postintervention period is accurately portrayed as low key, conciliatory, and largely neutral. U.S. officials shrewdly recognized that it was time to leave the Dominicans alone and trust that the judgment of the people would not harm our interests. One must, however, be careful in praising the restraint of the United States in the electoral process, because we were anything but neutral during the fighting, and most Dominicans knew where we stood with respect to Bosch and the constitutionalists. When the June elections were held, the Johnson administration could boast about its neutrality, but to the Dominicans their electoral decision was an easy one—Balaguer and a return to normalcy or Bosch and a return of the Americans.

Buying Friendship

The United States may have been cautious about its involvement in Dominican affairs in the immediate postintervention period, but once Joaquín Balaguer took office, the Johnson administration wasted little time in targeting the Dominican Republic for massive injections of economic aid. As Jerome Slater comments about U.S. assistance during the early years of Balaguer's rule,

From the inauguration of the Balaguer regime through November of 1968 the United States disbursed over $132 million in economic assistance to the Dominican Republic, some of it in grants and the rest in loans with mild repayment terms. Measured either since the 1965 revolution or in 1968 alone, the U.S. aid program was higher on a per capita basis than to any other Latin American country.[15]

Moreover, as Slater also observes, the United States during this period was also buying over 700,000 tons of Dominican sugar a year, more than from any other sugar-producing country in the world and at a price pegged at two cents a pound above the prevailing world price. The sugar policy of the United States provided the Balaguer government with an additional $28 million a year in export revenue.

Not surprisingly, the government of Joaquín Balaguer responded favorably to the American largesse by welcoming American businesses to the Dominican Republic and ensuring that they stayed by passing favorable investment laws, creating tax-free industrial zones, and implementing wage freezes and anti-union measures to hold down costs and increase profits. It is during these early years of the

Balaguer regime that multinationals such as Gulf and Western and Alcoa, major banks such as the Bank of America and Chase Manhatten, and scores of smaller assembly plants in the textile, leather, and clothing industries opened for business. These were the good days for U.S. business and for the U.S. government. It may have been costly to the United States in terms of large aid allotments for the Dominican Republic, but the dividends returned in investment profits and a favorable business climate were substantial.

Pouring dollars into a country ravaged by a war (especially one in which we had participated) is nothing new for the United States. But it is essential to examine the aid programs of the Johnson administration not only in terms of humanitarian concerns but also as a political investment in the future. The United States was consciously seeking to use the aid to turn attention away from political issues connected to the civil war and toward economic development. From the American perspective, a return to normalcy meant a depoliticization of the Dominican nation. Although President Balaguer was himself a master at creating a less-political climate in the Dominican Republic, the economic assistance and the arrival of U.S. investment further helped to shift attention away from the deep political divisions present in the country.[16]

With Balaguer—the master of normalcy—at the helm and the United States using dollars to shift attention away from the memory of the revolution, the Dominican Republic was quickly transformed; constitutionalists were sent into exile, the main political opposition (the PRD) became hopelessly factionalized, and the critics of the government were easily intimidated or coopted. The United States largely ignored the authoritarian policies of the Balaguer regime as concern over human rights gave way to concern over economic growth and investment potential. In this new environment, U.S. influence expanded significantly, and memories of the intervention began to fade. In return for our dollars the United States renewed a friendship, gained a valuable business partner, and defused an explosive political situation. In retrospect, it seemed an excellent investment.

Success Is What You Make of It

One certain way that policymakers justify their decisions and instil confidence among their constituencies is to claim victory: to declare their work a success. In the case of the Dominican intervention there is ample evidence that the Johnson administration fell prey to this temptation. From the White House to the U.S. embassy in Santo Domingo there was general agreement that the United States had acted admirably, if not nobly, in bringing peace to the war-torn Dominican Republic. Political scientist Samuel Huntington aptly described the mood of success when he stated:

Whether or not there was a threat of communist takeover on the island, we were able to go in, restore order, negotiate a truce among conflicting parties, hold reasonably honest elections which the right man won, withdraw our troops and promote a very considerable amount of social and economic reform.[17]

Success is, of course, a relative term that has many sides and is subject to contrary interpretation. From the American perspective, Huntington's observations are accurate. Despite numerous diplomatic setbacks and serious internal feuding within the administration over the proper means of handling the crisis, the United States was able to diminish the fighting capacity of the constitutionalists, forge an agreement that in effect brought an end to the revolution, see a pro-American president take office promising a return to normalcy, and send a message to all those in Latin America who were contemplating the use of force to achieve sociopolitical change that the United States was prepared to respond aggressively to such action. The United States apparently got all that it wanted out of the intervention.

But success cannot be measured only in terms of national security interests and power politics. It must also be judged within a larger context of national and international considerations and be connected to such issues as hemispheric relations, domestic values, and the impact on future foreign-policy initiatives. In these three areas there are serious questions as to what level of success the American intervention in the Dominican Republic attained. There was, for example, an almost immediate and profoundly negative response to the U.S. involvement in the Dominican crisis from the Latin American community of nations. Many moderate leaders not only openly castigated the Johnson administration for its use of force but also saw the intervention as a dangerous attempt by the United States to hold back the onrush of revolution in the region.[18] In 1965 much of Latin America was still enamored of the Cuban Revolution and the possibilities for similar radical change that it symbolized. The U.S. action in the Dominican Republic sent shock waves throughout the region as it became clear that this country would not tolerate another Cuba and was on the side of conservative interests. To the Latin Americans the intervention meant that achieving widespread sociopolitical change would be doubly difficult since intransigent elites opposed to reform were now joined by a powerful external foe who, in the name of national security, appeared willing to sacrifice the aspirations of those anxious to redirect their societies. What was defined as success in Washington was seen in many capitals in Latin America as a serious blow to the confidence of those convinced that the era of revolution had arrived and was in full swing.

The success of the Dominican intervention must also be assessed in terms of its impact on what can be called the prevailing philosophy of foreign policy. Because the Johnson administration could present a convincing argument about its success in handling the Dominican crisis, it became easier to ignore or downplay a number of traditional foreign-policy principles held in high regard by Third World nations, such as self-determination, a toleration of diversity, and, of course, nonintervention. At the conclusion of our occupation of the Dominican Republic there had already begun in policymaking circles a movement away from an automatic acceptance or endorsement of the Third World perspective. Increasingly, this country's approach to foreign policy accented Americans power, anticommunism, and a responsibility to establish a pro-U.S. order. With the sending of troops to the Dominican Republic and the successful completion of their mission, the United States in effect began to rewrite the rules of acceptable behavior in the Third World. But to critics of administration policy both in this country and abroad the intervention signaled that the United States had begun to deny the very principles upon which it had been founded and had promoted over the years.[19] This discernible shift in values was, to many, a terrible price to pay to control the spread of revolution in the hemisphere, tarnishing whatever success the Johnson administration claimed.

Finally, the claimed success of the Dominican intervention can be questioned because of the impetus that it created for our involvement in the Vietnam War. Although there is little direct evidence from Johnson administration papers or related materials to link the two interventions together, policymakers during the Dominican crisis did see the revolution in a global perspective and believed that the United

States was being challenged worldwide by the Soviets. What occurred in Santo Domingo would unquestionably send a signal to the
Soviets about our willingness to fight to restrain the North Vietnamese and their allies in the south. The fact that the United States did
control the spread of revolution in the Dominican Republic may not
have directly convinced the Johnson administration to intensify the
pressure on the Vietnamese Communists or even to enlarge our commitment, but certainly there is nothing like success to help strength-
en one's resolve and to enhance one's confidence in established policy. What the Johnson administration may have neglected to
recognize about its success in the Dominican Republic is that it
helped to foster the false belief that all revolutions are somehow
similar, manageable, and ultimately winnable. It would take the
United States nearly ten years after the Dominican intervention to
recognize that one success does not guarantee continued success.

Placing the Intervention in Perspective

The Dominican revolution and the crisis that it created quickly faded from national and international attention, and the United States
moved on to Vietnam. But despite the brief duration of the Dominican imbroglio it is important to remember that the U.S. involvement in the revolution cannot be viewed simply as an isolated event.
The intervention by the American military in 1965 was but another
example of the "special relationship" that has existed between the
United States and the Dominican Republic. From President Ulysses
S. Grant's attempt to annex the country to President Theodore
Roosevelt's receivership and to Woodrow Wilson's civilizing intervention, the United States has been intimately involved in Dominican affairs and more than willing to exert its influence in order to
shape the destiny of this poor and vulnerable country.

The departure of the American troops in September 1965 thus does
not close the book on intervention. In 1978 the United States again
showed its concern with the internal political situation in the Dominican Republic. In a strange turnaround from the Johnson administration's fear of communism, President Jimmy Carter placed enormous pressure on the Balaguer government to safeguard the
presidential elections, which had been stopped by the military after
the challenger, Antonio Guzmán, was shown to be mounting a considerable lead over the incumbent president. At no time was there a

threat of armed intervention, but there are other ways of intimidating a nation and controlling internal events. The Carter administration simply reminded President Balaguer of the considerable U.S.
assistance his government had received and would receive, along
with the numerous favorable trade and loan arrangements that had
been negotiated over the years. Calling attention to the close economic ties between the two countries and then using those ties as a
veiled threat was enough to force the government to resume the election and abide by its results. As a result of this indirect intervention
on the part of the Carter administration, Antonio Guzmán assumed
the presidency, and the Dominican Republic enjoyed its first peaceful democratic transition in generations of politics.[20] In Washington
the success of the Guzmán candidacy became a triumph of liberal
democracy, but one cannot ignore the fact that no matter how lofty
the goal, the United States continued to feel a responsibility to intervene in Dominican affairs.

What is perhaps most interesting about an examination of the
lengthy involvement of the United States in Dominican affairs is the
range of reasons (or excuses) this country has used to justify its intervention. For the Grant administration the Dominican Republic was
a real estate bargain that could not be passed up; with Roosevelt there
was the need to place Dominican finances in order; during the Wilson era it was an unstable government that could no longer be tolerated; for Lyndon Johnson intervention was required to stop Communist revolution; and for Jimmy Carter, who was reluctant to use
American force to enhance U.S. foreign policy, economic intervention was the appropriate tool to ensure that the Dominican Republic
would progress in a manner in accord with liberal democracy.

After years of experiencing the American rationale for intervention, the Dominicans have developed a sense of resignation about
the future of their relationship with the United States. They recognize that the United States sees their country in a manner approaching that of a former colony. Much like the French influence in northern Africa, the United States appears wedded to a kind of
suprasovereignty that entitles it to intervene in Dominican affairs
when internal conditions warrant.[21] The paternalism and arrogance
that fuel this attitude are so ingrained in the relationship that they
are unlikely to disappear from it. Various American administrations
may change the tactics and reword the rationale, but the principle
of suprasovereignty toward the Dominican Republic seems firmly

entrenched. As for the Dominicans, there is little they can do to restructure the relationship along more equitable lines. Living near the world's greatest power in a strategically important region with instability and revolutionary governments nearby makes the Dominicans captives of U.S. security interests and destined to continue to feel the effects of American power.

The Attempt to Regain the Hemisphere

Any revisiting of the intervention of 1965 would be incomplete without a mention of the lasting impact of the crisis on the manner in which this country responds to revolution in the hemisphere. Although some would dispute the emergence of anything like a Dominican "model" for handling outbreaks of leftist unrest in Latin America, there is little doubt that contemporary events in the Caribbean Basin and the U.S. response to those events bear a striking similarity to the 1965 crisis and the strategies that were employed to stop the fighting and the revolution. Because the Dominican intervention "worked" in terms of achieving its objectives, the approaches utilized to weaken the rebels, attain a favorable settlement, and install a pro-American government have not been forgotten. Therefore, by way of conclusion it may be helpful to bridge the gap of twenty years and show the connections between U.S. policy during the Dominican crisis and current approaches to crises in places like Grenada, Nicaragua, and El Salvador.

For example, the Dominican intervention showed Washington policymakers that leftist revolution can be defused through the quick and decisive use of American forces, especially in those situations in which the fighting is limited and the opposition is relatively small. By interjecting substantial American military personnel into an urban civil war, the Johnson administration proved that it is possible to suppress a revolution in the U.S. sphere of influence with little loss of life and minimal domestic criticism. Not surprisingly, there are numerous similarities between the Dominican intervention and the 1983 invasion of Grenada—a tiny island with a disorganized opposition, American citizens allegedly in danger, a lightning-fast United States military response, a quick victory with a small number of casualties, and the replacement of an anti-American government with one that plastered signs on public walls proclaiming "God Bless Ronald Reagan." Few in Washington credited the success of the invasion to any Dominican model of counterrevolution, but the intervention in Grenada to replace the pro-Cuban government of Bernard Coard owes much to the example set by the United States during the Dominican crisis. In both cases the United States showed revolutionaries in the hemisphere the possible consequences of American power.

Another current influence of the Dominican intervention can be found in our policy toward Nicaragua. Although one cannot make a comparison on grounds of U.S. military intervention in Nicaragua, the similarities with the Dominican Republic reside in the manner in which the Reagan administration has pressured neighboring countries into lending their support, the strategy behind the contra movement, and the involvement of the United States in the regional peace process. The Reagan administration, like the Johnson administration in 1965, is most concerned with developing a response to a perceived threat that does not make the United States appear to be standing alone. Mr. Reagan has not bullied the OAS, but he has revived the Central American military alliance, CONDECA, and has increased military assistance and training to neighboring countries in an attempt to strengthen those that are currently overwhelmed by the size and caliber of the Nicaraguan military. Furthermore, where Johnson formed the Inter-American Peace Force (IAPF), Reagan has encouraged the creation of a less formal organization, the contras, as a means of defeating the Sandinistas. In both cases the strategy is to weaken the revolution and present the United States as cooperating in a multilateral venture to protect its friends and restore democracy. If this country has learned anything from the Vietnam War, it is that unilateral military intervention creates too many image problems and places too heavy a burden on domestic politics.

Although relying on new military alliances and proxy freedom fighters, the Reagan administration has followed in the footsteps of the Dominican intervention by linking its military strategy with a visible commitment to achieving a negotiated settlement. Public support for the Central American peace effort, quiet talks with Nicaraguan leaders, frequent claims of negotiating in good faith, and consistent calls for a peaceful resolution of the conflict present a picture of the United States as actively involved in the peace process. But as was the case in the Dominican Republic, negotiations with the Sandinistas are closely connected with military operations, to the point where it is clear that the Reagan administration has little interest in achieving a diplomatic settlement with a firmly entrenched and confident Nicaraguan government. The contras have become the real negotiators with the Sandinistas, just as the so-called neutral American forces in 1965 were crucial to the success of the eventual settlement with the constitutionalists. The Reagan administration is apparently convinced that the contras are best used as a means of forcing the Sandinistas to limit their revolutionary applications and to break away from alliances that threaten American security interests—in effect, to cry "uncle," just as the constitutionalists did in 1965.

A final connection between current U.S. policy in this region and the Dominican intervention can be found in El Salvador. Again the link between 1965 and the present is not in the use of American military force but in the strategy employed to defeat the leftist rebels. The Reagan administration has decided that the most effective way to defuse the revolution is to construct a democratic framework in spite of right-wing terrorism, rebel opposition, and little if any tradition of self-governance. Tied closely to its campaign of democratization is the open effort of the United States to find a pro-American moderate to lead this new democracy and to conduct the war against the rebels. Luckily for the Reagan administration, José Napoleón Duarte fit the job description perfectly. The final step in the democratic strategy in El Salvador is the commitment of enormous sums of U.S. assistance to ensure that the new government will not founder from a lack of support. In fiscal 1986 the Reagan administration provided over $470 million in economic and military assistance to the Duarte government.

Twenty years earlier, the United States was in a similar predicament in the Dominican Republic, with popular leftist revolutionaries on the offensive. To regain the initiative, the United States not only sent in troops but also worked vigorously to rebuild a democracy that had disintegrated, sought out a pro-American conservative to return the country to normalcy, and then hoped that he would succeed. But when Joaquín Balaguer gained the presidency and ushered in a period of political calm, the United States provided the new government with millions of dollars in assistance, loans, and other grants. José Napoleón Duarte and Joaquín Balaguer cannot easily be compared in terms of their democratic values or the success of their respective governments in establishing a democratic system, but they are both products of a relationship with the United States, a relationship that fosters moderate leadership, encourages democratization, and supports both with American dollars.

The linkage between the events of 1965 and the contemporary struggle in the Caribbean Basin is made more meaningful if one returns to the beginning of this essay and the discussion of the U.S. reaction to the "new" Latin America. The Dominican intervention must be viewed in the larger context of this country's attempt to regain its preeminent position in the region. The Bay of Pigs invasion was the first effort to reassert domination over events in the hemisphere, but it failed. The "success" of the Dominican intervention thus marks the initial victory in this campaign to ensure that the American sphere of influence would remain intact and free of interference from other major powers. Since the intervention, the United States has challenged leftist governments in Chile, Grenada, and Nicaragua and is currently supporting a major counterrevolutionary effort in El Salvador. In each case the ultimate objective of U.S. policy is to hold the line, just as it was in the Dominican Republic.

The overall success of the American government in holding the line and regaining control over the U.S. sphere of influence is not yet clear. Despite outcomes in Chile and Grenada that have benefited U.S. interests, the revolutions in Central America have yet to run their course. Even though it is too early to arrive at a conclusion about the effectiveness of the campaign to regain control of the hemisphere, there is no doubt that the United States is continuing in the tradition of the Dominican intervention and maintaining its prerogative to secure the region closest to its borders.[22]

Notes

1. Often the significance and the impact of major foreign-policy decisions are not immediately or fully understood. In many instances, time and a more thorough examination of the decision yield new insights and produce different modes of analysis. But what is perhaps even more interesting about "revisiting" an important foreign policy event is that the actions taken abroad by a government reflect the basic premises upon which that government operates and views the world, and in many instances the actions leave a lasting mark on the manner in which it conducts its business in the international arena. By taking another look at an historical event, not only may our memory be refreshed and perhaps even enlightened, but also contemporary issues

and policies may be seen with a new perspective, one that recognizes the influence of the past on the present.

2. The three most helpful accounts of the U.S. intervention are Piero Gleijeses, *The Dominican Crisis: The 1965 Constitutionalist Revolt and the American Intervention* (Baltimore: Johns Hopkins University Press, 1978); Abraham Lowenthal, *The Dominican Intervention* (Cambridge: Harvard University Press, 1972); and Jerome Slater, *Intervention and Negotiation: The United States and the Dominican Revolution* (New York: Harper and Row, 1970).

3. See Howard Wiarda's discussion of these points in a review essay in the *Journal of Inter-American Studies and World Affairs* 22 (May 1980): 248.

4. Bruce Calder's recent book on the 1916–1924 intervention is a valuable guide to understanding the historical background of U.S. intervention in the Dominican Republic. See *The Impact of Intervention: The Dominican Republic during the U.S. Occupation of 1916–1924* (Austin: University of Texas Press, 1984).

5. Senator J. William Fulbright's criticism of the Johnson administration and its rationale for the intervention is valuable in understanding this fear of the unknown. See *The Arrogance of Power* (New York: Vintage Press, 1966), pp. 82–97.

6. Gleijeses, *Dominican Crisis*, pp. 203–17.

7. Juan Bosch, *Pentagonism: A Substitute for Imperialism* (New York: Grove Press, 1968).

8. Abraham Lowenthal, in *The Dominican Intervention*, pp. 137–62, gives perhaps the most detailed discussion of the No Second Cuba doctrine.

9. As quoted in Howard Wiarda, review essay, p. 247.

10. Gleijeses, *Dominican Crisis*, p. 258.

11. See Jerome Slater's account of this meeting in *Intervention and Negotiation*, pp. 29–30.

12. José Moreno's account of life in the embattled rebel-held sections of Santo Domingo reveals the hardships and the frustrations of the constitutionalists. See *Barrio in Arms: Revolution in Santo Domingo* (Pittsburgh: University of Pittsburgh Press, 1970).

13. For a good background study of these two political leaders, see John Barlow Martin, *Overtaken by Events* (New York: Doubleday, 1966).

14. Slater, *Intervention and Negotiation*, p. 169, describes the official policy of neutrality enunciated by the Johnson administration.

15. *Ibid*, p. 186.

16. Depoliticization as a strategy of the Balaguer regime is discussed in my article "Diversion, Subversion and Repression: The Strategies of Anti-Opposition Politics in Balaguer's Dominican Republic," *Caribbean Studies* 17 (April/June 1977): 83–104.

17. As quoted in Richard M. Pfeffer's *No More Vietnams* (New York: Harper and Row, 1968), pp. 2–3.

18. Some of these criticisms can be found in newspaper articles from the intervention period. See *New York Times,* 27 May 1965, p. 1, and 1 June 1965, p. 36.

19. See, for example, Theodore Draper, *The Dominican Revolt: A Case Study in American Policy* (New York: Commentary, 1968), and Fred Goff and Michael Locker, "The Violence of Domination: U.S. Power and the Dominican Republic," in Irving Horowitz et al., eds., *Latin American Radicalism* (New York: Vintage, 1969).

20. See my discussion of the election in "The 1978 Election in the Dominican Republic: Opposition Politics, Intervention and the Carter Administration," *Caribbean Studies* 19 (April/July 1979): 51–73.

21. The concept of suprasovereignty is further discussed in Howard Wiarda and Michael Kryzanek, *The Dominican Republic: A Caribbean Crucible,* (Boulder, Colo.: Westview Press, 1982), pp. 126–27.

22. For a discussion of the attempt by the United States to reeestablish its authority in the Caribbean Basin, see Abraham Lowenthal's article "Change the Agenda" in *Foreign Policy,* no. 52 (Fall 1983): 64–77. Also, see my article "The U.S. in Central America and the Caribbean: Regaining Our Sphere of Influence," *Bridgewater Review* 2 (March 1984): 4–8.

Paul E. Sigmund

Crisis Management: Chile and Marxism

The involvement of the United States in Chile over the last twenty-five years is one of the best-documented and most controversial areas of recent U.S. policy-making toward Latin America.[1] It raises fundamental questions about the nature of that policy making, the reasons that lie behind it, and the lessons that can be drawn from it. It has also had a lasting effect on the structure and content of U.S. foreign policy in ways that I hope to demonstrate here.

In addition, there are more specific questions about the U.S. role in Chile that have been the subject of continuing controversy. Most obvious is the issue of the relationship between U.S. involvement ("intervention") in Chile, and the tragic demise of Chilean democracy and the brutal repression that followed. It has become conventional wisdom that the United States worked unceasingly to "destabilize" the Marxist government of Salvador Allende and to promote the 1973 coup. The film *Missing*, not a great box office success but now widely available in videocassette form, even claims that the U.S. embassy ordered or cooperated in the murder of an American citizen after the coup in order to conceal its role. Three lengthy congressional investigations have been devoted to determining the U.S. role, and none has found any evidence of a direct U.S. involvement, but the myth persists. It may be useful, then, to summarize what we know about the U.S. reaction to Marxism in Chile, both for general and for specific reasons.

The U.S. economic role in Chile has been substantial for many decades, especially because of the ownership until 1971 of the largest concentrations of Chile's most important natural resource, copper, by two giant American multinational corporations—Kennecott and Anaconda. The copper connection meant that Chile was dependent on foreign decisions for the disposition of its principal source of foreign exchange, a situation that provided a continuing target for nationalist and leftist agitation and led to increasing pressure for nationalization. Politically, Chile was less important to the United States, because it is located farther away from the American east coast than is Moscow and is isolated by mountains, desert, and the Pacific Ocean from its neighbors (prompting Henry Kissinger's oft-quoted observation that "Chile is a dagger pointed at the heart of Antarctica"). However, Chile also possesses the largest and best-organized Communist party in the hemisphere, and once the cold war commenced, it naturally became the object of American political concern. As early as 1950 the Central Intelligence Agency began to become involved with the Chilean media,[2] and when the CIA's covert support for student, youth, and labor organizations in other countries was revealed in 1967, it was learned that Chilean organizations had long been centrally involved in the agency's Latin American activities.[3]

Covert actions of this kind had been common worldwide ever since the beginning of the 1950s, but they had a particular relevance in Chile because of its open democracy and the size of its Communist party. Indeed, because the newly legalized Communist party had formed a coalition with the Socialist party and nearly captured the presidency in 1958, the agency became increasingly concerned with Chile during the early 1960s. The 1975 staff report of the Senate Intelligence Committee *Covert Action in Chile* reports that in 1964 $2.6 million were spent in support of the Christian Democratic candidate for the presidency, Eduardo Frei, against the Communist-Socialist candidate, Salvador Allende. Aid also went to other political parties before and after that election. A total of $175,000 was spent to influence the 1965 congressional elections, and twice that amount was spent in the 1969 congressional elections. Thus by the time of the next important election—the presidential balloting of September 1970—the United States had a long record of covert involvement with many sectors of Chilean society. It also had openly endorsed the reformist goals of the Christian Democratic government, although that identification and support had been lessened by the adoption of a so-called low-profile policy in Latin America after Richard Nixon became president in January 1969. The policy had meant that the embassy's involvement with the Christian Democrats was much less intense than heretofore, leaving open its role in the 1970 elections and freeing it from identification with a party that seemed to be losing support.

When the presidential nominations were finally sorted out, it became clear that rather than the basically two-way race of 1964 between the Christian Democrats and the Marxists, Chileans would have to choose between three candidates—Allende again representing the left, Radomiro Tomic from the left wing of the Christian Democrats, and the rightist former president Jorge Alessandri. (The Chilean constitution prohibited Frei from running again.) Because of the low-profile policy, the embassy—including the CIA station—had not been in contact with the Christian Democrats as directly as in the past, and when it came time to decide on whether or how the United States should involve itself in the campaign, both the ambassador and the CIA recommended what they called a "spoiling" campaign involving anti-Allende propaganda but without direct support for either the Christian Democrats or the right. On 25 March 1970 and twice in June, money was authorized for the spoiling campaign and there was discussion of the use of CIA funds to "influence" (that is, bribe) the members of the Chilean Congress. This assumed that none of the three candidates would receive an absolute majority, and as the constitution provided, the race would go to the Chilean Congress to decide between the two front-runners. In that discussion the State Department argued against intervention in the electoral process, and a decision was postponed until after the 4 September election.

It is here that much of the postmortem controversy begins, so it might be useful at this point to review the structure of decision making by the U.S. government. Proposals for covert action usually came from the ambassador and the CIA station in Chile. They were reviewed and authorized by an interagency committee known first as the Special Group, then as the 303 Committee, and finally as the 40 Committee. It consisted of the director of central intelligence, the undersecretary of state for political affairs, the deputy secretary of defense, and the chairman of the Joint Chiefs of Staff, and it was chaired by the president's national security adviser. Congress was not involved, although a few key members of the Armed Services and Appropriations committees of the two houses were given general information in connection with the budget process. Besides the

CIA, therefore, four executive agencies were involved in the bureaucratic politics of covert action—State, Defense, the military chiefs, and the national security adviser and staff.

In Chile the number of players was smaller. They included the head of the CIA station, the army attaché, and the ambassador, with the ambassador as the "head of the country team." In his memoirs Henry Kissinger, who was the national security adviser at the time, blames the State Department and "the abstract theories of our better graduate schools" for the relatively limited U.S. involvement in the 1970 election. He is particularly critical of the Latin American Bureau in the State Department for its bias against supporting the conservative candidate.[4] He refers to Ambassador Edward Korry's expressed fears of an Allende victory but argues that the embassy and the CIA station were blocked in their efforts to take a stronger position by a "three-cornered minuet" that kept the problem from high-level attention until it was too late to do much to influence the outcome. On the other hand, the *Covert Action* report seems to indicate that the problem was the low-profile policy adopted a year earlier with strong ambassadorial support. No mention is made of "abstract" moral considerations or theories as possible reasons for the State Department's opposition to bribing the Chilean Congress, and given Kissinger's well-known views on the subject, these considerations were clearly not relevant to his decisions. In addition, as he admits, he knew and cared very little about Latin America and was lulled by Chilean polls that showed the rightist candidate, Alessandri, well in the lead.

Kissinger argues that the funds appropriated were "minor" compared to 1964 and since they were not devoted to the support of the stronger of the two non-Marxist candidates, probably only reinforced the three-way split that ensued. Again the *Covert Action* report indicates that large sums were spent—between $800,000 and $1,000,000—and these were supplemented by direct contributions totaling $700,000 to Alessandri's campaign by U.S. businesses. It was later revealed that the major U.S. business contributor, the International Telephone and Telegraph Company (ITT), approached the CIA with an offer to contribute a million dollars to be channeled through the agency. The CIA rejected the offer but put ITT in touch with the Alessandri campaign. On 7 August the 40 Committee met again to consider Chile but took no action to approve more money or to authorize exploratory contacts with the Chilean Congress. Chile was also considered, according to Kissinger's memoirs, by a senior review group that included, besides the 40 Committee members, the attorney general and staff members. Again Kissinger blames the State Department for U.S. inaction because it was responsible for the interagency paper presented at the meeting and took an ambivalent, if not tepid, view of the consequences of an Allende victory. Chile was still not seen as a crisis area, and the attention of policymakers was focused elsewhere.

Their attention was quickly focused on Chile, however, when the results of the 4 September election were known. Allende won the election by 39,000 votes (out of 3 million), gaining 36 percent of the vote, a scant 1.2 percent ahead of the right-wing candidate, Alessandri, with Tomic far behind. The election would therefore be decided in the Chilean Congress with a runoff between the two front-runners. Chilean tradition strongly favored the election of the leading candidate, but fifty days were to elapse before the congressional vote, and suddenly the United States was galvanized into action. On 14 September the 40 Committee authorized funds to promote the election of Alessandri (by this time he had announced that he would resign after the election, making it possible to have new elections in which the still-popular Christian Democratic president Eduardo Frei would then be eligible to run). It also authorized a propaganda campaign against Allende and economic pressures against Chile that were to be coordinated by an interagency working group involving the CIA, the State Department, the Treasury, and the National Security Council. This effort, which also later involved exploration of the possibility of Frei's resignation from the presidency in favor of a military cabinet that would call new elections, was dubbed Track I in the *Covert Action* report.

What the *Covert Action* report labeled Track II, a direct effort through the CIA and the army attaché to promote a military coup in Chile, constituted a significant—and shocking—departure from the normal bureaucratic procedures. It resulted from a meeting on 15 September between President Nixon and Richard Helms, the CIA director, Attorney General John Mitchell, and Henry Kissinger. Nixon gave Helms explicit orders to do everything possible to "save Chile." This was to include making "the economy scream" and taking any action necessary to prevent Allende from coming to power. These actions were to be taken without the knowledge of the ambassador or the 40 Committee and were understood to include the promotion of a military coup. Indeed, a coup was specifically mentioned in the CIA instructions to the Santiago station on 21 September.[5] The CIA station made use of the U.S. military attaché in Santiago to contact two groups of anti-Allende plotters, and agents were sent to Chile to assist. One of Kissinger's biographers also asserts, on the basis of hearsay evidence (an unidentified "close associate" of Helms), that an assassination plot against Allende was also developed, but this was vigorously denied by CIA director Helms in the 1975 hearings on Chile.[6] The net result of Track II was that U.S. support involving money, insurance policies, and in the case of one of the two groups, weapons, was given to civilian and military plotters, one group of which (though not the one to which the weapons had been given) tried to promote a coup by kidnapping General René Schneider, the army commander in chief, in a botched attempt that resulted in his assassination. The efforts to use economic pressures and to persuade the Christian Democrats to vote for Alessandri in the runoff also failed, and in fact, the murder of the army commander made the Chileans all the more determined to respect their constitutional processes. On 3 November 1970 Salvador Allende was sworn in as the first freely elected Marxist president of a Latin American country.

In his later testimony to Senate investigators and in his memoirs, Kissinger attempts to downplay the significance of Track II, arguing that both tracks aimed at a military coup and that the only difference between them was the bureaucratic question of embassy and 40 Committee approval. It is true that Track I did briefly explore the question of the resignation of Frei in favor of the military, but its primary emphasis was on the use of the Chilean constitution to prevent Allende's election by the Congress. On the other hand, the primary emphasis of Track II from the outset seems to have been the destruction of Chilean democracy and the seizure of power by extreme rightist military men and civilians. Bypassing the ambassador also violated the basic norms of American diplomacy and substituted the judgment of an impulsive and emotional president for the observation of those on the spot. (The CIA seems to have expressed doubt about the operation but was obliged to carry out a direct presidential order.) Along with other cases, that of Chile clearly suggested to later congressional investigators the need for a more formal review process of covert action as well as greatly increased congressional oversight.

After the failure of the effort to prevent Allende's accession to power, the Nixon administration continued its covert opposition to his regime. In early November 1970 National Security Decision Memorandum 93 called for the termination of new economic assistance—although military assistance was continued—and behind-the-scenes efforts to prevent the extension of new financial assistance or credits by multilateral agencies. U.S. Export-Import Bank credits were to be ended—in fact, they continued for a least another year—and private investors were to be "made aware" of the U.S. government's concern. The Inter-American Development Bank (IDB) made two small loans to Chilean universities in January 1971, and "pipeline" disbursements continued, but the IDB made no other new loans. The World Bank also made no new loans, although the paperwork on one such loan was nearly completed at the time of the 1973 coup. The International Monetary Fund continued to extend credits to Chile throughout the Allende period under its regular programs for countries with foreign-exchange difficulties. U.S. bank lending dropped precipitously, particularly after Chile declared a moratorium on the payment of its foreign debt in November 1971, but one American bank still had a credit line outstanding at the time of the September 1973 coup.

Thus what Allende described in his December 1972 speech at the United Nations as an "invisible blockade" should be more accurately described as a U.S.-initiated "credit squeeze"—a program of economic pressure but not a blockade.[7] Chile continued to export its products to the United States, and other companies resisted proposals by ITT for a genuine blockade when they were made at a meeting at the State Department after the nationalization of the American-owned copper companies. Chile was able to secure major credits from Western Europe, other Latin American countries, and to a lesser extent the Soviet Union and Eastern Europe. The U.S. pressures caused some shortages of replacement parts and alteration of supply sources, but the main economic difficulties of the Allende government were internal —especially a runaway inflation that had reached 323 percent by mid-1973, and strikes by shopkeepers, truckers, miners, and a whole range of organized groups in Chile that opposed his government.

Besides the economic measures decided immediately after Allende's accession to power, the United States also began a covert program of support for opposition parties, interest groups, and the media. Much of that assistance went to the major opposition newspaper, *El Mercurio* (beginning in September 1971), and to the principal opposition party, the Christian Democratic party, which began to publish its own newspaper with what we now know was CIA support. In the September–October 1970 period a small amount ($38,500) went to an extreme right quasi-fascist group and even smaller sums seem to have been passed to striking truckers against CIA wishes in October 1972 and possibly indirectly during a second strike, which lasted from late July 1973 until the coup. Ambassador Nathaniel Davis insists in his memoirs that he opposed support for the strikers because he knew that it would build up tension and lead to a coup.[8] Apparently the CIA favored such support, but there was no formal approval by the 40 Committee, and what help was given to the truckers in 1973 came from other opposition groups that received CIA money. Nevertheless, because of a story in the *New York Times* on 20 September 1974 that the "majority" of the CIA support went to the strikers, the myth persists that the U.S. support for the strikers played a major role in provoking the 1973 coup.

A more widespread myth that has already been mentioned is the belief that the United States itself instigated the coup. The first form that this myth took was the use of the term "destabilization" to describe the U.S. anti-Allende program. The term was first used in September 1974 by Congressman Michael Harrington, who revealed the CIA role in Chile after reading CIA director William E. Colby's earlier secret testimony to a congressional committee. Colby wrote a letter to the *New York Times* denying that he had ever used the term, but it stuck as a shorthand description of the CIA subsidies and economic pressures.

Was there more? Specifically, did the United States encourage or assist the 11 September 1973 coup? The Senate investigators in 1975 concluded that there was "no hard evidence of direct U.S. assistance to the coup, despite frequent allegations of such aid."[9] Indeed, the investigators found that the CIA station in Santiago had been specifically ordered to discontinue its contacts with the military in May 1973 to prevent just such an accusation being made. Nevertheless, the charge is repeated in various ways, although always without proof, and it forms a major element in the argument of a book (*The Execution of Charles Horman,* by Thomas Hauser) and a film (*Missing*) on the death of an American at the hands of the Chilean military after the coup "because he knew too much." The weakness of the argument has been demonstrated in Ambassador Davis's memoirs and in several reviews of the film, and the film is now the subject of a libel suit by the ambassador, but the myth persists.

Yet, even if the United States did not have a direct role in the coup and even if its economic pressures were not successful, there is no question that its policy was one of unremitting hostility to the Allende government—although this was occasionally concealed behind pious rhetoric, like President Nixon's February 1971 statement that "we are prepared to have the kind of relationship with the Chilean government that it is prepared to have with us." The State Department seems to have favored a more flexible position on a number of occasions, but Kissinger and Nixon were determined to oppose Allende with every available weapon. This was the case despite the repeated assertion by the CIA's National Intelligence Estimates that Chile posed no vital threat to American interests. Why such hostility?

There are a number of responses to this question. The Marxist left sees the U.S. opposition to Allende as a response to the threat that his program of nationalization posed to American business interests, while Kissinger speaks of the likelihood of the export of revolution to neighboring countries and the effect of the Chilean example on Western Europe. Others attribute U.S. actions to cold war anticommunism, which simply rejected an accommodation with a Marxist government. In the post-Watergate period it is also possible to refer to the particular psychological makeup of Richard Nixon, and this is confirmed by Ambassador Korry's account of Nixon's conduct in his meetings with him in October 1970. There is a large and controversial literature on the subject, to much of which I have contributed. Suffice it to say at this point that there is considerable evidence that U.S. business interests, although important, were not decisive, and that those interests were often divided in their views as to how to deal with Allende. (The conflict of opinion between ITT and the other U.S. companies doing business in Chile has already been mentioned.) It is also clear that a certain momentum had been built up by the accumulation of CIA "assets" in Chile over several decades, which made it difficult not to make use of them against a strongly anti-U.S. government. Henry Kissinger's well-known Realpolitik approach to international relations may also have contributed to such decisions as the use of Track II to subvert Chilean democracy, but Nixon's personal feelings seem to have been much more important. Thus, particular circumstances—including past CIA involvement, an emotional and militantly anticommunist president, and a national security adviser who believed that balance-of-power considerations were primary in determining foreign policy—as well as considerations of the duty of U.S. diplomacy to support American citizens (including business investors) who were receiving unfair treatment from foreign governments, all appear to be better explanations of U.S. policy than the simplistic reductionism of the left, which sees all U.S. actions in terms of the defense of American capitalism.[10]

The next question that may be asked now that we have so much information about the U.S. role in Chile is, Did it make a difference? In the case of the 1964 elections, the $2.6 million that was spent by the CIA went for radio programs, newspaper ads, and the creation and support of anticommunist groups; some money seems to have been spent and diplomatic effort exercised to keep a right-wing Radical party candidate in the race so that those anticlerical Radicals who could not bring themselves to vote for a Christian Democrat would have a non-Marxist alternative. (He got 5 percent of the vote.) Eduardo Frei secured 56 percent of the vote. What would he have received without CIA support? Perhaps less than an absolute majority but, given the traditional three-way division of the Chilean electorate, as long as the right was supporting him he was assured of a victory—if not in the election itself, then certainly in the congressional runoff. A less resounding victory might have led the Christian Democrats to make more compromises with the right in the ensuing six years and perhaps headed off a right-wing candidate in 1971, but given ex-president Alessandri's continuing appeal, it is difficult to see how the right could have avoided attempting a comeback with him at the head of the ticket.

In the years from 1964 to 1970, CIA activity seems to have had something to do with the split-off of the right wing of the Radical party in 1967 and possibly the division of the Socialist party in the same year. Neither of these events produced electorally significant parties, however, or affected the 1970 outcome. In the period before the 1970 election an effort might have been made to encourage the nomination of a Christian Democrat who was more acceptable to the right than Radomiro Tomic. However, Alessandri had already been nominated when the Christian Democrats chose Tomic, and as cofounder of the party he had had a long-standing commitment to be the Christian Democratic standard-bearer after Frei. Thus CIA or embassy involvement seems unlikely to have changed the outcome.

Would a more active role in support of Alessandri have made a difference, as Henry Kissinger implies in his memoirs? The *Covert Action* report notes that Alessandri received $700,000 from U.S. business interests in 1970 and that right-wing, women's, and "civic action" groups received CIA support from anti-Allende propaganda. The only differences from 1964 mentioned in the report are the lack of a polling effort by the CIA (though there were many polls in 1970, often with contradictory results) and an absence of grass-roots organizing and community development efforts. Given the closeness of the vote (a 1.2 percent margin), this might have made a difference, especially in inducing women voters to choose Alessandri rather than the Christian Democratic candidate, Tomic. The report also notes that Alessandri needed "help in managing his campaign," but the only serious example of mismanagement was a disastrous television interview which emphasized Alessandri's advanced age (through focusing on the effects of Parkinsonism on his hand). Active involvement by the CIA might have made some difference, but the case is not at all clear.

From 1970 to 1973, both Track I (the effort to get the Christian Democrats to support Alessandri in the congressional runoff so that he could resign and new elections could be called) and Track II (the effort to promote a military coup) failed; in the latter case, the death of General Schneider made it *more* likely that Allende would be chosen by the Congress. The support for opposition radio stations, newspapers, and professional and interest groups certainly encouraged the opposition, but with the exception of the two truckers' strikes that paralyzed the country, this did not make the coup more likely. (The truckers' strikes *did*, both by producing the involvement of the military in the cabinet in November 1972 and by further undermining the economy from the end of July until the September coup, but as far as can be determined only a small amount of CIA money went to the strikers.)

A crucial factor is the U.S. relation to the military. While military aid continued and new U.S. military assistance was extended, thus helping the military to resist Soviet offers of aid, the only CIA contacts with the military the Senate investigators discovered were the circulation of a packet of materials that included a forged letter in December 1971 and the monitoring of coup plotting, which was ended in May 1973. Despite unceasing efforts by the Chilean left and exiles, no other evidence of U.S. encouragement or promotion of a coup has been uncovered.

Even if there is no clear evidence that U.S. covert action made a significant difference, there remains the question as to whether it was justified in making the effort. Kissinger claims that the long-term goal of Allende and of his Communist allies was a totalitarian state, and he cites as evidence Allende's interview with Regis Debray published in 1971, in which he says that acceptance of the Statute of Democratic Guarantees, which was a condition of his election by the Congress, was "a tactical necessity" and that his ultimate goal was the overthrow of the bourgeois state.[11] Yet Kissinger does not mention Allende's commitment in his inaugural address to a democratic transition to socialism, which he supported with a quotation from Engels that argued that in some countries such a transition was possible. The Popular Unity Program called for a single legislative chamber, widespread nationalization, and popular courts, but despite his friendship with Fidel Castro, there is no evidence that Allende intended, as Kissinger claims, to create "another Cuba." And even if that was his goal, there remained the fact that two-thirds of the Chilean people had not voted for him in 1970 and that the armed forces were determined to retain their independence, hierarchical chain of command, and apolitical character.

A second argument that both Henry Kissinger and Richard Nixon use in their respective memoirs is that the Soviet Union and Cuba make use of covert action, and therefore we must do so as well. We know very little about the nature and instruments of Soviet support for the Chilean Communist party except that the relationship of that party with Moscow is very close. There have been reports of transfers of money through Uruguay and the channeling of income from visits by musicians and groups such as the Moscow Circus to support the party, and it is known that the party has a significant number of full-time employees in Chile. The *Covert Action* report also mentions CIA estimates that the Cubans provided $350,000 for Allende's 1970 presidential campaign, with the Soviets providing an "undetermined additional amount." Three responses to this argument are possible. First, conservatives will argue that we should fight fire with fire—responding in kind to Soviet-Cuban efforts at subversion. Liberals will respond that this puts us on their level and involves us in skulduggery that undermines the very values that support the democratic system. (The Senate investigation of the possible use of assassination as an instrument of national policy illustrates this problem.) The left, in turn, will argue that such methods should never be used (with the possible exception of an all-out war against a regime such as Hitler's) because they will inevitably be perverted to support the wrong regimes and will acquire a momentum of their own. The U.S. Congress finally adopted an intermediate position, refusing to abjure covert action completely but supporting it only after careful review.

A third argument in the Chilean case is a variation of the domino effect. Two weeks after Allende's election Kissinger argued publicly that an Allende takeover would present "massive problems for pro-U.S. forces in the whole Western Hemisphere" and that "there is a good chance that he will establish over a period of years some sort of Communist government . . . in a major Latin American country adjoining . . . Argentina . . . Peru . . . and Bolivia."[12] It is true that a reformist military coup had taken place in Peru in 1968, that Argentina was lurching toward a return to Perónism, and that a leftist military government had taken over in Bolivia. However, Chile is so sealed off by mountains and desert from the other countries that it is doubtful that it could have become much of a base for their subversion, especially since the Chilean armed forces were strongly committed to opposing internal subversion. Kissinger's remark about the Chilean dagger and Antarctica is relevant, although it does suggest that a different argument concerning the sea-lanes through the Straits of Magellan could have been made, though it was not.

The argument about direct threats to U.S. interests is a weak one, and the National Intelligence Estimates analyzed in the *Covert Action* report recognize as much. Ultimately a perception of a possible alteration of the worldwide balance of power seems to have motivated Kissinger, and a gut-reaction anticommunism to have determined Richard Nixon's response. How one finally reacts to the revelations concerning the U.S. role thus has much to do with one's basic philosophy of international relations.

How Congress reacted to those revelations was very important for the future conduct of U.S. foreign policy. From the day of the coup itself there were press reports of U.S. involvement, and as reports of a reign of terror filtered out of Chile, a number of congressional committees began to look more closely at the question of the U.S. role. There were complaints of a double standard when the United States granted Chile substantial Commodity Credit Corporation loans for wheat purchases (to replace those cut off by the Soviet Union) which had been denied to Allende. According to the *Covert Action* report, congressional oversight of intelligence activities was "inadequate."

Superficial briefings of the Intelligence subcommittees of the House and Senate Armed Services and Appropriations committees on eight out of thirty-three covert-action projects between 1963 and 1974 made absolutely no mention of the Track II effort to overthrow the Chilean government.

Suddenly all sorts of congressional committees began to hold hearings on Chile as thousands of letters, telegrams, and phone calls from university and church groups descended on Congress. On 28 September 1973, Senator Edward Kennedy held hearings of the Senate Judiciary Committee on human rights violations in Chile, and on 2 October he proposed an amendment to the foreign-aid legislation that cut off all nonhumanitarian aid to Chile until the president determined that Chile was protecting human rights in accordance with the UN's Universal Declaration of Human Rights. The amendment was not adopted, but the final version of the Foreign Assistance Act directed the president to urge the Chilean government to respect human rights. At the end of 1974, Congress voted to cut off military aid to Chile unless the president certified that it was making progress in human rights. In 1975 the aid prohibition was reasserted, and in 1976 a total ban on all Chilean military purchases or aid was adopted. That ban, in a stronger form enacted following the Chilean-inspired assassination of Allende's ex-ambassador in Washington in 1976, remains in effect eleven years later.[13]

Conservatives reacted by holding hearings in the Senate Internal Security Committee in November 1973 that focused on the Allende government's involvement in cocaine smuggling. The most important hearings were conducted in closed session in April 1974, when the director of the Central Intelligence Agency, William Colby, revealed that a total of $8 million had been authorized to be used against the Allende regime. When the contents of these hearings were revealed by Congressman Harrington in September 1974, an uproar ensued, especially since they seemed to contradict Henry Kissinger's testimony at his confirmation hearings as secretary of state in September 1973, in which he admitted U.S. involvement "in a minor way" in the 1970 elections in Chile but stated that "since then we have absolutely stayed away from coups." More damaging was the contradiction with the testimony of former CIA director Richard Helms during his confirmation hearings as ambassador to Iran when he responded to a question on whether the CIA had tried to prevent Allende's election in 1970 with the answer, "No sir."

The ultimate result of the congressional concern with the CIA role in Chile and elsewhere was that the Senate and House each established a Select Committee on Intelligence Activities to examine the role of the CIA and other intelligence agencies and to make recommendations concerning increased congressional oversight. Even before the Senate committee reported its recommendations, the 1974 Foreign Assistance Act included a provision that the CIA director must report all covert operations approved by the 40 Committee and the president to no less than six congressional oversight committees. After the Senate Select Committee reported and similar recommendations were made in the House, the two houses each set up an Intelligence Committee to review intelligence activities, which the CIA was required to report "in a timely fashion."

With slightly altered wording, those reviews continue today. In some cases, as in that of CIA aid to the Afghan resistance to the 1979 Soviet invasion, there is no criticism or public outcry. In others, however, most notably the aid to the Nicaraguan contras that began in December 1981, there is public debate over what *Newsweek* called on its cover in November 1982 "The Secret War in Nicaragua," and public votes are held on the amount and nature of "covert" assistance. The Chilean case has thus fundamentally altered the conduct of U.S. foreign policy, sharply limiting the range of covert operations available to the executive.

Besides Nicaragua, Angola was also affected indirectly by Chile. In the waning days of the Ford presidency in early 1976, and against the express wishes of Secretary of State Henry Kissinger, Congress adopted the Clark Amendment, which ended U.S. covert support of the Angolan opposition to the Marxist regime that was being installed with the aid of Soviet-subsidized Cuban troops. The amendment was repealed in 1985, but "covert" aid to the Angolan opposition is the subject of continuing public discussion and debate.

A further effect of the Chilean case can be seen in the attitudes and conduct of the Sandinistas in Nicaragua. Just as the Guatemalan intervention by the CIA in 1954 fundamentally affected the attitudes of Che Guevara (who was in Guatemala at the time) and of Fidel Castro as to the possibility of coexistence between the United States and a "revolutionary" government, so the Chilean experience alerted the Sandinistas to the need to achieve control of the armed forces and to secure alternative arms supplies from the Soviet Union. Thus, immediately after the July 1979 revolution, for example, the Nicaraguan army became the *Sandinista* Popular Army, and the police the *Sandinista* Police, and within weeks of the seizure of power the Sandinistas had sent a delegation to Moscow to seek military aid. As in the Cuban case, the perception of U.S. hostility became a self-fulfilling prophecy, which in the Nicaraguan case was reinforced by Sandinista aid to the Salvadoran guerrillas just at the time that the Reagan administration was coming into office.

A further long-term effect of the Chilean case is the continuing U.S. commitment to human rights. That commitment began in 1975—before the Carter administration—with the adoption of the Harkin amendment to the foreign aid bill, which cut off U.S. aid to governments that "engage in a consistent pattern of gross violations of human rights" as defined by internationally accepted standards. With variations, this has continued to be U.S. policy. It was intensified and given greater prominence by the Carter administration, while in reaction to the visibility of the Carter policy, the Reagan administration initially called for "quiet diplomacy" in support of human rights. However, the State Department continues to have a special bureau concerned with human rights and humanitarian assistance, and Congress continues to mandate an annual State Department report on the human rights situation in every country in the world, thus compelling every U.S. embassy to concern itself directly with the subject. One might argue that this is simply the result of post-Vietnam attempts to inject a larger moral element into U.S. foreign policy, but the evidence of the mid-1970s is overwhelming that the revelations of U.S. involvement in Chile and the hideous repression in that country following the coup had much to do with adding a new component to U.S. foreign policy.[14]

We may conclude from this review that U.S. involvement in Chile raised fundamental questions about U.S. foreign policy and produced an important shift in the way that it is conducted. While the United States neither destabilized nor overthrew Allende, its covert involvement led it to attempt to reverse the results of a free election and contributed to the polarization that led to a particularly bloody and repressive coup and the end of Chilean democracy. It led to a continuing debate on the appropriate U.S. response to Marxist regimes in the hemisphere and on the place of covert action in a democracy. It made it much more difficult for the executive to carry out covert activities of the sort that had been common in the postwar period. More positively, it committed the U.S. government much more strongly to the defense of human rights and the promotion of democracy. Chile may not be "the Spain of the 1970s," but it is an important case in point: For the left it is proof of unremitting U.S. hostility to all socialist regimes and preference for authoritarianism over democracy in Latin America; for the right it justifies continuing U.S. assistance to embattled democratic elements facing Soviet subversion. Characteristically, both sides overstate the importance and representativeness of the Chilean case, but there is no doubt that future historians will see it as one of the most significant and controversial examples of U.S. crisis management in Latin America.

Notes

1. The arguments center mainly around U.S. policy toward the Allende government (1970–1973). The best single collection of documents on the subject is U.S. Congress, House of Representatives, Committee on Foreign Affairs, Subcommittee on Inter-American Affairs, *The United States and Chile during the Allende Years* (Washington, D.C.: U.S. Government Printing Office, 1975), which includes hearings from 1971 to 1974, important governments documents, and twenty-seven of the most important articles on the subject. Major congressional investigations on related subjects include U.S. Congress, Senate, Committee on Foreign Relations, Subcommittee on Multinational Corporations, *Multinational Corporations and U.S. Foreign Policy: Hearings on the International Telephone and Telegraph Company and Chile, 1970–71*, 2 vols. (Washington, D.C.: U.S. Government Printing Office, 1973); U.S. Congress, Senate, Select Committee on Intelligence Activities, Staff Report, *Covert Action in Chile, 1963–1973* (Washington, D.C.: U.S. Government Printing Office, 1975); Select Committee on Intelligence Activities, *Alleged Assassination Plots Involving Foreign Leaders, Interim Report* (Washington, D.C.: U.S. Government Printing Office, 1975); Select Committee on Intelligence Activities, *Final Report* (Washington, D.C.: U.S. Government Printing Office, 1976), bk. 4, pp. 121–71. We also have important memoirs on the period, notably Henry Kissinger, *The White House Years* (Boston: Little, Brown, 1979), see chap. 17, and *Years of Upheaval* (Boston: Little, Brown, 1982) chap. 9; Richard Nixon, *RN: The Memoirs of Richard Nixon* (New York: Putnam, 1978); Nathaniel Davis, *The Last Two Years of Salvador Allende,* (Ithaca, N.Y.: Cornell University Press, 1985); and relevant sections of Seymour M. Hersh, *The Price of Power* (New York: Summit Books, 1983); and Thomas Powers, *The Man Who Kept the Secrets: Richard Helms and the CIA* (New York: Alfred A. Knopf, 1979). On the Allende presidency and the U.S. role, see Paul E. Sigmund, *The Overthrow of Allende and the Politics of Chile, 1964–1976* (Pittsburgh: University of Pittsburgh Press, 1977). Addi-

174 Paul E. Sigmund

tional background is provided in Anthony Sampson, *The Sovereign State of ITT*, rev. ed. (Greenwich, Conn.: Stein and Day, 1974), chap. 11, and David Phillips, *The Night Watch* (New York: Ballantine, 1977), chaps. 1, 9, 10.

2. See Phillips, *Night Watch*, chap. 1.

3. See Eduardo Labarca Goddard, *Chile Invadido* (Santiago: Editora Austral, 1969).

4. Kissinger, *White House Years*, p. 664.

5. *Alleged Assassination Plots*, pp. 227–29.

6. Hersh, *Price of Power*, pp. 259, 274; *Alleged Assassination Plots*, p. 228.

7. See Paul E. Sigmund, "The 'Invisible Blockade' and the Overthrow of Allende," *Foreign Affairs* 52 (January 1974): 322–40.

8. Davis, *Salvador Allende*, pp. 324–26.

9. *Covert Action*, p. 28.

10. For the debate between Elizabeth Farnsworth and myself on the U.S. role in Chile, see *Foreign Policy* 16 (Fall 1974), and Richard Fagen, "The United States and Chile: Roots and Branches," *Foreign Affairs* (January 1975) as well as my letter to the editor and Fagen's reply in the same issue. These and many other relevant articles are reprinted in *The United States and Chile during the Allende Years, 1970–1973*, cited in note 1 above.

11. Kissinger, *White House Years*, p. 656.

12. *New York Times*, 20 September 1970.

13. See Taylor Branch and Eugene M. Propper, *Labyrinth* (New York: Viking, 1982).

14. See Robert C. Johansen, *The National Interest and the Human Interest* (Princeton, N.J.: Princeton University Press, 1980), chap. 4; Lars Schoultz, *Human Rights and U.S. Foreign Policy* (Princeton, N.J.: Princeton University Press, 1981), and Paul E. Sigmund, "Chile: Successful Intervention?" in Robert Wesson, ed., *U.S. Influence in Latin America in the 1980s* (New York: Praeger, 1982), pp. 20–39.

Steve C. Ropp

Negotiating the 1978 Panama Canal Treaties: Contending Theoretical Perspectives

When the administration of Jimmy Carter announced at its inception that its top foreign policy priority would be the negotiation and ratification of new Panama Canal treaties, one result was an outpouring of writing about the event and its probable consequences. Most of this initial writing was polemical, with supporters of the idea attempting to bolster the historical and contemporary case for such a course and detractors attempting to undermine it. Only recently has a substantial body of academic literature emerged that seeks to explain the reasons behind the administration's push for ratification and the dynamics of the ratification process itself.

This chapter will focus on the problem of explaining policy formation and implementation in the Panama Canal treaty case through the use of three theoretical perspectives. The first is the international systems approach, which has been used by a number of authors but most extensively by Walter LaFeber in his classic 1978 volume on the canal treaties, and by William L. Furlong and Margaret E. Scranton in their more recent book on the negotiating process.[1] The second is that of linkage politics, as elaborated in David N. Farnsworth and James W. McKenney's study of U.S.-Panamanian relations.[2] And the third is the elite approach, found not only in a number of early journalistic writings but also scattered throughout more recent analytical treatments.

After giving a short chronological description of the major events along the road to treaty ratification, I will describe each of these three perspectives in general theoretical terms and then discuss their more specific applications to this particular case of foreign policy decision making. I will discuss areas of agreement and disagreement among the various authors, offer a critique of the three perspectives, and present my own personal synthesis. Finally, the chapter will examine the policy consequences of treaty ratification in terms of whether it can be considered a success or a failure.

The Road to Ratification

Although the Panamanian flag demonstrations of November 1959 are often used as a convenient starting point for a discussion of the negotiating process, it is clear that in the broadest historical sense, such negotiations began almost immediately after ratification of the original 1903 treaty. For it was quickly recognized by all patriotic Panamanians that the 1903 treaty constituted a legal superstructure that legitimized an overwhelming U.S. presence on the isthmus. Only through the dismantling of this legal superstructure could true independence be achieved.

Attempts to modify some aspects of the 1903 document almost succeeded as early as 1926, when a new treaty was negotiated. The Panamanian Assembly, however, refused ratification. Modest success was achieved in 1939 during the administration of Franklin Roosevelt when the Hull-Alfaro Treaty was ratified. Its primary effects were to do away with the U.S. right to intervene militarily in Panamanian domestic politics (in the spirit of the Good Neighbor Policy) and to increase the economic benefits that Panama received from the Canal.

Such incremental modifications of the original document continued through the 1950s. An additional treaty was ratified in 1955 during the Eisenhower administration, and this new treaty, together with its 1939 predecessor, had important consequences. But their impact was primarily on Panamanian domestic politics rather than on Panama's place in the international system. For example, the 1955 treaty opened up the market for consumer goods in the Canal Zone to Panamanian businessmen and further encouraged consumption there through higher wages. This in turn strengthened the national tax base and led to the rapid expansion of the Panamanian state.[3]

From Panama's point of view, however, the fundamental problem was that neither treaty touched on the international issue of sovereignty over the Canal Zone, a sovereignty that many North Americans saw (and many still see) as residing with the United States. Debate over this issue was much encouraged by the ambiguous language of the 1903 treaty, which stated that the United States would possess all of the rights and powers in the Canal Zone that it would have "if it were the sovereign of the territory within which said land and waters are located, to the entire exclusion of the exercise of the Republic of Panama of any such sovereign rights, power, and authority."[4]

That the sovereignty issue lay at the heart of the question of treaty revision became obvious in 1958 when a number of Panamanian university students engaged in a more or less peaceful attempt to place their national flag at various strategic locations throughout the Canal Zone. This was followed on 3 November 1959 (Independence Day) by an even more concerted effort to do so, which led to an outbreak of violence. Eventually, both the Canal Zone police and U.S. troops became involved in attempts to quell the riot, in which an estimated 120 Panamanians were injured.

At this point, the issue from the perspective of the United States was not one of granting Panama sovereignty over the Canal Zone (a nonnegotiable issue) but rather recognition of Panama's *titular* sovereignty. For several years President Eisenhower and others had been arguing that such recognition would constitute an important low-cost way of dealing with Panamanian sensibilities. However, congressional and public reaction in the United States to such palliative symbolic measures did not bode well for the future of the negotiating process. There was a strong and immediate outcry against the idea of two flags flying over the Zone, an outcry that President Eisenhower overrode in September 1959 when he declared that both were to be flown.[5]

The 1959 flag riots were the precursors of much more serious ones that occurred on 9 January 1964. Students from a Panamanian high school bordering the Zone marched over to Balboa High School to raise their flag beside that of the United States. In the ensuing struggle with U.S. students and their parents, the Panamanian flag was torn, word of which quickly spread to Panama City and Colón. Violent riots erupted.

Following this bloody confrontation, which left an estimated twenty-four Panamanians and four U.S. servicemen dead, President Johnson initiated a new process of negotiation that eventually led to the announcement of three new treaties on 26 June 1967. However, given the timing of the riots and the nature of his opposition in the upcoming presidential election, Johnson chose not to move openly on the matter until late in 1964. After his convincing victory over

Barry Goldwater, he announced in December that new treaties would be negotiated that would recognize Panamanian sovereignty over the Canal Zone, set a termination date for U.S. operation of the facility, and deal with the issue of its continuing defense.[6] Johnson's announcement was a watershed event in the treaty-negotiating process, shifting the U.S. position from one of bargaining over titular sovereignty to that of discussing the real thing.

This shift in thinking can largely be attributed to the advice that President Johnson received from his special representative to Panama, Robert B. Anderson. In a visit to the Oval Office on 2 December 1964, Anderson told the president that the 1903 treaty was anachronistic and needed to be replaced by a new one that would eliminate the perpetuity clause. Johnson responded to the challenge of such negotiations in the same fashion that Jimmy Carter would later, seeing the effort to negotiate such treaties as a struggle of heroic and hence history-making proportions.[7]

After several years of behind-the-scenes negotiations, the Johnson administration and that of Marco Robles in Panama publicly revealed drafts of three new treaties on 26 June 1967. The first set the year 2000 as the magic millenial date at which the United States would turn over control of the Canal Zone to Panama. The second dealt with the question of the U.S. defense of the Canal after the year 2000 by allowing for the continuing presence in the area of U.S. troops. The third allowed for U.S. construction of a new canal through Panama should there be a felt need.

In spite of the major conceptual breakthroughs embodied in these three treaties, they did not prosper in the increasingly hostile political environment existing in both countries and were never submitted to their respective legislatures for ratification. In the United States, opposition to the "transfer" of sovereignty over the Canal Zone quickly surfaced in Congress, and the president, increasingly preoccupied by Vietnam and having declared that he would not seek another term, was unwilling and perhaps unable to apply the needed pressure.[8] In Panama, the issue became caught up in the heated 1968 presidential election campaign that found firebrand nationalist Arnulfo Arias using this perennial national issue to rally support. According to William J. Jorden, the former U.S. ambassador to Panama, they soon became "the orphan treaties."[9]

During its early years, 1969 to 1971, the Nixon administration was so preoccupied with other, more serious global problems that it had inherited that it was in no position to move on the Canal issue even had it been inclined to do so. In any case, there seems to have been no such inclination associated with the Eurocentric vision of Richard Nixon and his national security adviser, Henry Kissinger. From their initial perspective, they viewed Latin America as a peripheral region, and Panama stood at the very edge of this periphery.

Developments in Panama itself, however, served as something of a counterbalance to this increased U.S. tendency to ignore the Canal issue. There, the newly inaugurated government of Arnulfo Arias had been overthrown by a military coup in October 1968. After several years of consolidating his hold over the government, General Omar Torrijos was in a position to apply increasing pressure on the United States to reinvigorate the negotiating process. Such reinvigoration was in fact part of his strategy to insure the consolidation of his regime.[10]

One of the key elements in Torrijos's approach to the negotiations was his effort to situate them in a broader global bargaining context. Before 1971 they had been conducted in traditional bilateral fashion, with only occasional attempts by the Panamanians to bring international pressure to bear. Torrijos set out to systematically cultivate allies among both Third World radicals and moderates. The first use of this strategy came in 1972 when Panama's ambassador to the United Nations gave a strongly worded speech at the United Nations Security Council meeting in Ethiopia. The speech compared U.S. colonialism in the Canal Zone to that prevalent in Africa. Torrijos followed this with a similar use of the world stage at the Security Council meeting the following year in Panama and by efforts to create a network of moderate regional allies.[11]

The renewal of serious bilateral negotiations came in late 1973. On 7 February 1974, Secretary of State Kissinger joined Panamanian foreign minister Juan Antonio Tack for the signing of a Joint Statement of Principles. This framework confirmed the decision to negotiate an entirely new treaty that would fix a date for the end of U.S. control over the Canal Zone. Panama would also assume a role in both the defense of the Canal and its operation, and would gain access to a larger share of the profits.[12]

In spite of another auspicious start, the two sides made little progress during 1975 and 1976 toward transforming the 1974 Joint Statement of Principles into new treaty drafts. U.S. negotiators, pressured by the Department of Defense, argued for a fifty-year lease on its mil-

itary facilities, a condition that was totally unacceptable to the Panamanians. There was also continued disagreement concerning the
amount of territory that these military facilities should occupy and
the terminal date for U.S. control of the Canal Zone. On the political
front, opposition surfaced once again in both the Senate and the
House, and the impending presidential election of 1976 established
an additional set of constraints. Perhaps most ominous for treaty
supporters was the fact that Ronald Reagan was able to make effective use of the treaty issue in his attempt to win the Republican nomination.[13]

With the election of Jimmy Carter, the treaty negotiations again had
a new lease on life under the guidance of Ellsworth Bunker and his
newly appointed conegotiator, Sol Linowitz. Carter made the issue
a top priority, and negotiations began again one month after he took
office. By August 1977 the two countries were able to announce
agreement in principle on the terms of two new treaties. One month
later, at an elaborate ceremony in Washington, they were signed by
General Torrijos and President Carter. Panamanian approval came
by way of a national plebiscite in October and Senate ratification in
the United States on 18 April 1978.[14]

The terms of the 1978 Canal treaties constituted an amalgam of the
ideas and principles embodied in the aborted 1967 treaties, the 1974
Joint Statement of Principles, and the 1977 negotiations themselves.
The first treaty, which was to remain in effect until the year 2000,
granted the United States the right to continue operating and admin-
istering the Canal. Administration was to be accomplished through
a new commission that would replace the Panama Canal Company
and that allowed for Panamanian participation (although with a permanent U.S. majority). The second treaty ensured the continued
neutrality of the Canal and continued U.S. access to it after the year
2000.[15]

Contending Theoretical Perspectives

Although the press analyzed the Canal treaties in great detail during
the ratification process, it has only been recently that scholars have
turned their attention to several key questions that were largely ignored in the early accounts. First, how does one explain the *timing*
of the U.S. decision to begin serious discussions with Panama about
the critical and previously nonnegotiable questions of sovereignty

and operation of the Canal? Second, how does one explain the *dynamics* of the ratification process itself and the ability of the Carter administration to get a treaty ratified where previous attempts had failed?

The literature on foreign-policy decision making is rich in perspectives that can be applied to this particular case, and there has been increasing application of a considerable variety of them. Here I will discuss three that seem to have some special utility and that have been occasionally, if not widely, used.

The International System Approach

The international system approach focuses on the general configuration of the system at any given time as the major causal factor determining the behavior of its constituent national elements. The foreign policy goals and objectives of nation states are considered to be shaped and constrained by various system characteristics. As these characteristics change over time, so, it is alleged, does the foreign-policy behavior of individual countries.[16]

In spite of the frequent use of this perspective in a general fashion by those who have sought to explain various discrete foreign policy decisions of the United States and other countries, surprisingly little rigorous use has been made of it with any attendant effort to develop specific theoretical propositions.[17] In the case of the Panama Canal treaties, no such proposition has been developed for the relationship that a number of analysts believe to have existed between changes in the international system and changes in U.S. foreign policy behavior. However, the implicit proposition is as follows: As the power of a nation declines relative to other systemic actors, its efforts to reach accommodations over major issues separating it from its international allies will increase.

The suggestive nature of this particular theoretical perspective is due to the fact (as a number of observers have noted) that the increased propensity of the United States to negotiate with Panama over the critical issues of sovereignty and operation of the Canal coincided with a period of relative decline in the international position of the United States. Further, the fact that this propensity to negotiate persisted across three seemingly quite different presidential administrations (those of Nixon, Ford, and Carter) suggests that all of them may have been influenced by international system imperatives.

Various students of post–World War II American foreign policy have argued that a general decline in the nation's relative power position led to frequent adjustments of the national leadership's key operative assumptions, adjustments that often spanned seemingly very different presidential administrations. For example, John Lewis Gaddis notes the existence of five distinct "geopolitical codes" identifiable in post–World War II administrations which responded to changes in the nation's position in the larger global context. Most germane for our analysis of the Canal treaty decision is the code that came to predominate during the Nixon administration and that Gaddis labels "detente." It tended to be more accommodationist in regard to relationships both with allies and with potential enemies because, unlike some of its predecessors, this code made a distinction between vital and peripheral national interests.[18]

Gaddis and others have noted that all three administrations from Nixon to Carter seemed to be locked into a set of foreign policy responses that were almost exclusively determined by the nature of the international system as manifested in the 1970s. This similarity of condition led to compulsive attempts by occupants of the Oval Office to distinguish their foreign policy from that of their predecessors.[19] As Kenneth Oye puts it:

Through rhetoric and action, the Nixon, Ford, and Carter administrations struggled to adjust to the emerging limits of American economic and military power. . . . Richard Nixon and Henry Kissinger spoke pessimistically about the inevitable "end of the postwar world." They formulated a narrow realpolitik foreign policy to control America's descent into an uncertain future. Jimmy Carter spoke with mild optimism of a "new world" where "we can no longer expect that the other 150 nations will follow the dictates of the powerful," and added a soupçon of idealpolitik to increase the palatability of a fundamentally realpolitik foreign policy. Although every administration seeks to distinguish its foreign policy from that of its predecessors, rhetorical and substantive differences should not be permitted to obscure the fundamental continuity of American policy during the 1970s.[20]

Perhaps the first academic observer to suggest that the Panama Canal treaty negotiations reflected such an attempt to reach an accommodation with an ally in the context of newly emerging perceived limits to American economic and military power was Walter LaFeber. LaFeber discusses changes in the international system in terms of three configurations of the cold war. During the first period (1945–1955), the United States confronted the Soviet Union directly in a series of crises that used the Third World as a stage but did not involve Third World participation. During the second period (1955–1970), Third World countries themselves, such as Cuba and North Vietnam, became U.S. adversaries in their own right. According to LaFeber, the primary characteristic of these two periods was the belief on the part of U.S. foreign policy makers that they had sufficient military and economic power to deal effectively with these adversarial relations.[21]

However, the period that LaFeber calls the Third Cold War (1970 to the present) was different in that various administrations continued to confront both the Soviet Union and Third World adversaries but with diminished economic and military power. In the instance of the Panama Canal treaties, the result of this combination of increasingly complex international problems coupled with a declining U.S. ability to manufacture instant military solutions was accommodation and adjustment.[22]

The case of those who argue for use of the international system perspective in explaining the propensity of three U.S. presidential administrations to seriously negotiate with Panama during the 1970s is further bolstered by evidence that key foreign policy groups and decision makers themselves were influenced by these system changes. For example, former ambassador to Panama William Jorden has attributed the willingness of Secretary of State Henry Kissinger to sign the Joint Statement of Principles in 1974 to a recognition of such changes:

> What made Kissinger willing to face reality in Panama? In two years in the White House working on Latin America, I never felt that he had any real interest in that part of the world. . . . But, with time, that perspective began to change. Great power politics, which shaped the 1950s and 1960s, was no longer adequate in coping with rising, assertive, ambitious, hungry, demanding peoples and nations. . . . Kissinger never liked that harsh fact, but he came to accept it. By 1973, he understood there was an important north-south dimension in world affairs, though he still continued to view the problems and the potential conflicts there in terms of their possible impact on greater power relations.[23]

As for the willingness of the Carter administration to negotiate new treaties, there were numerous statements reflecting the relationship viewed as existing between changes in international system structures and the need for a more flexible, accommodationist foreign policy. One of the most straightforward comes from the Commission on U.S.–Latin American Relations, which argued in 1975 that the relative power of other nations has increased. These nations, including some in Latin America, are playing increasingly effective roles on the international scene. . . . It is now clear that no single nation, not even one as strong and wealthy as the United States, can attain complete economic and political security in today's complex, unsettled, and interdependent world situation. . . . What is needed is greater cooperation among all nations, large and small.[24]

The international system perspective suggests that the relative decline of the global position of the United States influenced the nation's propensity to negotiate during the 1970s, but it does not tell us much about the concrete dynamics of this process. These dynamics resulted from the emergence after World War II of a large number of Third World countries whose view of historical patterns of unequal global relations (such as that which existed between the United States and Panama) was quite different from that of First World countries. Panama had an increasingly sympathetic international audience to play to, and the result was the internationalization of the treaty debate in the early 1970s.

Prior to the 1970s, Panamanian negotiators had not been remiss in attempting to internationalize the Canal issue. During their effort to promote a more equal treaty in 1926, the Panamanians had made an attempt to bring it before the League of Nations. The 1964 riots spurred another effort to bring local events to the attention of the world both through the Organization of American States and the United Nations.[25] However, both the structure of these organizations and the pattern of unequal global power relations that they reflected inhibited meaningful action.

It was the enhanced status of Third World countries within such organizations, a fact that in turn seemed to reflect changes in the global distribution of power, which opened the door for their use as a stage by countries such as Panama. Expansion of the United Nations Security Council in 1965 made possible Panama's strategy of using it as the major institutional vehicle for the dissemination of its case.[26]

As for the concrete impact of Panama's new strategy on the U.S. foreign policy decision-making *process,* Furlong and Scranton observe that it had four major effects. First, the increased international visibility of the issue forced it to higher levels in the bureaucracy, altering the mix of "players." Second, these players became more inclined to take a fresh look at their negotiating objectives. Third, internationalization encouraged sustained high-level U.S. attention to the issue. Finally, foreign-policy decision makers were encouraged to consider the Canal issue within a broader global context that encouraged its resolution.[27]

While the international system perspective has been used to explain certain aspects of treaty ratification (particularly timing) and appears to have considerable merit, there are a number of problems that bear mentioning. To demonstrate that changes in the international system affected the propensity of the United States to negotiate on this issue, one has to demonstrate that such a propensity is associated across time with changes in system structure. However, there are indications that the United States was willing to negotiate meaningful new arrangements with Panama (and for that matter, with the rest of Latin America) *before* any broadly held perception of a global power shift had developed. By December 1964, U.S. negotiators had accepted the concept of Panamanian sovereignty over the Canal Zone and of a fixed termination date for U.S. operation. This was several years before Vietnam began to affect general perceptions of the limits of U.S. power and a decade before the Arab oil embargo.[28]

Another general problem with the international system approach is that it is difficult to apply it to U.S. foreign policy behavior during the 1980s under the Reagan administration. If the proposition holds that there should be a one-to-one correspondence between a decline in objective measures of U.S. relative power and the propensity to accommodate the wishes of allies, then the proposition is obviously in trouble.[29] To explain the foreign policy behavior of the United States in the 1980s, considerable attention has to be paid to changes in domestic system characteristics, which in turn interact with changes in the global environment.

Finally, those who use the international system perspective can be faulted for placing too much emphasis on the behavior of nation states and their central decision-making structures. While this problem is not inherent in the international system approach, it is nonetheless true that there is a tendency to focus mechanistically on the nation states and patterns of interaction among them to the detriment of more subtle system forces. As we shall see, the elite perspective points toward the importance of such forces in the Canal treaty case.

The Linkage Politics Approach

The linkage politics approach to the study of foreign-policy decision making derives from the seminal work of James N. Rosenau in the 1960s. Its origins are to be found in dissatisfaction with the exclusive focus on the "national interest" embedded in writings of international relations scholars, a focus that tended to preclude serious concern with the domestic roots of that interest. The linkage politics approach aimed at overcoming the artificial boundaries between the analysis of international relations and national foreign policy by examining the relationship between elements of the total system at three distinct levels: the domestic political system to the national decision-making bureaucracy, national decision-making bureaucracies to each other, and national decision-making bureaucracies to the international system as a whole. Linkage politics was thus a comprehensive approach examining how the process at any given level impacted on the other levels.[30]

In their book on U.S.-Panamanian relations, David Farnsworth and James McKenney make the linkage politics perspective central to their analysis of the historical pattern of interactions between the two countries. Here I will focus more narrowly on certain aspects of the Canal treaty negotiation process in the 1970s that are illuminated by this perspective, particularly as it relates to national system-to-system linkages and domestic-to-national linkages.

To the extent that the linkage politics approach emphasizes national system-to-system linkages, it highlights an often-neglected aspect of the foreign policy decision-making process: the extent to which successful bilateral diplomacy is the result of the interaction of two decision-making units and the key individuals within them. While it has been noted that the international system context was favorable for the negotiation of new treaties during the mid-1970s, this would appear to be a necessary but not sufficient condition for ratification. Sufficiency was provided by (among other things) the regimes in power at the time in the United States and Panama and their respective leadership.[31]

While President Carter's role in obtaining treaty ratification is fairly well known, less attention has been paid to the remarkable involvement of General Omar Torrijos. In spite of the fact that international system-level developments and three successive U.S. presidential administrations favored movement toward new treaties, it took this unique individual first to partially create a favorable international climate and then to take advantage of it.

Torrijos's ability to internationalize the Canal debate in the early 1970s was due to a combination of personal talent and ideological predisposition. With regard to the former, he was an extremely personable and persuasive individual whose "country bumpkin" manners masked a quick mind. As for the latter, Torrijos was a national populist with whom a variety of Third World leaders (both democratic and authoritarian) could identify. Equally important was his appeal to First World leaders, who saw his populism as more palatable than Marxism-Leninism.

From this perspective, then, the existence of an appropriate international climate was not just a "given" of the 1970s. It was also the product of national-level activity by a very astute new Panamanian leader. According to William Jorden, "The general [Torrijos] said he based his strategy 'on a very simply principle.' That was 'to resolve a problem, the first thing that you have to do is *make* it a problem.'"[32]

In addition to highlighting the importance of national system-to-system interactions in explaining certain aspects of treaty ratification, the linkage politics approach directs our attention to an additional level of analysis. This is the domestic level, which involves the relationship between the national political system and the foreign policy bureaucracy. At this level, we find that the treaty ratification process in both Panama and the United States was very much colored by the *type* of foreign policy issue under discussion.

John Spanier and Eric Uslaner have identified three distinct types of foreign policy, which they have labeled crisis, non-crisis (security), and intermestic. The primary characteristics of crisis policy are their relatively infrequent occurrence and generally short decision time. These characteristics, coupled with the perception of extreme threat, predispose decision makers toward military responses rather than diplomatic negotiation.[33] The non-crisis (security) category differs from crisis policy with regard to its greater frequency of occurrence, lower level of threat to national survival, and longer decision-making time. Such characteristics dictate a sustained role for the president, the executive branch, and Congress, which places a greater premium on professional expertise.[34] Finally, there is intermestic policy, which consists of foreign policy issues with substantial domestic consequences. Such issues tend to affect broad groups of domestic political constituents directly in the form of prices, employment, and wages. Given these domestic consequences, the public is generally more "activated" in relation to intermestic policies and more predisposed toward viewing their resolution in zero-sum terms.[35]

The treaty negotiation and ratification effort under the Carter administration was very much influenced by the fact that the Canal issue in the United States combined aspects of both non-crisis (security) and intermestic policy. According to former secretary of state Cyrus Vance,

> The Panama Canal Zone problem was extremely complicated, bound up as it was with history, intense nationalism, and emotion. It involved far-reaching foreign policy and national security issues interwoven with sensitive political considerations. . . . The question demonstrated the increasingly close relationship between American domestic politics and the conduct of foreign affairs.[36]

The intermestic quality of the Canal issue in the United States was somewhat peculiar in that the public was involved through its general sense of the Canal as a national symbol rather than through more pragmatic and narrowly defined economic interests. This meant that the Carter administration faced a diffuse form of opposition that was a mile wide and an inch deep. Only in the case of residents of the Canal Zone, adherents of the New Right, and certain maritime interests was there a tremendous sense of urgency in opposing the new treaties.

In Panama, however, the situation was quite different. Unlike the United States, where the Canal issue was only partially intermestic, there it was totally so. Since the founding of the republic, there had been a direct relationship not only between the economic health of the nation and the Canal but also between the very definition of its nationhood and the Canal's existence. Thus, for Panamanian politicians, attention given to the Canal issue was attention given to domestic politics, with the attendant "activation" of the entire populace.

As a partially intermestic issue in the United States, the treaty negotiations held the attention of broad groups of Americans. This fact, coupled with the non-crisis (security) dimensions of policy and the fact that it was a new *treaty* being negotiated meant that Congress would also play a major role. As an analytical exercise, then, the task of academic observers has been to find a set of theories or perspectives that fine-tunes our understanding of the role that the public, Congress, and various foreign policy bureaucracies played in the decision-making process.[37]

Perhaps the strongest consensus to emerge from the academic literature on the treaty ratification process during the Carter years was that only a minimal linkage existed between public opinion and the final outcome. Despite the sustained attention the administration paid to its effort to convince the public that the new treaties were in the national interest, five out of every eight Americans remained firmly opposed to them.[38] According to Walter LaFeber, the linkage between the domestic political system and final treaty ratification totally excluded the public, thus constituting a classic example of organizational-institutional decision making. "In the end," LaFeber concludes, "the Senate accepted the agreements not because Carter's public education efforts succeeded. . . . Public opinion had little, if any, effect on the day-to-day Senate debate. . . . The decisive battles occurred in rooms off the Senate floor, not in the feverish public struggle over who could change the course of public opinion."[39]

Were this all there was to the matter, we would be dealing at best with another marginally interesting case of Burkean guided democracy at work, with "enlightened" members of Congress acting in what they perceived to be the best interest of the American public. More interesting, however, is the fact that the Canal treaties appear to have had no natural constituency either among the public at large or within traditional interest groups. As George Moffett puts it, "no *supportive* interest group had a sufficiently direct stake in the outcome of the treaty debate to engage in the kind of high-priority lobbying that might have eased the administration's task in the Senate."[40]

From a theoretical standpoint, the basic problem created by these observations is that the Panama Canal treaties appear to have been ratified *in spite of* the resistance of the American public and also considerable resistance within both Congress and the various foreign policy bureaucracies. Furthermore, as Moffett convincingly demonstrates, ratification occurred *in spite of* the apparent lack of a natural constituency for the treaties among the normal range of lobbying groups.

The absence of such domestic linkages points to the limits of the linkage politics approach for explaining treaty ratification to the extent that it relies on traditional models such as public pressure, organizational process, or bureaucratic politics. The most important remaining question is: Whose interests did ratification of these treaties serve if not the public's, that of Congress, the foreign policy bureaucracies, or traditional interest groups? This brings us to our final perspective.

The Elite Approach

As distinct from the international system and linkage politics perspectives, which stress the importance of factors external to the foreign-policy decision makers themselves, the elite approach focuses on key players. In its purest original form as derived from the work of sociologist C. Wright Mills, this approach stresses the common socioeconomic origins of a group of individuals capable of transforming their economic power into considerable influence over the government decision-making process.[41]

While the linkage politics perspective tends to emphasize the dynamics of interaction between the public and elected and appointed government officials, the elite perspective discounts the independent influence of all three groups. The public is portrayed as largely unconcerned with foreign policy initiatives and thus as susceptible to manipulation by the elite. As for elected and appointed officials, they are viewed as either being subject to elite influence or, in the case of high government appointees, representatives of the nongovernmental elite class itself.[42]

The variant of the elite perspective that seems most appropriate to the Panama Canal treaty decision posits the existence of a foreign policy elite that originated at the close of World War I. The United States had emerged from the war as the paramount Western power, yet the nation's traditional isolationist impulse rendered it ill-prepared to accept a larger global role. Responding to the tendency of Congress and the public to simply make peace and have done with the world, a group of East Coast (primarily New York) bankers and business leaders formed the Council on Foreign Relations in 1919 to educate the public to the need for a more sustained role.[43]

This particular model suggests, then, that there exists a "liberal establishment" centered around international banking and commercial interests which, through the Council on Foreign Relations and other similar organizations, has heavily influenced the formation and implementation of U.S. foreign policy for most of the twentieth century. Students of the Council argue that the books and policy studies that have emerged from its internal working groups have more often than not become government policy, implemented by members of the Council itself who occupy high government positions.

The case for use of the elite approach in analyzing the Panama Canal treaty decision derives from three observations. First, it appears that the liberal establishment became increasingly interested in the Canal question because of major changes in the structure of the world economy and the position that Panama occupied in relation to these changes. Second, various nongovernmental organizations associated with the liberal establishment gave strong support to the idea that new treaties were needed. And third, some of the key players associated with developing the policy of support for new treaties later occupied critical positions vis-à-vis this issue in the Carter administration.

The liberal establishment's increased interest during the 1970s in new Canal treaties derived from the fact that Panama's role in the world economy had rapidly changed from one of serving as an interoceanic artery to that of facilitating the activities of multinational corporations within an increasingly globalized economy. Within this globalized economy, Panama emerged as the center of an expanding "Latindollar" market. Since Panama's currency was the U.S. dollar, and since New York banks were located in the same time zone, the financial transactions of multinational corporations could be profitably and efficiently handled there out of reach of U.S. regulatory agencies.[44]

Although Panama's role within the international economy increasingly became one of serving as a banking intermediary, the sheer size of these financial transactions and the need for associated facilities, such as transhipment warehouses for multinational production, led to a rapid increase in U.S. direct investment. By 1978, U.S. direct investment in Panama was greater than that in all the rest of Central America and Peru combined. Per capita U.S. investment there was $1,300, eight times the amount invested in oil-producing Venezuela and twenty times that in Brazil and Mexico.[45]

In light of the rapid growth of the U.S. multinational corporations' economic interests in Panama and indeed throughout the hemisphere, the absence of satisfactory treaty arrangements appeared to be a major impediment to the routinization of the new regional relations. According to the elite perspective, the nongovernmental institutions associated with the liberal establishment thus found it appealing in the early 1970s to devise new policies that could be "suggested" to any incoming presidential administration. In mid-1974 the Rockefeller and Ford foundations funded the Commission on U.S.–Latin American Relations.[46] The resulting policy study, entitled *The Americas in a Changing World,* argued for revised treaty arrangements:

> Given present-day international realities, the Canal Zone is an anachronism. . . . The commission believes that reaching an equitable new agreement with Panama regarding the Canal would serve U.S. interests not only in Panama but throughout Latin America by removing one of the last vestiges of Big Stick diplomacy.[47]

The elite perspective, with its emphasis on the staffing of high-level government foreign policy positions by members of important nongovernmental institutions, is supported in the Panama Canal treaty case by a considerable amount of prima facie evidence. The Carter administration as a whole was very much influenced in its personnel decisions by the president's early affiliation with the Trilateral Commission, an offshoot of the Council on Foreign Relations. Former national security adviser Zbigniew Brzezinski notes of the commission that "The new President's specific views on foreign affairs . . . had been formed during his time with the Trilateral Commission."[48]

In staffing the National Security Council after the 1976 election, Brzezinski looked to the Commission on U.S.–Latin American Relations. Noting that the views of some of its key members were more liberal than his own, he asked Robert Pastor (the commission's staff director) to manage Latin American and Caribbean affairs. Sol Linowitz, who had served as the chairman of the commission, was appointed a special negotiator for the new treaties.[49]

As one observer suggested in arguing the elite perspective, the policy study produced by the commission was "not just another think-tank document to be stored away for future reference."[50] Rather, it was the direct reflection of the liberal establishment's most recent thinking on U.S. policy toward Latin America, and it was credible with the new president because of his ties to this establishment. Key commission personnel (Pastor and Linowitz) became central decision makers with regard to treaty policy in the Carter administration, with Pastor drafting the Presidential Review Memorandum in January 1977 that recommended rapid movement toward the conclusion of new Canal treaties.[51]

Despite the plausibility of the elite perspective, it has been explicitly or implicitly rejected by many academic observers. Most categorical in their dismissal are Farnsworth and McKenney, who state that "the assumption that there is a foreign policy establishment and that, if there is one, it can speak with one voice, is questionable."[52] LaFeber mentions the Commission on U.S.–Latin American Relations, referring to it as "privately funded" and in no way implying any elite status.[53] Furlong and Scranton mention neither the Trilateral Commission nor the Commission on U.S.–Latin American Relations.

A critique of the elite perspective as applied to the Panama Canal treaty case can be developed along a number of lines. For example, while George Moffett lends credence to this perspective by frequently citing the role of elite nongovernmental institutions, he ultimately rejects it because of a lack of evidence of active business pressure on Congress during the treaty ratification process.[54] In addition, the argument can be made that there is a lack of evidence for successful establishment manipulation of public opinion. While President Carter formed a blue-ribbon Committee of Americans for the Canal Treaties (COACT) to lobby for ratification, its impact appears to have been negligible.[55]

Those criticisms notwithstanding, the appeal of the elite model is that it purports to explain certain aspects of both timing and decision making that are not completely elucidated by either the international system approach or the linkage politics approach. With regard to timing, movement toward ratification is viewed as responding to new liberal establishment perceptions concerning the relative importance of strategic and economic concerns as they relate to the Canal question. Decision making is viewed as being critically influenced by policies developed in key nongovernmental organizations and then transferred via personnel changes under President Jimmy Carter into the governmental arena.

Conclusion

All three of the theoretical perspectives that we have examined here contributed to an understanding of both the timing of the Panama Canal treaty ratification and the nature of the decision-making process itself. The international systems perspective points to the importance of the climate of detente that existed in the 1970s. This climate, coupled with the perception of three presidential administrations that the growing relative power of Third World countries required movement toward accommodation on symbolically important issues helped create a favorable frame of mind for the Canal negotiations. The linkage politics perspective is particularly useful for examining both the bilateral bargaining between national decision-making bureaucracies and the impact that the unique intermestic nature of the issue in the United States had on the ratification process.

Neither of these two approaches by itself, however, can provide a totally satisfactory explanation for ratification. The international system perspective places too little emphasis on the relative autonomy of national decision makers, making it difficult to explain both the willingness of the Johnson administration to grant major concessions to Panama prior to changes in the structure of the system and the unwillingness of the Reagan administration to implement even more accommodationist global policies after these changes occurred.

Without superimposition of the elite perspective, it is extremely difficult to explain ratification of the new treaties, given that conventional analysis uncovers no key domestic groups whose interests would have been served. The American public, due to its perception of the symbolic importance of "giving away" the Canal in the wake of defeat in Vietnam, remained recalcitrant. The situation within Congress and the various foreign policy bureaucracies was more or less a standoff, and lobbying by interest groups in favor of the treaties was not intense.

It is not the absence of a natural constituency that explains the treaty ratification process but rather the nature of this constituency (the liberal establishment) and the role it played in the process. While the elite perspective has been criticized on the grounds that the liberal establishment did not openly lobby its position in Congress, the elite model suggests that such lobbying would have been viewed as unnecessary and even counterproductive.[56] The internalization of liberal establishment values by key members of both the administration and Congress was sufficient to render lobbying irrelevant, because such internalization made those who held these values the functional equivalent of an "interest group."[57] Also, lacking a proper "face" with which to present the Canal issue to Congress, any open lobbying from the multinational banking and business community would have amplified the populist reaction.[58]

Equally misplaced is the dismissal of the elite argument on the grounds that the liberal establishment failed to effectively use the blue-ribbon COACT commission to lobby the public for new treaties.[59] Their obvious lack of success in this regard only suggested that public opinion was so peripheral to the dynamics of treaty ratification that even a stopgap effort could create sufficient political space for an unwilling Congress to act. Furthermore, the lack of elite success with this particular aspect of the treaty ratification process does not disprove the general thesis that it exercised considerable influence during the policy formation phase.[60]

Most fundamentally, the focus of many academic observers on the process of policy *implementation* (from the inauguration of President Carter through treaty ratification) as opposed to the process of policy *formation* has skewed their analysis in the direction of acceptance of pluralist domestic politics models. While the liberal establishment was active during both phases, it was during the former that its influence was the most pronounced.

The key to understanding the ratification of the 1978 treaties is the temporary compatibility that existed in the late 1970s between the characteristics of the international system and the worldview of the Carter administration. At the global level, there appeared to be opportunities for compromise and accommodation. At the national level, the liberal establishment, through Jimmy Carter and the Trilateral Commission, was able to temporarily reestablish the old foreign policy order. As Robert Schulzinger points out, the establishment was "at bay," but it still had sufficient bite to ward off its pursuers through one more presidential administration.[61]

A number of other factors facilitated treaty ratification in spite of an unenthusiastic Congress and a hostile public. Despite the fact that the nongovernmental institutions of the liberal establishment were increasingly pulling in different policy directions in the wake of the Vietnam debacle, there was general agreement as to the value of new Canal treaties.[62] Furthermore, the fact that President Carter and his foreign policy advisers chose to make the Canal treaty issue an early test of their ability to achieve victory in the more important matter of the ratification of SALT II meant that they could take full advantage of the presidential honeymoon period with Congress.[63]

The liberal establishment's ability to control the agenda of treaty negotiation and ratification was greatly facilitated by the fact that the issue was largely handled apart from routine foreign policy channels. While Brzezinski remained almost exclusively concerned with more important global issues—such as arms control, U.S. relations with the Soviet Union and China, and the Middle East—Sol Linowitz and others associated with the Commission on U.S.–Latin American Relations proceeded on an independent track with the Canal question.[64] From such a perspective, implementation of this policy proved to be a special case of elite influence within a broader foreign policy decision-making environment less conducive to its complete exercise.

Did this decision-making process produce treaties that can be deemed successful? Certainly the foreign policy officials associated with the Carter administration have considered them so. According to Brzezinski, "Ratifying the treaty was seen by us as a necessary precondition for a more mature and historically more just relationship with Central America, a region which we had never understood too well and which we occasionally dominate. . . . It was a new beginning, and I was proud of our achievement."[65] Although disagreeing with Brzezinski on a number of issues, former secretary of state Vance concurred on this one: "It is difficult to imagine how the United States could deal in any affirmative way with the turbulence in Central America and the Caribbean today if, in addition to problems in Nicaragua and El Salvador, we also confronted Panamanian nationalism directed against the canal and the Canal Zone."[66]

Vance is no doubt correct in his assessment of the negative consequences for the U.S. position in Central America had the treaties not been ratified. But it is also clear that the Carter administration did not view the Canal question as part of its Central American policy.[67] The administration's Central American policy emphasized the universal application of human rights principles and, as such, antagonized regional authoritarian governments in Nicaragua, Guatemala, and El Salvador.[68] Because treaty opponents in the United States wished to use the human rights issue to undermine the ratification process by branding General Torrijos a repressive dictator, the administration had to be careful to compartmentalize the case of U.S.-Panamanian relations. From this point of view, there would appear to be a certain amount of ex post facto justification by former Carter foreign policy officials of the treaties' success as a component of a broader Central American strategy.

Whether the Panama Canal treaties will continue to serve as a force for stability in a turbulent region very much depends on whether they survive the crisis now facing the military regime in Panama. In 1987 the political opposition held large public demonstrations following accusations that the commander in chief of the defense forces, General Manuel Antonio Noriega, was involved in assassinations, drug trafficking, and electoral fraud.[69] As the crisis deepens, politicians are increasingly tempted to revive the Canal issue and to question the permanent status of the 1978 treaties. Since treaty relations with the United States continue to be an important intermestic issue in Panama, it remains to be seen whether any successor regime will recognize their continuing validity.

Judging success or failure in the very long term is a task that will have to be left to a future generation of historians. The treaties will create a relationship after the year 2000 between the United States and Panama similar to that which existed between the United States and Colombia following signing of the Bidlack-Mallarino Treaty in 1846. U.S. power will be exercised not through a physical military presence but through the Neutrality Treaty, which guarantees unimpeded transit across the isthmus. Whether a treaty relationship that served U.S. interests well in the middle of the last century will do so in the next remains to be seen.

Notes

1. Walter LaFeber, *The Panama Canal: The Crisis in Historical Perspective* (New York: Oxford University Press, 1978), and William L. Furlong and Margaret E. Scranton, *The Dynamics of Foreign Policymaking: The President, the Congress, and the Panama Canal Treaties* (Boulder, Colo.: Westview Press, 1984).

2. David N. Farnsworth and James W. McKenney, *U.S.-Panama Relations, 1903–1978: A Study in Linkage Politics* (Boulder, Colo.: Westview Press, 1983).

3. From this perspective, it was the strengthening of the state through previous treaty changes that later put the state under Omar Torrijos in a position to negotiate the 1978 treaties.

4. U.S. Congress, Senate, Committee on Foreign Relations, *Hearings on the Panama Canal Treaties*, 95th Congress, 1st session, September 1977, Part I, p. 588.

5. LaFeber, *Panama Canal*, pp. 124–28.

6. Ibid., pp. 143–46; and William J. Jorden, *Panama Odyssey* (Austin: University of Texas Press, 1984), pp. 99–102.

7. Jorden, *Panama Odyssey*, p. 100.

8. Furlong and Scranton, *Foreign Policymaking*, pp. 32–33; and LaFeber, *Panama Canal*, p. 184.

9. Jorden, *Panama Odyssey*, p. 91.

10. Ropp, *Panamanian Politics: From Guarded Nation to National Guard* (New York: Praeger, 1982), p. 10.

11. These regional allies played a critical role in the negotiation process because Torrijos was careful to pick the heads of democratically elected governments. They included presidents Alfonso López Michelsen of Colombia, Daniel Oduber of Costa Rica, and Carlos Andrés Pérez of Venezuela. Ropp, *Panamanian Politics*, p. 104.

12. Just as with the conceptual shift in President Johnson's thinking concerning the Canal issue, a critical role was played by individuals who did not share the limelight with Nixon and Kissinger in February 1974 when the joint statement was signed. Panamanian foreign minister Juan Antonio Tack actually proposed this new framework in May 1973, and it was Kissinger's special representative to Panama, Ellsworth Bunker, who gave it strong inside support. Jorden, *Panama Odyssey*, pp. 203–16.

13. LaFeber, *Panama Canal*, pp. 185–90.

14. Furlong and Scranton, *Foreign Policymaking*, pp. 36–37.

15. Ropp, *Panamanian Politics*, p. 105.

16. Maurice East, "The International System Perspective and Foreign Policy," in Maurice A. East, Stephen A. Salmore, and Charles F. Hermann, eds., *Why Nations Act: Theoretical Perspectives for Comparative Foreign Policy Studies* (Beverly Hills, Calif.: Sage Publications, 1978), p. 143.

17. Ibid., p. 150.

18. John Lewis Gaddis, *Strategies of Containment: A Critical Appraisal of Postwar American National Security Policy* (New York: Oxford University Press, 1982), p. 346.

19. Gaddis says of the Carter administration that "there was among leaders . . . an almost desperate determination to establish a distinctive identity for it, to break out from under the lengthy and intimidating shadow of Henry Kissinger." Ibid., p. 346.

20. Kenneth A. Oye, "International Systems Structure and American Foreign Policy," in Kenneth A. Oye, Robert J. Lieber, and Donald Rothchild, eds., *Eagle Defiant: United States Foreign Policy in the 1980s* (Boston: Little, Brown, 1983), pp. 3–4.

21. LaFeber, *Panama Canal*, p. 197.

22. James Kurth also takes a broad historical perspective on the Canal treaty negotiations. Kurth argues that the hegemonic system that the United States established over the Central American countries, including Panama, had largely disappeared by the 1970s and that policymakers in all presidential administrations had by that time rejected the foreign-policy assumptions that hegemony produced. From Kurth's perspective, negotiation of the Panama Canal treaties was an effort to preserve as much of the hegemonic system as

possible under current conditions. "Like Roosevelt in Mexico," Kurth states, "the Carter administration recognized in the Panama Canal issue the value of a satisfied Panama still nestled within a wider American strategic and economic framework." James Kurth, "The United States, Latin America and the World: The Changing International Context of United States–Latin American Relations," Latin America Working Paper no. 148, the Wilson Center, 1984, mimeographed, p. 12.

23. Jorden, *Panama Odyssey*, p. 206.

24. *The Americas in a Changing World* (New York: Center for Inter-American Relations, 1975), p. 14.

25. Farnsworth and McKenney, *U.S.-Panama Relations*, pp. 122–23.

26. Ibid., p. 121.

27. Furlong and Scranton argue, for example, that Defense Department officials were more encouraged to view the Canal in the context of the possibility there of guerrilla war. *Foreign Policymaking*, p. 49.

28. Another possible explanation for the 1964 policy shift is benevolence. Part of the problem of explaining U.S. policy in terms of American benevolence seems to be a broadly based academic skepticism of U.S. motives. After Vietnam it was increasingly difficult for the academic community to imagine that the United States could make concessions that were not forced on it or otherwise act magnanimously toward weaker countries.

29. Recent U.S. foreign policy toward New Zealand and Australia is a case in point.

30. James N. Rosenau, ed., *Linkage Politics: Essays on the Convergence of National and International Systems* (New York: Free Press, 1969), p. 3.

31. Furlong and Scranton argue that a "bargaining window" was created during the early 1970s for U.S. and Panamanian negotiators due to the existence of detente. This window had closed by the late 1970s with the change in the East-West climate. *Foreign Policymaking*, p. 13.

32. Jorden, *Panama Odyssey*, p. 176.

33. These general characteristics of crisis policy making are sometimes altered in specific cases. For example, the Iranian hostage crisis during the Carter administration combined the perception of extreme threat with long decision time. John Spanier and Eric M. Uslaner, *American Foreign Policy Making and the Democratic Dilemmas* (New York: Holt, Rinehart and Winston, 1985), pp. 12–13.

34. Ibid., pp. 17–18.

35. Ibid., p. 13.

36. Cyrus Vance, *Hard Choices: Critical Years in America's Foreign Policy* (New York: Simon and Schuster, 1983), p. 140.

37. To deal with this analytical problem, Furlong and Scranton propose an eclectic approach. They first stress organizational dynamics, including those related to the separation of powers, different points of view held by competing bureaucracies, and the existence of policy coalitions that cut across bu-

reaucracies. To this they add a bargaining approach that emphasizes the conditions necessary for the internal resolution of conflict over any such issue. *Foreign Policymaking,* pp. 4–10.

38. The best study of public opinion on the issue is Bernard Roshco, "The Polls: Polling on Panama—Si; Don't Know; Hell, No" *Public Opinion Quarterly* 42 (Winter 1978): 562. As Roshco puts it, "The trend that was confirmed most strongly [in U.S. opinion on the Canal treaties issue] could have been graphed with a straight horizontal line" (p. 562).

39. LaFeber, *Panama Canal,* p. 234.

40. George D. Moffett III, *The Limits of Victory: The Ratification of the Panama Canal Treaties* (Ithaca, N.Y.: Cornell University Press, 1985), p. 14.

41. Barry B. Hughes, *The Domestic Context of American Foreign Policy* (San Francisco: W. H. Freeman and Co., 1978), p. 13.

42. Ibid., pp. 13–14.

43. Robert D. Schulzinger, *The Wise Men of Foreign Affairs: The History of the Council on Foreign Relations* (New York: Columbia University Press, 1984), pp. 1–30; and Laurence H. Shoup and William Minter, *Imperial Brain Trust: The Council on Foreign Relations and United States Foreign Policy* (New York: Monthly Review Press, 1977), pp. 1–12.

44. Ropp, *Panamanian Politics,* p. 108.

45. Ibid.

46. That the Commission on U.S.–Latin American Relations was in general agreement with (if not a direct clone of) the Council on Foreign Relations seems clear from the fact that three members of the commission were also directors of the council. They were W. Michael Blumenthal, Nicholas Katzenbach, and Peter G. Peterson. *The Americas,* pp. 3–4; and Laurence Shoup, *The Carter Presidency and Beyond: Power and Politics in the 1980s* (Palo Alto, Calif.: Ramparts Press, 1980), p. 291.

47. *The Americas,* p. 31.

48. Zbigniew Brzezinski, *Power and Principle: Memoirs of the National Security Adviser, 1977–1981* (New York: Farrar, Straus, and Giroux, 1983), p. 49.

49. Ibid., pp. 74–75, 135.

50. Alan Howard, "The Real Latin American Policy," *Nation,* October 15, 1977, p. 365.

51. Brzezinski, *Power and Principle,* p. 51.

52. Farnsworth and McKenney, *U.S.-Panama Relations,* p. 255.

53. LaFeber, *Panama Canal,* p. 194.

54. Moffett states that "as it happened, U.S. businesses never did play a major role, either in the formulation or in the ratification of the new Panama policy." Of all the recent studies of the treaty negotiation process, Moffett's is the only one to seriously flirt with the elite perspective, but he ends up backing away from the theoretical implications of his own analysis. Moffett, *Limits of Victory,* p. 147.

55. The chairman of this committee was Averell Harriman, dean of the liberal foreign-policy establishment. Steve C. Ropp, "Ratification of the Panama Canal Treaties: The Muted Debate," *World Affairs* 141 (Spring 1979): 286.

56. Moffett makes the absence of business lobbying central to his case against the elite perspective. However, to demonstrate that traditional business groups such as the National Association of Manufacturers did not lobby strongly for ratification ignores critical differences within the "business community" along a domestic-international interest axis. *Limits of Victory*, pp. 162–63.

57. This was particularly true in Congress with regard to certain senators on the Foreign Relations Committee.

58. Ropp, "Ratification," p. 287.

59. See Moffett, *Limits of Victory*, p. 84.

60. COACT was really an outward manifestation of the more important liberal establishment consensus already institutionalized within the Carter administration bureaucracy through certain key appointments. It had little importance in its own right.

61. Schulzinger, *Wise Men of Foreign Affairs*, pp. 209–42.

62. Moffett argues that "within the ranks of the nation's Establishment foreign-policy elite, the treaties were the object of the first broad-based consensus since the Vietnam War." *Limits of Victory*, p. 10.

63. Furlong and Scranton, *Foreign Policymaking*, p. 85.

64. It is clear that the Panama Canal treaty was not a matter that Brzezinski himself spent a great deal of time on. He viewed it as a second-tier issue, important in its own right for improving relations with Latin America but more important as a symbol of President Carter's ability to deal effectively with larger global issues. When the Senate vote on the treaties was taken on 18 April, he noted that "If we had lost, there is no doubt that our policy on SALT and most importantly on the Middle East would have been dead ducks." *Power and Principle*, pp. 138–39.

65. Ibid., p. 139.

66. Vance, *Hard Choices*, p. 156.

67. Richard Feinberg states that "the Carter administration's first policy thrusts in the Central American region were the negotiation and ratification of the new Panama Canal Treaties and the initiation of a process of normalizing relations with Cuba. Neither was seen as a Central American issue per se." Richard E. Feinberg, "The Recent Rapid Redefinition of U.S. Interests and Diplomacy in Central America," in Richard E. Feinberg, ed., *Central America: International Dimensions of the Crisis* (New York: Holmes and Meier, 1982), p. 60.

68. Ibid., pp. 60–61.

69. Steve C. Ropp, "General Noriega's Panama" *Current History* 85 (December 1986).

Jack Child

War in the South Atlantic

The Unfolding and Managing of the Crisis

The Background to 1981

The historical literature on the South Atlantic War is rich, especially from the Argentine side, but it yields little information on the U.S. role, which was minimal until 1982.[1] Nevertheless, the Argentine recollection of that role is an unhappy one, based on the incident in December 1831 when a U.S. warship expelled a group of Argentine settlers from the Falkland Islands and paved the way for the beginning of British occupation in January 1833. Further, when that occupation came, the Argentines were disappointed that the United States made no effort to apply the recently proclaimed Monroe Doctrine.

From the British perspective, the issue was quiescent until the first Perón administration, when Argentine claims to the Falkland/Malvinas Islands (as well as the other South Atlantic islands and Antarctica) were revitalized as part of Juan Perón's nationalistic "Third Position" policies. The Argentines won a diplomatic victory with UN Resolution 2065 of 1965, which labeled the islands a "colony" and urged the governments of Argentina and Great Britain to make progress toward their eventual decolonization.

By the mid-1970s this indeed seemed to be happening, based on a 1971 bilateral agreement to gradually integrate the islanders into Argentine economic and transportation systems. Talk of a Hong Kong "lease-back" solution was in the air in the late 1970s, although the kelpers (i.e., the islanders) opposed it. Further complicating matters were perceptions of increasingly important energy and food resources, and the approach of the symbolic date of 1983, which to the

Argentine people represented a century and a half of unjust deprivation of something that was unquestionably theirs.

Historically, U.S.-Argentine relations have never been close, and they became considerably strained during the Jimmy Carter years over a number of issues, most notably severe U.S. criticism of Argentina's deplorable human rights record during the period of the "dirty war" against left-wing subversives. Thus the November 1980 Reagan victory was greeted with delight by Argentina's military rulers, who were pleased by visits from Reagan emissaries in the early part of his administration, and indeed even during the transition process.[2] General Roberto Eduardo Viola assumed the Argentine presidency only a few months after Ronald Reagan became president, and Viola was the subject of some courting even before that time.[3] The essence of the message being sent in these early days of the Reagan and Viola presidencies was that the United States was seeking to improve the ties strained during the Carter years and that there was interest in having Argentina play an important part in supporting U.S. policies in the hemisphere, especially in Central America.

Galtieri and the Junta, 1981

Lieutenant General Leopoldo F. Galtieri was an otherwise unremarkable commander of the Argentine army who possessed a key trait: he was the most pro-American of the Argentine military leadership at a time when the new Reagan administration was forging its close relationship with Argentina. Thus, partly out of ideology and personal relationships and partly out of opportunism, General Galtieri became the Reagan administration's perfect "man in Buenos Aires." In an historic interview after the defeat on the islands, Galtieri referred to himself as Washington's "niño mimado" ("spoiled child" or "favored one"), who had done important favors for the Americans and who received preferential treatment.[4]

In August 1981 Galtieri traveled to the United States at the special invitation of U.S. Army Chief of Staff General Edward Meyer and received strong assurances of Argentina's growing importance in U.S. strategic plans for the hemisphere. Three months later Galtieri was back in Washington to attend the XIV Conference of American Armies, where he was again the object of considerable high-level attention by U.S. officials.

The key topic at most of these meetings was the Reagan adminis-

19 March: Argentine salvage workers land in South Georgia. British send HMS *Endurance* to evict them.

1 April (Thursday): Great Britain calls for UN Security Council session. President Reagan calls General Galtieri (8:21 EST) asking that he stop the invasion.

2 April (Friday): Argentina invades the Islands, U.K. breaks relations with Argentina. The European Economic Community condemns Argentine actions.

3 April (Saturday): UN Security Council adopts British proposal (Resolution 502) demanding Argentine withdrawal, cessation of hostilities and diplomatic solution.

8–19 April: Haig shuttle diplomacy between Washington, London, and Buenos Aires.

13 April: OAS resolution expresses concern over developments; splits are exacerbated between the English- and Spanish-speaking nations in the OAS.

25 April: British retake South Georgia.

26 April: OAS meets; Costa Méndez is received effusively, Haig gets cold reception. Resolution on 28 April backs Argentine position.

30 April: U.S. announces sanctions against Argentina and promises to respond positively to British requests for military aid.

2 May: Peruvian and UN (Pérez de Cuellar) peace initiatives launched; cruiser *Belgrano* sunk.

21 May: British forces land on the islands.

28 May: Meeting under Rio Treaty procedures; OAS passes a resolution which condemns U.K. and the support provided by U.S.

2 June: Argentines seek ceasefire through UN.

4 June: Vote on UN ceasefire: British veto; U.S. (Kirkpatrick) initially vetoes then tries to change vote.

11 June: The final battle for Port Stanley begins.

14 June: Argentines surrender at Port Stanley.

Figure 1. Key Events of the South Atlantic War, 1982

tration's perception of the subversive Marxist-Leninist threat in Central America and the role that the Argentine military could (and did) play in countering that threat through an ambitious program of overt and covert activities in Honduras, Nicaragua, and El Salvador. Although his hosts stressed the Central American crisis area, Galtieri's personal agenda included a great deal more than countering guerrillas there. Galtieri was in effect assuming a burden in exchange for Washington's support of a greater subregional geopolitical role for Argentina in the Southern Cone and the South Atlantic.[5]

Shortly after these two key trips to the United States, Galtieri pushed aside the ailing President Viola and assumed the presidency in December 1981. A key element in this changing of the president-generals was the personal support given Galtieri by the hard-line commander of the navy, Admiral Jorge Anaya. The price of Anaya's support appears to have been that Galtieri would back Anaya in his personal dream of recovering the Malvinas before the 150th anniversary of British control in 1983. It is in this context that Washington's messages of support for Argentina must be interpreted.

These messages intensified in late 1981 and early 1982. They included visits to Argentina by Ambassador-at-Large General Vernon Walters, UN Ambassador Jeane Kirkpatrick, Assistant Secretary of State Thomas Enders, Army Chief of Staff General Edward Meyer, and many others. At the same time, General Galtieri's man in Washington, military attaché General Mallea Gil, was receiving similar messages from his impressive range of contacts high in the administration.

In the wake of the conflict, much attention has focused on the content of these "messages" and on whether they included explicit or implicit assurances that the United States would support Argentina in its plans to retake the Falkland/Malvinas Islands, or at least remain neutral. The issue is important because it forms the basis for Argentine accusations of betrayal by the United States. In this connection it is illustrative that Galtieri himself stated that he never asked for an explicit assurance and was never given one.[6] At the less explicit level it can be argued that the sudden warming of Washington's relations with Buenos Aires was in effect a "wink and a nod" that the Argentine military, with their inherent tendency to believe what they wanted to believe, could reasonably take as support for their Falkland/Malvinas plans.[7]

January–February 1982: The Warning Signs

The first two months of 1982 were a period in which U.S.-Argentine cooperation continued in Central America and elsewhere. It was also the period in which the junta finalized its plans for taking the islands by force and attempted to test the U.S. reaction to such a contingency.

The most obvious such test was a late January column in the prestigious daily *La Prensa* written by a journalist with good government contacts.[8] Titled "The Foreign Offensive," it laid out what in hindsight turned out to be the junta's grand scheme: In the very near future Argentina would present Great Britain with a demand for meaningful negotiations on Malvinas sovereignty; should the British refuse, Argentina would break off the talks and would be free to take the islands by force. Part of this plan was the belief that Washington understood Argentina's position and had expressed support for its actions. The column went on to note that the military operation would be relatively easy and that the kelpers would support it. The *Prensa* column duly appeared in the Central Intelligence Agency's unclassified English-language *Foreign Broadcast Information Service* the following week and was also presumably the subject of classified reports from the U.S. embassy in Buenos Aires.

At about the same time, the Argentines were entertaining a U.S. congressional delegation passing through Buenos Aires on a vacation junket. Foreign Minister Nicanor Costa Méndez seized the opportunity to brief the senators and congressmen on the high priority that Argentina placed on recovering the islands. To his dismay, they were not even aware of the existence of the islands, and did not seem to care much about them.[9]

March 1982: The Enders Visit and the Georgia Incidents

From the Argentine perspective, the visit of Assistant Secretary of State Thomas Enders to Buenos Aires in early March 1982 was a key one, and there is some controversy over exactly what transpired during that visit. Enders was making a fairly routine swing through South America, and the principal items on his Argentine agenda had to do with U.S.-Argentine cooperation in Central America. However, Argentine sources claim that Costa Méndez told him that the Malvinas issue was going to heat up soon and specifically asked him what the U.S. attitude would be. According to these Argentine sources, Enders's reply was "hands off," which the Argentine government interpreted to mean that the United States would not attempt to stop Argentina from recovering the islands.[10] British government sources, which tended not to trust the "Latinamericanists" in the U.S. State

Department, have also indicated that Enders gave the Argentines encouragement during this visit.[11]

By late March the British were becoming alarmed over the incidents involving Argentine workers who raised their flag while removing scrap metal under contract on the island of South Georgia and the hard-line Argentine response to British attempts to get them off the island. On 28 March the British asked Washington to intercede with Buenos Aires to cool the issue; by the thirtieth, U.S. intelligence was picking up indications of unusual Argentine troop movements.[12]

1–2 April: Last-Minute Attempts to Stop the Invasion

Clearly, the U.S. government had been caught off guard by the Argentine preparations to invade the Falkland/Malvinas Islands. There had been ample diplomatic and intelligence warnings, but they had not made much of an impression in the White House or the State Department. For some British observers, the explanation was more sinister and had to do with suspicions that Washington so valued the Central American support of its newfound Argentine ally that it was condoning its actions.[13]

On the eve of the invasion (Friday, 1 April) Secretary of State Alexander M. Haig set up a telephone conversation between Presidents Galtieri and Reagan. After a two-hour delay in which Galtieri was "unavailable" to speak to Reagan, he finally came on the line. It was a little past 8 P.M. in Washington (10 P.M. in Buenos Aires). The extraordinary conversation, which began with Galtieri's halting English and quickly switched to using interpreters, lasted almost an hour; it was reportedly the longest phone conversation Reagan had ever had with a chief of state.[14] In it Reagan expressed his concern, warned that an Argentine invasion would harm relations with the United States, and gave Galtieri his frank assessment that Prime Minister Margaret Thatcher would respond with force. Galtieri was polite but evasive and refused to give Reagan an assurance that Argentina would not invade; Galtieri knew that the invasion was already under way and could not be stopped.

3–7 April: Initial Reactions

Once the initial shock had worn off, the reaction in much of official (as well as unofficial) Washington was to make light of a crisis that was seen as anachronistic, if not downright comic opera. But the British government saw little humor in the situation and quickly made requests for strong U.S. action. The State Department demurred, arguing that it would exercise more effective leverage with Argentina by remaining neutral.[15]

The British were successful in getting a quick UN Security Council Resolution (502) on 3 April. It condemned the Argentine use of force and called for immediate withdrawal of all Argentine forces from the islands. The resolution was important because Great Britain and the United States based much of their subsequent actions on the resolution's demand for Argentine withdrawal. The vote also showed how badly Argentina's leaders had misjudged their support from the start, since they had apparently counted on a veto from the Soviet Union (because of its trade relationship with Argentina) and had hoped for a U.S. abstention. There were indications that in the inner circles of the U.S. government Ambassador Kirkpatrick had argued for a U.S. abstention, or at least a delay in the vote.[16] It is telling that Kirkpatrick was absent from the UN during the debate and voting.

8–19 April: Haig's Shuttle Diplomacy

The twelve days of Haig's shuttle diplomacy between Washington, London, and Buenos Aires were a unique period in the history of U.S.–Latin American relations. Rarely has a hemispheric problem consumed so much of the time, attention, and energies of the U.S. secretary of state, and never before has a U.S. official of this rank employed the mechanism of continuous travel in this manner in Latin America.

President Reagan and Haig made the decision to undertake shuttle diplomacy on 6 April. In his memoirs Haig says that he was under considerable pressure from both the British and Argentine governments to take a direct role; others have less charitably suggested Haig was eager to show that he could play at shuttle diplomacy just as well as his mentor, Henry Kissinger.[17] The mission got off to a rocky start with a squabble over the aircraft Haig would use. Haig rejected the first aircraft made available to him because, he said, it lacked adequate communications and office facilities, but according to his critics it was because it had no windows and was not prestigious enough.

The general problem faced by Haig and his shuttle team was to bridge a profound gap between two stubborn opponents who rightly perceived that political or military defeat could bring about the fall of their government. A formula had to be found that would allow one (or both) sides to back away from extreme positions without seeming to do so. For Argentina the key issue was sovereignty: Galtieri could not survive politically if he accepted a solution that did not give Argentina sovereignty, or at least a guarantee of sovereignty in a relatively short period of time. For the Thatcher government the paramount concerns were that Argentine aggression not be rewarded by sovereignty and that the islanders be free to choose the form of government they desired (obviously British).

What emerged from Haig's shuttle diplomacy came to be called "Haig I" or the "five-point plan." The basic elements addressed by the proposal were:

(1) a cease-fire and a withdrawal of Argentine and British forces from the islands to some specific point;
(2) interim administration of the islands by some form of tripartite arrangement, with British and Argentine participation;
(3) restoration of normal communications and transportation links to the mainland;
(4) a commitment to negotiate the long-term status of the islands with the assistance of a third party;
(5) consultation with the kelpers to find out their views.[18]

Haig went first to London (on 8 April), where he found a determined Margaret Thatcher not inclined to accept a compromise until the Argentines complied with UN Resolution 502 by withdrawing from the islands. Haig reassured the British that the United States supported them on the basic issues of principle, and that, unlike in Suez, the United States was a trustworthy ally. He also recognized that the Argentines would have to make significant concessions if an agreement was to be reached, especially on the sovereignty issue.

Upon arriving in Buenos Aires on 9 April the Haig team was faced with some Argentine realities: the whole nation was deeply committed emotionally to the recovery of the Malvinas, and any retreat from that recovery was practically impossible. Haig was also deeply frustrated in dealing with the Argentine government because of the peculiar (indeed, sometimes nonexistent) decision-making process involved. Costa Méndez had no real authority, and commitments made by him would consistently be overruled by the junta. Within the junta, Admiral Anaya was the most unyielding; the air force commander, Brigadier Basilio Lami Dozo, was consistently more flexible; and General Galtieri seemed to bend and vacillate as different pressures were placed on him. The U.S. delegation also learned that even the junta's power was limited, since any important matters first had to be cleared with senior military commanders, who exercised a veto.

Haig's return trips to London (12–13 April) and Buenos Aires (15–19 April) produced some concessions on both sides but not enough to bridge the gap as the British task force neared South Georgia and time ran out. The Argentines began to show increasing distrust and even hostility to Haig as basic U.S. support for Great Britain became clear. The Argentine press in particular stressed that no concessions could be made on sovereignty and that the Haig team was only stalling to gain time for the British fleet. Ironically, a similar current of opinion in London held that the Argentines were using Haig to stall until winter and bad weather would make British military efforts impossible.

Midway through the Haig shuttle effort, the OAS took its first formal action: a bland resolution of concern on 13 April, which offered the friendly cooperation of the OAS to assist in getting peacemaking efforts under way. The OAS motion came out of the Permanent Council, in which there was an obvious split between the Latin American and the English-speaking nations. It was clear to the Argentines that if they wanted strong OAS support, they would have to use the forum of the Rio Treaty's Organ of Consultation, which would have the effect of eliminating from the debate the majority of the English-speaking nations.

20–28 April: The OAS and "Haig II"

The failure of the Haig shuttle odyssey was followed by Costa Méndez's refusal to see Haig and an Argentine rejection of another trip to Buenos Aires by the secretary of state. Coming on the heels of Buenos Aires' rebuff of the last proposals from London, these steps hardened the U.S. attitude and contributed to the late April break with Argentina.

U.S.-Argentine tensions were exacerbated when Buenos Aires called for an OAS meeting under Rio Treaty procedures on 20 April.

The session would include only the twenty-one signatories of the Rio Treaty, and thus only two English-speaking member states (the United States and Trinidad-Tobago). The United States lobbied hard to meet under OAS charter procedures, but the Argentines were able to get a favorable vote on a motion to meet under the Rio Treaty. Over the weekend the British task force entered the geographic limits of the Rio Treaty and retook South Georgia, thus strengthening Argentina's case for invoking the treaty.

The Rio Treaty's XXth Meeting of Consultation of Foreign Ministers held its first session from 26 to 28 April, and in a sense it was a defeat for both Argentina and the United States—for Argentina because she did not get the strong resolution of Latin American support she had hoped for, and for the United States because of the cold reception given Haig. Costa Méndez capitalized on Great Britain's retaking of South Georgia, calling it unwarranted aggression and a clear violation of the Rio Treaty.[19] He was strongly supported by Venezuela, Nicaragua, and Panama, which, for their own reasons, saw some benefit in supporting an "anticolonial struggle." Several key nations (most notably Brazil, Mexico, and Chile) were restrained in their support of Argentina, although only one delegation (Colombia) criticized her.

Haig, stung by Argentina's rebuffs, committed the tactical error of offending many of the OAS nations by emphasizing his own peace-making role (which he said was "continuing") and by arguing that UN Resolution 502 was the best road to peace, thus implicitly criticizing the OAS.[20] He also labeled Argentina the aggressor. The silence that greeted the end of Haig's speech was in stunning contrast to the ovation that followed that of Costa Méndez.

It soon became clear, however, that Argentina did not have the two-thirds majority vote that sanctions require under the Rio Treaty. The result of this first session of the Meeting of Consultation was a relatively mild resolution with no sanctions, though reports circulated that many Latin American delegates delivered private messages of criticism to their Argentine colleagues, much to their shock.[21] The resolution urged Great Britain and Argentina to cease hostilities and deplored the sanctions imposed on Argentina by the European Economic Community. The vote was seventeen in favor, none opposed, and four abstentions (the United States, Trinidad-Tobago, Chile, and Colombia).

During the OAS sessions the United States presented what became known as "Haig II." Dated 27 April 1982, these were the most formal, detailed, and specific U.S. proposals offered during the whole conflict.[22] Although they were similar to Haig I, they were considerably refined. The British clearly had problems with Haig II but were reluctant to reject it. Thus they told Haig that they would be willing to give it serious consideration. The Argentines, still hanging on to their firm position on sovereignty, replied on 29 April that they could not accept Haig II, because it did not give them either effective interim control or assurance of eventual sovereignty. Costa Méndez was later to say that he never "rejected" Haig II but only "made certain observations" on unacceptable provisions, such as giving the islanders a veto power over Argentine sovereignty.[23]

The last few days of April saw a consolidation of profound pro-British sentiment in the U.S. press and Congress, which pushed the Reagan administration into its final break with Argentina on 30 April. The U.S. media had been pro-British from the beginning and frequently criticized Haig and Reagan for their attempts at "evenhandedness." Cartoonists such as Herblock and Oliphant were especially effective, portraying the Argentines as jack-booted dictators. (See cartoon.)

Congress was not far behind. Senate Resolution 382 was approved on 29 April with only one negative vote (that of Jesse Helms). The resolution stated in part that "the United States cannot stand neu-

Copyright, 1982, Universal Press Syndicate. Reprinted with permission. All rights reserved.

tral" and called for implementation of UN Resolution 502 and "full withdrawal of Argentine forces."[24]

29 April–1 May: The Argentine-U.S. Break

After the OAS session and the definitive rejection of Haig II by the Argentines, Haig told the president that hopes for a negotiated peace had practically disappeared and accordingly there was no longer any point in staying neutral. In the face of growing congressional, media, and public pressure, the moment had come to side openly with Britain.

The first steps in this were the imposition of sanctions against Argentina on 30 April. The formal announcement stated that "the United States cannot and will not condone use of unlawful force to solve disputes."[25] The sanctions against Argentina included suspension of commercial military sales (some $5 million per year), further delay in military training funds ($50,000 in such funds was pending certification), and suspension of Export-Import Bank loans and Commodity Credit Corporation loan guarantees (some $235 million was involved). The announcement also stated that the United States would respond positively to British requests for material support, although there would be no direct U.S. military involvement.

The Latin American reaction to the sanctions varied by country and was clearly linked to each nation's interests. As expected, the Argentine response was the loudest and most indignant. But most Latin Americans were not surprised when the United States came out on the British side. They had been expecting this step, and with the failure of Haig's shuttle diplomacy and the arrival of the task force, the time was clearly ripe. There was, however, some feeling that the U.S. proclamations of evenhandedness in April had been deceptive, and there was a belief that it would have been more honest for the United States to have made its sympathies clear from the outset. The sanctions against Argentina caused much resentment, and many Latin Americans believed they were gratuitous, vindictive, and exaggerated. There was also much concern over the nature and amount of U.S. military assistance to the British.

The full extent of this assistance did not emerge until well after the conflict ended. From the beginning the Argentines argued that U.S. assistance was decisive and that they could not reasonably be expected to defeat the world's third most powerful military, supported by a superpower. Understandably, both the United States and Great Britain minimized the importance of the support, especially during the fighting.

In March 1984 the respected British journal *The Economist* carried a startling article that stated flatly: "The British operation to recapture the Falklands in 1982 could not have been mounted, let alone won, without American help."[26] The article detailed the extent and significance of this aid and the fact it began well before the 30 April sanctions. As one example, the United States was apparently prepared to provide the Royal Navy with an American carrier if the British should lose the *Invincible* or the *Hermes*. Secretary of Defense Casper Weinberger, an ardent Anglophile, played a key role in U.S. support for Britain, according to *The Economist*. In the early period the United States provided much of this support secretly in order to keep the "Latinists" in the State Department from finding out about it.

2–26 May: Peruvian and UN Initiatives

After the two major ship losses the first week of May (the ARA *Belgrano* and the HMS *Sheffield*), there was an increasing sense of urgency among both peacemakers and adversaries to use the little time remaining to find a peaceful way out of the conflict. The United States could no longer be considered an evenhanded mediator. Consequently, the Argentines and some of their more vociferous Latin allies increased their verbal hostility toward the United States to the point that any peace plan involving the United States was suspect. The numerous efforts of the various peacemakers operated sometimes at cross-purposes, with the Argentines or British playing one off against the other to gain a perceived advantage. The fact that the principals involved in the two major peace plans of May (President Fernando Belaúnde Terry and UN Secretary-General Javier Pérez de Cuellar) were both Peruvians and onetime political rivals, further complicated matters.

For the United States, Haig's efforts in April could be described as overt attempts at peacemaking. But Haig had not given up hope with their failure and with the U.S. tilt toward Great Britain. Instead, the U.S. peace effort went into its covert stage in May, using the Peruvian president and later the UN secretary-general as its instruments.

This gave rise to the label of "Haig in a poncho" for the proposals that emerged in May, especially that of Belaúnde Terry. The Peruvian plan was quite close to Haig II. Some specific differences involved the creation of a third-party "contact group" and a definitive settlement within a year.[27] For Argentina, the close similarity to Haig II and the continuing role of the United States posed problems. Nevertheless, the U.S.-Peruvian plan apparently came close to being accepted by both sides until it sank in the cold waters of the South Atlantic on 2 May along with the *Belgrano* and the *Sheffield.*

The circumstances surrounding the loss of the *Belgrano* on 2 May remain controversial to this day. Argentine sources claim that she was deliberately sunk on specific orders of the Thatcher government to destroy the last chance for peace.[28] The fact that she was sunk outside the exclusion zone, and the close communications between the submarine captain and London during the thirty hours during which she was stalked lend credence to this argument, which has been picked up by opposition Members of Parliament.[29] The Argentines, and a number of Latin American critics of the United States, also argue that the *Belgrano* was found thanks to U.S. satellite and signal intelligence, and that part of the blame therefore rests with the United States.

The Peruvian plan was publicly released on 5 May, but by that time it was already dead, and the principal diplomatic focus shifted to the UN. Pérez de Cuellar operated with caution, slow motion, and vagueness, much to the alarm of those who saw that combat in the South Atlantic was acquiring its own dynamic. There were some indications of Argentine flexibility on the issue of sovereignty, but ultimately the UN effort, like those that had preceded it, fell apart because of this issue and the issues of self-determination for the islanders, timetables, and geographic boundaries.[30]

U.S.-Argentine relations continued to deteriorate in this period. There was more bitterness directed toward the United States (the "traitor" nation that had deceived Argentina) than Great Britain, which was seen as acting as a natural enemy could be expected to. The extent of U.S. aid to Great Britain was emphasized and indeed exaggerated in the Argentine press, to the point that some observers saw this as an attempt to set up the United States as the scapegoat in case of an Argentine military defeat.

27–29 May: The OAS Again

In late May the OAS entered the picture again at a moment when the British forces were ashore in the Falkland/Malvinas Islands and had begun their slow and steady push toward Puerto Argentino/Port Stanley. In the Rio Treaty's XXth Meeting of Consultation of Foreign Ministers, the Argentines found a supportive Latin American forum. Although their purpose was somewhat unclear, they presumably were seeking to pressure the United States, promote unified Latin American support for their cause, and possibly come away with formal Rio Treaty sanctions against Britain and the United States. They were not able to get sanctions, although they put the United States in an awkward position. The Argentines were also able to portray the South Atlantic War as a continuation of the historic Anglo-Saxon–Latin conflict, presenting it as a North–South anticolonialist struggle. Moreover, the British colonialists had neocolonial U.S. allies. The U.S. concerns over Latin unity and Anglo-Saxon–Latin hostility included the possibility that some Latin nations, most likely Peru and Venezuela, might push for sanctions calling for military action in support of Argentina and might under these provisions send military forces to help Argentina.

The OAS sessions on 27 through 29 May produced some of the bitterest anti-U.S. rhetoric ever heard in that forum.[31] In an emotional tirade that lasted forty-five minutes, Argentine foreign minister Costa Méndez attacked Great Britain's "irrational armed aggression" and accused the United States of turning its back on Latin America. The standing ovation for Costa Méndez was seen as a direct attack on Haig and the United States.[32] Haig attempted to be conciliatory in his speech, but he also argued that Argentina had used force on 2 April and had blocked several promising peace initiatives through its inflexibility.

There was intense lobbying by both Argentina and the United States over the final resolution. Much to Argentina's disappointment, the emotional rhetoric by many Latin American countries did not translate into meaningful and specific action in the form of sanctions under Article 8 of the Rio Treaty.[33] Faced with the probability that sanctions would not receive the necessary two-thirds majority, the Argentines retreated and settled for a general resolution condemning the British for their "unjust and disproportionate attack on Argentina," urged Latin America to support Argentina, and called on the United States to stop helping Great Britain and lift its sanctions. The vote was identical to that of 28 April: seventeen in favor, none against, and four abstentions (U.S., Trinidad-Tobago, Chile, and Colombia).

30 May–14 June: The Last Desperate Search for Peace

As British forces advanced on Puerto Argentino/Port Stanley, the Argentines and their Latin allies in the United Nations mounted a last-ditch attempt to obtain a cease-fire before the final collapse of Argentine resistance. In this process the Argentines showed increasing flexibility in their demands, reaching a point where they apparently were willing to withdraw their forces in exchange for an interim UN administration of the islands. None of this appealed to Mrs. Thatcher, who saw it as an attempt to snatch victory from the grasp of "her boys." The Reagan administration, concerned over the damage that an overwhelming British victory would do to U.S.–Latin American relations, urged that Britain be "magnanimous in victory" and consider a last-minute compromise.[34] The specific UN action was a draft Security Council resolution Spain and Panama produced in early June which called for an immediate cease-fire and a phased military withdrawal by both sides.

The resolution reached a vote on 4 June and led to an incident that has widely been described as the low point in U.S. diplomacy in the UN.[35] Ambassador Joane Kirkpatrick was under firm instructions from Haig to join Great Britain in vetoing the Spanish-Panamanian draft cease-fire resolution. Kirkpatrick, supported by Thomas Enders, had argued against this approach, feeling that it was unnecessary and harmful to U.S.–Latin American relations. When the vote came, she followed her instructions and vetoed the resolution. However, at the last moment Haig (in Paris for the Versailles summit) changed his mind and authorized an abstention, which would have been less galling to the Latin Americans. Because Haig chose to relay his instructions through the State Department rather than trying to reach Kirkpatrick directly, the new instructions arrived after the veto had been cast.

Several subsequent events made the situation worse. For one, Kirkpatrick announced in the Security Council that although the United States could not change its vote, it wanted to go on record that it now preferred an abstention; when reporters got to her after the session, she said, "You don't understand it? I don't understand it either." She later described U.S. diplomacy as that of a "bunch of amateurs." Second, the incident brought into the open the long-simmering squabble between Haig and Kirkpatrick. When Haig was asked why he had not given Kirkpatrick her voting instructions directly, he used a sarcastic military analogy, saying, "You don't talk to a company commander when you have a corps in between." Lastly, when reporters asked President Reagan at a luncheon in London about the incident, he cheerfully admitted knowing nothing about it (he had been asleep when Haig changed his mind, and no one had bothered to tell him). Margaret Thatcher, sitting next to him, was not amused by this blatant example of U.S. diplomatic ineptness. The net result was the worst of both worlds for the United States. It had managed to offend both sides at the same time as it revealed U.S. indecisiveness and splits within the administration.

The Haig-Kirkpatrick fight was exacerbated by a *Newsweek* article that reported a bitter conversation between them. In it Haig accused Kirkpatrick of being unable to think clearly on the Falkland/Malvinas issue because of her emotional ties to the Latin Americans. Kirkpatrick replied that Haig was incapable of understanding the Latin Americans because he had subordinated U.S. foreign policy to British interests.[36]

The British government, meanwhile, was beginning to ponder postvictory realities and suggested that the United States might play a role in defending the Falklands after the Argentines had been thrown off the islands.[37] Conscious of the damage this would cause to its hemispheric relations, the Reagan administration responded negatively, although the mere suggestion caused alarm in Latin America. Ironically, the U.S. push for British "magnanimity in victory" also had a negative impact in Latin America, where it was seen as insulting and patronizing.

The Aftermath

One immediate result of the collapse of Argentine resistance on 14 June 1982 was the fall of the junta and the slow return of Argentina to democracy. With Haig's resignation as secretary of state in late June, many Latin Americans felt that there was a real opportunity for a fresh start in the U.S.–Latin American relationship. Fairly or unfairly, Haig was seen as duplicitous because of the way he had presented himself as evenhanded at a time when the United States was clearly supporting Great Britain.[38]

Under his successor, George Shultz, the State Department indicated a desire for closer relations with Argentina, and the United States quickly lifted the economic sanctions imposed on 30 April. The Argentine transitional government led by retired general Reynaldo Bignone reciprocated by backing away from the Third World and the Non-Aligned Movement stances of the last days of the Galtieri regime. Within a relatively short period, Argentina was back to its normal foreign policy orientation, which stressed independence and a certain correct distance from the United States.[39]

Other issues quickly replaced the Falkland/Malvinas Islands as priority concerns for Latin America: the international debt, Central America, Grenada, migration, drugs, and a host of other problems. For individual Latin American nations, their own national interest and their bilateral relationship with the United States were far more significant than the Falkland/Malvinas Islands or Latin American solidarity. This solidarity was described as being like the River Plate: very broad but not particularly deep.

Within international organizations, the United States took steps to heal the damage caused during the South Atlantic War. The United States supported OAS and UN General Assembly resolutions in the fall of 1982 and subsequent years calling for renewed negotiations between Argentina and Great Britain over the Falkland/Malvinas Islands. These resolutions were seen as diplomatic victories for Argentina because they put pressure on Great Britain to address the sovereignty issue. The November 1982 UN vote was particularly significant as a measure of U.S. good will and intentions toward Argentina and Latin America just before President Reagan's hemisphere trip.[40] The U.S. vote was courted by both Argentina and Great Britain (which wanted at least a U.S. abstention). Prime Minister Thatcher personally appealed to Reagan and was reported to be dismayed when the United States voted with the Latin Americans in favor of the resolution.

Although the war soon faded from the headlines, Latin America (and the Argentines in particular) continued to be concerned over the future of the islands and the possible U.S. role in "Fortress Falklands," which was being installed by the Thatcher government. The greatly enlarged airfield at Port Stanley was a key point. The British insisted that the airfield was being extended to permit air links from

Ascension or the British Isles without expensive and potentially risky in-flight refueling. The Argentines and many Latin Americans saw it differently, arguing that the airfield was intended as a NATO base to control the South Atlantic and protect British, U.S., and NATO interests in that area, the interoceanic passages, and Antarctica.[41]

Key Factors in Managing the Crisis

The Conflict between Pan-Americanism and North Atlantism

The South Atlantic War has often been described as being an especially difficult crisis for the United States to manage because it presented the United States with the classic dilemma of being caught between two warring allies. However, the dilemma was more profound than this analogy suggests, since it was also a question of the United States being caught between two fundamental currents of its foreign policy: Pan-Americanism and North Atlantism.

The Reagan administration's attempt to be a friend of both Argentina and Great Britain and to take an evenhanded approach in the early period of the conflict was essentially an effort to have it both ways by trying to avoid pitting the Pan-American link against the North Atlantic one. If Haig's shuttle diplomacy—or even the U.S.-Peruvian plan—had been successful, he might have pulled it off and finessed the deeper issue of which current had the priority. But Haig was not able to bridge the gap between the Argentine and British positions, and eventually the United States had to give priority to the more fundamental alliance.

There was, however, a price to pay when the United States came out solidly in favor of Great Britain. The immediate price was the end of Argentine support for U.S. policy objectives in Central America. Given the nature of some of those objectives, this was perhaps one of the few positive outcomes of the South Atlantic War. However, the Latin American resentment over U.S. support for Great Britain and the clear preference for the North Atlantic tie has weakened the commitment toward Pan-Americanism and has accelerated the trend toward greater Latin American independence. There is, after the South Atlantic War, less of a likelihood that the Latin American governments will follow U.S. policy initiatives unless it is clearly in their own interest.

The conflict between Pan-Americanism and North Atlantism

showed up during the South Atlantic War in another dimension: within U.S. foreign policy bureaucracies. Most markedly in the State Department, but also in other agencies, individuals and offices took adversarial positions in the conflict. Thus, there was talk of the "Latino Lobby" of hemisphere specialists at State facing off against the "Europeanists" or "NATOers."[42] Assistant Secretary of State Thomas Enders and UN Ambassador Jeane Kirkpatrick were the most prominent Latinists, while Assistant Secretary Lawrence Eagleberger and Defense Secretary Caspar Weinberger were the chief advocates of the North Atlantic priority. Secretary of State Haig straddled the fence for a while, torn between his natural inclination toward the North Atlantic link and his desire to protect the Argentine contribution to his Central American policy initiatives.

The Role Of Pan-Latinism

A key factor in the South Atlantic War crisis was played by another current: Pan-Latinism. Although few U.S. foreign-policy makers will address the issue, it is clear that an enduring tenet of U.S. policy toward Latin America is to make sure that Pan-Latinism does not become the mechanism for effectively organizing anti-American sentiments. Put another way, it is basic U.S. policy to prevent the Latins from ganging up on their northern neighbor, and Pan-Americanism is thus an antidote to Pan-Latinism. The South Atlantic War saw an important strengthening of Pan-Latinism.

With historic roots going back to Simón Bolívar, Pan-Latinism has a contemporary institutional embodiment in the Latin American Economic System (SELA), which is unique among hemisphere institutions in that it includes Cuba but not the United States. It is significant that SELA received much attention during and after the Falklands/Malvinas crisis as a possible vehicle for effective coordination of Latin American approaches to the United States.[43]

During the South Atlantic War, Argentina made strong and explicit appeals to Pan-Latinism, especially after the United States came out in favor of Great Britain. After the key 30 April U.S. sanctions against Argentina, the war was increasingly portrayed by Argentina as pitting the Latins against the Anglo-Saxons (i.e., the United States and Great Britain). It is not a coincidence that one of the themes in Argentine propaganda was that the Anglo-Saxon "pirates" were continuing their centuries-old forays against the Hispanics. This theme acquired a distinctly racist tone, with the Anglo-Saxons portrayed as decadent and materialistic, while the Latins, led by Argentina, were painted as idealistic, noble, and self-sacrificing. Many Latins found some irony in this Argentine propaganda theme because of Argentina's reputation in the hemisphere for believing itself racially superior to those Latin nations with strong infusions of native Indian or African blood.

The Argentines also attempted, with mixed success, to link their Pan-Latinist cause to Third Worldism via the Non-Aligned Movement (NAM). Here the linkage was through the colonialist theme, and the Argentines thus portrayed the Falkland/Malvinas Islands fight as a North-South struggle to rid the hemisphere of one of the last vestiges of colonialism. The Argentines also had some success in using the tenets of dependency theory to argue that the United States was supporting Britain to protect its economic and strategic interests in the hemisphere. As was the case with the racist theme, however, Argentine credibility was somewhat in question because until the war she had been aloof from the NAM.

Finally, the latent anti-Americanism present in much of Latin America was fanned by the South Atlantic War. One of the startling features of the conflict was that there was more antagonism and resentment against the United States than Great Britain. The war seemed to provide a lightning rod for much of this unfocused sentiment by giving it a specific issue.[44]

The Role of the U.S. Media and Public Opinion

U.S. media and public opinion were overwhelmingly in favor of the British side in the South Atlantic War and exerted considerable pressure on the Reagan administration when it was still trying to be the friend of both sides.[45] This inevitably found an echo in Congress, as in the Senate and House Foreign Affairs Committee resolutions of 29 April supporting Britain, and this in turn undoubtedly influenced the Reagan administration to tilt toward Great Britain.

Opinion in the United States went through some well-defined stages. In the early days of the war there was amusement at the comic-opera, anachronistic aspects of the conflict. Images of swaggering tinhorn Latin military dictators squaring off against Victorian, Gilbert and Sullivan Colonel Blimps were prominent in editorial cartoons. So were penguin and sheep jokes. These acquired a more serious tone after the shock of the deaths on the *Belgrano* and the *Sheffield,* and when it became clear that the United States had an important stake in the conflict. In its latter days the conflict was seen as something of a cross between a football game and a morality play, with public opinion and the media rooting for the British "good guys."

A number of reasons explain this clear-cut support of Great Britain. For one, they were seen as the aggrieved party on 2 April. Attempts by academic analysts in the media to explain the historical roots of the Argentine position were not well received. The Argentine use of force in the invasion (although restrained) was quickly condemned by UN Resolution 502, and the effective employment of this resolution by the British was a key element in portraying the Argentines as the aggressors. The image of the Argentine regime as a brutal military dictatorship with a bloody past of human rights violations further swung the balance. It was all too easy to satirize and ridicule the Argentines and their military establishment. There was also a gut admiration for British determination and competence, which contrasted sharply with U.S. military failures in places such as Vietnam and Iran. Thus the British were in a sense surrogates for the American desire for a win.

All of these elements were extraordinarily well managed by the British and their ambassador to the United States, Nicholas Henderson, who ran a sophisticated and highly effective lobbying and public relations campaign.[46] In contrast, the Argentine effort was almost counterproductive, as when full-page ads in major newspapers employed shoddy translation and bombastic rhetorical phrases that did not carry well from Spanish to English.

Idiosyncratic Personality Factors

The key idiosyncratic element in the U.S. management of the Falklands/Malvinas crisis was the personality of Alexander M. Haig. His military background and tutoring under Henry Kissinger on the National Security Council had given him a dynamic "take charge" style that came to the fore during the crisis. This feature of his personality also won him the enmity of White House insiders, who had been eager for an opportunity to cut him down to size, or even, as Haig charges, force him out of office.[47] During the period of shuttle diplomacy there was considerable unkind commentary that Haig was attempting to emulate (and outdo) his mentor's own Mideast shuttles. But the distances were too great, and the psychology of the feuding parties (Latin pride and machismo versus Anglo-Saxon offended principles) was quite different from that of the Middle East hagglers Kissinger had dealt with. The distances involved produced exhausting jet lag, and Haig, who had undergone serious heart surgery not long before, seemed to have an obsessive need to show that these physical factors could not sap his energy.

One key feature in Haig's internecine struggles was his feud with UN Ambassador Jeane Kirkpatrick, noted previously. The academic and the retired general both had strong personalities, their areas of bureaucratic turf overlapped, and they disagreed sharply over a number of issues. Kirkpatrick had done her doctoral dissertation on the Peronist movement in Argentina, and she considered herself the Reagan administration's leading specialist in Latin American affairs; she had also gone to considerable lengths to cultivate the Argentine military regime and its representatives in Washington and at the UN. Thus, when the South Atlantic crisis broke, both Haig and the British were suspicious of her links to the Argentines and the likelihood that as the leader of the "Latino Lobby" in the State Department, she was undermining the efforts of the North Atlanticists in the administration.[48]

The great absentee in the South Atlantic crisis was President Reagan. He seemed to be blandly unconcerned about managing the crisis, made few statements about it, and was seemingly content to let Haig and Kirkpatrick slug it out. Reagan's amiable personality was not particularly effective in dealing with either Galtieri or Thatcher. Thatcher's strong determination was much admired by the administration, and on several occasions Reagan's attempts to urge British moderation were overwhelmed by her single-mindedness.

Dealing with the Argentine Junta

Initially there were some illusions that dealing with a military dictatorship like the Argentine junta would be simpler than dealing with an open democratic government like Great Britain's Ironically, the reverse proved to be true.

The illusions stemmed in part from the mistaken belief that Haig, as a military man, would have some special relationship with the military men who ran Argentina. This belief was bolstered by the fact that Galtieri had studied at U.S. Army schools and that he was the most pro-U.S. Argentine general in recent memory. Further, it was naively believed that the decision-making process in a military dictatorship would be swift and efficient.

Several factors worked against this optimistic view. For one, at key moments the junta was badly split. Costa Méndez, who had been Haig's primary contact, turned out to have relatively little influence on basic decisions, and the Haig shuttle team wasted a great deal of time dealing with him. One U.S. diplomat was quoted as saying that "we literally did not know who we should be talking to."[49]

Even when a position was tentatively agreed on by the three junta members, they were obliged to take it to their subordinate commanders for clearance. These individuals had not been involved in the original decision to invade and were not present at the sessions with the U.S. representatives. Thus they were not well informed of the discussions and harbored some resentment at having been excluded from the original decision. Their reaction was to take extreme positions and veto anything the junta proposed which smacked of backing down. This was especially true on the issue of sovereignty, and it accounts for much of the Argentine inflexibility on this key point. Haig notes the profound frustration he felt on several occasions when, having painstakingly reached an agreement with Costa Méndez and Galtieri, he would learn later that the Argentine position had been changed by these faceless subordinate commanders and that it was back to the starting point.[50]

Multilateral versus Bilateral Channels

In managing the South Atlantic crisis, the United States showed a traditional preference for bilateral over multilateral channels of diplomacy. The reasons for this preference are clear: bilateral channels permitted the United States to bring its weight to bear more effectively, while the multilateral forums gave Argentina the opportunity to marshal Latin American and Third World solidarity against the United States and Great Britain.[51]

In choosing between the two principal multilateral forums, the United States showed a clear preference for the UN, where the U.S. and British veto in the Security Council would effectively block damaging action (although, as the 4 June cease-fire fiasco showed, using the veto could bring a different set of problems). The UN Security Council also provided a far less emotional forum than the OAS, with its Latin American majority and the possibilities for outpourings of strong Pan-Latin rhetoric.

When forced to become involved in the OAS, the United States showed an equally understandable tendency to prefer the OAS Permanent Council rather than the Rio Treaty's Organ of Consultation. There were two reasons for this. For one, the United States believed that UN Resolution 502 was the appropriate basis for negotiations and that Rio Treaty resolutions or sanctions would detract from the UN decision. Further, the OAS Permanent Council is composed of all the member states of the OAS, which at the time of the South Atlantic crisis numbered thirty (of these nineteen were Latin and ten were English-speaking). With the exception of Grenada, all the English-speaking OAS nations basically backed Great Britain. On the other hand, there are only twenty-one Rio Treaty signatories, and of these only two are English-speaking (the United States and Trinidad-Tobago). Thus the more favorable forum for Argentina was the Rio Treaty, which explains the U.S. reluctance to follow this route.

U.S. Communications and Intelligence Failures

The South Atlantic crisis once again showed up the U.S. failures in communications, intelligence, and understanding with regard to Latin America. These were brought out in an especially glaring way in the U.S. failure to anticipate the crisis and the possible unintended messages sent to Argentina prior to the invasion. As Haig himself noted in his 27 May speech at the OAS, a lesson to be learned from the conflict is that it could have been averted "if there had been better communications and confidence among American states."[52] The deeper reality was that the unintended messages, the ignored intelligence indicators, and the mishandling of many aspects of the crisis were but further examples of the U.S. tendency to pay inadequate attention to Latin America until a crisis breaks.

Conclusions

The Range of Assessments

One notable aspect of the South Atlantic crisis is the range of assessments it produced concerning the impact the conflict would have on the hemisphere, the Inter-American System, and U.S.–Latin

American relations. The assessments tended to be pessimistic during the crisis itself but swung more toward the optimistic when the fighting stage ended and things returned more or less to normal.

The pessimistic view was based on much of the rhetoric emanating from Argentina and her principal supporters (Venezuela, Panama, and Nicaragua) in April, May, and June 1982. The central theme in this current of opinion was that the Latin Americans strongly believed that the United States had "betrayed" them and the Inter-American System by first declaring evenhandedness and then swiftly switching over to a decidedly pro-British stance. Many thoughtful Latin Americans were prepared to accept the inevitability of U.S. support for her oldest ally and mother country, but what was not acceptable was the switch, the gratuitous sanctions against Argentina, and the heavy (and initially hidden) level of military support for the British task force. To many, the United States was all too quick to sacrifice the carefully constructed foundations of Pan-Americanism to North Atlantism. To those inclined to find cynical motives in the U.S. behavior, Margaret Thatcher provided one when she called for U.S. involvement in constructing Fortress Falklands: according to these cynics, the United States supported Great Britain because of the strategic significance of a NATO base in the South Atlantic from which to project power into key sea-lanes and Antarctica. For those inclined to seek anti-American themes, the crisis offered a wealth of them: colonialism, neocolonialism, dependency theory, imperialism, North-South conflict, and a continuation of the centuries-old struggle between Latin and Anglo-Saxon.

The optimistic assessment was fairly consistently presented by U.S. policymakers (at least in public), and by those who noted that the expressions of pro-Argentine solidarity in the crisis were somewhat restrained. Proponents of this perspective discounted much of the anti-U.S. solidarity as emotional rhetoric welling forth in the midst of a dramatic crisis and fueled by the Argentine propaganda machine. The optimists concentrated instead on the more dispassionate messages coming through bilateral U.S.–Latin American channels, which strongly undercut the more spectacular rhetorical support for Argentina. As the fighting ended in the South Atlantic, the optimists seemed to be vindicated as Latin America's attention returned to focus on more fundamental issues, such as the debt crisis, and to bilateral problems. The positive moves taken by the United States in late 1982 (OAS and UN votes and Reagan's trip to Latin

America) helped to restore normality. The optimists also tended to stress the long-term possibilities of an anti-Argentine "backlash" based on the historical aloofness of that nation toward the rest of Latin America and on the belief that the crisis was an unnecessary one stemming from internal Argentina political dynamics.

In addition to these two positions, there was a strong realistic current that argued that each Latin American nation's position during and after the crisis was determined by its national interest; rhetorical support for Argentina was tempered by more permanent national concerns. This realistic current placed emphasis on each nation's bilateral relations with the United States (as opposed to its relations with Argentina). Thus the strong support for Argentina evinced by Venezuela, Panama, Nicaragua, and Cuba can be explained (in part, at least) by the impact of the Falklands/Malvinas crisis on their own foreign policy concerns with regard to territorial aspirations or relations with the United States. Likewise, the anti-Argentine positions taken by Chile were driven by strains in the Argentine-Chilean relationship, and those of Colombia by concerns over the parallel between the Falkland/Malvinas Islands and her dispute with Nicaragua over the San Andrés archipelago.

With the benefit of hindsight, the realists now seem to have been the ones closest to the truth. Rhetorical and emotional Latin American messages of support for Argentina can now be seen to have several components. First, there is general agreement that the Falkland/Malvinas Islands should belong to Argentina, and that Argentina deserves Latin American political help in getting them back. Second, there is a great deal of nervousness over the use of force to settle a long-standing territorial dispute, since almost every Latin American country has an historical dispute of one kind or another with a neighbor. Third, no Latin American country was seriously disposed to commit its military forces to Argentina's fight, or even to seriously jeopardize relations with Great Britain or the United States in support of Argentina's cause.

The South Atlantic crisis, as dramatic as it was, may have merely illuminated the generally declining state of U.S.–Latin American relations over a decade or more and shown how much Latin American independence had increased as the U.S. ability to influence hemisphere events weakened. Thus it should perhaps be seen historically more as a symptom than a cause of difficulties in the U.S.–Latin American relationship.

The Impact on Multilateral Relations

Clearly, the multilateral components of U.S.–Latin American relations were damaged by the South Atlantic crisis. The OAS and its peace and security elements have been especially hurt, along with the idealism that supported the Pan-American principles upon which the OAS was founded.[53] In the aftermath of the crisis, the United States and indeed the majority of the hemisphere nations seem less interested in using multilateral channels in any meaningful way. The more extreme calls for moving the OAS or expelling the United States which were heard at the height of the crisis have disappeared, but there is no doubt that significant damage has been done. There is also the danger that the OAS will throw itself into another lengthy and sterile attempt to revise its basic juridical instruments while ignoring the reality that the problem lies with fundamental political relationships, not legal documents.

The Rio Treaty was a special target for attack by many Latin American critics, who felt that the Falklands/Malvinas crisis clearly showed that the treaty would be called on only when it suited U.S. interests.[54] It was now extremely unlikely that the United States would be able to muster the necessary two-thirds majority that the Rio Treaty requires to support anti-Marxist sanctions, as it had been able to do in 1962 and 1964. It is revealing that in the next hemisphere security crisis (Grenada in 1983) the United States apparently did not even consider going to the OAS but instead used selective multilateralism by employing the little known security provisions of the treaty of the Organization of Eastern Caribbean States (OECS). And in the continuing Central American crisis, the United States has avoided the OAS, choosing instead to use covert means or subregional allies, while the principal Latin American initiative, the Contadora process, has also developed outside of the OAS. These events would have been very unlikely in the 1960s or 1970s.

The crisis had a strong impact on the Anglo-Latin (or English-Spanish) polarization that has always existed in the OAS. There were hard feelings between these two groups, and the fact that most of the English-speaking Caribbean nations are not Rio Treaty signatories (and are not likely to be in the future) further polarized the OAS and undercut the effectiveness of the treaty. The Falklands/Malvinas crisis also derailed the promising candidacy of a Caribbean representative to be the new secretary-general and made it less likely that the three remaining English-speaking nations presently outside of the

OAS (Canada, Guyana, and Belize) would seek, or be permitted, membership.

The South Atlantic crisis did not kill the OAS or the multilateral relationship, but it did weaken them, especially those elements involved with peace, security, and military and strategic relationships. The continuing decline and lack of relevance of the OAS suggests that it may die not with a bang (as some suggested during the tense moments of the Falklands/Malvinas crisis), but with a whimper as member states send their less qualified people and continue to delay their financial contributions, as they did in mid-1985.

At the same time, certain subregional and Latin-only bodies have acquired renewed vigor as a result of the South Atlantic crisis. The importance of the OECS was noted above; attempts to revive the Central American Defense Council also respond to the same desire on the part of the United States for more reliable subregional bodies. SELA has become more politically and diplomatically active since the Falklands/Malvinas crisis despite the fact that it is supposedly only an economic body. There is a real possibility that as a result of the South Atlantic crisis, SELA (or a similar coordinating body) will be the Latin Americans' channel for unifying their positions on issues of major significance, such as resolving the international debt crisis.

The Impact on Bilateral Relations

The paramountcy of bilateral relations with the United States for most of the Latin American nations was noted previously. The United States remains the principal source of capital, trade, and technology and the focal point of a host of other issues (such as migration and drugs). Few if any of these agenda items were affected by the South Atlantic crisis.

U.S.-Argentine bilateral relations are, of course, a special case. But even here the lasting damage from the South Atlantic crisis was less severe than many expected. The departure of Secretary Haig and the junta shortly after the crisis cleared the air. Argentina's return to democracy under the Alfonsín regime further hastened the reestablishment of traditionally formal and not particularly close relationships with the United States. But the plateau at which the new relationship has stabilized has been affected by the South Atlantic crisis, and there is no doubt that in the case of future strains between the United

States and Argentina there will be a tendency to open up the old wounds caused by the conflict.

The Potential Impact on Future Conflicts

There is some ambivalence in any attempt to evaluate the impact of the South Atlantic crisis on possible future conflicts in the hemisphere. At one level, Argentina's dismal failure to recover the Falklands/Malvinas and the strong position taken by the United States (and to a lesser extent other nations) on the use of force, have been valuable object lessons. As such, they diminish the probability that other nations will attempt to solve territorial or other disputes by force. And yet, some nations, or their military establishments, may draw other lessons from the South Atlantic crisis. They may, for example, focus on the value of high-technology weapons, such as the Exocet or Sidewinder missiles, as equalizers between a Third World nation and a major power. They may also see the value of a conflict to unite a nation (albeit temporarily in the Argentine case) and may believe that the lesson of the war lies in preparing the ground more carefully for a military conquest.

Regardless of which sets of lessons are learned, and by whom, the Falklands/Malvinas crisis has brought renewed attention to the twenty or so potential conflicts between states in the hemisphere. It has also highlighted the diminished ability of the United States to stop or influence the course of these conflicts. Within Latin America's military establishments, the Falklands/Malvinas crisis also brought home the dangers of excessive dependency on a single source of weapons. Thus it has stimulated the drive to diversify arms suppliers, decrease the dependency on the United States, and develop indigenous arms sources. Ominously, it has also sparked talk of the desirability of nuclear military technology ranging from nuclear submarines to "peaceful nuclear devices," and to actual weapons.

Although the South Atlantic war resolved the Falklands/Malvinas issue, the solution is a short-term one. Argentina has not accepted that the military defeat on 14 June 1982 means giving up the long-term battle to regain the islands. Significantly, postage stamp cancellations in Argentina on the first anniversary bore the legend "2 April—anniversary of the *first* recovery of the Malvinas." The Argentine struggle to recover the islands will continue, and it is not inconceivable that this may again take the form of military action, especially as the British grow tired of spending large sums of money on Fortress Falklands.

The Falklands/Malvinas crisis also has links to broader conflicts in the South Atlantic and Antarctica.[55] The latter issue is especially troublesome since it involves a large number of nations (including the United States and the Soviet Union), the perception of important natural resources, competing territorial claims (those of Argentina, Chile, and Great Britain), and the pressures of the 1991 date for possible revision of the Antarctic Treaty. Argentine and Latin American distrust of U.S. and British goals in Antarctica may be yet another price to be paid for the Falklands/Malvinas crisis of 1982, and may in turn lead to a more serious and wide-ranging conflict.

Notes

1. For bibliographic sources on the historical background of the South Atlantic crisis, see Raphael Perl, ed., *The Falklands Dispute in International Law and Politics: A Documentary Source Book* (New York: Oceana Publications, 1983); Roberto Etcheparaborda, "La Bibliografía Reciente Sobre la Cuestión Malvinas," *Revista Interamericana de Bibliografía* 34, nos. 1, 2 (1984): 1–52, 227–88; and Sara de Mundo Lo, *The Falkland/Malvinas Islands* (Urbana, Ill.: Albatross, 1983).

2. Paul Eddy and the *Sunday Times* Insight Team, *The War in the Falklands: The Full Story* (New York: Harper and Row, 1982), p. 58; Richard Ned Lebow, "Miscalculations in the South Atlantic: The Origins of the Falklands War," *Journal of Strategic Studies* 6 (March 1982): 23.

3. I recall the warm attention given General Viola at the XIII Conference of American Armies in Bogotá in 1979, at a time when it was an open secret that Viola was about to become the next Argentine military president.

4. *Clarín* (Buenos Aires), 4–10 April 1983, pp. 8–9. An English version is available in *Foreign Broadcast Information Service* (hereafter *FBIS*), 11 April 1983, pp. B-9 to B-19.

5. Oscar R. Cardoso, *Malvinas: La Trama Secreta* (Buenos Aires: Planeta, 1983), pp. 22–30; Rogelio García Lupo, *Diplomacia Secreta y Rendición Incondicional* (Buenos Aires: Legasa, 1983), pp. 180–83; *Washington Post,* 16 April 1982, p. A-1; *Latin American Weekly Report,* 12 February 1982, p. 1.

6. *Clarín* (Buenos Aires), 4–10 April 1983, p. 8.

7. Anthony R. Cordesman, "The Falklands Crisis: Emerging Lessons for Power Projection and Forces Planning," *Armed Forces Journal International* 120 (September 1982): 30.

8. *La Prensa* (Buenos Aires), 24 January 1982, pp. 1, 5. The English version is in *FBIS*, 2 February 1982, p. B-1.

9. Cardoso, *Malvinas*, p. 58.

10. Ibid., pp. 61–62.

11. Eddy et al., *War in the Falklands*, p. 24.

12. Alexander M. Haig, *Caveat: Realism, Reagan and Foreign Policy* (New York: Macmillan, 1984), pp. 261–63.

13. Henry Raymont, "The Falklands Dilemma: Errors All Around," *New Republic*, 28 April 1982, p. 9.

14. *Washington Post*, 3 April 1982, pp. 1, 6. The best account of the substance of the conversation is in Cardoso, *Malvinas*, pp. 96–100.

15. Haig, *Caveat*, p. 266.

16. Cardoso, *Malvinas*, p. 131.

17. Max Hastings and Simon Jenkins, *The Battle for the Falklands* (New York: W.W. Norton, 1983), p. 104.

18. For details, see Enders, "South Atlantic Crisis," pp. 78–90; also, the testimony of Assistant Secretary of State Thomas Enders to the House Foreign Affairs Committee, Subcommittee on Inter-American Affairs, 5 August 1982, published in *Hearings, Latin America and the United States after the Falklands/Malvinas Crisis*, pp. 109–66.

19. Jack Child, "Present Trends in the Inter-American Security System and the Role of the Rio Treaty," *Anuario Jurídico de la OEA, 1983* (Washington: OAS, 1984).

20. Hastings and Jenkins, *Battle for the Falklands*, pp. 139–40; *La Nación* (Buenos Aires), 27 April 1982, p. 1.

21. *New York Times*, 28 April 1982, p. 1; Juan E. Guglialmelli, "La Guerra de las Malvinas," *Estrategia*, nos. 71–72 (April–September 1982): 42–44.

22. Enders testimony, *Latin America and the United States*, pp. 119, 129–31.

23. Nicanor Costa Méndez in *La Nación* (Buenos Aires), 1 and 2 September 1983.

24. *Congressional Record*, Senate, 29 April 1982, pp. S4315–S4324.

25. N. H. Peterson, "Background on the Falkland Islands Crisis," *Department of State Bulletin* 82 (June 1982): 88.

26. *Economist*, 3 March 1984, p. 29.

27. T. Enders, "The South Atlantic Crisis," *Department of State Bulletin* 82, no. 2067 (October 1982): 84; *La Nación* (Buenos Aires), 8 May 1982, p. 1.

28. Virginia Gamba, *Malvinas Confidencial* (Buenos Aires: Comité pro Soberanía de las Malvinas, 1982), p. 23; Nicanor Costa Méndez, writing in *La Nación* (Buenos Aires), 2 September 1983, p. 7.

29. *New Statesman*, 13 May 1983, pp. 8–10; *Latin American Weekly Report*, 1 July 1983, p. 3.

30. Hastings and Jenkins, *Battle for the Falklands*, pp. 169–71; Enders, "South Atlantic Crisis," pp. 84–88.

31. *Washington Post*, 28 May 1982, p. 1; *New York Times*, 30 May 1982, p. 1.

32. Economist, 12 November 1983, p. 41.

33. Peter Calvert, The Falklands Crisis (New York: St. Martin's Press, 1982), p. 135.

34. Ibid., pp. 137–39; Economist, 12 November 1983, p. 41.

35. Hastings and Jenkins, Battle for the Falklands, pp. 172, 258–59; Washington Post, 6 June 1982, p. 1.

36. Newsweek, 7 June 1982, pp. 29–31.

37. Washington Post, 4 June 1982, p. 1.

38. New York Times, 1 July 1982, p. A-10.

39. Washington Post, 7 July 1982, p. 1.

40. New York Times, 5 November 1982, p. 1.

41. La Nación (Buenos Aires), 29 May 1983, p. 1. Washington Post, 17 May 1985, p. A-28.

42. Economist, 12 November 1983, p. 32.

43. Washington Watch, 7 September 1982, p. 3.

44. See, for example, Elizabeth Reimann, Las Malvinas: Traición Made in U.S.A. (Mexico: Ediciones El Caballito, 1983), chap. 1.

45. Jorge Alvarez Cardier, La Guerra de las Malvinas: Enseñanzas para Venezuela (Caracas: Enfoque, 1982), pp. 184–86.

46. Hastings and Jenkins, Battle for the Falklands, pp. 112–13.

47. Haig, Caveat, pp. 271, 298.

48. Ibid., p. 269; Economist, 12 November 1983, p. 37.

49. Newsweek, 17 May 1982, pp. 30–31.

50. Haig, Caveat, p. 289.

51. Francisco Orrego Vicuña, "El Elusivo Entendimiento entre América Latina y los Estados Unidos," Estudios Internacionales (Chile) no. 60 (October 1982): 519–32; New York Times, 18 June 1982, p. A-11.

52. Alexander M. Haig, "Prospects for Peace in the South Atlantic," Speech to the OAS, 27 May 1982, Department of State Current Policy No. 397, p. 2.

53. For a more detailed analysis, see the author's "Present Trends in the Inter-American Security System and the Role of the Rio Treaty," Anuario Jurídico de la OEA, 1983 (Washington, D.C.: OAS, 1984), pp. 43–82.

54. Alvarez Cardier, Guerra de las Malvinas, esp. pp. 56–68; Viron P. Vaky, "Inter-American Security: Lessons from the South Atlantic," Worldview, January 1983, pp. 17–20. Francisco Orrego Vicuña, "La Crisis del Atlántico Sur y su Influencia en el Sistema Regional," Estudios Internacionales, no. 60 (October 1982): pp. 493–94.

55. See the author's Geopolitics and Conflict in South America: Quarrels among Neighbors (New York: Praeger, 1985), esp. chap. 6, and his article "South American Geopolitical Thinking and Antarctica," ISA Notes (International Studies Association) Fall 1985, pp. 23–28.

Part Three

**Toward the
Twenty-first Century:
Challenges and
Opportunities**

Riordan Roett

The Debt Crisis: Economics and Politics

By early 1985 the debt crisis that began with the worldwide recession of 1981–1982 had become routinized, at least from the perspective of the United States and its industrial allies. Latin American and Caribbean states, financially overextended, had finally been forced to "adjust," to accept International Monetary Fund (IMF) guidelines for domestic austerity programs that triggered either new capital from private commercial banks or a restructuring of existing debt. The United States, supported by its more conservative allies such as West Germany and the United Kingdom, refused to admit any role for government-to-government negotiations. The debt issue was to be addressed by the individual debtor countries and the private commercial banks via the IMF.

As the crisis entered its third year, many observers and participants in the North believed that the earlier perceived threat to the international banking system had diminished. Alarmist predictions of social and political chaos in Latin America had not come true—although there has been demonstrable hardship and misery in all of the countries of the region as a result of the debt and the adjustment process. Had the Reagan administration been correct in believing that the crisis would respond to orderly, if painful, adjustment and adequate levels of international financing?

Suddenly in mid-1985 the key actors in the drama of the debt crisis were recast. Secretary of the Treasury James Baker announced at the annual meeting of the World Bank and the IMF in Seoul, South Korea, that the United States now recognized that major debtor states required both economic growth and adjustment, not merely the latter. The change in the U.S. position reflected a new set of realities. The expected return of Mexico to voluntary borrowing, following its three years of austerity, was not going to take place. Peru's new president, Alan García, inaugurated in July 1985, announced a dramatic and challenging new approach to servicing his country's debt. Secretary Baker spoke with a number of Latin American political leaders at García's inauguration in Lima and returned convinced that a new approach was needed. The suggestions contained in the October speech in Seoul opened a new round of discussions among the private commercial banks, the international financial institutions, the creditor governments, and the indebted nations that would extend into 1986 and beyond. Whether new solutions will be identified in a timely fashion remains to be seen.

In this chapter, we will briefly review the origins of the 1981–1982 crisis. With that discussion as background, we will consider the interplay of economics and politics in Latin America as country after country has attempted to cope with the crisis under the existing "rules of the game." The kinds of responses from the international financial system will then be considered, and a final section will deal with alternatives—both those stemming from Latin American and Caribbean initiatives and those that have been suggested in the United States, Western Europe, and Japan. Particular attention will be given to the U.S. initiative announced by Secretary Baker in Seoul in October 1985.

It is my position that the debt crisis is not over. In the course of the discussion we will examine how the damage limitation approach adopted by the United States and the North since 1982 has allowed everyone to "muddle through" the situation. But the social and political costs in both Latin America and the industrial North may yet fall due for what has been, to date, a technical financial response to the greatest crisis to hit Latin America since the Great Depression of the 1930s.

The Origins of the Crisis

The Latin American countries became most heavily indebted in the decade of the 1970s, after the first oil crisis. While a good deal of the world went into a recession, the Latin American economies continued to grow. Much of the growth was financed with capital borrowed from the private commercial banks of the United States and Western Europe. There is a school that argues that the debt crisis is due entirely to the Latin American governments' propensity to overspend, combined with poor management. Others argue that the evidence points to the private commercial banks, and by extension the industrial countries, as the parties responsible for the current and continuing debt crisis. From my perspective, the current Latin American debt crisis is due to both internal and external factors.[1]

Because of the massive international liquidity generated by OPEC-accumulated surpluses in the 1970s, the private commercial banks entered an unprecedented period of recycling of petrodollars. This was the principal external factor. OPEC surpluses brought new life to international capital markets, particularly through the newly created Eurocurrency markets. Since no new public international institutions were created to deal with the new liquidity, the private commercial banks became, by default, the mechanism for recycling. Competition among the banks and the lure of high profits in international banking led to fierce competition to make new loans, often under questionable credit conditions.

Internally, Latin American governments took immediate advantage of the newly available international financing. They saw external credit as a way of surmounting the shocks that followed the first oil price rise in the mid-1970s. Countries borrowed to maintain relatively high levels of growth. The money borrowed went into a wide variety of undertakings. Some investment projects were justifiable in development terms but carried a long lead time; others were overambitious or were excessively optimistic regarding market behavior. Some countries borrowed to expand imports, which often included a higher proportion of consumer goods. One of the most dangerous trends was the encouragement of exchange overvaluation policies, which were easier to follow than alternative methods of fighting inflation. In a number of countries, macroeconomic policy decisions led to an almost total loss of confidence in the government and subsequently to a massive flight of capital. This flight of capital led to a loss of reserves and a further increase in external debt. A large share of the capital flight was also due to corruption. Arms purchases contributed significantly to the increase in debt in a few countries.

Latin America had escaped the recession of the 1970s—at a cost. That cost was an external debt that amounted to about $200 billion by the early 1980s, but neither the indebted countries nor their creditors showed much concern. High growth rates, particularly in regional leaders such as Mexico and Brazil, and excellent export performance inspired confidence that such trends would continue. The advent of the Reagan administration in January 1981 and the adoption of new economic policies in Washington in 1981 and 1982, however, dramatically altered the situation of Latin America's indebtedness. Interest rates increased rapidly. Much of the Latin American debt had been incurred at variable interest rates, which meant an immediate adjustment upward of annual service payments.

High interest rates in the United States damaged Latin America in two ways. First, the rates made recovery in the industrialized countries a slow and drawn-out process, which tended to reduce the demand for Latin American exports. Second, by increasing the cost of servicing the foreign debt for Latin America, the rates greatly increased the deficit on current account and contributed to the considerable transfer of resources from Latin America to the exterior. Countries began to borrow new capital at higher interest rates to service the old loans. At the same time, the terms of trade turned against Latin America, further exacerbating the debt repayment burden. Without foreign exchange earned from exports, it became necessary to dip deeply into reserves—or to borrow more from the private commercial banks. Thus, debt service obligations began to climb precipitously at the very moment when income from exports dropped. By 1983, Latin America was forced to use more than 35 percent of its total export earnings to service the outstanding debt.

As the international financial system reacted to the combination of Reaganomics and world recession, the private commercial banks reduced their levels of lending. Capital inflows, which had amounted to $37.9 billion in 1981, had dropped to only $3.2 billion by the end of 1983. Latin America was starved for capital. Why? Debt servicing obligations mounted quickly and surpassed the total inflow of new capital from the private commercial banks, multinational corporations, and international financial institutions.[2]

On the trade front, as recession in the industrial countries resulted in a cutback in consumption, Latin America's capacity to sell decreased.[3] Pressures for protectionist measures also grew in the United States and Western Europe, since Latin American exports were viewed as a threat to domestic production in the industrial nations.

Protectionism has become a key issue in evaluating the possibilities of stable recovery for Latin America and other developing countries. At the September 1984 meetings, both World Bank president A. W. Clausen and IMF managing director Jacques de Larosière warned that continued and growing protectionism in the industrial countries threatened to jeopardize future growth. De Larosière stated that so-called protectionist decisions tend to "become entrenched and spread. They do not just poison the trading climate in certain industries, but weaken the fabric of international economic and political cooperation as a whole."[4] Clausen echoed the managing director's position by arguing that Third World recovery will be a "pipe dream" if the richer nations continue their protectionist measures instead of liberalizing trade. "It is now of crucial importance," Clausen warned, "that governments stop simply making general declarations of interests, and start taking concrete steps to liberalize trade."[5] Unfortunately, the trend is clearly in the other direction. In the last three years, the United States alone has placed restrictions on stainless steel, textiles, and food products, all of importance to Latin America. While the United States is a major figure in the growing protectionist trend, the European Community has maintained tough protectionist policies for some years and will continue to do so because of internal structural immobility—particularly if the slow pace of recovery in Europe continues in the coming years.[6]

Once again the countries of Latin America face a dilemma. If they are to earn the foreign exchange required to finance their debts, they must trade. But protectionist tendencies in the industrial countries hinder trade. Private commercial banks are reluctant to provide new money for already heavily indebted countries in the region. Where will the Latin American countries turn for viable alternatives? The grim economic situation severely limits the ability of Latin American governments to respond to pent-up social demands within their societies. After three and often four years of extreme austerity, political considerations have priority in many— if not all—of the indebted countries of Latin America.

It is essential to understand that the military regimes that borrowed, with little understanding of the obligations they were incurring, are now gone or going. The successor democratic governments are now burdened with the mistakes and debts of the past. The new governments must simultaneously cope with the implications of the global economic recession of the mid-1980s and with the pent-up demands of their citizens that the democratic process satisfy both political and socioeconomic needs. Not to respond may lead either to their losing power in the short term, which does not appear to be the greatest risk, or to a severe weakening of the fabric of democratic rule in the medium and long term, which is the greater risk. Weak democratic governments, confronted internally with a series of escalating pressures and unable to respond, will do little to institutionalize democracy. Moreover, they run the risk of either strengthening the extremes, who will appeal for popular support, or falling into a state of immobility, waiting for the armed forces to act.[7]

There is a fundamental disparity between the promises of the democracies and their immediate tasks in the hemisphere. Latin American countries have been encouraged by the United States and Western Europe to return to democracy and have been widely applauded when they did so. The greatest problems they confront are the repercussions of the world economic crisis generally and the foreign debt specifically. With the applause of the United States and Western Europe still ringing in their ears, Latin American democratic leaders are then turned over to the private banks and the international monetary institutions to work out appropriate programs of austerity. No one argues that adjustment is not needed. The issue is how much and at what pace.

Adjustment policies will always take different forms in different societies. What is evident is the commitment to reform in many of Latin America's democratic societies. Issues such as exchange-rate policy, the public deficit, spending by state corporations, regulations regarding direct foreign investment, and related issues are on the agenda for discussion and change. Innovation comes slowly in all societies. What is critical at this moment is to offer new governments, or governments severely impacted by the debt crisis, incentives to change existing procedures and explore new policy alternatives. Space to grow economically will give beleaguered governments the opportunity to introduce substantial policy changes that were highly improbable prior to the onset of the debt crisis.

The Interplay of Politics and Economics

By 1981 the warning signals were apparent to those who wanted to see them. While the ratio of debt service to export earnings in countries such as Indonesia, Korea, and Malaysia remained below the "safe" level of 15 percent, the debt service ratios in Brazil and Chile rose above 50 percent and reached 35 percent in Mexico and Argentina. World Bank estimates indicate that a single percentage point change in short-term dollar interest rates has an impact each year of more than $1.2 billion on the combined net debt service of Mexico, Brazil, and Argentina, Latin America's three largest borrowers. From 1979 to 1981 the debt servicing of these three key countries rose by $10 billion, or 170 percent.[8]

The cascading process of indebtedness ended in August 1982. Abruptly, the government of Mexico proposed a moratorium on $19.5 billion of principal payments due in 1982 and 1983. The lame-duck administration of President José López Portillo admitted defeat and sought an international solution to the country's inability to finance its existing level of external debt. A set of ad hoc arrangements was quickly patched together. An advisory committee of private banks convened to negotiate on behalf of all the banks with exposure in Mexico. The U.S. government agreed to a prepayment of $1 billion for oil imports from Mexico. Further, the U.S. Treasury contributed a "bridging" loan of $925 million for one year, an amount matched by the Bank for International Settlements, pending approval of the adjustment program then under discussion with the IMF. Central banking authorities brought pressure to bear on the international banks, as well as on the smaller banks with exposure in Mexico, to maintain existing lines of credit for the government.[9] The IMF communicated to the private commercial banks that they would be expected to participate with new lending as the international financial community sought a stopgap response to the debt. In bits and pieces, Mexico was brought back from the brink of declaring itself unable and/or unwilling to repay its outstanding debt. Such a declaration by Mexico would have had immediate and deleterious implications for both the private commercial banks and for the international financial system.

The international response to the Mexican debt was repeated thereafter for almost all of the Latin American and Caribbean countries, as well as for many other states of the Third World. But Latin America was particularly vulnerable in the early 1980s, and it is in the Western Hemisphere that the drama of debt and adjustment, contrasted with a return to democratic political institutions, has been played out.[10]

The emergency efforts undertaken by the international financial community to protect their exposure in Latin America and the Caribbean inevitably led to the involvement of the IMF. The IMF's highly controversial role became crucial in rescheduling the debt of the

Latin American countries.[11] In exchange for a set of orthodox adjustment measures that emphasized lowering the rate of inflation,
cutting the public deficit, reducing the money supply, and other
measures, the IMF provided standby financing for the indebted nation. That signal from the fund triggered a process of the private
commercial banks' rescheduling the outstanding debt in direct negotiations with the indebted government.

The adjustment measures coincided with a major change in the
political orientation of Latin American political systems that it is
crucial to understand. Populist regimes in the 1950s and 1960s over-
spent and overpromised. Limited resources were often poorly used.
A wave of military regimes replaced democratic governments on the
continent—Brazil in 1964, Argentina in 1966 and 1976, Peru in 1968,
Ecuador in 1972, and Chile and Uruguay in 1973. Ecuador and Peru
can be classified as military populist governments; the others were
right-wing authoritarian. The record is clear. The authoritarian governments affronted and violated the community of values and norms
that stands as an important bond among all the states of the hemisphere. In Central America military regimes continued in power or,
in the case of Nicaragua, the Somoza family governed with the full
support of the National Guard. Only Costa Rica remained an exception.

In all of the countries, representative political institutions were
either closed or emasculated. Political parties were banned or were
given little room for freedom of action. Political adversaries were exiled (if fortunate), jailed, tortured, and frequently murdered, or made
to "disappear." Judicial systems were truncated, and the media and
press fell victim to censorship and intimidation. These deliberate
violations of the traditions of Western culture were heralded by the
new regimes as policies that would promote efficiency, rapid economic growth, and the control of subversion and social disorder.

By the end of the 1970s it was obvious that the military regimes
had not only broken faith with the minimal standards of decency but
had also failed to achieve permanent, sustainable economic growth.
The protests and social demonstrations that accompanied the falter-
ing of the economic models the regimes espoused led to their demise, or appear to be doing so in those countries that remain under
military rule.

Peru and Ecuador were exceptions to this process in most ways.
In Peru, a basically nonrepressive regime undertook bold social and

economic experiments. But in uprooting tradition, the regime failed to construct suitable or permanent institutional substitutes. The transition back to competitive politics has been marred by the legacy of the revolutionary period and appears to threaten the survival of democratic institutions in Peru more than in any other country on the continent. The Ecuadorean military was more pliable and susceptible to compromise. Military rule, while inefficient, was bland and relatively short-lived.

It is imperative to understand that the South American perspective on the current debt crisis differs fundamentally from the apparent positions of the United States and Western Europe.[12] The Latin American states view the crisis as potentially posing a fundamental threat to the continuation or installation of democratic regimes. It is particularly exasperating to the Latin American countries that the industrial states seem to have forgotten the circumstances under which the debt was originally incurred, and by whom. For the Latin Americans, it is as if the banks and their governments know nothing of recent history in Latin America. The memories are all too poignant for a number of the states in the region. It is commonly believed that bankers have no interest in or concern for the nature of specific political systems. One government is a good as another as long as it maintains scheduled interest payments and does not jeopardize the private banks' portfolios.

Latin America's Response to the Crisis

As the social and political implications of the debt crisis became apparent to the region's political leaders—and as the attitudes of the industrial countries remained unresponsive to the sacrifices being asked of Latin America—the hemisphere's leaders turned to political action.[13]

The UN's Economic Commission for Latin America and the Caribbean (ECLAC) and the Latin American Economic System (SELA) had both undertaken extensive analyses of the economic situation in Latin America and of the effects of the oil-price shocks, the recession in the industrial world, and the fiscal and monetary changes instituted during the first Reagan administration. However, the opening salvo in the effort to seek a common political response to the crisis came from Ecuador's Christian Democratic president Osvaldo Hurtado, who wrote on 11 February 1983 to the executive secretaries of

ECLAC and SELA, Enrique Iglesias and Carlos Alzamora, respectively. In his letter he stressed the social and political implications of the economic crisis:

If the high growth indexes of the past decades . . . did not eliminate this deep wound of misery, injustice and underemployment or unemployment which divides our societies, imagine what will happen in the future if the economic depression is prolonged beyond 1984, as is feared. What is at stake, then, as never before, is the social peace of the nations and the instability of the democratic system—in brief, the fate of vast human communities which are seeing their unresolved social problems grow worse day by day, and are fearfully becoming aware of the possibility of total disaster.[14]

Hurtado requested that the two organizations "prepare as soon as possible a set of proposals designed to develop the response capacity of Latin America and to consolidate its systems of co-operation."[15] In response, ECLAC and SELA proceeded to prepare a basic document, "Bases for a Latin American Response to the International Economic Crisis" (16 May 1983), with the support of other regional organizations, including the Latin American Integration Association (ALADI); the Board of the Cartagena Agreement, the so-called Andean Pact (JUNAC); the Center for Latin American Monetary Studies (CEMLA); and the Latin American Energy Organization (OLADE).

Meanwhile, the Inter-American Economic and Social Council (CIES) of the Organization of American States met in Washington on 13 May 1983. CIES called for the organization of a "Specialized Conference on External Financing in Latin America and the Caribbean." CIES instructed its secretariat to "take into account" the recommendations of the VI United Nations Conference on Trade and Development (UNCTAD) as well as the ECLAC-SELA report prepared at the suggestion of President Hurtado. This CIES conference met in Caracas, Venezuela, from 5 to 9 September 1983.

Following the Caracas conference, many Latin American delegates concluded that the OAS was an inappropriate forum for a realistic study of the debt crisis. As a member of the organization, the United States did not share the general Latin American perspective on either the origins of the crisis or the available solutions. Moreover, the bureaucracy of the OAS did not possess a reputation for either boldness or great imagination in defining issues such as the economic crisis. Indeed, the closing address at the meeting by the chairman of the U.S. delegation, Undersecretary of the Treasury Beryl Sprinkel, indicated the differences in viewpoint. While the Latin Americans were still deeply concerned about the deterioration of their economies and their societies, Mr. Sprinkel stated that the issue had basically been resolved:

I . . . want to emphasize that this extreme situation is temporary. Once significant adjustments are made, the underlying strength and promise of our economies will re-emerge with dynamism and vitality. Most importantly, confidence is being restored.

We look forward to working with you to hasten the arrival of that day, and to working with you thereafter in achieving the potential of this beautiful hemisphere.[16]

The Latin American Economic Conference

Formally linked to the Caracas conference of September 1983, the January 1984 Quito meeting transcended the OAS in that the United States was not invited to participate. The Declaration of Quito struck a note of urgency when it stated that

the most harmful social effects of this situation take the form of an increase in unemployment figures unprecedented in our history, of a substantial reduction of real personal incomes and of living standards, with serious and growing consequences for the political and social stability of our peoples, the persistence of which will, in time, result in further deterioration of our economies.[17]

The plan of action prepared at the conference boldly stated the political tone of the deliberations:

Responsibility for the external debt problem must be shared by the debtor and developed countries, the international private banking system and the multilateral finance organizations.

The Latin American and Caribbean countries have already assumed their responsibility by making extraordinary adjustments in their economies and enormous efforts to meet their international obligations, despite the high social, political, and economic cost involved.

The magnitude of the regional economic recession and the persistence of adverse external factors make it imperative that any external debt arrangements and negotiations . . . should harmonize the requirements of debt servicing with the development needs and objectives of each country, by minimizing the social cost of the adjustment processes under way.[18]

The Quito meeting dramatically shifted the focus of the discussion about Latin America's debt from the technical and financial to the social and political. It also directly implicated the creditors and the international financial institutions in seeking a mutually agreeable outcome. The presidents and foreign ministers assembled in the Ecuadoran capital were communicating a message: the debt is political.

The Quito meeting took place in the midst of great uncertainty about the capacity of the Latin American countries to continue servicing their debt. Venezuela had refused to go to the IMF. Argentina was entering a period of stop-and-go negotiations with the private commercial banks and was balking at any adjustment program imposed by the IMF. Brazil's letters of intent with the IMF required continuous rewriting as targets were not met. Finally, Peru appeared unable to muster either the political will or the economic performance required to reschedule or to meet existing obligations.

The growing solidarity among the major debtor countries had been reinforced in March 1984 during the meetings of the Inter-American Development Bank in Punta del Este, Uruguay. A default by Argentina had been prevented at the last minute by an imaginative package of support put together under the leadership of Mexico, which included contributions by Mexico, Colombia, Brazil, and Venezuela. It is widely believed that the U.S. Federal Reserve System and its chairman, Paul Volcker, were involved in executing the package. By early 1984, Volcker saw the need for relief for Latin America but had to work behind the scenes to avoid open conflict with the U.S. Treasury.

The urgency of a coordinated response to decisions over which Latin American governments had little control became evident as the U.S. prime lending rate climbed from 11 percent in early March 1984 to 12.5 percent in May. For the first time, Latin American heads of state and their key advisors coordinated statements and public reactions. The lead, it was noted, was taken either by the presidents of the Latin American states or their foreign ministers, not by the finance or planning ministers as had been customary in the past. Two weeks later, four Latin American presidents issued a joint letter in which they called for the convening of a ministerial-level meeting to identify initiatives to be taken in the area of debt and finance.

The letter—signed by President Raúl Alfonsín of Argentina, João

Figueiredo of Brazil, Belisario Betancur of Colombia, and Miguel de la Madrid of Mexico—stated:

> We have confirmed that the successive increases of interest rates, the perspective that there will be new increases and the proliferation and intensity of protectionist measures have created a somber scenario for our nations and for the region as a whole.
>
> Our countries cannot accept these risks indefinitely. . . . we do not accept being pushed into a situation of forced insolvency and continuous economic stagnation.[19]

The four heads of state requested "adequate amortization and grace periods, and a reduction in interest rates, margins, commissions and other financial charges" on the foreign debt.[20] A meeting of key ministers was scheduled for Bogotá, Colombia, in June 1984.

Prior to the convocation of that Latin American meeting, the tenth annual Economic Summit took place in London. In an effort to focus the London summit on the debt issue, seven Latin American presidents addressed a short but sharp letter to the London participants. In it they called for the summit members to give highest priority to the debt issue. The chief executives of Argentina, Brazil, Colombia, Ecuador, Mexico, Peru, and Venezuela called for a "constructive dialogue among creditor and borrowing countries." They said that it was impossible to imagine that their financial problems could be resolved only by "contacting banks or through the isolated participation of international financial organizations."[21]

Even though summit participants such as French president François Mitterand called for a thorough review of the international monetary system, and sympathy for the plight of the Latin American debtors found in informal comments by other heads of state, Mrs. Thatcher and President Reagan carried the day. The final communiqués offered help to the Latin American debtors but only if they reduced government spending and worked to put their houses in order. It included no criticism of the U.S. deficit. The case-by-case approach, each country being dealt with separately by the private banks and the international financial institutions, remained the standard procedure after the summit. The frustration over the meager results of the London Economic Summit was evident in the preparations under way for the next major conclave of the Latin American debtor countries.

The Cartagena Consensus

By mid-1984 it was evident that many Latin American governments were convinced that the private commercial banks, perhaps with the support of the U.S. government, had decided to pursue a "divide and conquer" strategy within the region. The banks' strategy was to reward cooperative countries with lower interest rates and easier repayment terms while standing firm against recalcitrant governments. It appeared to be a strategy of isolating those countries, such as Argentina, that were unwilling to cooperate, and holding out the carrot of better terms for those governments able and willing to impose strict austerity measures on their people and to comply with IMF conditions.

Subsequently, the Cartagena meeting convened in June 1984 during a period of perceived weakening of the ties between the Latin American debtor countries and their creditors. Argentina remained adamant against signing an austerity agreement with the IMF, and Bolivia and Ecuador had suspended debt payments. Following widespread rioting and looting in Santo Domingo, the Dominican Republic had broken off its conversations with the IMF. In contrast, major debtors like Mexico, Brazil, and Venezuela were proceeding to work on individual arrangements with the banks. The seven participants at Cartagena—Argentina, Brazil, Colombia, Ecuador, Mexico, Peru, and Venezuela—represented about $286 billion of the region's estimated $340 billion foreign debt. Four other countries— Chile, Bolivia, Uruguay, and the Dominican Republic—attended as observers.

The foreign ministers, or political spokesmen, were clearly in charge of the Cartagena meeting. At the opening meeting, President Belisario Betancur stated that "Latin America's foreign debt service has become so burdensome that it threatens the very stability of the international monetary system and the survival of the democratic process in various countries."[22]

The final communiqué stated that Latin America would honor its debts and ruled out collective renegotiation. But there was no threat of a cartel of debtor countries. The Cartagena delegates called for government-to-government negotiations on the debt. The Cartagena Consensus, signed by the finance and foreign ministers of the eleven participating countries, reemphasized the Declaration of Quito in setting out specific remedies, such as lower loan costs, a concerted effort by the industrial countries to reduce interest rates, and an emphasis on fighting protectionism and promoting free trade.

In what appeared to many as a tragic parody, the prime rate rose by a half point to 13 percent a short time after the Cartagena meeting ended.

The Mar del Plata Meeting

The collegial sense of cooperation among the Latin American debtor countries resulted in a call for another meeting of the Cartagena group, which took place at Mar del Plata in Argentina immediately prior to the World Bank and IMF annual meetings in Washington in September 1984. President Raúl Alfonsín's beleaguered government hoped to gain some political support by holding the meeting in Argentina while the government was engaged in a duel with the IMF over austerity measures.

It was clear that the mood had changed between Cartagena and Mar del Plata. Mexico had reached an agreement with leading foreign banks on favorable conditions for a major restructuring of its commercial debt, and Brazil and Venezuela appeared to be on the way to satisfactory deals with their creditors. Even the Argentine government, in September 1984, appeared to be making some headway in its talks with the IMF. The most significant outcome of the meeting was a call for a collective meeting between the Latin American debtors and the industrialized countries in 1985 to help solve the ongoing crisis. The ten-point declaration issued at the end of the meeting called for a return to "realistic and reasonable" interest rates, a loosening of protectionist trade measures, and the renewal of short-term credits.

The call for direct political talks was carried to Washington by the Latin American debtors during the 1984 annual meetings of the World Bank and the IMF. To avoid further confrontations, the top policymaking bodies of the two institutions agreed to hold a special session on debtor countries' problems in April 1985, but spokesmen for both groups agreed in Washington that the meeting would be symbolic. The United States promoted the plan in order to blunt pressure for a more sweeping creditor-debtor conference.

A meeting of the foreign ministers of the Cartagena group in Brasília was convened in November 1984 at the same time as the annual conference of the OAS. It was clear that this meeting was deliberately held outside of the discussions of the OAS. The foreign ministers also met with Secretary of State Shultz. Despite the lack of concrete results, Colombian foreign minister Ramírez Ocampo said with satisfaction that it was the first contact between Latin American debtors and Shultz in which he recognized that the debt problem had political consequences.

The February 1985 meeting held in Santo Domingo in the Dominican Republic was notable for its lack of relevance to the debt debate. Rhetorical statements dominated the proceedings. One positive fact that followed the meeting, however, was the appointment of Enrique Iglesias as the coordinator of the Cartagena Group. A former executive secretary of the Economic Commission for Latin America and the Caribbean (ECLAC) in Santiago, Chile, Iglesias has been an important and balanced presence in the debates about the Latin American debt since the beginning of the crisis. He now serves as foreign minister of Uruguay.

As predicted, the April 1985 meetings in Washington with the IMF and the World Bank proved useless, and no progress was made. In preparation for the industrial nations' summit in Bonn in mid-1985, another letter was addressed to President Reagan and his colleagues by the Latin American heads of state, again to no avail. In part, the drifting down of U.S. interest rates in 1985 had lessened the sense of urgency for some countries. It was also clear that the Latin American states had rejected confrontational tactics and were seeking a medium-term strategy to deal with the problems of economic growth and social discontent at home.

Momentary moral and political support was provided in June 1985 by former U.S. secretary of state Henry A. Kissinger, who called for a Marshall Plan for Latin America in a series of provocative and widely quoted newspaper articles and television interviews.[23] As expected, little resulted; the view prevailed that the crisis had passed and that the outstanding debt was a topic for negotiation between the private banks and the indebted countries. That perspective was reinforced by the dramatic austerity program announced in June 1985 by the government of Argentina and by the agreement between the government of President Alfonsín and the IMF on a medium-term set of adjustment measures.

By the summer of 1985 it was difficult to find significant support within the U.S. government, the IMF, the World Bank, or the leading states in the Organization for Economic Cooperation and Development (OECD) for any new approach to ameliorating the impact of the debt burden on the Third World. Most observers thought that the IMF and World Bank meetings scheduled for Seoul, South Korea, in the autumn of 1985 were unlikely to yield new initiatives. The combined psychological impact of declining interest rates and lower oil prices appeared to have created a false sense of confidence that the debt was indeed manageable both now and in the foreseeable future.

The U.S. Initiative in Seoul

July through September 1985 saw in Latin America a marked shift in attitude toward the debt burden as a result of a startling role reversal. A renegade Argentina adopted a stringent adjustment program, while International Monetary Fund disciple Mexico fell out of compliance with the IMF. New governments in Peru and Brazil reiterated the need for growth in their economies to generate foreign exchange needed to service their debts. In his inaugural speech as president of Peru, Alan García declared that his country would allot no more than 10 percent of export proceeds toward the $1.3 billion it owed in interest payments for 1985.[24] Increasingly the region's leaders appeared to be in revolt against the economic adjustment policies imposed by the IMF.

At the fortieth anniversary of the United Nations, on the eve of the annual meeting of the IMF and the World Bank in Seoul, South Korea, two Latin Americans articulated their resistance. Brazilian president José Sarney stated that

Brazil has taken its position. . . . We have chosen to grow without recession, without submitting ourselves to those adjustments which would imply relinquishing development. Brazil will not pay its foreign debt with recession, nor with hunger. We believe that in settling this account, at such high social and economic costs, we would then have to surrender our freedom, for a debt paid for with poverty is an account paid for with democracy.[25]

Brazil's intransigence on internal monitoring of its economy by the IMF did not yet imply a break with the fund. But Peruvian president Alan García assumed a more aggressive position:

We therefore reiterate that the International Monetary Fund shall not be the intermediary between us and our creditors. In the dialogue with our creditors we shall not accept the mortgaging of our economic independence by signing letters of intent which contain negative policies for our people. . . .

Under current conditions, as a result of its unjust beginnings and because of the methods by which it has been increased, the foreign debt can never be paid off by any one of our countries, because the effort to service it on time will keep our democracies trapped in misery and violence. Thus we are faced with a dramatic choice: it is either debt or democracy.[26]

Simultaneous with events at the United Nations, the 1985 Inter-American Development Bank report *Economic and Social Progress in Latin America* concluded that the adjustment policies of 1982 through 1984 were to a large extent negative and had not yet produced the basis for a longer-term structural transformation of the Latin American economy capable of setting the region on a new growth path. The report noted that the transferral of resources had come largely at the expense of investment and that the attempt to service large debts in the present prejudiced the nations' continuing ability to pay in the future.[27]

Annual reports by ECLAC documented the effects of the adjustment policies since 1981 and illustrated why the Latin American democratic regimes feared greater and ongoing austerity: "The crisis unleashed in 1981 has in fact been the severest, most widespread and longest crisis suffered by Latin America in the past half century and has proved to be very costly both economically and socially."[28] According to the 1984 study, "this pronounced slowdown went hand in hand with a sharp rise in open unemployment—which in some of the main urban centers rose to over 15 percent and even 20 percent of the labor force—and an increase in the various forms of underemployment. Moreover, the negative social effects of the deterioration of the employment situation were further aggravated, in many countries, by a simultaneous decline in real wages."[29] Figures for the end of 1984 indicated that

Latin America's per capita product was almost 9 percent lower in 1984 than in 1980 and was similar to that already obtained by the region in 1976. . . . [P]rice increases once again speeded up in Latin America, attaining record rates. The simple average rate of increase of consumer prices soared from 66 percent in 1983 to 145 percent in 1984, while the average rate weighted by the population went up between those years from 130 percent to over 175 percent.[30]

Clearly, the costs of austerity in Latin America have been severe. Drops in production and income have been so sharp that, even with considerable effort, it is not certain that standards of living seen in the 1970s will be achieved again by the end of the 1980s. It is possible in several countries to speak of the 1980s as a "lost decade" from the perspective of social and economic progress.

The UN's run-up to the IMF and World Bank meetings took place amid speculation that the United States was preparing a bold new approach to dealing with the debt crisis. Considerable suspense was generated by closed-door meetings in Washington to formulate the proposal Treasury Secretary Baker would unveil in Seoul.

The Baker proposal set forth a three-pronged attack on the debt. First, debtor countries were to put their financial houses in order by implementing policies that would lead to growth without inflation. The traditional prescriptions were to reduce the role of the state sector in the economy, stimulate investment through tax policies, allow the market to determine foreign-exchange rates, and welcome direct foreign investment. Once these were under way, the private commercial banks would be encouraged to lend an additional $20 billion over a period of three years for debt service and new investment. Finally, the World Bank and the Inter-American Development Bank would provide an additional $9 billion over the same period.[31]

In the fall of 1985, the framework Treasury Secretary Baker envisioned was generally regarded as an inadequate remedy for the debt stalemate. The proposal failed to attack the debt crisis at its roots: the huge U.S. budget deficit and the overvalued dollar. Further, it predicated new lending on more austerity in Latin America, precisely what the countries of the region declared they could not accept as a prerequisite for growth. The recognition of the need for internal adjustments was unanimous, but the evidence that austerity had not led to economic recovery was impressive. None of the major debtors—Brazil, Argentina, or Mexico—had recovered its financial health since the imposition of austerity in 1982. Indeed, the Mexican presence in Seoul underscored this fact, as the failure of the three-year adjustment program in that country was apparent.

The significance of the U.S. initiative was the repeated emphasis on the word *growth,* commented Brazilian finance minister Dilson Funaro in Seoul.[32] But whether sufficient resources could be mobilized through the World Bank and the reluctant commercial banks to make a difference remained to be seen. An "enhanced" role for the World Bank hinted at a general capital increase that would permit it to lend much larger sums to the Third World than the eleven to twelve billion dollars of 1983–84. However, Congress at present seems unlikely to approve any significant increase in the U.S. commitment to the World Bank.

Conclusion

By early 1986 the debt crisis had not disappeared. Countries have reacted differently to the prolonged period of austerity that began in 1982. Columbia undertook a successful adjustment program, as did Ecuador during the first two years of the Febres Cordero administration, although Ecuador's initial success was compromised by a severe earthquake, which caused a significant fall in exports and consequently in the country's ability to service its debt. Argentina's radical adjustment efforts, begun in June 1985, appeared on the way to success. But sustaining even these positive signs will depend on continued flows of capital, open world markets, and ongoing adjustment within each of the debtor countries.

These signs, however, are countered by a number of negative trends. As Morgan Guaranty's *World Financial Markets* stated in late 1985, "Exports of the ten major debtors, after recovering by more than 11 percent in 1984, are declining again to 11 percent below the 1980–81 level. LDC export volumes generally have increased, but neither steadily nor strongly."[33] The debt continued to be a heavy burden for the Third World as it absorbed large portions of export earnings: "the share of . . . export earnings absorbed by scheduled interest payments has not declined significantly since 1982 despite the steep fall in nominal interest rates."[34] Further gloomy news indicated that

the debtors' export earnings are being dampened by the currently sluggish pace of economic growth in the major industrial countries. OECD real GNP growth this year [1985] is unlikely to be much above 2.5 percent, little more than half the 1984 result. On the basis of present policies, OECD growth is unlikely to be much above 2.5 percent, little more than half the 1984 result. On present policies, OECD growth is unlikely to be better in 1986.[35]

The continued sluggishness in the economics of the industrialized nations since 1985 has added further uncertainty to the debt situation for Latin America and the Caribbean.

What is required is a bold decision by the United States to view the Latin American debt issue as a political issue, and ultimately as a matter of national security. The situation calls for a carefully coordinated program on the part of the United States, supported by Japan and Western Europe, that will provide the resources for sustained growth in Latin America. Simultaneously, a medium-term adjustment program of structural changes by Latin America will need to be identified. The support of the international financial institutions on a sustained basis is a *sine qua non* for such an undertaking. In the United States, the government's commitments to cutting the federal deficit and to continuing to oppose protectionist pressures are essential elements in any successful effort to address the debt question.

The United States should view the debt in national security terms, because a stable, democratic, economically prosperous Western Hemisphere is in its best interest. It is neither a romantic notion nor one driven by a desire to be charitable. Working to ameliorate the impact of the debt serves U.S. interests as well as those of Latin America and the Caribbean. Only when this dimension is added to our analysis of the debt question will a satisfactory response be possible. Without it we continue to run the risk of further social malaise, economic deterioration, and political instability.

Acknowledgment

I wish to thank Sarah K. Brown for her research assistance in the preparation of this chapter.

Notes

1. For a recent discussion of this point of view, with which I am in agreement, see Enrique V. Iglesias, "Latin America: Crisis and Development Options," in Colin I. Bradford, Jr., ed., *Europe and Latin America in the World Economy* (New Haven, Conn.: Yale Center for International and Area Studies, Yale University, 1985).

2. Ibid., Table 1, "Real Interest Rates and Net Capital Inflow," p. 50.

3. See Riordan Roett, "The Case of Latin America," in Joseph J. Norton, ed., *World Trade and Finance* (New York: Matthew Bender, 1985), chap. 24, pp. 19–28.

4. Quoted in Hobart Rowen, "See Threat to Recovery," *New York Times*, 25 September 1984, p. D-4.

5. Ibid.

6. *Financial Times*, 5 September 1985, p. 1.

7. I have developed these themes in "Democracy and Debt in South America: A Continent's Dilemma," *Foreign Affairs: America and the World, 1983*, vol. 62, no. 3 (1984): 695–720.

8. M. S. Mendelsohn, *The Debt of Nations,* A Twentieth Century Fund Paper (New York: Priority Press Publications, 1984), p. 31.

9. The Mexican debt case is very well summarized in Lance Taylor, "Mexico's Adjustment in the 1980s: Look Back before Leaping Ahead," in Richard E. Feinberg and Valeriana Kallab, eds., *Adjustment Crisis in the Third World,* Overseas Development Council, U.S.–Third World Policy Perspectives, no. 1 (New Brunswick and London: Transaction Books, 1984).

10. I develop these themes in "The Foreign Debt Crisis and the Process of Redemocratization in Latin America," in William N. Eskridge, Jr., ed., *Dance along the Precipice: Political and Economic Dimensions of the International Debt Problem* (Lexington, Mass.: Lexington Books, D. C. Heath and Co., 1985).

11. For a better understanding of the role of the international financial institutions, see Tony Killick et al., "The IMF: Case for a Change in Emphasis," in Feinberg and Kallab, eds., *Adjustment Crisis.*

12. For a Latin American perspective, see the collection of essays on adjustment in Argentina, Brazil, and Mexico in John Williamson, ed., *Prospects for Adjustment in Argentina, Brazil and Mexico: Responding to the Debt Crisis* (Washington, D.C.: Institute for International Economics, 1983); and Aldo Ferrer, "Debt, Sovereignty and Democracy in Latin America: The Need for a New Orthodoxy," in Bradford, ed., *Europe and Latin America.*

13. See Riordan Roett, "Latin America's Response to the Debt Crisis," *Third World Quarterly* (London) 7 (April 1985): 227–41.

14. Enrique V. Iglesias and Carlos Alzamora Traverso, "Bases for a Latin American Response to the International Economic Crisis," Organization of American States, Inter-American Economic and Social Council (CIES), Reference document for the Special Specialized Conference on External Financing in Caracas, Venezuela (5–9 September 1983): Annex, pp. 1–2.

15. Ibid., p. 4.

16. "Statement by the Under Secretary of the Treasury, Beryl Sprinkel, at the OAS Special Specialized Conference on External Financing," Organization of American States, Inter-American Economic and Social Council (CIES), OEA/Ser. K/XX.1, CONFINAN/34.

17. "Declaration of Quito," Latin American Economic Conference, Quito, 9–13 January 1984, p. 3, published by the SELA Permanent Secretariat.

18. "Plan of Action," Latin American Economic Conference, Quito, 9–13 January 1984, pp. 1–2, published by the SELA Permanent Secretariat.

19. "Joint Presidential Statement calling to a meeting of Latin American Foreign Ministers and Financial Authorities to discuss the international debt crisis," copy distributed by the Embassy of the Argentine Republic in Washington, D.C., 19 May 1984.

20. Ibid.

21. *Journal of Commerce,* 8 June 1984, p. A1.

22. *New York Times,* 8 June 1984, p. A11.

23. Henry A. Kissinger, "A Plan of Help, Hope for This Hemisphere," *Los Angeles Times,* 23 June 1985.

24. "Peru Creditors Wary of Garcia Strategy of Confrontation," *Washington Post,* 3 November 1985, p. E1.

25. "Address by His Excellency José Sarney, President of the Federative Republic of Brazil, to the XL Session of the General Assembly of the United Nations, New York, 23 September 1985, Mimeographed, p. 21.

26. "Address by His Excellency Alan García, President of the Republic of Peru at the Fortieth Session of the General Assembly New York," 23 September 1985, Mimeographed, pp. 12–13.

27. *Economic and Social Progress in Latin America; External Debt: Crisis and Adjustment* (Washington, D.C.: Inter-American Development Bank, 1985), pp. 89, 143.

28. United National Economic and Social Council, Economic Commission for Latin America, "Preliminary Overview of the Latin American Economy during 1984" CEPAL, no. 409/410, January 1985.

29. United Nations Economic and Social Council, Economic Commission for Latin America, "Adjustment Policies and Renegotiation of the External Debt," E/CEPAL/SES.20/G17, 22 February 1984, p. 5.

30. UN, "Latin American Economy."

31. See Riordan Roett, "Bolder Move Is Needed to Deal with Mounting Financial, Political Risks," *Los Angeles Times,* 20 October 1985, pt. 5. p. 3.

32. "Few Banks Rush to Aid Latin America," *Washington Post,* 13 October 1985, p. D1.

33. *World Financial Markets,* published by the Morgan Guaranty Trust Company of New York, September/October 1985, p. 3.

34. Ibid., p. 4.

35. Ibid.

Abraham F. Lowenthal

The United States, Central America, and the Caribbean

The small nations of the Caribbean Basin—the islands of the Caribbean and the nations on Central America's isthmus—are once again at the heart of U.S. foreign policy, as they were for the first quarter of the century. Beginning with the Carter administration, and with greater attention during the Reagan period, official Washington has rediscovered its border region.

Economic and military assistance from the United States to the countries of the Caribbean and Central America has multiplied more than tenfold since 1977, even while overall foreign aid figures have been declining. Except for Israel and Egypt, the countries of the Caribbean Basin are the largest recipients of U.S. assistance in the world. El Salvador is the fourth largest recipient of U.S. aid.

The Reagan administration has even intervened militarily in the Caribbean Basin, deploying some 7,000 marines and army paratroopers to occupy tiny Grenada in October 1983. Although the troops were ostensibly sent to protect U.S. citizens, undoubtedly their primary aim was to reverse the island's alignment with the Soviet Union and Cuba. In addition to the operation in Grenada, the Reagan administration has repeatedly undertaken extended military and naval exercises involving several thousand U.S. troops, in Honduras and off the coasts of Nicaragua. It has also built new military bases and airfields in Honduras and pre-positioned thousands of tons of materiel. Washington has engaged in a prolonged and hardly covert war against the Sandinista government in Nicaragua, and there is good reason to believe that the U.S. government prepared itself in the mid-1980s for the possibility of direct military intervention. Neglected by Washington for so many years, the countries of Central America and the Caribbean are today receiving lavish attention from the United States. This country is becoming increasingly embroiled once again in the domestic turmoil of its Caribbean Basin neighbors.

Caribbean and Central American realities have changed considerably during the past sixty years, as have U.S. interests in these regions. But U.S. policies toward the Caribbean Basin still resemble those of the 1920s in many respects. If adequate U.S. policies to deal with Central America and the Caribbean in the future are to be fashioned, up-to-date assessments are needed of exactly what is at stake for the United States in this region and how U.S. aims can best be advanced.

The Insular Caribbean

In most respects the countries of the insular Caribbean are very different from those of Central America. The two regions have distinct cultural and national histories, as well as different economic structures, demographic compositions, social organizations, and politics. The Central American countries share a common history, and their citizens interact frequently across national boundaries. Similarly, the countries of the insular Caribbean (especially the former British colonies of the Commonwealth Caribbean) share many experiences and traits among themselves and project a sense of common regional identity. But interchange, even communication, between these two regions is rare. Policies that treat the Caribbean and Central America together in an undifferentiated way are bound, therefore, to miss the mark.

The insular Caribbean includes some thirty-two political entities with a population totaling about 30 million people. (Belize, which is more Caribbean than Central American in its background, culture, and traditions, will be grouped with the Caribbean islands for the purposes of this chapter). Sixteen of these units are now independent countries, with four achieving their independence in the 1960s and nine since 1970. The Caribbean islands are remarkably diverse, yet in some ways they are overwhelmingly alike. Except for Cuba and Hispaniola (the island that includes both the Dominican Republic and Haiti), most are very small. Grenada is not much larger in area than the District of Columbia or Martha's Vineyard, and its entire population could fit into the Rose Bowl. Trinidad is smaller than Rhode Island. Jamaica is the size of Connecticut. Even Cuba, by far the largest Caribbean island, is only about the size of Virginia.

Table 1. The Caribbean Countries and Dependencies

Country	Year of Independence	Area (Sq. Km.)	Pop./Ann. Increase (No./%)	Pop. Density (Per Sq. Km.	Pop. under 20 Yrs of Age[2] (%)	Literacy Rate (%)
Anguilla	(U.K.)	91	6,000/—	72.0	—	80
Antigua & Barbuda	1981	280	82,000/2.6	293.0	—	90
The Bahamas	1973	13,934	235,000/1.8	17.0	49.6	89
Barbados	1966	430	253,000/0.5	588.0	41.1	99
Belize	1981	22,963	168,000/2.2	7.3	—	90
British Virgin Islands	(U.K.)	153	12,000/1.0	78.4	—	98
Cayman Islands	(U.K.)	259	22,000/2.8	85.0	35.0	97
Cuba	1902	114,471	10,221,000/1.1	89.3	39.7	96
Dominica	1978	753	74,000/0.4	98.3	—	80
Dominican Republic	1844	48,734	6,785,000/2.5	139.2	58.7	68
French Guiana	(France)	90,909	88,000/4.1	1.0	42.2	73
Grenada	1974	334	86,000/−0.4	250.0	–	85
Guadeloupe	(France)	1,779	334,000/0.5	187.7	43.9	70
Guyana	1966	214,970	771,000/0.3	3.6	–	85
Haiti	1804	27,249	5,870,000/1.9	211.5	48.9	23
Jamaica	1962	10,991	2,288,000/1.0	208.2	50.6	76
Martinique	(France)	1,100	328,000/0.1	298.2	41.6	70
Monserrat	(U.K.)	–	12,000/0.2	117.6	41.3	77
Netherlands Antilles[1]	(Neth'lnds)	1,821	300,000/1.3	270.0	–	88
Puerto Rico[1]	(U.S.)	8,897	3,283,000/1.5	369.0	42.1	88[3]
St. Kitts-Nevis	1983	261	40,000/−1.2	153.3	50.2	80
St. Lucia	1979	619	123,000/1.1	198.7	59.2	78
St. Vincent and the Grenadines	1979	389	103,000/0.9	264.8	–	82
Suriname	1975	163,265	381,000/1.7	2.3	52.7	65
Trinidad and Tobago	1962	5,128	1,204,000/1.5	234.8	46.6	89
Turks and Caicos	(U.K.)	430	7,436/1.9[2]	22.1	53.7	99
U.S. Virgin Islands	(U.S.)	344	110,800/1.3	324.0	29.9	–

Source: Unless otherwise stated, figures are from the Central Intelligence Agency, *The World Factbook, 1986* (Washington, D.C., 1986).

[1]Figures on Netherlands Antilles (including Aruba, independent since 1986) and Puerto Rico, and figures on tourist receipts, are from Caribbean/Central American Action, *Caribbean and Central American Databook* (Washington, D.C., 1986).

[2]Population growth rate for Turks and Caicos, and figures on percentage of population under 20 years of age, and from the United Nations, *UN Demographic Yearbook, 1984* (New York, 1986).

[3]Puerto Rican literacy rate is from the 1980 U.S. Census.

None of the insular Caribbean territories is ethnically or culturally homogeneous. Five racial groups (black, white, Oriental, native Indian, and East Indian) and their numerous subgroups and combinations mingle with varying degrees of integration and hostility, and

Table 1. (continued)

Infant Deaths (Per 1,000 Births)	Per Capita GDP in U.S. Dollars (Year)	Imports c.i.f. (In Millions of U.S. Dollars)	Exports f.o.b. (In Millions of U.S. Dollars)	GDP Growth[4] (%; same year as for Per Capita GDP)	Av. Ann. Per Capita GDP Growth 1965–84[4] (%)	Tourist Receipts, 1985[1] (In Millions of U.S. Dollars)
–	1,000 (1983)	–	–	–	–	–
31.5	1,990 (1984)	147.0	41.0	( )	−0.1	158.0
20.2	7,950 (1984)	3,000.0	2,300.0	4.5	1.6	1,428.0
26.3	4,650 (1984)	656.0	390.0	( )	2.5	3,089.0
56.0	1,200 (1985)	126.0	93.0	1.5	2.5	23.0
–	6,425 (1983)	50.0	2.0	( )	–	65.0
–	8,333 (1983)	140.0	2.4	–	–	19.0
15.0	1,530 (1982)	8,100.0	6,200.0	1.4	–	82.0
24.1	1,034 (1984)	56.0	26.0	4.3	0.3	4.5
63.0	1,090 (1984)	1,400.0	866.0	−2.0	3.2	371.0
–	1,940 (1976)	246.0	35.4	–	–	–
16.7	940 (1984)	55.6	18.9	0.6	1.7	–
18.6	3,760 (1980)	560.0	89.2	15.7	–	95.0
41.0	510 (1984)	222.0	212.0	4.0	–	–
107.0	240 (1984)	284.0	166.0	2.0	1.0	69.0
16.8	890 (1984)	1,100.0	706.0	−1.0	−0.4	583.0
12.6	4,540 (1980)	703.0	123.0	( )	( )	–
124.0	2,760 (1983)	20.0	1.6	2.0	–	4.8
–	9,140 (1983)	4,500.0	4,400.0	1.0	–	–
18.6	4,301 (1985)	10,100.0	10,500.0	2.8	–	710.0
–	1,563 (1985)	47.3	30.6	4.0	–	13.0
27.4	1,105 (1984)	106.8	49.7	5.0	3.1	56.0
–	781 (1983)	71.4	42.0	3.0	1.9	35.0
23.0	2,980 (1984)	346.0	356.0	−1.0	4.2	–
197.0	7,370 (1984)	1,900.0	2,200.0	−7.4	2.6	197.0
–	2,020 (1980)	20.9	2.5	–	–	12.0
–	7,780 (1985)	3,700.0	3,300.0	( )	( )	698.0

[4]Figures on percentage GDP growth and average annual per capita GDP growth are from the World Bank, *World Development Report, 1986* (Washington, D.C., 1986).

with considerable consciousness of color and shade. Numerous languages and dialects are spoken within the region, including Dutch, English, French, and Spanish and their derivatives, plus the Creole mixtures with African and Indian tongues. Caribbean religious sects are similarly diverse.

The economic organization of the Caribbean islands runs the gamut from the tax havens of the Bahamas to Cuba's brand of socialism. The Dominican Republic, where long-time dictator Rafael Trujillo's personal fiefdom passed to government ownership after his assassination in 1961, has a large public sector as a result. Both Jamaica and Guyana, which in the 1970s chose to build mixed economies with a heavy dose of state ownership, have been trying since then to attract and stimulate private investment again.

Economic productivity in the insular Caribbean ranges from the depths of Haiti (the only nation of the Americas that is among the very poorest countries of the world) to the uneven but impressive performance of Martinique and Guadeloupe, the Bahamas, Puerto Rico, Trinidad-Tobago, and Barbados. The region includes four of the six countries with the lowest per capita GNP in the Americas (Haiti, Dominica, Grenada, and Guyana), but also eight territories among the highest (Martinique, Trinidad-Tobago, Netherlands Antilles, Guadeloupe, Puerto Rico, Surinam, Bahamas, and Barbados). Poverty is widespread. Two-thirds of Haiti's rural population were reported in 1978 to have annual per capita incomes below forty dollars; 50 percent of children under five are said to suffer from protein calorie malnutrition, with 17 percent classified as severely malnourished. Figures from other countries are not quite as appalling, but per capita income figures in many nations are low.

Overall, the regional economies are in deep trouble. World demand is stagnant for two major Caribbean exports—sugar and bauxite—and prices are low. The region's share of world tourism revenues fell in the late 1970s and has not recovered. High prices for petroleum and other vital imports, coupled with rising interest rates, have placed additional strains on most Caribbean economies. Jamaica had seven consecutive years of negative growth during the 1970s. Haiti's per capita income is at about the 1960 level.

The Caribbean units share a number of painful characteristics. Almost all are heavily dependent on exporting a few primary products and are vulnerable to international market fluctuations and to the vagaries of disease and weather. Most of the islands have only a few known resources, apart from the sun and the sea. All have limited domestic markets and small local savings. Agriculture is weak and declining throughout most of the region. Per capita food production has dropped in most of the insular Caribbean, and regional imports of food have risen.

But while agriculture has declined, so has the push toward industrialization. The regionwide burst of "industrialization by invitation" during the 1960s reached the limits of import substitution and market scale, and quickly ran out of steam. Unemployment and underemployment, consequently, are high throughout the insular Caribbean. Most of the Caribbean islands are extremely overpopulated, and emigration from all is high.

Although a few of the Caribbean islands have been independent since the nineteenth century, many have achieved independence only during the past few years, and a few are still colonies today. All the Caribbean islands are to some degree dependent on close relations with a metropole; they are satellites in search of an orbit, requiring a regularized pattern of relationships with a central power. In recent years, that power has increasingly been the United States, which has seen its influence grow as the presence of Great Britain and other former colonial mentors has receded. The United States is closely involved with practically all the Caribbean islands, increasingly dominating their trade and investment. U.S. trade with the insular Caribbean totaled $12 billion in 1981, and U.S. direct private investment there (not counting that in Puerto Rico) reached some $7.7 billion in 1983.

The most dramatic link between the insular Caribbean and the United States is the steady stream of Caribbean immigrants to the mainland. Since World War II, close to five million Caribbeans have entered the United States. One out of every eight living persons born in the insular Caribbean currently resides on the mainland of the United States. Some 20 percent of legal immigrants to the United States, and an equal or higher percentage of illegal entrants, come from the insular Caribbean.

Five of the six countries in the world with the highest per capita rates of migration to the United States in the 1980s are from this region. Almost two million Puerto Ricans have come in, as well as over one million Cubans, about one million West Indians, well over half a million Dominicans, and more than 400,000 Haitians.

The Caribbean islands have been restless during the last few years. Regional economic difficulties have been a factor, to be sure, but underlying the Caribbean's unease has been conflict among fundamental goals and frustration about not achieving them. Caribbean people, of whatever race, religion, or nationality, want economic growth, improved equity, full employment, political participation, enhanced national autonomy, and more self-respect. These goals are all understandable, but for the present they are probably not compatible in the Caribbean. Cuba has achieved nearly full employment and considerably improved equity but at the cost of economic growth, personal freedom, and national autonomy. Martinique is relatively prosperous, but in large part this is because it is not autonomous. Barbados has grown rapidly but not equitably. Puerto Rico, which was once thought to be advancing on most of these lines, has in recent years found progress hard to sustain. No development strategy has been very successful in the insular Caribbean. Progress has everywhere been elusive, and increased frustration understandably has resulted.

Central America

The Central American nations are quite different from those of the insular Caribbean. They are somewhat larger than most of the Caribbean islands; most are the equivalent of small to medium-sized states of the United States. Except for Guatemala, where half the population is Indian, and the Miskito Indian enclave in Nicaragua and the Kuna Indian region in Panama, they are ethnically more homogeneous and less influenced by African immigration than the Caribbean islands. They are all Spanish-speaking and have many cultural, economic, and political links with each other; indeed, they are in a sense a nation divided, for all but Panama once formed a regional unity. Their economies are more industrialized than those of the insular Caribbean and are more diversely integrated into world markets.

The Central American nations have been independent since the nineteenth century, and their cultural and political identities are more secure. Although several of the Central American countries are very densely populated—El Salvador's figure of 580 persons per square mile is among the world's highest—their resource base is richer than that of most of the Caribbean islands. Their rate of emigration has been considerably lower than that of the insular Caribbean, though it is rising fast as a result of the bitter conflicts now under way.

Most of the Central American nations experienced very rapid economic growth and social change during the 1960s and until the late 1970s. From 1950 to 1978, the nations of Central America averaged an annual real rate of economic growth of 5.3 percent and a doubling of real per capita income. Physical infrastructure in Central America—including roads, port facilities, electrical energy, and mass communications—expanded remarkably. The rate of adult literacy

Table 2. The Central American Countries

Country	Area (Sq. Km.)	(Pop./ Ann. increase (No./%))	Pop. Density (Per Sq. Km.)	Pop. Under 20 Yrs. of Age[1] (%)	Lit'cy Rate (%)	Infant Deaths[3] (Per 1,000 Births)	Total Net Official Development Assistance, 1984[2] (Millions of U.S. Dollars)	Preliminary GDP Growth Estimates, 1985[3]	Average Annual Per Capita GDP Growth, 1965–84[2] (Percentage)	Per Capita GNP[2] In 1984 U.S. Dollars
Costa Rica	50,700	2,714.000/2.6	53.5	46.7	93	18.8	217	1.6	1.6	1,190
El Salvador	21,041	5,105,000/2.5	242.6	55.3	65	35.1	263	1.6	−0.6	710
Guatemala	108,780	8,600,000/5.0	79.1	55.6	50	56.0	65	−1.1	2.0	1,160
Honduras	112,088	4,646,000/3.3	41.5	58.4	56	78.6	290	3.0	0.5	700
Nicaragua	130,000	3,342,000/3.3	25.7	58.8	66	87.0	114	−2.6	−1.5	860
Panama	77,080	2,227,000/2.1	28.9	49.9	90	20.0	72	3.3	2.6	1,980

Source: Unless otherwise stated, figures are from the Central Intelligence Agency, *The World Factbook, 1986* (Washington, D.C., 1986).

1. Figures on percentage of population under 20 years of age are from the United Nations, *UN Demographic Yearbook, 1984* (New York, 1986), except for figures on El Salvador, which are from the United Nations Population Division, *World Population Prospects: Estimates and Projections as Assessed in 1982* (New York, 1985).

2. Figures on total net official development assistance, average annual per capita GDP growth, and per capita GNP are from the World Bank, *World Development Report, 1986* (Washington, D.C., 1986).

3. Figures on infant deaths and preliminary GDP growth estimates are from the Inter-American Development Bank, *Economic and Social Progress in Latin America: 1986 Report.*

rose from about 44 percent to 72 percent over these years. Urbanization increased at a similar pace, from 16 percent of the population living in urban areas in 1950 to 43 percent in 1980.

In the mid-1970s, however, economic expansion in Central America slowed and in some countries reversed. The easy phase of import substitution was exhausted in most of these countries by about 1970. The economic benefits of the Central American Common Market, of considerable importance in the early 1960s, gave way in the late 1960s to intraregional tensions, which were exemplified by the 1969 "Soccer War" between El Salvador and Honduras. Further, Central America, without any oil resources except in Guatemala, was hard hit by the worldwide increase in energy costs; the region's oil bill climbed from $189 million in 1973 to about $1.5 billion in 1980, while the prices of the region's main exports lagged.

Central America's economic woes have worsened dramatically since the late 1970s. The region's terms of trade have deteriorated severely, by almost 50 percent between 1977 and 1984. The volume of Central America's exports has decreased, by some 20 percent since 1980, and intraregional trade has dropped almost 35 percent. Central America has been very hard hit, too, by other consequences of the international recession. These include a dramatically increased regional debt of $14 billion and burgeoning debt service costs, which reached $1.5 billion in 1982, equivalent to 33 percent of the region's export earnings. Capital flight has also increased, to an estimated $3 billion since 1979. Per capita incomes in Costa Rica and Guatemala are down to the level of 1972, Honduras is back to that of 1970, and in Nicaragua and El Salvador—wracked by civil strife—they have fallen to the levels of the early 1960s.

As economic difficulties have mounted, the striking socioeconomic inequities in most Central American nations (except for Costa Rica) have become more extreme and have aggravated internal tensions. The size of the average plot owned by the highland Indians in Guatemala, for example, was cut in half between 1955 and 1975; the number of landless peasants in El Salvador grew from 11 percent of the rural population in 1961 to 40 percent in 1975. In most Central American countries, the real per capita income of the poorest 20 percent of the population fell during the 1970s. Estimates from the UN Economic Commission for Latin America (ECLA) have suggested that 65 percent of Central America's population should be classified as economically "poor" and 42 percent as "critically poor." A total of

52 percent of Central America's children, according to ECLA, are malnourished.

The desperate poverty and the increasing concentration of land ownership and income in Central America are part of a syndrome. Small groups have monopolized political power (often with U.S. support) and have used it to reinforce their dominance over the export-based economies. Production of cash crops for export has been crowding out small-scale agriculture since the late nineteenth century. The process intensified in the 1950s and 1960s, when the oligarchies manipulated their control of the banking and judicial systems (and the military) to cash in on booming world prices for cotton and beef. While a few plantation owners and ranchers enriched themselves, small farmers lost their lands and were forced to become rural wage laborers. The Central American Common Market stimulated some foreign investors in the 1960s to set up industries that produced for the expanded regional market, but migration to the cities by landless peasants outstripped industrial employment.

As income distribution in Central America has worsened, conflicts have intensified. As a consequence, both political repression and insurgency have increased. Central America has been wracked since the late 1970s by bitter internal struggles. Nicaragua's broke out first, in part because of the excesses of the Somoza dynasty. El Salvador has for several years experienced an intense civil war, pitting Marxist-led guerrilla groups against the country's armed forces. Leftist groups in El Salvador, as in Nicaragua during the late 1970s, have received some Cuban encouragement and support, but the main impetus has been local. A series of coups in Guatemala has not appreciably reduced that country's prolonged bloodletting. Honduras, the poorest of the Central American nations, teeters near violence. Even Costa Rica, long tranquil, is beginning to experience incidents of terrorism.

The disruption that accompanies civil turmoil, moreover, has further clouded economic prospects in most of Central America. Central America's internal wars during the past decade have killed almost 150,000 people, displaced at least one and a half million more, and caused hundreds of millions of dollars of damage. The crumbling of Central America's remaining oligarchies and the further polarization of Latin America's most bitterly divided countries contrast with the muted unease of most of the insular Caribbean.

Although historically the United States has exerted considerable influence on the political and economic history of the Central American isthmus, the region is less closely tied to the United States, or to any metropolitan power, than are the Caribbean islands. U.S. economic involvement in Central America has remained modest in recent decades. After a surge in the 1960s, direct U.S. investment in the countries of Central America except Panama slowed again in the 1970s and decreased in the early 1980s. It amounts to less than $800 million, or about 2.5 percent of U.S. direct investment in Latin America, 10 percent of U.S. investment in the insular Caribbean, and only 0.3 percent of U.S. investment worldwide. The financial involvement of U.S. banks in Central America amounts to less than 2.3 percent of their total exposure in Latin America and the Caribbean, and it has been declining further in the face of the region's turmoil. Nor is U.S. trade with Central America very significant; in 1982 it amounted to about $4 billion, which is only 5.4 percent of U.S. trade with all of Latin America, 36 percent of U.S. trade with the insular Caribbean, and 1 percent of the worldwide commerce of the United States. The economic stake of the United States in Central America today is modest, less than in the insular Caribbean and much smaller than in Brazil and Mexico.

The Politics of National Insecurity

Although they are different in many respects, the countries of the Caribbean and Central America are similar in one very important way. Clustered around the Caribbean Sea—America's Mediterranean— they constitute the "third border" of the United States. The proximity of the Caribbean Basin to the United States has been its defining characteristic ever since this country burst onto the international scene as a significant power in the nineteenth century. The United States rose to international prominence precisely by exerting its influence in the Caribbean region, starting with Cuba and Puerto Rico. The region remains fundamental to the perception many U.S. leaders have of this country's world standing. As President Reagan put it in his April 1983 address to a joint session of Congress: "The national security of all the Americas is at stake in Central America. If we cannot defend ourselves there, we cannot expect to prevail elsewhere. Our credibility would collapse, our alliances would crumble, and the safety of our homeland would be put in jeopardy."

During the late nineteenth and early twentieth centuries, the Caribbean Basin was necessarily a major focus of U.S. foreign policy. A considerable share of U.S. foreign investment and trade was then concentrated in the Caribbean and Central America. This nation's most important overseas military installations were the network of coaling stations and naval bases established to protect U.S. interests in the region, especially access to the Panama Canal. A primary aim of U.S. foreign policy, therefore, was to prevent extrahemispheric powers from expanding their influence in the Caribbean region. The annexation of Puerto Rico, the Platt Amendment imposed on Cuba, the promulgation of the Roosevelt Corollary to the Monroe Doctrine, the repeated U.S. military interventions in the Dominican Republic, Haiti, and Central America —all were part of a sustained U.S. effort to secure absolute control of its border region. By the time Franklin Delano Roosevelt launched the Good Neighbor Policy in 1934 to shore up hemispheric relations in a troubled international context, the United States could afford to change its approach to the Caribbean Basin. This shift was possible precisely because the United States was not being effectively challenged in its border region.

The United States emerged from World War II dominant in the whole Western Hemisphere, and indeed in much of the world. The United States extended its influence throughout Latin America and spread its investment, financial, commercial, diplomatic, military, and cultural presence around the globe. Because the United States undertook such a large international role in the postwar period, its involvement in the Caribbean Basin paled into relative insignificance and was largely taken for granted. The U.S. government paid very little attention to the Caribbean Basin from the mid-1940s until the mid-1970s, except for sporadic bursts of activity when it appeared to Washington that leftists aligned with the Soviet Union were coming to power: in Guatemala in 1954, in Cuba from 1959 on, in British Guiana in the early 1960s, and in the Dominican Republic in 1965. In Guatemala, a covert military operation removed the left-leaning Arbenz government and installed a client regime. In British Guiana (later Guyana), clandestine U.S. involvement helped to thwart the political ambition of Dr. Cheddi Jagan. In the Dominican episode, 23,000 U.S. troops were landed to prevent what some in Washington feared might become a Communist takeover, and they remained to stabilize the local situation until national elections could put a trusted Dominican political figure back into power.

The case of Cuba was different, however, and it has changed the nature of U.S.-Caribbean relations. Beginning in 1959, and especially from 1960 on, Washington tried a variety of techniques to try to coopt, reverse, abort, or destroy the Cuban revolution, all to no avail. The strategic and tactical skill of Fidel Castro, blunders in U.S. policy, and a Soviet decision to provide unstinting assistance to Castro's regime combined to permit the firm consolidation of an anti-U.S. government in what had formerly been a U.S. client state. Unchallenged U.S. hegemony in the Caribbean Basin ended for all practical purposes in April 1961 when the U.S.-supported Bay of Pigs invasion collapsed. The "understandings" between the United States and the Soviet Union at the end of the October 1962 missile crisis—in which the Soviet Union agreed to remove its missiles and not to reintroduce a strategic threat to the United States in exchange for a U.S. pledge not to invade Cuba—reinforced the end of U.S. hegemony. Many opinion leaders in the United States still do not accept the loss of absolute U.S. control over the Caribbean Basin, but it has been a fact for more than twenty-five years.

During the period from the mid-1940s to the mid-1970s, tangible U.S. interests in the Caribbean and Central America changed a great deal. The region's military importance diminished as new technology (especially intercontinental ballistic missiles and nuclear submarines) drastically reduced the significance of proximity. Preserving U.S. access to the Panama Canal remains an important aim, but it is no longer considered a "vital interest." Today's aircraft carriers and supertankers are too large to transit the Canal, and the share of U.S. commerce passing through the Canal has declined to less than one-sixth of this country's total oceanic trade. Some U.S. bases and other military assets in the Caribbean region are still useful, especially for training purposes and as listening posts, but their diminished significance was made evident in the 1970s by the Pentagon's decision to downgrade or close several Caribbean facilities and to reduce the number of U.S. military personnel stationed in the region.

The sea-lanes that pass through the Caribbean remain important to the United States, because 44 percent of all foreign cargo tonnage and 45 percent of the crude oil imported into the United States transit them. But absolute control of each Caribbean Basin country is no longer needed to protect these lanes. A Caribbean Basin nation (such as Cuba or Nicaragua) that sought to disrupt the sea-lanes would find itself instantly vulnerable to the overwhelming power of the United

States, only minutes away. It is hard to imagine a credible scenario in which the Caribbean sea-lanes would be disrupted. Even if the Soviet Union were to undertake the risky enterprise of interfering with U.S. shipping, it would be more likely to do so in the North Atlantic than in the Caribbean, where the relative disparity in easily projectable power is so favorable to the United States.

U.S. economic interests in the Caribbean Basin have also declined, both in absolute and in relative terms. U.S. investment in the insular Caribbean accounts for less than 2.5 percent of the total book value of all direct U.S. foreign investment, and even that figure would be much lower if the essentially paper investment in the Bahamas were excluded. The U.S. investment stake in Central America, as has been noted, is even smaller and has been declining in recent years. Likewise, the relative importance of Central America and the Caribbean as sources for products and materials has diminished because the worldwide involvement of the United States has produced multiple suppliers, and synthetics have replaced many natural products.

Two newer U.S. interests in the Caribbean Basin have emerged in recent years, particularly with regard to the insular Caribbean. One is diplomatic: the Caribbean nations wield many votes in the United Nations, the Organization of American States, and other bodies. Though the Caribbean democracies have consistently supported U.S. positions on a number of international issues, a shift to hostility would be irritating. A second U.S. stake in the insular Caribbean, and to a lesser extent in Central America, is demographic. Over 10 percent of all the Caribbean population as a whole—not simply Cuba's population—has immigrated to the United States since 1959. The United States has an interest in regulating migration from the Caribbean Basin because large groups of immigrants are increasingly a source of local anxieties and tensions in Florida, New York, New Jersey, and other states.

In sum, traditional U.S. interests in the insular Caribbean and Central America have declined over the last generation, although they are still emphasized in official documents and discussions. Newer U.S. interests in these regions, particularly diplomatic and demographic concerns, have increased in significance but not yet in salience; President Reagan's key address to the OAS on the Caribbean Basin Initiative did not even mention migration, for instance. The main reason that U.S. policymakers have rediscovered the Caribbean and Central America flows instead from an almost reflexive U.S. concern: the desire to retain overwhelming predominance in the border region.

Most U.S. political leaders believe that an administration identified as having "lost" a country previously in the U.S. orbit, as having permitted a "second Cuba" to emerge, would suffer a high domestic political cost. The urge to retain tight control is further strengthened by a calculus of international prestige. U.S. officials do not want the United States to be perceived abroad as unable to maintain dominance so close to home. To some extent, recent U.S. administrations have been caught in a credibility trap of their own making, as they have voluntarily raised the declared stakes for the United States in the Caribbean Basin and then escalated U.S. involvement to match the stakes.

Official discussions of U.S. policy in the Caribbean Basin are laced with assertions of a vital U.S. "national security interest" in the region, although the exact nature of the interest is rarely specified. It may be that the underlying rationale of recent U.S. policy can be understood best not in terms of national security as it is usually discussed but rather in terms of national *in*security. What is fundamentally at stake, more than any tangible and objective challenge, may be the psychological and subjective difficulty of coping with a loss of control in the border region. U.S. policymakers have considered it important to retain control of the internal politics of Caribbean Basin countries, even though the object of this control is far less significant than it used to be. Further, the United States has sought to retain its overwhelming control even though the domestic and international costs of perpetuating this stance are increasing in the face of nationalist revolutionary movements. That is the heart of the matter in the Caribbean Basin.

The U.S. Stake in the Caribbean Basin

Discussions of U.S. relations with the Caribbean Basin often suffer from a tendency to treat ideal visions of the region as realistic objectives of U.S. policy and thus to confuse unattainable preferences with core U.S. interests. The vision that the report of the National Bipartisan Commission on Central America (the Kissinger Commission) holds out as the correct aim of U.S. policy in Central America, for example, is one of peaceful, democratic, reform-oriented, stable, prosperous, congenial neighbors. The basic problem, however, is that this goal is utterly unrealistic. Except for Costa Rica, Central America's nations are conflict-wracked, repressive, polarized, economically depressed, and unstable, and they harbor a deep resentment toward the United States. The goals posited by the Kissinger Commission report and by other recent official articulations of U.S. policies toward Central America and the Caribbean are not merely unrealistic; they are like a mirage, ever receding as we approach them.

To fashion a successful U.S. policy toward the Caribbean Basin, it is essential to define the core objectives of the United States. The primary U.S. interest in the Caribbean Basin, today as in the past, is to prevent hostile extrahemispheric forces from using the Basin as a platform for damaging activities directed against the United States or its allies. In contemporary terms, this means assuring that no bases, strategic weapons or facilities, or combat forces are introduced by the Soviet Union or its allies into the border region of the United States. In fact, given the presence of missile-toting Soviet submarines off the Atlantic coast, such facilities or forces would probably not very markedly increase the Soviet military threat to the United States. But the presence of threatening bases or facilities in the Caribbean Basin would pose some additional danger, and at a margin where each increment matters. Equally important, in a world where perceptions can create realities, the United States would appear weak if it could not keep direct security challenges out of its immediate vicinity.

The second core interest of the United States in the Caribbean Basin today is to assure continuing access to the assets of Central America and the Caribbean, primarily the Panama Canal but also the sea-lanes. Historically it has been important for the United States to maintain secure access to these advantages without a major investment of resources, and this objective remains a priority. It is doubtful, however, that tight control of the internal affairs of Caribbean Basin nations is still the most effective means of achieving this goal. On the contrary, the Panama Canal treaties of 1978 suggest that accommodating nationalist impulses in the Caribbean Basin region is a more effective means of protecting U.S. interests than is resisting such nationalist currents. It is also important for the United States to reduce the risk of a regional conflagration in the Caribbean Basin, for such an outbreak would be far more likely to disrupt U.S. access to the region's assets than any domestic political change within the individual Caribbean nations.

The third important U.S. interest in the Caribbean Basin is to decrease the pressure for immigration into the United States, a pressure created by continued economic decline and violent turmoil in the region. The causal connections between development and migration are complex, and the United States cannot be confident that pressures for migration from the Caribbean Basin will diminish as soon as economic development in the region picks up. It is clear, however, that worsening economic conditions will heighten pressures for emigration and that increasing polarization and strife will increase migration regardless of the results of a civil war.

This interest in stemming the flow of migration from the Caribbean Basin leads to a fourth and broader U.S. interest: to promote economic development and long-term political stability in the Caribbean Basin countries so that they can become self-sufficient. Access to Caribbean Basin resources is no longer the most important issue to the United States. Rather, the United States has an increasing interest in helping Caribbean and Central American nations use their own resources to achieve regional development.

If these four U.S. interests in the Caribbean Basin are fundamental, other aims of U.S. policy, though often repeated by Washington officials, are or ought to be less important. The United States should support democracies, but U.S. policy cannot create democracy in countries that lack the traditions and institutions required or that are still in the midst of civil wars. Moreover, although the United States would prefer that its neighbors share its perceptions of world problems, favor free enterprise and foreign investment, and disdain the Soviet Union and its policies, such regional conviviality is not crucial. If countries in the Caribbean Basin area choose to adopt socialist economies or even to embrace the Soviet Union but not to offer military advantages to the Soviet Union or Cuba, that can be tolerated by the United States.

Options for U.S. Policy

The United States has four main options for advancing its interests in the Caribbean Basin: intermittent intervention, sustained disengagement, activist expansion of immediate U.S. influence, or an emphasis on long-term development. The policy of intermittent intervention combines a low degree of interest in Caribbean socioeconomic development with a high degree of concern for U.S. security interests, narrowly defined. The policy of sustained disengagement features a low degree of U.S. concern with the Caribbean Basin on both socioeconomic and traditional security dimensions. The activist policy involves a high degree of U.S. concern with both socioeconomic and security aspects. Finally, the developmental policy combines a high degree of U.S. concern with socioeconomic questions with a relatively minimal preoccupation with classic security issues.

Intermittent Intervention

Intermittent intervention was, in effect, the policy of the United States toward the Caribbean Basin from the turn of the century until the late 1970s. The traditional stance meant ignoring the Caribbean Basin countries most of the time, sending diplomats who were without stature in the region, offering few if any economic concessions, and often letting private interests dominate national concerns. Whenever change threatens to undermine U.S. control, or even to generate significant unpredictability, the traditional policy calls for U.S. power to restore this country's domination. The intermittent interventionist approach to the Caribbean and Central America has its advantages. Most of the time it ties up few resources, and it frees policymakers to concentrate on other matters unless they think key U.S. interests are directly engaged.

One main difficulty has always plagued the traditional U.S. approach to the Caribbean Basin, however. Weak, dependent entities like those dotting the Caribbean are precisely those most vulnerable to instability and hence to outside influence. By themselves, these territories have never been able to resist the encroachments of external powers that Washington considers threatening, but neither have they been able to undertake the development and integration that might make them less vulnerable to foreign penetration. Although the United States has traditionally regarded the area as strategically important, it has never adopted the positive long-term measures this concern might imply. That is why the United States has so often been drawn into unpleasant Caribbean entanglements, including military intervention. The seeds of future interventions germinate in the underlying conditions that Washington persistently ignores.

The periodically intrusive nature of U.S. policy toward the Car-

ibbean Basin has had its costs. Each U.S. intervention tends to undermine national development. Each distorts the local distribution
of power and resources, often in ways unsupportive of long-term and
self-sustaining growth. Each U.S. intervention, whether overt or
covert, fuels anti-American movements not only in the affected
country but also elsewhere in the region. These episodes often strain
the domestic U.S. consensus on foreign policy, and each episode
makes more distant the day when international laws against military
coercion will have real force.

The traditional approach, in sum, has been shortsighted, counterproductive, and ultimately expensive. It amounts, in effect, to putting out fires in the region without removing the flammable material
and even, indeed, while leaving some smoldering embers behind. It
is an increasingly infeasible approach. The large Caribbean diaspora
in the United States makes it hard to ignore the region. Most important, both domestic and international constraints make it impossible
for the United States to exercise force in Central America and the
Caribbean as easily and effectively as it once did. The brief U.S. intervention in Grenada was in some ways the exception that proves
the rule, for it involved sending U.S. forces into a ministate with a
makeshift armed force of less than a thousand men, and this was done
under optimal political circumstances. In Nicaragua since 1979,
however, the United States government has felt the constraints that
limit the possibility of armed intervention. These limits have also
sharply narrowed the U.S. options in dealing with the Marxist groups
in El Salvador and, most obviously, with Castro's Cuba.

Sustained Disengagement

Under sustained disengagement the United States would limit its
involvement in the Caribbean Basin to a conventional diplomatic and
commercial interchange. This view holds that U.S. economic interests in the Caribbean Basin are not overwhelmingly important and
would probably remain largely unaffected even if some governments in the area became hostile to the United States. These governments will almost inevitably maintain economic relations with the
United States unless Washington itself imposes economic sanctions, as it has done in the case of Cuba and Nicaragua. U.S. policymakers, attentive publics, and eventually the electorate at large
should therefore be educated to accept a substantial U.S. withdraw-

al from Caribbean involvement. The United States should not preoccupy itself with either the economic development or the political direction of the Caribbean Basin countries but should treat them with the kind of benign neglect it accords to small countries in central Africa.

The disengagement formula has some abstract appeal, for it relates instruments and resources to objective interests more logically than the traditional approach. It is evident, too, that the kind of frenetic U.S. intervention in Caribbean Basin affairs that characterized the 1920s and the 1960s has been counterproductive. But the disengagement option is blatantly unfeasible. The United States cannot simply withdraw unilaterally from involvement in its border region.

Geography—strongly reinforced by history, politics, economics, and culture—makes the United States a major presence in the Caribbean Basin. The countries of this region cannot escape the shadow of the United States, whether it be benign or stifling. Nor can the United States escape involvement in the Caribbean, with which this country is so interconnected. Whatever policy an administration adopts, immigration from the Caribbean Basin would not stop, tourism would continue, and other business flows would prompt fuller U.S. involvement. More important, public opinion in the United States, both at the attentive public and at the mass level, would feel uncomfortable about Washington's abandoning these countries to their fate. The international reputation of the United States, both among allies and rivals, would also be damaged by such a passive U.S. stance. Great powers simply do not behave that way; disengagement would prove impossible to sustain.

Activist Expansion of Immediate U.S. Influence

Although they adopted differing emphases, both the Carter and Reagan administrations actively expanded U.S. involvement in the internal politics and the economies of the Caribbean Basin countries. The basic tenets of this approach are that the United States should concern itself with the immediate situation and stability of the Caribbean Basin, acting to shore up current U.S. influence wherever possible, and that it should also increase and sustain longer-term economic and technical assistance to the region in order to contribute to its long-range stability. Rather than wait for instability, revolutionary conditions, and anti-American movements to intensify, it is argued, the United States should head off problems in the Caribbean Basin by helping these nations cope with their problems while at the same time moving to counter Cuba and its influence.

The Carter administration took a number of early steps to expand the U.S. presence and influence in the insular Caribbean. High officials were sent to the region to indicate interest and to show that Washington accepted "ideological pluralism" in the Caribbean. The Latin American Bureau of the State Department was reorganized to assure greater concern for the Caribbean, and the number of U.S. diplomats assigned to the region expanded. U.S. economic assistance to the region was doubled, and Washington took the lead in establishing a multilateral consortium to channel aid to the region. The Carter administration also began to explore a limited improvement in bilateral relations with Cuba while making it clear that Cuba's efforts to support revolutionary movements would be strenuously opposed.

The gathering strength of the anti-Somoza movement in Nicaragua and of the insurrectionary groups in El Salvador eventually convinced the Carter administration to include Central America in its new Caribbean policy. Significant economic aid packages were designed for Nicaragua, El Salvador, and the other Central American countries in the hope of preempting revolutionary movements or coopting them where they had emerged. The cooptive approach to the revolutionary movements in Grenada and Nicaragua failed to produce quick results, however. Cuba remained actively involved in Africa despite the Carter administration's overtures and signals. Similarly, leftist insurgents in El Salvador stepped up their attacks. The Carter administration responded to these developments by backing away from its forthcoming posture on change and gradually reverted to a more conventional anticommunist approach to the Caribbean Basin.

The Reagan administration was preoccupied from the start with the Caribbean Basin, especially with Central America and El Salvador. From its first days the administration intensified its war of words and at least a few actions against Cuba, and it drew a line in El Salvador against the further expansion of Soviet and Cuban influence. The Reagan administration's overall approach, unveiled by the president in his Caribbean Basin Initiative (CBI) of 1982, has been to beef up the U.S. presence throughout the Caribbean and Central America: militarily, politically, economically, and culturally. As originally proposed, the CBI included major adjustments in trade and tariff policy—even "one-way free trade" on a number of products—as well as tax incentives to stimulate U.S. investment in the region. Significant public-resource transfers were also proposed, mainly through bilateral channels. The U.S. Congress, however, removed the investment tax incentives and excluded selected products from the free-trade provisions, thus reducing the economic impact of the CBI.

An East-West focus has characterized every aspect of the CBI. Allocations for assistance have depended much more on a country's attitudes toward Cuba and the United States than on its economic need or development prospects. The insignificant aid offered to Haiti, the poorest country in the Caribbean region, illustrates this point, as does the outright exclusion from the plan of Nicaragua—and of Grenada until the leftist government there was ousted. Over 70 percent of the assistance has gone to El Salvador, Jamaica, and Costa Rica. Moreover, the entire aid supplement has taken the form of Economic Support Funds—simple transfers of funds to recipient countries' treasuries without reference to specific development projects. The CBI's thrust is to shore up immediate U.S. political influence; it is not primarily a strategy for the region's long-term economic and social development.

When it comes to combating leftist gains in Central America and the Caribbean, the Reagan administration's approach has been avidly to support anticommunist governments and movements. The United States is deeply involved in the politics of El Salvador, in addition to providing arms, training, and advisers to that country's military. It has converted Honduras into a major base for U.S. military training and for operations against neighboring Nicaragua. The Reagan administration has revived the Central American Defense Council (CONDECA), sought to restore military aid to Guatemala's military regime in the early 1980s, and has provided military equipment and training to Costa Rica despite that country's misgivings.

The U.S. government channeled covert aid to counterrevolutionaries in Grenada during the period of the New Jewel Movement and seized the opportunity to unseat the leftist regime there in October 1983. U.S. assistance to the armed partisans fighting against the Nicaraguan government (the contras) has continued despite congressional restrictions. Mindful of congressional and public opinion, the administration has frequently reiterated that it does not plan to send U.S. combat forces into Central America. Some U.S. officials, however, began in the mid-1980s openly to discuss the possibility that U.S. troops might eventually have to be used there.

The differences between the Carter and Reagan variants of the activist approach to the Caribbean and to Central America should be noted. The Carter stance on leftist regimes in the Caribbean Basin area was (especially at first) more accommodating; Washington was willing to accept ideological diversity even in this border region. The Reagan administration strongly favors procapitalist and pro-U.S. regimes, and ignores or punishes the others. The Carter administration supported multilateral economic and technical assistance; the Reagan administration prefers visible bilateral assistance. The Carter administration, although willing to commit U.S. resources to counter unwanted trends in the Caribbean and Central America, respected the sovereignty of the Caribbean and Central American nations. The Reagan administration, on the contrary, made it plain from the start that it might use force as a means of reversing unacceptable developments in this region.

These significant differences should not obscure important similarities between the Carter and Reagan variants of the activist approach, however. Both administrations lumped together the insular Caribbean and Central America. Both showed a high degree of concern with socioeconomic and security issues. Both emphasized short-term political considerations and the aim of countering Cuba. Both proposed that the United States should take the lead in orchestrating regional security and development initiatives in order to combat revolutionary inroads.

The recommendations of the Kissinger Commission epitomized the activist approach by calling for more U.S. involvement in practically all aspects of that region's life. The Commission argued that Central America needs major social changes and massive economic development, as well as considerable security assistance, in order to beat back the challenge of Marxist-oriented insurgent movements. It urged the United States to play a pivotal role in promoting economic growth, social change, and political democracy, and to provide a "security shield" behind which progress could occur. It called for the United States to lead a process of regional transformation in order to preempt revolutionary movements.

The activist approach to the Caribbean Basin has obvious advantages over both the interventionist and the disengagement options. Focusing sustained attention and resources on the Caribbean Basin should enable the U.S. government more effectively to influence U.S. relations with the region. The scale of Caribbean Basin entities is such that even limited U.S. moves can have an impact. Many Caribbean countries are so dependent that an infusion of U.S. resources is likely to fix the region even more firmly in the U.S. orbit, at least in the short run.

But the activist approach involves important risks. First, it may arouse unrealistic expectations within the region. Prime Minister Edward Seaga of Jamaica, for instance, called for a long-term program of aid to Central America and the Caribbean at a level of $3 billion per year, and the Kissinger Commission called for $8 billion over five years. In a period of massive U.S. federal deficits, however, aid transfers to the Caribbean Basin will be much more modest. Aid to shore up military regimes, moreover, often produces a need for more aid. The activist approach may thus produce a troublesome gap between rhetoric and expectations, on the one hand, and implementation and impact on the other. The American public will surely not long support an expensive effort to transform Caribbean Basin realities.

Second, the preoccupation of U.S. policymakers with Fidel Castro's Cuba exacerbates severe political strains. Insular Caribbean leaders typically perceive Castro primarily as a Caribbean actor, not a Cold War instrument. At times they have found "playing the Cuban card" useful to increase legitimacy with domestic constituents or to strengthen Third World ties. The persistent failure of U.S. government officials to assess Caribbean perceptions of Castro accurately and the recurrent U.S. readiness to focus on Cuba rather than on the region's underlying needs inevitably breed resentment. To the extent that U.S. interest in the Caribbean Basin appears to be purely instrumental, the chances increase that an activist U.S. presence in the region will backfire, triggering nationalist reactions.

The activist approach has three other important drawbacks.

First, despite the Reagan administration's repeated assurances that U.S. combat forces will not be used, the risks of an escalating U.S. military involvement in Central America are inherent in the policy of direct confrontation with insurgent movements and unrelenting hostility toward Cuba and Nicaragua. The prospect that the United States will eventually have to choose between humiliation and escalation is built into the activist stance.

Second, the more fully the United States is engaged in the internal affairs of the nations of the Caribbean Basin, the greater is the likelihood that this country will have to absorb larger flows of refugees from the continuing civil wars. As the United States involves itself more deeply in the region, it creates increasing political and moral imperatives to assist the victims of violence.

Third, an increasingly interventionist U.S. stance, even if it stops short of direct military action, contradicts the respect the United States must show Latin America if it is to secure greater cooperation from the hemisphere's major countries. Gunboat diplomacy in the Caribbean Basin may win back Grenada or perhaps even Nicaragua, but such "successes" may alienate Brazil, Mexico, Colombia, Argentina, Venezuela, and other Latin American nations. The one event that could push Mexico into a strongly nationalist, anti-American mode would be a U.S. military intervention in Central America. The consequences throughout South America would also be harmful.

Emphasis on Long-Term Development

A fourth possible approach to Central America and the Caribbean would involve a sustained U.S. commitment to the economic and social development of the nations in the Caribbean Basin without an attempt to exercise tight control over their internal affairs. This approach posits that the core U.S. interest in its border region is to exclude security threats—to keep hostile bases, combat forces, and strategic facilities out of the area. It would accept diverse sociopolitical and economic approaches in the Caribbean Basin, even Marxist ones, as long as no direct security threats are introduced into the region. It would accomplish this aim not by controlling the area's domestic politics but by making it clear to the Soviet Union or other potential adversaries that the introduction of threatening forces and facilities would trigger an immediate U.S. response and by negotiating regional agreements to exclude such items.

The second proposition of the developmental approach is that the United States will benefit if the countries of the Caribbean Basin are able to grow economically and build effective social and political institutions. The improved viability of Caribbean Basin nations would decrease pressure for migration to the United States and would facilitate a fruitful economic, cultural, and social exchange with the United States.

The developmental approach assumes as well that geography, history, and economics will tie the countries of the Caribbean Basin to the United States so long as the United States does nothing to expel them from its orbit. Caribbean Basin nations, regardless of their domestic or even their international politics will send most of their exports to the United States and buy most of their imports from this country as long as they are permitted to do so. They have an interest, therefore, in avoiding hostile relations with the United States.

The developmental approach to the Caribbean Basin would concentrate on long-term economic and social progress rather than on immediate political alignment. It would distinguish between those countries that are ready for significant economic advance (presently, this would include most of the insular Caribbean nations, along with Costa Rica, Guatemala, and perhaps Honduras on the Central American isthmus) and those where civil turmoil precludes effective economic progress in the near future.

With regard to the former group of countries, those ready for economic and social development, the United States would extend to all—regardless of ideology, domestic social or political organization, or foreign policy—the provisions for free access to the U.S. market contained in the Caribbean Basin Initiative as originally proposed. An attempt would be made to reverse congressionally imposed restrictions that have reduced the impact of the CBI for precisely those products on which Caribbean Basin nations have achieved a comparative advantage. The United States and other interested countries would provide assistance for the development of infrastructure and human resources in the Caribbean Basin. Foreign assistance would be provided mainly through multilateral rather than bilateral channels in order to reduce politicization and to extend the time horizons beyond the U.S. electoral cycle. Rather than increase its visibility, the United States would gradually lower its profile in the Caribbean Basin. Washington might then be less of a focus for nationalist and integrative impulses in the region.

With regard to the strife-torn nations of Central America, the United States would cut back its intense involvement of recent years. It would aim primarily to stop any of the Central American conflicts from providing an occasion for the introduction of extrahemispheric military threats and to prevent the Central American conflicts from escalating, broadening, or becoming part of a general East-West confrontation. The main instrument of U.S. policy would be diplomatic, not military. In particular, Washington would genuinely support the efforts to mediate Central America's conflicts.

The United States would fully back attempts to negotiate a regional political solution that would protect the territorial integrity of existing states and their governments (including Nicaragua and El Salvador) against insurgent movements. Such an accord would bar both overt and covert attempts to overthrow established governments. It would also, by regional agreement, keep threatening bases, forces, and facilities out of the Caribbean Basin. As part of the agreement, the United States would assure the government of Nicaragua that U.S. efforts to destabilize the Sandinista regime would end.

Such an accord would extend to the whole Caribbean Basin region the basic principles embodied in the U.S.-Soviet understandings of 1962, 1970, and 1979 affecting Cuba; that is, that Soviet strategic bases or facilities will not be introduced into the region, that conventional forces will not be augmented so as threaten regional security, and that the territorial integrity of every state in the region will be respected by all. The draft treaty presented by the Contadora nations (Colombia, Mexico, Panama, and Venezuela) in June 1986 goes a long way toward this kind of regional solution. Properly verified and enforced, the proposed treaty provisions would protect core U.S. interests.

With regard to Cuba itself, the developmental approach would counsel mutually respectful diplomatic relations without undue cordiality. Pragmatic attempts would proceed in an effort to resolve immediate problems between the two countries regarding migration, fishing rights, hurricane tracking, hijacking, narcotics control, and other issues. Conventional diplomatic relations would be restored, and efforts would be made to involve Cuba constructively in regional peacekeeping agreements. As long as Cuba remained aligned with the Soviet Union, the United States would not warm its relations with Havana or include Cuba in the proposed regional provisions for preferential economic treatment. In time, however, as the improved regional relationship with the United States took hold, it might become possible, in effect, to threaten Cuba with peace. Cuba might be induced to weaken its close relationship with the Soviet Union, particularly its military ties, in exchange for increasing access to U.S. markets, capital, and technology.

Finally, the United States would ask all the countries of the Caribbean Basin to work cooperatively with Washington to regulate migration. The United States would consult with Caribbean Basin nations on means of keeping migration to this country within legal bounds and preventing the exploitation of illegal aliens. The United States would target U.S. foreign investment, trade policy, and foreign assistance to foster labor-intensive development in the region. Local family-planning programs would also be supported.

The developmental approach to the Caribbean Basin—concerned as it is with both preventing direct strategic threats to U.S. security and promoting the long-term viability of the insular Caribbean and Central America—would protect the core interests of the United States immediately and in the long term. It would do so without engaging the United States unnecessarily in these regions' internal struggles. It would keep the U.S. focus on those problems of the Caribbean Basin that should matter most to us and that we can still affect. Most important, this approach would enable the United States to deal with its border region without distracting its attention from the major economic and political issues affecting U.S. relations with Mexico and South America. The challenge for U.S. policy in Central America and the Caribbean is less a test of national will and credibility than of our sense of perspective and priorities.

Acknowledgments

This essay is excerpted and adapted from chapter 6 of my book *Partners in Conflict: The United States and Latin America* (Baltimore: Johns Hopkins University Press, 1987). Support for the research on the book was provided by a number of sources, particularly the Twentieth Century Fund and the Woodrow Wilson International Center for Scholars. I am grateful to Robertico Croes, Charles Becker, and David Ayón for research and editorial assistance.

Wayne S. Smith

Castro, Latin America, and the United States

In Cuba's renewed efforts to normalize relations with the other Latin American governments, one can see the metamorphosis of the Cuban Revolution. The overthrow of those same governments and the creation of a Latin American revolutionary bloc were once Castro's most deeply felt goals. As he came to power in 1959, it was this which drove him. It was important to carry out reforms in Cuba itself, but that was more a means to achieve the greater end. Castro had to put forward a revolutionary model of his own, had to have a national stage of his own from which to project himself into the larger international arena. But there was never any question as to which was the most important, his domestic or his international programs. No, even as he carried out his domestic reforms, Castro looked outward, his gaze on the southern horizon. As one of his more sympathetic chroniclers, Herbert Matthews, put it in 1961: "Fidel has all along felt himself to be a crusader, if not a saviour. He is out to achieve a second liberation of Latin America."[1]

Castro saw himself in the role of a Bolívar, with nothing less than the "liberation" of all Latin America as his goal—a goal encapsulated in the slogan, "The Andes will become the Sierra Maestra of Latin America." It was from U.S. economic domination that he intended to free it, just as Bolívar had freed it of Spanish political control almost a century and a half earlier. But while the United States was the real enemy, Castro believed that to break its hold, one first had to overthrow the bourgeois, *vendepatria* governments that served it. Just as he had rid Cuba of Batista, so would he have to rid the other countries of such governments. To accomplish this, Castro did not intend to march across the continent with a growing army behind him, as had Bolívar and San Martín; rather, he believed the Cuban example would in itself spark revolutions elsewhere, and he of course stood ready to give them both moral and—on a clandestine basis— material support.

These early Cuban foreign policy objectives were both dynamic and static in nature. On the one hand, not even the liberation of "Nuestra América" was an end in itself; rather, the creation of a great new Latin American revolutionary bloc with himself as its spiritual leader was but the core of Castro's plan to project himself onto the world stage as a major player. Castro as the leader of a small island might go unnoticed; Castro as the recognized spokesman of a revolutionary hemisphere could leave his mark on the world.

But if there was an outthrusting, even something of a global outthrusting, implicit in early Cuban foreign policy, so too were its objectives defensive in nature. Castro was aiming to do no less in Latin America than to curtail U.S. economic interests and challenge the U.S. political leadership. He did not expect the United States to sit passively by as he did so. Sooner or later, he surmised, it would move against him unless there were some restraining factor, and for this Castro initially counted on a show of Latin American revolutionary unity. A Cuba standing alone would be totally vulnerable; a Cuba supported by other revolutionary governments might not be. In numbers there would perhaps be strength. Thus he believed that Cuban survival depended upon the near-term triumph of other revolutionary movements in Latin America. The extension of the Revolution to the rest of the hemisphere, therefore, was not only crucial to the advancement of Cuban foreign policy objectives, it was also imperative for its very survival—or so he believed.

It should be emphasized that these early objectives were Castro's; the Soviet Union had nothing to do with them. As the Cuban Revolution had been nationalist in content, so too was Castro's international vision fueled by nationalism. The other revolutions he hoped for would spring from the soul of Latin American nationalism. The great new revolutionary bloc he expected it to form would be antiimperialist and anti-U.S., yes, but it would be inspired by the thought of José Martí, Simón Bolívar and Rubén Darío, not of Marx or Lenin.

Castro was, of course, correct in his assumption that the United States would react strongly to his efforts to turn the Andes into the Sierra Maestra of Latin America. It began to gather its allies in the Organization of American States, and at a meeting of that organization's foreign ministers in August 1959 the Cuban problem was taken up for the first time. From that point forward, the OAS moved steadily in the direction of isolating Cuba. The United States, meanwhile, also tried to solve the problem by more direct means, launching a Cuban exile invasion at the Bay of Pigs in April 1961, and, when that failed, resorting to all sorts of clandestine operations against Cuba—everything from attempts to assassinate Castro to radio broadcasts calling on the Cuban people to rebel.

In the face of this increasingly active response, Castro had few options. By the end of 1959 it had become clear to him (if it had not before) that the United States was indeed gearing up to move against him and that it would in time have the support of the OAS in doing so. Further, he saw he would stand alone. The other revolutions he had counted on for support had not taken place and, it was increasingly clear, were not likely to win in the near term even should they break out. The United States and the Latin American governments were forewarned and had already taken defensive countermeasures.

Castro was thus left with two choices if he wanted to survive: (1) he could give up his foreign policy objectives, or (2) he could turn to a more powerful patron for a shield against U.S. might—a shield behind which he might continue to pursue those objectives. Castro chose the latter course, eventually even declaring himself to be a Marxist-Leninist in an effort to force a greater security commitment out of the Soviets.[2]

Of course, Cuba's growing association with Moscow further sharpened suspicions and raised tensions, not only between Cuba and the United States but also between Cuba and the Latin American governments. In January 1962 the OAS countries in effect expelled Cuba from their midst, voting to suspend its membership in the organization. Castro's reply was immediate and vitriolic. In what came to be called the Second Declaration of Havana, issued on 4 February 1962, he virtually declared war on the other governments of the hemisphere, as well as on the United States. The United States and its *vendepatria* allies in the region might try to prevent it, he declared, but the fact was that hemispheric revolution was inevitable. He concluded with a rousing call to all revolutionaries to "get out and fight."[3] Castro backed up his rhetoric with concrete actions. Guerrilla fronts soon appeared in Guatemala, Venezuela, Colombia, Peru, Bolivia and Argentina. Most were native in origin, but in all cases Castro had encouraged their establishment and provided them with at least some support. The war, in effect, was on.

Castro had expected the Soviets to applaud his revolutionary efforts in Latin America. Rather than that, he found that the Soviets had their own tactics and allies in the area, which they expected him to accept now that he was their associate. Rather than aiding him, the Soviets were constantly trying to restrain him. Castro wanted to assist and work through radical left-wing revolutionary groups patterned after his own 26th of July movement. The Soviets wanted him to work with the orthodox Communist parties, whose cautious tactics Castro despised. In an effort to strike a compromise, the Soviets maneuvered Castro into holding a meeting of Latin American Communist parties in September 1964. There, a bargain appeared to have been reached. In six countries, Cuba's tactics of armed struggle were deemed appropriate, and in those six (Guatemala, Honduras, Colombia, Paraguay, Haiti, and Venezuela) the Communist parties themselves supposedly would support guerrilla warfare. In all other countries, however, popular-front tactics were to be followed, and Castro was to work through the orthodox parties.

Most observers expected that the parties to the agreement would soon abandon it, and they were right. It was most often honored in the breach. Further, in less than eighteen months, at the Tri-Continent Congress in January 1966, Castro outmaneuvered the Soviets and overturned the agreement altogether. Ostensibly this congress was to have been a meeting at which "progressive" movements from Latin America would be added to those already comprising the Afro-Asian People's Solidarity Organization, thus converting it to a tricontinental entity. For tactical reasons related to their rivalry with Peking, the Soviets left the invitation list and agenda entirely in Castro's hands. That was a mistake. They had expected him to invite groups sympathetic to Moscow. Rather than that, Castro invited every radical revolutionary group he could think of, including a number that were decidedly out of favor with Moscow. The traditional Communist parties were largely bypassed, and Soviet positions were ignored. He turned the congress into a Fidelista circus, with call after call for armed struggle and confrontation with the imperialists on every front. Castro insisted that these across-the-board calls for guerrilla warfare superseded the cautious compromise of 1964, and to the embarrassment of the Soviets, he demanded that they honor those calls.

For their part, the Latin American governments were of course angered and alarmed by the fire-breathing exhortations at the January congress. Except for Mexico, none had diplomatic relations with Havana, so they could not call Cuban ambassadors on the carpet. Soviet diplomats were present in most of the major capitals, however, and government after government called them in to demand an explanation of Moscow's apparent endorsement of these calls for the overthrow of existing governments. In all cases the Soviets disavowed the Tri-Continent Congress resolutions, insisting that only Soviet "social" organizations had attended. The Soviet government had not been represented and therefore was not bound by any of the congress's resolutions.

Castro reacted with scorn to this backtracking on Moscow's part. Whatever others might say or do, Castro declared, he considered the Havana resolutions binding and would carry them out. Those who did not so regard them, he noted pointedly, were guilty of betraying their people.[4]

In early 1966, Castro began efforts to form an axis with two other small, radical members of the Communist camp: North Korea and North Vietnam. Together, he seemed to believe, the three of them might prod Moscow toward a harder, more revolutionary line. One might say that the culmination of this trend came in 1967 when Castro published a major treatise on the question of revolution in Latin America in which he openly rejected Soviet theoretical constructs and made it clear that he would ignore questions of affiliation with the world Communist movement in his dealings with Latin American revolutionaries.[5]

Then, in January 1968, Castro expelled from the newly reconstituted Cuban Communist party a number of old-line Communists who were known to be sympathetic to Moscow's views. With this open affront to his Soviet protectors, an open break between Havana and Moscow appeared inevitable. In fact, however, it never came. One reason was that Castro understood that, all else aside, Soviet economic support was a *sine qua non* to his survival. He had wished to maintain a separate position and his own identity, but it must have been clear to him all along that if push came to shove, he would have little choice but to accommodate Soviet concerns. Push had indeed come to shove. The Soviets began to cut back on Cuba's petroleum supplies. That Castro had immediately taken the point became clear in his 23 August speech of that year. Most had expected him to condemn the Soviet invasion of Czechoslovakia. Rather than that, he supported it. Signs of a warming trend in Soviet-Cuban relations soon followed, and by the end of 1969, Castro was giving effusive thanks for Soviet aid and had dropped calls for armed uprisings in the rest of the hemisphere.

This shift doubtless resulted not just from Soviet pressure but also from the painful recognition that after almost a decade of effort, armed struggle had failed as a tactic; it had not produced a single victory in Latin America. Che Guevara's 1967 defeat in Bolivia dramatized this failure and must have led to deep soul-searching on Castro's part. And as his own tactics had failed, others had worked. Castro had always argued that the only way to bring about a social revolution was through the barrel of a rifle and that the first step a revolutionary government had to take was the destruction of the traditional armed forces. In 1968, however, the Peruvian military took power and instituted a series of popular reforms, including the expropriation of the International Petroleum Company, an American subsidiary.

In a speech on 19 July 1969, Castro had to admit that the Peruvian military seemed to be leading the country toward a true revolution, thus implicitly recognizing for the first time that both the tenets he had advanced so confidently were wrong. Meanwhile, Soviet popular-front tactics and emphasis on state-to-state relations had paid off handsomely. Moscow had established diplomatic relations with Colombia, Venezuela, Bolivia, Ecuador, Costa Rica, and Guyana, as well as with Peru and Salvador Allende's Chile, while Castro had wasted his time trying to overthrow governments. As Castro surveyed the scene, he must have concluded that it was time to begin breaking out of his own diplomatic isolation in Latin America.[6]

To accomplish this, he deemphasized the export of revolution as a policy and armed struggle as a tactic. Cuban assistance to guerrillas and other subversive groups was drastically reduced if not stopped entirely. By 1970, Venezuela's guerrilla leader, Douglas Bravo, was bitterly complaining of Castro's refusal to provide further support. Castro also put out peace feelers to several of the other governments, emphasizing his willingness to coexist with them and to respect their sovereignty if they would respect his.

This profound shift in Cuban foreign policy did not, of course, take place overnight; rather, Castro effected it over a period of several years. Nor did the other Latin American governments immediately respond. Most were deeply suspicious of Castro's intentions and feared that this new moderation on his part might be nothing more than a tactical maneuver. Gradually, however, as they perceived that it reflected a real change in policy, they began to adjust their own postures accordingly. Many of the same countries that had once felt themselves to be the targets of Cuban policy, began to resume diplomatic and trade relations with Havana and to insist that the multilateral sanctions imposed by the OAS be lifted.[7]

Against this background of declining Cuban aggressiveness, the United States also began to shift its position. In 1975, for example, the United States voted with the majority in the OAS to lift the multilateral sanctions, thus leaving it up to each government whether it would maintain relations with Cuba. This further encouraged renewal of ties with Havana, and by 1980 Cuba had full diplomatic relations with eleven of the governments of this hemisphere: Argentina, Peru, Colombia, Venezuela, Panama, Mexico, Ecuador, Nicaragua, Grenada, Jamaica, and Guyana.[8] All save Guyana were members of the OAS. In addition, Costa Rica had established consular relations and maintained a consulate general in Havana. The United States did not reestablish diplomatic relations with Cuba, but it did open an interests section in Havana that maintained direct communications with the Cuban government and in fact did (and still does) everything an embassy would have done except fly the American flag and call itself an embassy.

While the 1960s can be characterized as a decade of sharp animosity and tension between Cuba and the other hemispheric states, the decade of the 1970s was most definitely one of rapprochement. Not that even those countries that opened embassies in Havana necessarily considered themselves to be on a friendly basis with Castro. By the end of the decade, Nicaragua and Grenada had become sister revolutionary republics. Relations between Havana and Panama, Mexico, and Jamaica (under Michael Manley) were also warm and cordial. Relations with the others, however, were correct but were still tempered with a good deal of suspicion and reserve on both sides. Nonetheless, even in these latter cases the underlying assumption seemed to be that the fraternal bonds that united them were stronger than the different systems and conflicts of interest that divided them—so long as Cuba did not interfere in their domestic affairs. As a Colombian diplomat put it in 1979:

Cuba has chosen a different political system but remains a sister republic. It is entirely appropriate, and in fact in everyone's interest, including that of the United States, that we treat her as a member of the family again if she

wishes to be so treated and provided she adheres to the basic rule of not meddling in her neighbors' affairs. What could be gained by continuing to exclude her? Nothing. To do so would be to take a false position and to deny
the instincts of blood and history which bid us stretch forth our hand to a
sister with whom we have quarreled but who is nonetheless one of us.[9]

The U.S. opening to Cuba proved to be short-lived. The Ford
administration had not only agreed to the lifting of the multilateral
sanctions but had also held a series of secret talks with Cubans to
determine whether there were in fact grounds for a significant easing
of tensions between the two countries. These were broken off, however, after Cuban forces began arriving in Angola in 1975. Despite
the fact that the CIA had been up to its neck in touching off the civil
war in the first place, and despite the fact that the South African forces
had crossed into Angola first—without provoking any protest at all
from Ford and Kissinger—President Ford said the Cuban intervention was the act of an international outlaw and that we would have
no further dealings with Cuba until those troops were removed.

The Carter administration, which was elected in 1976, took a different position. There would be no preconditions for talks. How,
after all, could we hope to resolve the problems between us if we did
not discuss them? It was made clear to the Cubans, however, that the
presence of their troops in Africa, along with a number of other aspects of their foreign policy, remained of serious concern to the
United States and that little progress could be made toward improving relations until these conflictive issues were worked out. But, in
the event, they were not worked out. The fault for that lay as much
with the United States as with Cuba. Be that as it may, however, the
result was that by 1978 the normalization process had been halted.

The Latin American countries were not concerned by the presence of Cuban troops in Africa. On the contrary, their reaction—a
rather amusing one in its frank practicality—was that it was better
"to have them over there than over here." What was of principal interest to them was that Cuba stay out of *their* internal affairs. Neither
did they see Cuban assistance to the Sandinistas in the Nicaraguan
civil war to oust Somoza as a violation of that principle; rather, it
was accepted by most of the other governments as "kosher." They
could hardly regard it otherwise, since several of them were as deeply involved as were the Cubans in supporting the anti-Somoza rebels. The fact was that Somoza was regarded as a special case, one of

the last of the old-style caudillos; the other governments were willing to bend the rules—and to have Cuba bend them—if that contributed to his ouster.

Castro doubtless regarded the Sandinista victory in 1979 as a belated windfall. During the 1960s, he had *expected* guerrilla struggles reminiscent of his own to win power in country after country. But his expectations went unfulfilled. The Cuban example was not repeated in a single country. Now, two decades later, and a full decade after he himself had come to doubt the hemispheric efficacy of guerrilla warfare, it had indeed produced another revolutionary government. Might Castro now feel that his earlier advocacy of such tactics had been vindicated? And, the other governments wondered, would this perhaps encourage him to return to the policy of exporting revolution that he had followed in the 1960s?

Their concerns were sharpened in 1980 as they observed a military buildup in Nicaragua, and it became apparent late that year that both Nicaragua and Cuba had mounted a major effort to support the guerrillas in El Salvador. Did this indeed presage a new effort to turn the Andes into the Sierra Maestra of Latin America? At that point there was reason to think so, for 1980 had been a tumultuous year in Cuba's relations with the rest of the hemisphere. Beset by economic difficulties and rising emigration pressures, Castro at the beginning of the year had also suffered a grievous personal loss—the death of his long-time friend and confidante, Celia Sánchez. For many months thereafter, Castro was simply not himself, and during that period he made a number of decisions that he probably regretted later. There was, for example, the episode of the Peruvian embassy. In their efforts to leave the country, Cuban citizens had with increasing frequency managed to gain access to Latin American embassies in Havana and ask for political asylum. Castro's refusal to grant them safe conduct out of the country left them stuck as permanent houseguests of the various embassies and led to serious disagreements between Havana and the respective governments—especially those of Venezuela, Colombia, and Peru—that accused Castro of violating existing international conventions regarding asylum.

That was bad enough, but Castro made it worse by removing the guards at the Peruvian embassy, saying that he was not going to risk the lives of Cuban policemen to keep asylum seekers out; if the Peruvians wanted to admit such people, he said, that was their business. But as a result of his decision, the Peruvian embassy was within a few days inundated by a flood of ten thousand Cubans asking to leave the country. Embarrassed and in a towering rage, Castro reacted by lashing out at unseen enemies both at home and abroad. He described the ten thousand inside the embassy as scum whose conduct aided the imperialists. He encouraged Cuban citizens to manifest their repudiation of the ten thousand and of anyone else who wished to leave.

Castro accused the other governments of encouraging incidents at their embassies, and when Costa Rica offered to set up an airlift to take the ten thousand to Costa Rica for processing as refugees, Castro saw it as a maneuver to embarrass him further. He scathingly rejected the offer and accused the Costa Rican government of bad faith. When the Costa Rican consul general was roughed up at the Havana airport, the consulate general was closed. Subsequently, Costa Rica broke off relations altogether.

In April, Castro turned the situation against the United States by declaring that the ten thousand inside the Peruvian embassy, and in fact anyone else who wished to leave the country, were free to depart through the port of Mariel. Friends and relatives in the United States could come down by boat and pick them up there. Between April, when the exodus began, and September, when Castro closed it off, some 125,000 Cubans left for Florida. The United States was hard pressed to process and absorb so many in such a short period, and the whole episode was politically embarrassing to President Carter, who was again accused of showing weakness in dealing with Castro.

But if the Mariel exodus was embarrassing to the Carter administration, it was much more so to the Castro government, whose image abroad was severely damaged by the fact that so many Cubans so desperately wished to leave and by Castro's arbitrary and callous handling of the exodus. External perceptions further suffered when it was revealed in mid-1981 that a number of Colombian guerrillas had, at the very least, received training in Cuba during 1980. These were the same guerrillas who had seized the Dominican embassy in Bogotá in February 1980 and held a number of diplomats hostage, including the American ambassador. In April a deal had been worked out under which the Colombian government had the guerrillas flown to Havana, accompanied by their diplomatic hostages. The diplomats were released upon arrival and returned to their home countries. The guerrillas, it later became known, asked for and were given training in guerrilla warfare. They then returned to Colombia and opened operations against the government, in the course of which a number were captured and under interrogation confessed to their Cuban connections. Again embarrassed, the Cuban government acknowledged that the group had received instruction in Cuba, but it heatedly denied having armed them or assisted in their return to Colombia. Even if one took the Cuban explanation at face value (and few did), providing training was in itself a foolish thing to have done. Supporting Nicaraguan rebels in the overthrow of Somoza had been one thing; this was quite another. Somoza had been regarded as a tyrant. The Colombian government, by contrast, was a democratic one elected by the people and with which Cuba maintained full diplomatic relations. Assistance of any kind in efforts to overthrow it was definitely taboo in the eyes of the other governments.

Privately, a number of Cuban officials attributed their government's faux pas to the extreme personal antipathy between Castro and President Julio César Turbay. While this may indeed have been a factor that led to the Cuban miscalculation, in no way did it alter the fact that it had been an error. Certainly it did not minimize the consequences. Colombia quickly broke diplomatic relations with Cuba, and several other governments registered strong concern with Havana.

By mid-1981, then, Cuba's relations with its neighbors had reached their lowest point in many years. Costa Rica had closed its consulate general. Colombia had broken diplomatic relations. Peru, Venezuela, and Ecuador had withdrawn their ambassadors. More important than the immediate state of relations, however, was the looming uncertainty with respect to Castro's long-range intentions. Did the events and immediate aftermath of 1980 suggest that Castro had indeed reverted to more confrontational policies?

During most of 1981 the answer to that question remained in doubt. True, by the fall of 1980, Castro's political instincts seemed to be working again—at least to the point of realizing that by further embarrassing President Carter he might be helping to elect Ronald Reagan, whom he described as the "war candidate." He therefore closed Mariel and made a number of conciliatory gestures toward the United States. Without question, this was in part a ploy aimed at helping Carter's electoral chances, but it was not only that, for even after Reagan was elected, Castro continued to emphasize through diplomatic channels his desire to ease tensions and improve relations with the United States, irrespective of who was in the White House.

At the same time Castro put out peace feelers to a number of Latin American governments. It was difficult to place much credence in these overtures while Castro was still going all out to support the Salvadoran guerrillas. Once the January 1981 guerrilla offensive had failed, however, clearly both the Cubans and the Nicaraguans reevaluated their positions. Arms shipments soon declined drastically, and both signaled their disposition to seek a political settlement in El Salvador. By December 1981 the Cubans had gone so far as to suspend all military shipments even to Nicaragua and indicated they were doing so in hopes of improving the atmosphere for regional negotiations.[10]

More important to the other Latin American governments, it became increasingly apparent that any reversion on Castro's part to support for guerrilla warfare was limited to the area of conflict in Central America. Elsewhere, he studiously avoided any repetition of the mistake he had made in Colombia: he did not provide further assistance to subversive groups struggling to overthrow duly elected governments. And even with Colombia, once Turbay had been replaced in the presidency by Belisario Betancur, Castro made his peace. By 1984, Betancur was saying he was satisfied that Cuban support for the guerrillas had ceased.[11]

Cuba's resumption of a moderate approach was given doctrinal cachet at a meeting of Latin American Communist and revolutionary parties held in Havana in 1982. Cuban theoreticians proclaimed that conditions for revolution existed in only two Latin American countries—El Salvador and Guatemala. Only in those countries would it be appropriate for Marxist-Leninist groups to assist revolutionary organizations.[12] Thus any doctrinal shift back toward armed struggle had relevance only for those two countries. Even in those cases, Cuba had sharply curtailed any support it was giving and signaled its willingness to cooperate with diplomatic efforts to find peaceful solutions—something it would have been unlikely to do in the 1960s.

Clearly, then, the events of 1980 had represented but a brief divergence from the policies of detente adopted by Castro at the end of the 1960s. With that made clear, by mid-1982 Cuba was able to repair most of the damage done to its relations in Latin America. Its repair efforts were given a further boost by the war over the Falkland/Malvinas Islands, which broke out between Great Britain and Argentina in May 1982. The Cubans had little sympathy for the Argentine military government. The issue, however, went beyond the particular government in power in Buenos Aires; rather, it had to do with hemispheric solidarity and a defense of sovereignty in the face of what most Latin Americans perceived to be external aggression. Latin Americans may have had reservations about Argentina's wisdom in retaking the islands by force, but few doubted that she had a right to them.

Still, as it became apparent that Great Britain would send a major military expedition to invade the islands, not all Latin American governments were willing to give Argentina material support in her struggle to retain them. Castro made it clear that Cuba *was* willing to give such support. Cuba would come to Argentina's assistance militarily, he said, provided the other Latin American governments also extended such support. It was an offer cleverly phrased and from which Castro could not possibly lose. He probably calculated that few of the other governments were likely to fulfill that condition and thus that he would have to provide no material support at all. At the same time, he was unlikely to be criticized for not doing so, since the onus for his inaction would be on the other governments. How could they fault him if they themselves had not come to Argentina's aid? Meanwhile, Castro could only gain from the crisis. It suddenly put him on the same side of the barricades as all the other Latin American countries and dramatically emphasized the historical factors that united them.

At the same time that Castro was making the Falklands/Malvinas war work for him, the U.S. position in Latin America was damaged, not seriously perhaps and not permanently but nonetheless damaged. Just as the war put Cuba on the same side of the barricades as the other republics, so did it put the United States on the other. Nor was the irony of the situation lost on Latin America. Here was the United States supporting a European country in reasserting its control over a territory in this hemisphere which rightfully belonged to a sister republic. What ever had happened to the Monroe Doctrine? Further, while the United States had for years talked of invoking the Rio mutual defense treaty *against* Cuba, suddenly it seemed more likely that the treaty would be invoked against Great Britain, and, by extension, against its American ally. The face of the enemy had for a moment changed, and it was a moment the Latin Americans would not quickly forget. As an Argentine diplomat put it: "The next time you talk about the need for a solid front against Cuba or that you threaten to invoke the Rio pact against Cuba, we'll tell you to take your Rio pact and sit on it."[13]

During 1983 and 1984, Cuba continued to improve its standing with most of the Latin American governments by indicating its willingness to cooperate with the Contadora process, launched by Mexico, Panama, Venezuela, and Colombia in an effort to produce a negotiated settlement in Central America. In a broader context, Castro urged the need for detente between East and West and on several occasions offered to contribute to that detente by negotiating, or at least airing, his differences with the United States. When asked in an interview in 1984 whether detente was a crucial goal of Cuban policy, Castro replied without hesitation that it was. "Even if the two [superpowers] never come to the nuclear exchange that would mean the end of the world," he said, "East-West tensions divert attention from other pressing problems, and the arms race leads the world toward economic disaster."[14]

With respect to the turmoil in Central America, Castro emphasized Cuba's preference for an accommodation acceptable to all sides. Such an accommodation, he went on, would of course have to take into account U.S. security. "The grounds for an accommodation acceptable to all are there," he said. "Negotiations, however, can only succeed if the will exists on both sides to make them work. And, frankly, our experience with the present United States Administration has been such as to make us very skeptical. . . . Still, if there is ever any seriousness of purpose on the other side, Cuba is prepared to cooperate in the search for peaceful solutions in Central America."[15]

No one can say whether Castro did in fact want a negotiated solution. Perhaps such assurances represented nothing more than a tactical feint. If so, U.S. intransigence played into Castro's hands, leaving the rest of the world with the image of a Castro who was making peaceful overtures and a Reagan administration that was refusing to respond. Castro's stock with most of the other Latin American governments rose another notch.

Castro's image was further enhanced by his growing inclination to concentrate on issues of economic underdevelopment rather than on geopolitical questions. At a time when the developing countries were increasingly concerned over their very economic survival, the United States insisted that communism, not hunger, was the principal threat they faced. Castro, on the other hand, spoke a language that had increasing appeal to Third World countries and that tended to project him as a champion of the South in the North-South equation rather than as Moscow's partner in the East-West conflict. In a 1983 interview, for example, he seemed to chide both Washington and Moscow. He said,

Rather than joining forces to tackle the real challenges faced by mankind— food supply, disease, energy and protection of the environment—East and West are locked in sterile political conflict. While the poor nations become poorer and the imbalance between North and South grows ever more dangerous, the superpowers continue to squander resources on the construction of still more nuclear weapons, as if there weren't already enough of them.[16]

In another recent major foreign policy initiative—his campaign related to the international debt—Castro continued to concentrate on development issues. In speech after speech during 1985 he stressed the idea that the debt owed by various Latin American countries to foreign banks simply could not be paid and that in their efforts even to pay interest the other governments would undermine their chances for development and cause hunger among their people. Further, if the situation were allowed to drift, Castro warned, outright default would eventually become inevitable and with it possibly the collapse of the international banking system. That, Castro noted, would be a disaster for everyone. To avoid it, he urged that the governments of the industrialized creditor nations should take over and make themselves responsible for the debts to their banks. They could easily do so, he went on, simply by devoting a fraction of their military budgets to the payment of the debt.[17]

Castro doubtless hoped that championing the cause of the debtor nations would increase his political stock in the rest of the hemisphere. In that, his expectations were fulfilled. It was an issue that again placed him squarely on the side of the sister republics. On balance, the other governments appreciated his speaking out on their behalf. By saying things they could not, and by taking the extreme position that they should pay nothing, Castro made any less radical proposals of theirs appear positively moderate. That in itself was a useful service and raised his acceptability in the hemisphere.[18]

But Castro may have expected more. In March 1985 he predicted: "The economic crisis and the debt will unite the Latin American countries, much more than did the War of the Malvinas. . . . In the case of Latin America's economic crisis and foreign debt . . . the solution is a matter of survival for the Latin American countries."[19] He may even have had some hopes that it would unite them behind his leadership, at least on this one issue. If so, he was to be disappointed. The other governments were happy enough for Castro to speak out on the matter, but they had no intention of joining in a debtors' crusade led by Castro. Each was inclined to work out its financial problems in its own way. Thus when Castro called an international conference of debtor nations in July 1985, the other governments did not send representatives.

That, however, was a minor setback. Without question, Castro has gained new respectability in the hemisphere. Peru, Venezuela, and Ecuador have returned ambassadors to Havana. Brazil, Uruguay, and Bolivia have all reestablished diplomatic relations and opened embassies in Havana. As of mid-1987, then, Castro could be well pleased with his position in the hemisphere. No longer isolated, Cuba is now regarded by most Latin American governments as a newly returned member of the family—albeit one who has taken up a life-style not necessarily to their liking.

Conclusion

Demonstrably, both Castro and his foreign policy have evolved. It would be strange if that were not so. All things in nature change, even political leaders. Castro is no exception. For over a quarter of a century now, he has dealt with the world as it is rather than as he would wish it to be. He will doubtless always consider himself a revolutionary, but over the years he has become more patient and more pragmatic. In the 1960s he called for worldwide revolution and scathingly denounced the whole idea of detente. Today he is one of its most fervent advocates. In the 1960s the overthrow of the other Latin American governments was a consuming passion. Today he seeks to increase his influence with those governments. The imperatives that fueled his earlier policies are gone. He saw the creation of a Latin American revolutionary bloc as a prerequisite to his projection onto the world stage as a major player, but he long ago achieved such a role on his own. His ultimate success in the Third World, and in the world at large, proved not to depend upon the creation of such a bloc.

Castro gives evidence of being in search of a new role. Increasingly he seems to wish to project himself as a champion of the underdeveloped countries, and in a North-South rather than an East-West context. After twenty-five years in power, Castro knows full well that when a revolution achieves power, it has only begun to face the staggering problems of development, that there is no certainty whatsoever that it will succeed in solving them and that it is likely to need capitalist technology, investments, and trade advantages if it is to do so. In the real world, revolutionary credentials alone do not create jobs or put bread on the table. Hence, rather than global confrontation, Castro is now urging detente so that the governments of the world can devote their attention and resources to development and conservation, the real problems that haunt the world's future.

The U.S. government appears appallingly oblivious to all this. It seems to have made up its mind on an a priori basis that Castro has not changed and never can change, that Cuban policy is not and never will be subject to moderation. As a State Department representative put it at a conference in 1983: "Cuba remains as committed to fomenting revolution throughout the region as it was in the 1960s. . . . The fundamental goals of the Cuban leadership have not changed in nearly 25 years; Cuban tactics have simply become more sophisticated and pragmatic."[20]

Given this rigid mind-set, the Reagan administration refuses even to discuss the issues with the Cubans. Castro offers to exchange views on Central America, for example; the United States will not. Such obduracy makes little sense. One would think discussions with the Cuban government would be a logical step in any diplomatic process aimed at resolving the conflicts in Central America. It stands to reason that any proposed solutions would have a better chance of succeeding if they could count upon Cuban acquiescence. For this if for no other reason, it would be in the interest of the United States to discuss the matter with the Cubans. To refuse is to stick our heads in the sand.

None of this is to say that we must trust Castro or take him at his word. Of course not. Even if he has changed, the United States and Cuba are not destined to be friends. We are adversaries and likely to remain so for the foreseeable future. Trust is not likely to be a notable ingredient in our relationship for a very long time to come. But that does not mean that the differences between us could not be reduced through careful diplomatic engagement. Even the bitterest of adversaries often find accommodations to be in their mutual interest.

At the very least, we ought to deal realistically with Castro as he is today rather than addressing an outdated image distorted by our ideological preconceptions. The Latin American states have been sufficiently pragmatic to adjust to the new Cuban reality. Surely the United States, with immensely greater power and thus less to fear, should be able to show the same good sense.

Notes

1. Herbert Matthews, *The Cuban Story* (New York: George Braziller, 1961), p. 191.

2. It is interesting to note, however, that even after declaring himself to be a Communist, Castro continued to take a nationalist line. Even the Second Declaration of Havana, for example, was nationalist, not Marxist-Leninist, in content. Nowhere in the declaration does one find any reference at all to Marxist-Leninist theory. On the contrary, Castro had a good deal of implied criticism for the orthodox Communist parties, which were, in Castro's eyes, simply too cautious.

3. For the text of Castro's speech, see *Cuba Socialista* (Havana), March 1962.

4. United Nations Document S/7134, 11 February 1966. Quoted in D. Bruce Jackson, *Castro, the Kremlin, and Communism in Latin America* (Baltimore: Johns Hopkins University Press, 1969), p. 93.

5. Jackson, *Castro*, pp. 21–22.

6. Much of this is taken from my paper *Castro's Cuba: Soviet Partner or Nonaligned?* (Washington, D.C.: Woodrow Wilson Center, 1984), pp. 22–24.

7. These were sanctions under which all member states had been required to sever diplomatic and trade relations with Cuba. Only Mexico, all through the years, had refused to comply.

8. Chile and Cuba had established diplomatic relations when Salvador Allende was elected president of Chile in 1970. Relations were broken when he was overthrown in 1973.

9. Statement to the author in August 1979 in a conversation with Clara Ponce de León, then the Colombian ambassador in Havana.

10. Wayne S. Smith, *The Closest of Enemies: A Personal and Diplomatic History of the Castro Years* (New York: W. W. Norton, 1987), pp. 253–54.

11. See "A Talk with Colombian President Betancur," *Business Week*, 27 August 1984, p. 56.

12. *Prensa Latina*, dispatches of 27 and 28 April, 1982.

13. Conversation between the author and an Argentine diplomat in Havana in June 1982.

14. From the author's interview with Fidel Castro. See "Time for a Thaw," *New York Times Magazine*, 29 July 1984.

15. Ibid.

16. Ibid.

306 Wayne S. Smith

17. Fidel Castro, in an interview granted to the Mexican daily *Excelsior;* printed in its entirety by Editora Política, Havana, 1985.

18. Tad Szulc, in the *New York Times,* 5 May 1985, sec. 4, p. 25.

19. Fidel Castro's interview granted to *Excelsior.*

20. *Report on Cuba,* Findings of the Study Group on United States–Cuban Relations (Boulder, Colo.: Westview, for the School of Advanced International Studies, Johns Hopkins University, 1984), p. 14.

John D. Martz

Images, Intervention, and
the Cause of Democracy

Images of the mind nourish the assumptions and preconceptions of U.S. policymakers toward Latin America. Whether founded on fantasies, realities, or an admixture of both, these constitute the foci about which hemispheric relations have revolved. As the twentieth century draws to a close, conflicting mind-sets continue to cloud the comprehension and sensibilities of diplomats and political leaders. Where Washington perceives an historic mission to guide its neighbors toward its customarily ethnocentric vision of democracy, Latin American capitals experience actions and activities that repeatedly smack of cultural, political, or economic intervention.

For the United States, there has been an historic compulsion to assist Latin America in a cleansing of nondemocratic practices through the institutionalization of elections and support for constitutionality. Throughout this century, moreover, there have been periodic outbursts of crusading zeal in the Americas. As Pike has written, "the United States passes through alternating cycles of trying to make the world safe for its type of democracy and of endeavoring to make its type of democracy safe from the world."[1] In recent times, the report of the National Bipartisan Commission on Central America has provided a reminder of U.S. attitudes. This analytic exercise was consistent with many earlier policy reviews. Henry Kissinger and his associates thereby presented once more the familiar portrait of the United States in what Lloyd Etheredge has called a "managerial role, boldly transforming Central American societies to become liberal, democratic, progressive, and prosperous—more like the United States."[2]

Attention to the internal affairs of hemispheric states has been episodic. Federico G. Gil contends that "periods of rising interest in and concern with Latin America on the part of the United States have invariably been followed by periods of declining interest, increasing conflict, and almost total disregard for the fate of these nations."[3] Washington turns its eyes toward the south only at times of a perceived threat to geopolitical security interests. Its advocacy of democratic practices has mirrored pragmatic political judgments. A contemporary example is the shifting stance of the Reagan administration toward elections in Nicaragua. At first there was pressure for the swift convening of national elections. When the Sandinistas finally scheduled the vote for November 1984, the United States reversed itself on the grounds that the opposition needed more time to organize. It also quietly persuaded Arturo Cruz, the strongest announced opposition candidate, to withdraw from the race and cast his lot with the contras.

The point here is not the soundness of policy judgments by Washington but rather the reliance upon political circumstances and opportunity to produce decisions allegedly based on democratic values and principles. The use of democratic rhetoric as a rationalization for diverse acts of intervention or interference is by no means unique to the Reagan administration. Its repetition through the years, however, has left an indelible mark on the Latin psyche. Even such leaders as Woodrow Wilson and John F. Kennedy, often hailed as ardent defenders of democracy and individual freedom, hesitated not at all to intervene. The former deliberately dispatched troops under General John J. Pershing to northern Mexico and marine detachments to Haiti, the Dominican Republic, and Nicaragua. Kennedy's actions included supporting Cuban exiles with invasion plans, sending ships to Santo Domingo to show the flag, and withholding diplomatic recognition from regimes of which he disapproved.

In the light of these and numerous comparable events, it is small wonder that Latin Americans take a jaded view of democracy as personified by U.S. diplomacy. Kalman Silvert has made the point with characteristic insight:

The very word *democracy* . . . has come to symbolize hypocrisy. Democracy is only for those who can afford it; it is a luxury that comes at the end of a long process of economic development. The world's democratic countries may be partially democratic for themselves—"bourgeois" democracies—but for the poorer parts of the world, they are only the extra actors of surplus value, the imposers of colonialism, the buyers of local elites, the prompters of worldwide dislocation, as they move about in the ceaseless search for economic advantage and military security.[4]

And this also means, he argues, that democracy viewed in terms of international practice becomes a password for the right, suggesting authoritarianism and economic exploitation. While some would prefer a less pejorative explanation, Silvert's basic point is undeniable. If Latin Americans have too often been exposed to intervention, interference, and pressure in the name of democracy, small wonder that images have become blurred.

To be sure, there is a level of generality sufficient to elicit some consensus as to the meaning of democracy. The belief that society should be ruled through the consent of its members has been a dominant credo in both the industrialized and the developing worlds. Forms designed to achieve self-determination have been multiple, each seeking to operate through constitutions, laws, parties, and elections. Furthermore, conventional notions of democracy enshrine the rights of the individual, calling for the observance of civic freedoms and the respect of basic liberties. Some have also argued that democracy must extend beyond the realm of the political. Equality, social justice, and economic well-being are to be included. This seems consistent with *demokratia,* the Greek derivation of the word, which calls for a government with full participation by all, including the lowliest sectors of society.

A less sweeping interpretation prefers that the concept of democracy be limited to the political regulation of conflict and power. This emphasis on institutionalization has been described by Wilde in the following fashion:

"Democracy" can be defined in more restricted, procedural terms as those rules that allow (though they do not necessarily bring about) genuine competition for authoritative political roles. No effective political office should be excluded from such competition, nor should opposition be suppressed by force. More specifically, such rules would include freedom of speech, press, and assembly, and the provision of regular institutional mechanisms for obtaining consent and permitting change of political personnel (normally, elections).[5]

John Peeler recently expressed a similar view, in which "liberal democracy" is seen as including adult universal suffrage, electoral competition for major policymakers, and the freedom to organize or join parties and interest groups while acting to influence public policy.[6] If this falls short of populist or participatory democracy, it has the benefits of readily identifiable mechanisms for the shaping of policy consistent with the interests of the majority.

It remains a central contention of this chapter, however, that the policy relationship between the United States and Latin America is marked by a mutual lack of understanding of this basic concept. There is no monopoly on myopia here, for neither party fully comprehends the character of democracy as embedded in the fabric of a different and distinctive culture. It is one thing to criticize flawed or distorted understanding, but it is quite another to rethink problems within the framework of present and future policy. To do so, three areas must draw our immediate attention: (1) the origins and character of democracy in Latin America, (2) the cyclical shifts in electoral forms, and (3) the permanence of interventionism and the missionary impulses on which it rests.

The Etiology and Ethos of Latin American Democracy

Etiology, we recall, is the study of causes, origins, or reasons. Scholars and political practitioners have debated for over four centuries the intellectual predispositions underlying Iberian and Latin culture. The earliest forms reflect the monist or organicist tradition, which emanated from Roman law, the Thomistic tradition, feudalism, and the prolonged struggle to expel the Moors. By the mid-1500s the Dominican Francisco de Vitoria was espousing traditions of Spanish law, Thomism, and a monist view of authority. He was followed by the Jesuit theologian and jurist Francisco Suárez, who personified an Hispano-Catholic view of man, society, and the state based on hierarchy and inequality, on organicism and patriarchalism. All of this led to a civic deference toward the power of the ultimate authority, the *patrón*. Natural inequality in society meant, for the monists, a well-ordered political community in which authoritarian rule would be necessary.[7]

The Enlightenment tradition was communicated to the New World somewhat later. Well before the revolutionary wars of independence, however, the ideas of Locke, Montesquieu, and to a lesser extent Rousseau had become familiar to intellectuals in the colonies. The liberal pluralist strain thus began to take shape, competing alongside its monist rival. The transmission of Enlightenment ideas to Latin America registered an impact on Latin American universities and seminaries, with older Thomist principles subjected to challenge. Toward the close of the colonial period, both French and U.S. revolutionary struggles drew the attention of Latin American leaders. Paine, Jefferson, and Franklin joined the panoply of leaders and pamphleteers whose ideas were extensively disseminated.

In other writings I have contended that Latin America reveals a blending of intellectual traditions: the monist and the liberal pluralist traditions from colonial and revolutionary times, and subsequently the more radical outlook embodied in Marxism. The fortunes of each have fluctuated, but at no point has one set of ideas fully displaced another. To understand the Latin American worldview at the time of independence is to recognize the blending of both monist and pluralist elements. In the present century, the Marxist must also be heard. The threads of the three orienting traditions are tightly interwoven, and their durability and persistence across the years would suggest that contemporary analytic models should heed the behavior produced by all three worldviews.

Approaches which champion only one of the traditions will continue to be flawed. Whatever the philosophical and ideological bases from which the individual, society, and state are to be visualized, it is urgent that sources of conceptual complementarity be sought. The imperative for integrative conceptualizing is powerful.[8]

In short, the intellectual perspectives on democracy in Latin America are diverse, and they challenge the validity of easy or direct assumptions.

Varied or, indeed, contradictory views can readily be drawn from eminent political figures. One perspective, for instance, holds that although the democratic ideal is to be preferred, it requires a level of education and civic awareness that cannot be assumed. As early as 1812, Simón Bolívar was explaining the collapse of the first Venezuelan republic as the result of impractical efforts to construct a federal system of government. Also, the Liberator continued, "Popular elections became . . . another obstacle in the way of the smooth functioning of the federation, . . . for the peasants are so ignorant that they vote without knowing what they are about, and city dwellers are so ambitious that everything they attempt leads to factions."[9]

When the early years of independence were dotted with a succession of classic caudillos, it was natural to extend the argument while reiterating the importance of socioeconomic and political realities. According to Arturo Uslar Pietri, the stereotypical strongmen were logical products of the land and tradition, responding to historic necessity. As he saw it, these rulers owed their immense power to their incarnation of the reaction of a rural world that had severed connections with the Spanish empire in hopes of implanting liberal republican institutions without roots in the past. As the Venezuelan put it:

Latin America saw the emergence of a form of social organization that was contrary to the republican ideas that had been fashioned in Europe, but that perfectly suited the American economic and social structure.... Men like Don Porfirio or Rosas emerged because they reflected the thoughts, the inclination, the deep feeling of the majority of their people; in the fullest sense of the term, they were their spokesmen, their representatives, the symbol of the dominant collective feeling of the time.[10]

In point of fact, Mexico's Porfirio Díaz had himself insisted to a North American interviewer that he was a believer in democracy as "the one true, just principle of government, although in practice it is possible only to highly developed peoples." He then explained that he had inherited a government whose people were "unprepared" for democratic principles. For Díaz, the masses were not yet capable of sustaining the responsibility of self-rule.[11] This opinion was later corroborated by such despots as Anastasio Somoza García, founder of the Nicaraguan dynasty. According to "Tacho," to provide democracy prematurely was tantamount to feeding a newborn infant a hot tamale; with time and the proper tutelage, both democracy and digestion would be possible. Such was scarcely the practice of *somocismo* under either father or sons, of course.

If the etiology of Latin American democracy, then, is based on interlocking intellectual traditions as further informed by particularistic historical and socioeconomic conditions, it is inevitable that its ethos cannot be a mere reproduction of Anglo-American principles. A dictionary definition of ethos speaks of the disposition, character, or attitude peculiar to a specific people or culture; fundamental values or mores distinguish it from other groups or peoples. It is not condescending to accept the importance of cultural relativism in the theory and practice of Latin American democracy. There is no more reason to expect a mechanistic reproduction of the U.S. model in Latin America than to suggest that the North American citizenry should or will imitate the patterns of their neighbors to the south.

To speak of a Latin American democratic ethos is not to deny the existence of certain panhumanistic values that fit a variety of constitutional structures. These clearly include meaningful competition among individuals and groups for government power; regularized elections for the free choice of leaders and policies; and the observance of basic civil liberties on behalf of the freedoms of expression, press, assembly, and association. In the final analysis, it is the perceived inadequacy of such formalistic institutional features which has periodically occasioned the advocacy of more revolutionary political action. As the late Ecuadoran president Jaime Roldós Aguilera once observed, his nation's impending return to constitutionality in 1979 following nine years of both civilian and military dictatorship was a mere beginning, an institutional framework within which the exercise of true democracy and civic involvement might be nurtured.[12]

In any cultural environment, the policy is confronted by a basic question: how to resolve the extent to which power is placed in the hands of the people. Is mass participation to be encouraged, or at least permitted, as a given in the daily unfolding of political affairs? Or, alternatively, should a presumably enlightened and educated elite wield the power of the state, only sporadically calling upon the citizenry at large for a judgment at the ballot box? There is an inescapable tension between the principle of rule by the people and that of rule by the privileged or hypothetically most highly qualified. The concept of human equality of political rights has been exceptional in the contemporary world. If pure egalitarianism and majority rule must inevitably clash, this fact also underlines the differences of terminology and comprehension between the United States and Latin America.

Especially in light of the contemporary impetus for change and reform in Latin America, the existence of political radicalism and of important revolutionary forces cannot be avoided. However, the very words *democracy* and *freedom* carry divergent meanings. In a recent critique of U.S. attitudes toward Central America, Burbach puts it cogently:

In the contemporary revolutionary societies, . . . democracy is often prefaced by the word "popular," meaning that participation in the direction of society can occur in various forms and at different levels. . . . The local organizations that exist in these and other areas enable people to participate in decisions that affect their daily lives. While bourgeois democratic societies, on the other hand, do have some organizations that influence local decisions, . . . the term "democracy" is predominantly identified with electoral politics; it means the right of everyone to go to the ballot box every few years, even if the majority of the populace finds it irrelevant to exercise that right.[13]

This view helps to underline the plurality of democratic perspectives and formulas for Latin America. They range from revolutionary democracy, with a reliance on both pacific and violent tactics, to an elitist version that pays mere formalistic lip service to externalities, and from participatory, mass-based democratic organizations to that bourgeois liberal democracy that allows occasional but carefully controlled pluralistic competition. Through the experience of the recent past, Latin America has further documented this plurality of approaches while undergoing cyclical shifts away from, then back toward, democratic forms. It has also testified to the surrealistic quality of electoral democracy in societies that retain an attachment to the Iberian cultural tradition.

The Ebb and Flow of Democratic Formalism

An inordinately oversimplified democracy-vs.-dictatorship dichotomy has been expressed by both analysts and Latin American politicians over the past four decades. It has sometimes produced exaggerated assessments of the democratic ethos. In the immediate post–World War II period, authoritarians who fell before a wave of democratic movements included, among others, Getúlio Vargas of Brazil, Guatemala's Jorge Ubico, and the Venezuelan Isaías Medina Angarita. In less than a decade, however, a large array of dictatorial regimes dotted the scenery: Marcos Pérez Jiménez in Venezuela, Manuel Odría in Peru, Colombia's Gustavo Rojas Pinilla, the Cuban Fulgencio Batista, and Juan Domingo Perón in Argentina. They joined such durable veterans as Generalissimo Rafael Leónidas Trujillo of the Dominican Republic, Paraguay's Alfredo Stroessner, and two generations of Somozas in Nicaragua.

For the United States, foreign relations in the 1950s were dominated by Dwight D. Eisenhower's secretary of state, John Foster Dulles, who moralistically presided over a policy that supported staunch rightist authoritarianism. Imbued with the crusading anticommunism of the Cold War—which was also claiming domestic victims in the United States during this period—Washington ignored the subtleties of Latin American politics. Overgeneralizing with a vengeance, it unwisely concluded that the best defense against the inroads of international Marxism was unwavering support for military repression. In electoral terms, Pérez Jiménez could falsify 1952 returns to reverse his popular defeat and could rig an unconstitutional plebiscite in 1957; Rojas Pinilla could proscribe both Conservatives and Liberals while seeking to adopt a corporatist constitution enshrining his Colombian dictatorship; Odría in Peru could extend the arbitrary proscription of that country's mass-based APRA party and its popular leader, Víctor Raúl Haya de la Torre. Examples could be multiplied ad nauseum.

By the turn of the decade, however, the pendulum had swung back once more. Pérez Jiménez, Rojas Pinilla, Odría, Perón, Batista, Trujillo—by 1961, all were gone. It was a time when folk wisdom held that a veritable "twilight of the tyrants" was marking an historic watershed, one that was to give way in definitive fashion to a lasting democratic order.[14] The decisive model, consistent with the anticommunist developmentalism of John F. Kennedy and the Alliance for Progress, was that of democratic reformism—the Democratic Left, as it was known, led and inspired by such men as Rómulo Betancourt of Venezuela, José Figueres of Costa Rica, and Puerto Rico's Luis Muñoz Marín. When it later appeared that these social democratic movements were losing momentum, Washington's favor turned toward Christian democracy. The latter's alleged "solution" for democracy and social justice was, indeed, encouraged by generous funding from the Central Intelligence Agency for the electoral campaigns of Eduardo Frei and the Chilean Christian Democrats.

Where the 1960s had initiated unrealistic proclamations that electoral democracy was the wave of the future, in time it was replaced by the flawed and ill-informed pessimism of the 1970s. The two great powers of South America, Brazil and Argentina, were by this time both under harsh military rule. Generals commanded the state in Ecuador, Peru, and Bolivia. General Stroessner continued into his third decade in Asunción. Most damning of all for the advocates of democracy was the shattering of long-established liberties and freedoms under the jackboots of the military in Chile and Uruguay. Amid this shambles, it was predictable that scholars and political observers would undertake a new series of broad-based explanations and rationalizations.[15] While there were certainly grounds to challenge earlier formulations equating socioeconomic development with political democracy, it was specious to assert that democracy was simply alien to the region. In time, the events of the 1980s helped to debunk this gross oversimplification.

Across the hemisphere there was a progressive retreat by the military from government to the barracks. Sometimes reluctantly, occasionally eagerly, but always with a sense of inevitability, the generals and admirals turned over responsibility for government to civilians. Elections provided the means for the transmission of power. The Ecuadorans in 1979, followed by the Peruvians in 1980, helped to show the way. Of particular significance was the reestablishment of Argentine electoral democracy in 1983, that of Uruguay a year later, and then the 1985 inauguration of civilian government in Brazil. By the close of 1985 the record showed, as I have reported elsewhere, that the fortunes of democratic institutions in the region were prospering.

Constitutional government solidly remained in Venezuela, Colombia, and Costa Rica, . . . Brazil, Uruguay, and Argentina had undertaken a transition. . . . In Peru, Ecuador, and Bolivia recently elected administrations struggled to deepen democratic practices. A host of governments in the eastern Caribbean also continued the democratic traditions inherited from the legacy of Great Britain. . . . [T]he region as a whole has never before witnessed such extensive observance of democratic practices and institutions.[16]

Continuity from one elected government to another was demonstrated with the inauguration of new presidents in Peru, Ecuador, and Bolivia—in each case, a critic or opponent of the outgoing chief of state. There was also a noteworthy programmatic range and diversity in these new leaders. Alan García of Peru was a young, charismatic populist with a determination to modernize his country; Ecuador's León Febres Cordero, in contrast, was a staunchly conservative, pro-business free trader whose outlook was combined with an aggressive personal style; and Víctor Paz Estenssoro, twenty-three years after first assuming the Bolivian presidency as a democratic reformer, returned to office and began to implement an austerity program that contradicted his policies of earlier years.

None of this is to suggest that the cyclical process had necessarily ground to a halt. There is persuasive evidence that several military regimes allowed themselves to be escorted out of power in the wake of economic mismanagement and failure. In Argentina the calamitous outcome of the South Atlantic War had played an important part. Only the long-established dictatorships of Chile and Paraguay managed to retain power in the face of foreign indebtedness and domestic recession. In time, an inability of democratic regimes to reverse the course of economic hardship and social deprivation may very well promote the recrudescence of military authoritarianism.

Furthermore, in a number of cases there has been more form than substance to the democratic experience. The mere convening of elections, while not to be ignored, tends to demonstrate an initiation of democratic formalism rather than the implantation of a system that reaches beyond the sporadic solicitation of national approval by recourse to the ballot box. Conducting elections has been no guarantee that meaningful popular rule and civic participation is in the offing. Often the manipulative power of a regime colored the representative nature of the process itself. Charades that distorted or denied the true expression of popular will have not been unknown in the Latin American experience, to understate the case. Neither has there been a reluctance to evaluate a given election in terms of partisan outlook. The United States in particular has shown a striking talent for interpreting elections to suit its own purposes, and the policymakers themselves have differed over the extent to which democratic governments might be congenial to U.S. interests.

The perceptions of the Kennedy administration were alluded to previously. The administration adamantly insisted that the reforms of the Alliance for Progress were to be political as well as socioeconomic. Thus the preamble to the Charter of Punta del Este, signed on 17 August 1961, urged "accelerated economic progress and broader social justice within the framework of personal dignity and political liberty." The twelve fundamental objectives of the Alliance were designed to achieve "maximum levels of well-being, with equal opportunities for all, *in democratic societies adapted to their own needs and desires*" (italics mine).[17] Yet a close collaborator of the president would later write that Kennedy's avowed championing of democratic regimes was less than total. In time, Kennedy came to believe that the Latin American military was often more competent, and more pro-U.S., than civilian governments. For Kennedy,

some military usurpers . . . were neither unpopular nor reactionary; and those able and willing to guide their countries to progress he wanted to encourage. Unfortunately, he had learned, many of the more progressive civilian governments in Latin America (as elsewhere) were less willing or less able to impose the necessary curbs on extravagant projects, runaway inflation and political disorder.[18]

Twenty years later, the Reagan administration displayed its own creativity in assessing electoral processes. The turbulence of Central American politics elicited highly disparate declarations concerning El Salvador and Nicaragua. U.S. support for elections in the former produced both moral and material aid to José Napoleón Duarte and his forces. It was felt that any elected government would oppose the embattled guerrillas; Duarte was seen as the best option, and Washington's approval was frequently expressed in fulsome terms. The absence of conditions in which leftist forces might participate in elections was ignored or undervalued. This is not to deny the excesses and injustices emanating from the FMLN rebels but rather to note that the Reagan administration framed its actions in terms of its preferences more than stark political reality.

This was underlined by the contrasting Nicaraguan case. Earlier U.S. administrations had usually found little to criticize in the electoral frauds of *somocismo;* moreover, such loyal Reaganites as Jeane J. Kirkpatrick regarded these practices as less unacceptable than those of the Sandinistas. In the wake of the November 1984 elections, the administration went to exceptional lengths to denounce the process. But for all its shortcomings, the Nicaraguan exercise was no less representative than that of El Salvador earlier in the year. Notwithstanding the self-serving statements of North American officials, there were many international observers who agreed that the Sandinista electoral triumph essentially reflected the wishes "of the majority of the people and that, at best, only its large margin of victory would have been modestly reduced by fuller participation of exile groups backed by the United States."[19]

The contemporary U.S. practice of viewing Latin American elections through self-serving lenses is consistent with well-established patterns. There is an ineradicable conviction that the United States can and should export its institutions in toto to other nations and, moreover, that Latin America is eager to adopt the practices and structure of the Colossus of the North. Characteristically, the U.S. Congress in November 1983 created the so-called National Endowment for Democracy which in the eyes of its more ardent champions would transfer Anglo-American forms to its neighbors—"political parties like our own, honest and competitive elections, pluralistic interest groups, the full gamut of representative institutions, and the social programs of an advanced industrial society."[20]

Certainly U.S. diplomacy repeatedly demonstrated an unwillingness to recognize or accept the notion that Latin American conceptions of democracy are drawn from their own historical experience rather than being arbitrarily imposed from abroad—no matter how altruistic Washington's motives might be. From the Latin American perspective, their own traditions are understandably regarded as distinct from those of the United States. The Liberator was among those who cautioned against efforts to emulate North American institutions and attitudes. In the famous 1819 Angostura Discourse, Bolívar was explicit:

I must say that it has never for a moment entered my mind to compare the position and character of two states as dissimilar as the English-American and the Spanish-American. . . . Does not *L'Esprit des Lois* state that laws should be suited to the people for whom they are made; that it would be a major coincidence if those of one nation could be adapted to another; that laws must take into account the physical conditions of the country, climate, character of the land, location, size, and mode of living of the people . . . ? This is the code we must consult, not the code of Washington.[21]

Another famed revolutionary hero voiced similar disquietude more than a half century later. In the words of José Martí,

Spanish America owes its inability to govern itself entirely to those of its leaders who sought to rule nations that have conquered their identity through violence with laws based on four centuries of freedom in the United States and nineteen centuries of monarchy in France. A decree formulated by Hamilton will not keep a horse of the pampas from bucking, nor will a pronouncement of Siéyes stir the thick blood of the Indian race. . . . Government must grow upward from the land itself. The spirit of a government must be based on the true nature of the country.[22]

While, as explained earlier, there are divergent views of democracy in Latin America, few would deny Martí's insistence on the fundamental relevance of the hemispheric experience. One of the major consequences has been the dissonance between U.S. diplomacy and Latin American political reality. While across the decades the fortunes of democracy in the region have ebbed and flowed, there has been a consistent North American compulsion to interfere as a means of presumably promoting the cause of democracy.

U.S. Activism and Interventionism

The thrust of U.S. diplomacy toward Latin America has inevitably—and not improperly—reflected a commitment to the national interest. It is the definition and articulation of this interest, of course, which contains the seed of misunderstanding or flawed policy making. Action and inaction, unilateral and collaborative measures, are all responsive to perceptions of the national interest. These have notably reflected geopolitical and security considerations, as described in Gil's classic formulation: "The policy of the United States has had two unchanging objectives: to prevent the influence of extracontinental powers in the Western Hemisphere and to make Latin America a special sphere of influence of the United States, the latter to be accomplished by a variety of means, among which have been trade and investment diplomacy, and military objectives."[23]

The emergence of international communism and the Cold War rivalry between the United States and the Soviet Union compounded, but did not basically alter, the historical pattern. For the United States, both the Third World in general and Latin America in particular generated close attention to security goals. These emphasized a determination to block the rise of power of radical revolutionary movements, along with an insistence that host nations permit the continuing presence and participation of North American political and economic interests. In the immediate post–World War II era, Washington's efforts were crowned with success, but by the 1960s this had begun to change. In Latin America the Pax Americana was confronted by the Cuban Revolution, and later by fallout from the Vietnam War. Even before the 1980s, the United States found its maneuverability in world affairs reduced from earlier levels. The use or threat of military force concomitantly received a higher priority. Consequently, Roger Burbach has concluded, Ronald Reagan's emphasis on increasing military power and "adopting a tough posture abroad is in large part a logical consequence of the fact that the United States finds itself in a weakened position in the world."[24]

There has been a tendency to underemphasize traditional diplomatic efforts, although Reagan policymakers have contended that dialogue has not been thwarted and that, indeed, there is a two-track approach—that is, a reliance on both political and military leverage. Earlier chapters have discussed Reagan's policies in Central America, the Caribbean, and beyond. The administration's threat of force or clandestine intervention has not muted the usual rhetoric about democracy and elections. The first Reagan secretary of state, a hardliner, came to office believing that in El Salvador, for one, economic reform and democracy faced the "stark alternatives" of either leftist totalitarianism or a renewed rightist oligarchy. For Alexander Haig, the Salvadoran provisional government of early 1981 provided the only hope for a democratic transfer of power. "If it survived, elections could follow. No one—least of all the insurgents themselves—imagined that the leftist insurgents, if they won, would hold free elections to decide the future of the country."[25]

Another advocate of "tough" measures, although frequently a bitter bureaucratic opponent of Secretary Haig, was Jeane J. Kirkpatrick. She recognized that in the politically less developed countries, elections and parties were sometimes no more than a "democratic facade," with "the impact of democratic forms . . . modified by varying degrees of fraud, intimidation, and restrictions on who may participate."[26] Yet she had few qualms about denouncing the FSLN for its long denial of the electoral process in Nicaragua. When the Sandinistas did proceed to hold elections in November 1984, Washington's criticisms, as already cited, centered on the degree of opposition and of meaningful competition, not on the fact of elections itself.

U.S. activism and interventionism is not the exclusive preserve of any one administration. The sometimes erratic pursuit of human rights by the Carter administration, aside from its uneven impact on assorted Third World and Latin American countries, was in itself a form of interventionism. Adherents will argue that it was instrumental in the saving of many innocent Argentine lives during the harshness of military repression in the late 1970s. Critics can maintain that there was little significant response from Chilean and Paraguayan dictatorships, that relations with such nations as Brazil were damaged, and that violations were highlighted in such rightist regimes but underplayed in the Cuban case.

The fundamental willingness to employ U.S. power and influence in behalf of "democracy" has provided the justification for a wide array of actions through the years. Interventionism has thereby assumed many different forms, as even a selective listing readily testifies. Return for a brief traversal of the last seven North American administrations. In 1954 the CIA achieved a swift and effective ouster of Guatemala's Arbenz government. President Eisenhower promised aid in making the country a showcase for democracy, while John Foster Dulles vowed "to support the just aspirations of the Guatemalan people." He further pledged the United States "to help alleviate conditions in Guatemala and elsewhere which might afford Communism an opportunity to spread its tentacles throughout the Hemisphere. Thus we shall seek in positive ways to make our Americas an example which will inspire men everywhere."[27] This was the same administration which, that very year, awarded Venezuelan despot Pérez Jiménez the Legion of Merit for his leadership in the Caribbean. Eisenhower's letter of commendation praised the dictator's economic, public works, and anticommunist policies.

With Kennedy, the orientation was different but the rationalization was similar. When the Peruvian military seized power in 1962, U.S. pressure, which included the recall of the U.S. ambassador to Lima, merely angered nationalists over the uninvited Yankee intervention. Less than a year later the CIA clandestinely undermined the constitutional Ecuadoran government, contributing to the creation of a military junta that would rule nearly three years. Conditions were somewhat similar in the Dominican Republic, where Kennedy's representatives threatened retaliation should the elected government of Juan Bosch be toppled. Such efforts to save a democratic, if sadly disorganized, government were also unavailing. Later, when the Salvadoran military ousted a mildly reformist government, Kennedy merely shrugged that "governments of the civil-military type of El Salvador are the most effective in containing communist penetration in Latin America."[28]

The zeal of Kennedy's Alliance reformism was already waning when his assassination brought Lyndon B. Johnson to office. In a matter of months his key Latin American policymaker, Thomas Mann, was highlighting anticommunist goals while downgrading the emphasis on democratization. The civil turmoil that shredded the Dominican political fabric in April 1965 ultimately led to the dispatching of U.S. troops to maintain the status quo. The anticommunist card was played once again when Johnson declared on television that another Communist government had been in the offing and was unacceptable. He also argued that the United States was favorable to change but insisted that it come via peaceful means. A rather different means of combating communism was being exercised in Chile, where CIA millions to the Christian Democrats from Kennedy through Johnson to Nixon were expended as a means of averting a possible Marxist government.

It remained possible for a dedicated public servant and ranking policymaker to reiterate Washington's "all-out support for constitutional democracy" in the Americas. According to Sol Linowitz, Johnson's ambassador to the OAS, the Alliance would "stand or fall on the capacity of the progressive democratic governments, parties, and leaders of Latin America."[29] Johnson himself would eventually write from retirement that for Latin America, "the old days, when they had looked to the United States to solve their problems, had ended. We would now be a junior partner in Latin American economic and social development."[30] Nonetheless, in actual practice Johnson's approach was best suggested by his sending troops to restore stability in the Dominican Republic.

For the Nixon-Ford years, as Francis explains in chapter 2, Latin America was relegated even more to a position of peripheral interest. Following the vaguely noncommittal speech of Richard Nixon in the wake of the Rockefeller mission, the administration continued to view foreign relations from an East-West perspective. There was little sensitivity to, or appreciation for, the democratic ethos in the Americas. So it was that a presidential toast at the White House could publicly praise Brazilian military rule as a model to be emulated across the hemisphere. This produced an icy wrath from such democratic governments as Venezuela, Costa Rica, and Colombia—but to no evident effect.

Intervention in assorted shapes and sizes was acceptable to Henry Kissinger and his colleagues in the case of the Marxist government in Chile. National security was invoked, albeit rather obliquely; it seemed as if the idea of such a regime was perhaps more to be anathematized than its realistic potential as a threat to the United States. The very idea seemed insulting to North American officials, producing such sentiment as the demand that the United States make the Chilean economy "scream." The secretary of state explicitly stated that Washington's duty was to correct the misguided or naive electoral choice of the Chilean citizenry. His perspective, then, was less than congenial for Latin America.

When Jimmy Carter reached the White House, he brought a different outlook on the Third World. As Pastor details in chapter 3, there were renewed calls for a recrudescence of democracy, elections, and individual liberties. Constitutionality was to be encouraged, and the administration was candid in pressuring military leaders to relinquish power, as in the case of Ecuador. Leverage was subsequently exerted on Joaquín Balaguer to accept the 1978 election results in the Dominican Republic, and elsewhere the promotion of human rights was also stressed. At the same time, there was internal strife over basic policy approaches: the East-West proclivities of national security adviser Zbigniew Brzezinski, for one, ran counter to those of such figures as Cyrus Vance and Andrew Young, whose sympathy toward the Third World was pronounced.

Inconsistencies in the application of human rights policy were manifest in responding to hemispheric politics. Thus, if Carter felt the need to invite all chiefs of state to White House ceremonies in promotion of the Panama treaties, this also provided General Pinochet with "photo opportunities" that could be and were manipulated in his favor back home. There were further indications of dissent, as when separate State Department and UN representatives produced disparate assessments of internal Chilean politics before Santiago journalists within weeks of one another. Even setting aside such substantive and bureaucratic issues, however, there was a sense that Washington's image of Latin American democracy should be readily adopted and implanted throughout the region. This familiar attitude was writ even larger when Ronald Reagan arrived in town.

The Reagan administration's attitudes toward elections in El Salvador and Nicaragua have already been noted. Where efforts in the former were handsomely assisted by both technical and financial resources dispatched from the United States, the electoral processes in the latter were disparaged. The involvement of the United States was repeated in the Honduran elections of November 1985, when some 1.9 million voters chose a new president and a 132-person congress. An estimated one million dollars was expended to pay for ballot boxes, paper, ink, and the participation of electoral observers. This, it was hoped, would help to promote Honduras as an alternative model to the Marxist system next door. The results, however, were ultimately shaped predominantly by the particulars of domestic Honduran politics.[31]

In the wake of these events, it could scarcely be said that the U.S. effort to enhance Honduran democracy had been an overwhelming success. More important, however, policymakers continued to believe that Washington had both the duty and the capacity to shape events as it saw fit. Similar activism and interventionism has been produced by a succession of administrations. Neither Republicans nor Democrats have exclusive rights—whether for bragging or for apologies. Policymakers with diverse ideological bases have continued determinedly to urge their views upon Latin America. By the decade of the 1980s, some observers were proposing that, for the sake of convenience, at least three competing positions could be identified: the confrontationalist, the liberal interventionist, and the neorealist.[32] Despite the inevitable risks of oversimplification, these labels are useful.

The first accords generally with the Reaganite view that the Western Hemisphere is but another theater for the global contest with the Soviet Union. There is a conviction that Cuba, and Nicaragua by extension, are basically surrogates of the "evil empire" of the East. The stress on security interests and scenarios makes inevitable a lessened concern over democracy; it also brings a willingness to use electoral contests as a means of projecting U.S. interests. This contrasts with the liberal interventionist position, which is espoused by some of the former Carter advisers. They give greater credence to domestic problems as a source of turbulence, although still viewing the Soviet role with suspicion, and urge greater emphasis on diplomacy as a means of resolving conflicts. This includes the overt encouragement of democracy and its institutional processes, but again as a means of enhancing U.S. interests. There is the omnipresent willingness to insert Washington's perceptions of Latin American political realities. It becomes the responsibility of the United States to pass judgment on governments and to act accordingly.

Adherents of the neorealist school are marginally less receptive to interventionism.[33] There is a willingness to believe that the complexities of contemporary international affairs suggest very real limitations on the ability of the United States to shape events at will. National interests are not to be ignored but rather to be served through an allegedly more practical approach to policy. Consequently, it may even be necessary upon occasion to accept revolutionary movements as an alternative preferable to that rightist fascism which, in the end, can only degenerate into chaos. For the neorealists, there are also times when U.S. military involvement and public diplomatic support for unsavory authoritarianism should be terminated before the nation is drawn into a quagmire not originally of its own making.

It might be argued that any U.S. administration that pursues an active role in Latin America will in effect be serving nondemocratic forces in the region. Peeler states, for example, that the basic thrust of the United States in Latin America is "unquestionably conservative." Therefore, he continues, "any time a U.S. administration pursues a policy of nonintervention, the forces of change are likely to benefit. And even if it is inconsistently pursued (as with Carter), a policy favoring the defense of human rights will tend to provide the

forces demanding change with more space in which to operate safe-
ly."[34] If this is so, it must at the same time be recognized that no U.S.
administration in living memory has been unwilling to impose its
views on the countries to the south. The degree of provincial eth-
nocentrism on the part of North American officials has varied in intensity, but it has seldom wavered from the bedrock conviction that,
in the end, the United States knows best.

Conclusion

There is in the tradition of U.S. foreign policy a belief in the obligation to share national values with others—if necessary, with energetic insistence. This is projected in different forms and fashions,
but it readily becomes attached to democracy, constitutionalism, and
electoral processes. North Americans are imbued with the sense that
their country has a higher mission to perform in addition to its pursuit of the national interest. It is all well and good to agree upon a
neorealist—or tougher—stance, one regarded as worthy by Hans
Morgenthau, George Kennan, or even Machiavelli. But that does not
change the fact that, as Stanley Hoffman has written, "American idealism will not go away."[35] It is a thread that has been woven into the
national fabric for the better part of a century.

Reflect, if you will, on the words of an eloquent critic of U.S. policy in another Third World country, the Philippines:

Extending the Blessings of Civilization to our Brother who Sits in Darkness
has been a good trade and has paid well, on the whole; and there is money
in it yet if carefully worked—but not enough, in my judgment, to make any
considerable risk advisable. The People that Sit in Darkness are getting to be
too scarce and too shy . . . they have become suspicious of the Blessings of
Civilization.[36]

This was written, not about U.S. relations with the dictatorship of
Ferdinand E. Marcos in the mid-1980s, but rather as a sardonic
mockery of imperialism at the turn of the century. The author was
Mark Twain.

A primary U.S. architect of the policies that espoused the missionary duties of global civilizing put it—again with regard to the
Philippines—in the following terms:

We took arms only in obedience to the dictates of humanity and in the ful-
fillment of high public and moral obligations. We had no design of aggran-

dizement and no ambition. . . . The lustre and the moral strength attaching to a cause which can be confidently rested upon the considerate judgment of the world should not under any illusion of the hour be dimmed by ulterior designs which might tempt us into excessive demands.[37]

If President William McKinley lived in an age simpler than the late twentieth century, his declaration amply illustrates the durable attitudes of the United States. Similar if more subtle declarations could be cited from each of the many administrations that followed. Whatever the circumstances of the moment, the U.S. drive to project its own ideals upon foreign nations and societies has been relentless. This has been especially true for Latin America, which has somehow continued to be viewed paternalistically as part of "our" hemisphere.

Through one administration after another, the powerholders in Washington have continually fueled the movement back and forth from benign neglect to professed preoccupation. They have, in Lowenthal's words, "pledged greater attention, . . . vowed their support for Latin America's economic development, and expressed their interest in the region's political evolution. . . . The next phase of this historic cycle generally sees the newly announced policy toward Latin America set aside."[38] Furthermore, the civilizing spirit is renewed with each new policy thrust—be it the Good Neighbor Policy, the Alliance for Progress, the Mature Partnership, the New Dialogue, or what have you. It inevitably draws nourishment from electoral or constitutional processes misconstrued because of the distortion of North American optics.

The result has been the reactivation of either covert or open interventionism while, sadly, misshapen images continue to be projected. It sometimes seems politically and personally impossible for North Americans to view other regions—most especially those of the developing world—without succumbing to the temptation of proffering advice. To be sure, it is neither realistic nor rational to suggest that Washington policymakers simply leave Latin America alone. National interests cannot be casually forfeited. At the same time, it is incumbent upon the U.S. political leadership to understand and respond to the realities of hemispheric affairs. To do otherwise is to suggest that, even with the best of intentions, the United States will ill serve the cause of democracy in Latin America. If history is to be our guide, the prospects are much more a cause for lamentation than for optimism.

Notes

1. Fredrick B. Pike, *The United States and the Andean Republics: Peru, Bolivia and Ecuador* (Cambridge: Harvard University Press, 1977), p. 303.

2. Lloyd S. Etheredge, *Can Governments Learn? American Foreign Policy and Central American Revolutions* (New York: Pergamon Press, 1985), p. 185.

3. Federico G. Gil, *Latin American–United States Relations* (New York: Harcourt Brace Jovanovich, 1971), p. 284.

4. Kalman H. Silvert, *Essays in Understanding Latin America* (Philadelphia: Institute for the Study of Human Issues, 1977), p. 58.

5. Alexander W. Wilde, "Conversations among Gentlemen: Oligarchical Democracy in Colombia," in Juan J. Linz and Alfred Stepan, eds., *The Breakdown of Democratic Regimes: Latin America* (Baltimore: Johns Hopkins University Press, 1987), p. 29.

6. John A. Peeler, *Latin American Democracies: Colombia, Costa Rica, Venezuela* (Chapel Hill, N.C.: University of North Carolina Press, 1985), p. 5.

7. For further discussion, see Richard M. Morse, "The Heritage of Latin America," in Louis Hartz, ed., *The Founding of New Societies* (New York: Harcourt, Brace and World, 1964), pp. 156ff.

8. John D. Martz and David J. Myers, "Understanding Latin American Politics: Analytic Models and Intellectual Traditions," *Polity* 16 (Winter 1983): 241.

9. Simón Bolívar, "Memoria dirigida a los ciudadanos de la Nueva Granada por un caraqueño," in Vicente Lecuna, ed., *Proclama y discursos del Libertador* (Caracas: Litografía y Tipografía del Comercio, 1939), 1:22.

10. Arturo Uslar Pietri, "El caudillo ante el novelista," *El Nacional* (Caracas), 11 May 1975, p. D-1.

11. Díaz's famous interview with James Creelman was published in the March 1908 issue of *Pearson's Magazine*. Excerpts may be found in Lewis Hanke, ed., *History of Latin American Civilization: Sources and Interpretations*, vol. 2, *The Modern Age* (Boston: Little, Brown, 1967), pp. 258–59.

12. Roldós elaborated upon the point at length in a 1979 preinaugural statement at the Wilson Center in Washington during a presentation in which the author participated. Roldós's thoughtful if unremarkable views helped contribute to the ill-founded perception on the part of Ecuador's traditionalist elite of the allegedly dangerous leftism of the reformist Roldós. A more extended treatment of the Roldós administration is included in my forthcoming work on the politics of petroleum in Ecuador.

13. Roger Burbach, "Introduction: Revolution and Reaction," in Roger Burbach and Patricia Flynn, eds., *The Politics of Intervention; The United States in Central America* (New York: Monthly Review Press, 1984), pp. 19–20.

14. For an account by an experienced journalist who shared this outlook, see Tad Szulc, *Twilight of the Tyrants* (New York: Praeger Publishers, 1959).

15. Among the most influential was Guillermo A. O'Donnell, whose first major statement was *Modernization and Bureaucratic-Authoritarianism: Studies in South American Politics* (Berkeley: Institute of International Studies, 1973). The current of corporatist theorizing is effectively represented in two edited volumes: James M. Malloy, ed., *Authoritarianism and Corporatism in Latin America* (Pittsburgh: University of Pittsburgh Press, 1977); and David Collier, ed., *The New Authoritarianism in Latin America* (Princeton, N.J.: Princeton University Press, 1979). It might be noted that the first has no entry for "democracy" in its seven-page index. An incisive review that delineates distinctive corporatist perspectives is that of Charles W. Anderson in the *American Political Science Review* 72 (December 1978): 1478–79.

16. John D. Martz, "Latin America and the Caribbean," in Robert Wesson, ed., *Democracy: A Worldwide Survey* (New York: Praeger, 1987), p. 49.

17. The text is included in a useful work by one of the architects of the Alliance. See Lincoln Gordon, *A New Deal for Latin America: The Alliance for Progress* (Cambridge: Harvard University Press, 1963), esp. pp. 118–19.

18. Theodore C. Sorensen, *Kennedy* (New York: Harper and Row, 1965), pp. 535–36.

19. Etheredge, *Can Governments Learn?* p. 182.

20. Howard J. Wiarda, "At the Root of the Problem: Conceptual Failures in U.S.–Central American Relations," in Robert S. Leiken, ed., *Central America: Anatomy of Conflict* (New York: Pergamon Press, 1984), p. 272.

21. For the text, see Harold A. Bierck, Jr., and Vicente Lecuna, eds. and comps., *Selected Writings of Bolívar* (New York: Colonial Press for the Banco de Venezuela, 1951), 1:179–80.

22. José Martí, *Nuestra América* (1891), as quoted in Carlos Rangel, *Del buen salvaje al buen revolucionario* (Caracas: Monte Avila Editores, 1976), p. 180.

23. Gil, *Latin American–United States Relations,* p. 283.

24. Roger Burbach, "U.S. Policy: Crisis and Conflict," in Burbach and Flynn, eds., *Politics of Intervention,* p. 68.

25. Alexander M. Haig, Jr., *Caveat; Realism, Reagan, and Foreign Policy* (New York: Macmillan, 1984), p. 126.

26. Jeane J. Kirkpatrick, *Dictatorships and Double Standards: Rationalism and Reagan in Politics* (New York: Simon and Schuster, 1982), p. 66.

27. *New York Times*, 1 July 1954, pp. 1, 8.

28. Cynthia Arnson, *El Salvador: A Revolution Confronts the United States* (Washington: n.p., 1982), p. 19.

29. Sol M. Linowitz, *The Making of a Public Man: A Memoir* (Boston: Little, Brown, 1985), p. 27.

30. Lyndon B. Johnson, *The Vantage Point* (New York: Holt, 1971), pp. 350–51.

31. An agreement sanctioned by the Tribunal Nacional Electoral (TNE) gave the presidency to the leading candidate of the most-voted-for party. This meant victory to the Liberals' José Azcona, for he and the other party candidates

outdistanced those of the National party. Yet Rafael Leonardo Callejas of the latter led Azcona by more than 10 percent of the vote. If scarcely consistent with basic democratic practices, it was an outcome shaped by domestic politics. One can imagine the furor had a similar procedure and outcome been the product of Sandinista policies in Nicaragua.

32. Burbach, "U.S. Policy," p. 69.

33. For an exposition of the neorealist approach, see Richard Feinberg, *The Intemperate Zone: U.S. Policy toward the Third World* (New York: W.W. Norton, 1983).

34. Peeler, *Latin American Democracies,* p. 60.

35. Stanley Hoffman, "Fights and Diplomacy," *New York Times,* 31 December 1978, p. F-17.

36. From Frederick Anderson, ed., *A Pen Warmed-Up in Hell: Mark Twain in Protest* (New York: Harper and Row, 1972), pp. 64–65, as quoted in David Haward Bain, *Sitting in Darkness: Americans in the Philippines* (Boston: Houghton Mifflin, 1984).

37. As quoted in Margaret Leech, *In the Days of McKinley* (New York: Harper and Brothers, 1959), p. 331.

38. Abraham F. Lowenthal, "Latin America and the Caribbean: Toward a New U.S. Policy," in J. Lewis and Valeriana Kallab, eds., *U.S. Foreign Policy and the Third World Agenda* (New York: Praeger, 1983), p. 51.

The Contributors

Jack Child is an associate professor Spanish and Latin American studies at the American University. He was born in Buenos Aires and lived in South America for nineteen years. He holds a B.E. degree from Yale and a Ph.D. in International Relations from American. A retired U.S. Regular Army officer, he had several assignments related to Latin America. His research interests include conflict and its resolution in Latin America, the impact of geopolitical thinking, and the international politics of Antarctica and the sub-Antarctic islands, which he visited in 1986. Among his recent publications is *Geopolitics and Conflict in South America: Quarrels among Neighbors* (Westview, 1985).

Michael J. Francis is a professor and chairman of government and international studies at the University of Notre Dame. He received his Ph.D. from the University of Virginia and works in the area of international relations, with a concentration on Latin American affairs. He is a fellow of the Kellogg Institute and has held research grants from the Social Science Research Council and the University Consortium for World Order Studies. He is the author of *The Limits of Hegemony* (Notre Dame, 1977), *The Allende Victory* (Arizona, 1973), and numerous articles in English and Spanish journals.

Federico G. Gil is Kenan Professor Emeritus of political science at the University of North Carolina, Chapel Hill. Born in Havana, he was educated in Cuba and Spain. A widely published author throughout his career, he was recently the editor of an issue on Latin American relations in the *Journal of Inter-American Studies and World Affairs* (1985). A founder and president of the Latin American Studies Association, in 1985 he was awarded the Kalman H. Silvert

Award for a career of distinguished service and scholarship on Latin American affairs. He continues to write and lecture, and to serve extensively on a host of boards, committees, and advisory directorates.

Margaret Daly Hayes is director of the Washington office of the Council of the Americas. She served as principal staff person for the Western Hemisphere on the Senate Foreign Relations Committee from 1981 to 1984. She was also the associate director of the Center of Brazilian Studies at the John Hopkins University School of Advanced International Studies, and was senior associate of a Washington consulting firm. She is the author of *Latin America and the U.S. National Interest: A Basis for Foreign Policy* (Westview, 1984). She is currently writing a book on Congress and the making of Central American policy for the Council on Foreign Relations.

Michael J. Kryzanek is a professor of political science at Bridgewater State College in Massachusetts. He received his Ph.D. in 1975 from the University of Massachusetts in Amherst. He has written extensively on the politics of the Dominican Republic and on U.S. policy in the Caribbean. He is a coauthor with Howard Wiarda of *The Dominican Republic: A Caribbean Crucible* (Westview, 1982). His latest book is *United States–Latin American Relations* (Praeger, 1985).

Abraham F. Lowethal is a professor of international relations at the University of Southern California and executive director of the Inter-American Dialogue. From 1977 to 1983 he was the founding director of the Latin American Program at the Woodrow Wilson International Center for Scholars in Washington. Before then he served with the Ford Foundation in Latin America and has been the director of studies at the Council on Foreign Relations. He is the author of numerous books and articles on Latin American and inter-American affairs.

John D. Martz is a professor of political science at Pennsylvania State University. From 1975 to 1980 he was the editor of the *Latin American Research Review*. Among the more recent of his many publications are *Regime, Politics and Petroleum: Ecuador's Nationalistic Struggle* (Transaction, 1987); and with coeditor David J. Myers, the second edition of *Venezuela: The Democratic Experience* (Praeger, 1986).

Robert A. Pastor is a professor of political science at Emory University and director of the Latin American and Caribbean Program at

Emory's Carter Center. He was the Director of Latin American and Caribbean affairs on the National Security Council from 1977 to 1981 and the Executive Director of the Linowitz Commission on U.S.–Latin American Relations in 1975–76. He received his Ph.D. from Harvard University, is the author of *Condemned to Repetition: The United States and Nicaragua* (Princeton, 1987), and is editor of *Latin America's Debt Crisis* (Lynne Rienner, 1987).

Riordan Roett is a professor of political science and director of the Latin American Studies Program and of the Center of Brazilian Studies at the Johns Hopkins School of Advanced International Studies in Washington, D.C. The third edition of his *Brazil: Politics in a Patrimonial Society* appeared in 1984; in 1985 he coedited (with Wolf Grabendorff) and coauthored *Latin America, Western Europe, and the U.S.: Reevaluating the Atlantic Triangle* (Praeger, also 1985).

Steve C. Ropp has been Milward Simpson Distinguished Professor of Political Science at the University of Wyoming. He is the author of *Panamanian Politics: From Guarded Nation to National Guard* (Praeger/Hoover, 1982) and coeditor with James A. Morris of *Central America: Crisis and Adaptation* (New Mexico, 1984). He has served as a contributing editor on Central America for the Library of Congress's *Handbook of Latin American Studies* and is coauthoring a volume on the Latin American military.

Paul E. Sigmund is a professor of politics and director of the Latin American Studies Program at Princeton University. He is the author of *Multinationals in Latin America: The Politics of Nationalization* (Wisconsin, 1980). He has written extensively on the politics of Chile, including *The Overthrow of Allende and the Politics of Chile, 1964–1976* (Pittsburgh, 1977).

Wayne S. Smith was a career foreign service officer from 1958 to 1982, at which time he left the service because of serious disagreements with Reagan administration policies on Cuba and Central America. He was the State Department's leading expert on Cuba, having served in Havana as third secretary of the embassy from 1958 until the United States broke relations in January 1961; on the Cuban Desk from 1964 to 1966; as Director of Cuban Affairs from 1977 to 1979; and as chief of the U.S. interests section in Havana from 1979 to 1982. Dr. Smith is adjunct professor of Latin American studies at the Johns Hopkins School of Advanced International Studies in Washington, D.C.

Index